SILICON DREAMS

INFORMATION, MAN, AND MACHINE

SILICON DREAMS

INFORMATION, MAN, AND MACHINE

• • • • • • • • • • •

ROBERT W. LUCKY

**EXECUTIVE
DIRECTOR
OF RESEARCH
AT&T BELL LABS**

A THOMAS · DUNNE BOOK

ST. MARTIN'S PRESS NEW YORK

SILICON DREAMS: INFORMATION, MAN, AND MACHINE. Copyright © 1989 by Bell Telephone
Laboratories, Inc. All rights reserved. Printed in the United States of America. No part of this
book may be used or reproduced in any manner whatsoever without written permission except
in the case of brief quotations embodied in critical articles or reviews. For information, address
St. Martin's Press, 175 Fifth Avenue, New York, N.Y. 10010.

Library of Congress Cataloging-in-Publication Data

Lucky, R.W.

    Silicon dreams : information, man, and machine / Robert Lucky.
      p. cm.
    "A Thomas Dunne book"
    Includes index.
    ISBN 0-312-05517-X
    1. Computers and civilization.   2. Information technology.
  I. Title.
  QA76.9.C66L83   1991
  306.4'2—dc20   90-19224
                                                          CIP

10 9 8 7 6 5 4 3 2

CONTENTS

• • • • • • • • • • •

C O N T E N T S

CONTENTS

PREFACE

● ● ● ● ● ● ● ● ●

The motivation to write this book came from a single, compelling source. In 1987 the Marconi Foundation awarded me the 13th Marconi International Fellowship. Unlike most honors, where the convention is for the recipient to take the award and disappear, the Marconi Fellowship is designed to send the awardee on some kind of quest in aid of the profession. This book is my quest. I discovered, however, that having a quest was a wonderful thing. The quest became an end in itself, and I shall miss writing this book, even as it lapses into obsolescence and uncovered error.

I knew that the only way that I could satisfy the implied moral charter of the Marconi Fellowship was by writing a book. But about what? After years in management I was left with scant remaining expertise. This was a situation unlike that of most of my associates, who fill themselves with a subject over many years, and then effect an informational catharsis by putting forth a book on their specialty. They start with a subject, and decide to write a book. I started with a book, and then had to decide on a subject.

I had long been fascinated with the idea of information—formless, intangible, and undefinable, yet our most important conduit and currency. One of my chemist friends likes to remind people of the importance of his work in materials by beginning his talks with a slide that says "Everything must be made of something." But it makes me wonder. Many *things* today are made of *nothing.* They are made of conceptual thought; they are forged from information.

So in the back of my mind I wanted to write a book about information. The only problem was that I knew so little about information, only a little about the hard edges of the technology. Specifically, I knew something about dealing with information in electronic format. Taking this small kernel of expertise, I started upon the course of weaving these hard edges a little way toward the amorphous, unknowable central concept of information. My little hard edges—communications, information theory, coding—the things I knew something about—did not go very far. I was soon adrift in a sea of subjects about which I knew almost nothing.

The audacity of venturing so far from my home turf was crystallized when my son, an engineer himself, interrupted me in an attempt to take over my computer for his own work. Resisting, I explained that my fingers were not on the keyboard at that precise instant because I had to read some more of the papers in front of me before I knew what to write. He was obviously mystified and disillusioned that I had to read something before I could write something. "How can you write a book about stuff you don't know?" he asked skeptically. It was a good question, and one that still bothers me to some degree. The response that I gave myself was that there was no one who knew the breadth of subject matter contained in what I wanted to write about. I told myself that I could do as good a job of learning and integrating the material as anyone. Unfortunately, I knew that it was also true that for every subject I touched upon, there would be many people who knew much more than I did. It is an intimidating thought that discourages all of us from time to time, and many times during the writing I had to shake off the worry that I would be looked down upon by this or that group of experts. For any scientist or engineer this is a fearful threat.

While I was writing the book people would occasionally ask me what it was about. Every time I responded that it was "about information" I got a blank stare. Eventually I came to the realization that not everyone had the same concept of "information" that I did. Ask a securities analyst, a schoolteacher, a reporter, or a librarian, for example, and each will think of information in a quite different way. My viewpoint here is with the *representation* of information in appropriate formats for people and for computers. I am concerned with the symbols of information—the bits and bytes that computers manipulate, and the writing, speech, and pictures that we ourselves use to store and communicate information. In contrast, I am not so concerned with the meaning of the information itself. For example, in analogy to the daily newspaper my considerations would be those of the layout editor. What should be the format of the newspaper? How many stories could be run in a given number of pages? How many pictures could accompany these stories, and how effective would the pictures be in comparison to using the same space for text? As important as the headline might be on a given day, its particular content would not be my concern. I found this to be a delicate distinction not always appreciated by my friends in other occupations.

Now that the book has been written, and has been read by a number of experts, I have a better understanding of its strengths and weaknesses. I still believe that there is no single person who is expert in all of the subjects included here. While I feel reasonably confident about the technological portions, I am less sure about the parts that deal with human issues, and there are a great many personal opinions scattered throughout. I asked each expert who read a portion of the book to be sure that the material was "not wrong." I felt that was a much better criterion for my imagined readership than for it to be "right." Experts universally like to qualify all of their statements to make them precisely correct. It is very hard to resist this temptation to write for your peers, and in so doing to lose the patience and understanding of everyone else. In the end most of my experts agreed reluctantly that the material was "not wrong," but I could see that they were not especially happy with the liberties that I had taken. What did make me glad was that every reviewer seemed to want to read other portions of the book that were outside their own specialities. They usually found this other material interesting and provocative. Thus even though the book is uneven in its authoritative merit, the corollary is that I believe everyone will learn something. That is my real aspiration.

I have tried to make the book accessible to all determined readers with a general education. I wish I could say that I had succeeded, but there are several sections that I believe will be difficult for the nonengineer. Specifically these hard parts are the latter third of Chapter 2, where I discuss the philosophy of error-correcting codes, and the middle third of Chapter 6, which deals with the conversion of speech signals into bit streams. I think that if you are not an engineer but you persevere through these two sections, then you deserve a good deal of credit. It is not that the material requires knowledge of math (there is almost none), but rather that it helps to have the background knowledge of day-to-day engineering or computing. With these exceptions, much of the book deals with matters in which we all have experience, such as the structure of our English language, and the psychology of speech and vision.

I have also tried to make the tone of the book light, but at the same time thoughtful, or even occasionally philosophical. It is a combination that does not always go together, but I have enforced the blend with the inclusion at the end of each chapter of a tongue-in-cheek editorial column taken from a regular series of such columns that I have written for the *IEEE Spectrum Magazine.* On the other hand, in trying to be thoughtful I have concentrated on creating a "how come" book, rather than a "how to" book. This is in no sense a handbook for information users.

Since there is much opinion and anecdotal argument in the book, all of my readers have been anxious to argue this or that with me. Generally, I take this as complimentary. I am not sure that I have sought consciously to be provocative, but I do want to make the reader think for himself. There is no correct explanation or interpretation for many of the phenomena that I discuss. Please feel entitled to form your own opinions. It is also possible that I am wrong here and there; this is the chance I have taken.

This book is itself a prototypical information age task. It is probable that there are not many original facts contained here. There are, I believe, original conjectures, thoughts, and, of course, opinions, but that is quite a different matter. Instead, my contribution is, first, *selection,* the most valued function amidst the flood of data posing as knowledge in the information age. Moreover, I have provided *translation* into a common language and *interpretation* with respect to a particular framework. It would have been much easier to get an expert to write each different section in this book, but my own experience with books of this sort is not good. Thus I had to learn something about each topic, then translate the knowledge into terms and frameworks that I understood, and then retell a subset of the knowledge here.

Having an information age job myself, I seldom get the sense of measured, day-to-day accomplishment. Seeing the pages of this book grow has been extraordinarily satisfying. I can see behind me the trail of bytes, like bread crumbs, reminding me of where I have been. I see the aimless wanderings, the circlings of the trees, the evasions of the unclimbable problems, and the detours to friendly, known places along the way. But on the whole, I like it. I learned a lot on that path. I hope you will too.

ACKNOWLEDGMENTS

● ●

I would like to thank Mrs. Gioia Marconi Braga and the Marconi Foundation for giving me the incentive and support to write this book. Among the people who gave me helpful comments on the manuscript were Jack Salz, Jacob Ziv, Israel Bar-David, Jim Flanagan, Larry Rabiner, and Bruce Ballard. Jon Bentley went through the entire manuscript in great detail. Among other things, he taught me the difference between the words "which" and "that." I should have known from the table of word usage in Chapter 3 that I had too many "whiches."

Pictures for the last chapter were provided by Aadrian Ligtenberg and Hemant Bheda. Finally, I would like to acknowledge the help from my secretary, Marlene Gannon, and the support of my wife, Joan, and my children, David and Karen, throughout the preparation of this manuscript.

SILICON DREAMS

INFORMATION, MAN, AND MACHINE

1

THE INFORMATION ECOLOGY

• • • • • • • • •

THE INFORMATION AGE

The silent, uncomplaining spacecraft aims its camera at the moving earth far below. The salesman in the hardware store patiently records a sale in his ledger. Tapes spin in a computer complex, their slight whir unheard beneath the roar of air-conditioning, as volumes of newborn financial transactions are given their freedom in the electronic network beyond. The teenager with a towel wrapped around her wet hair scans with anticipation the daily television listings in the newspaper, while millions of her counterparts in the daylit regions of the world listen, work, and dream in crowded classrooms. All about us information is being generated, processed, and exchanged. Who can doubt that information has become the cultural and economic ether of our time?

When I was a youth I lived at the end of a new street in the suburbs. Civilization ceased at our dead end; the woods beyond were there to serve as the playground to which our neighborhood gang was obviously entitled. But every morning I would see crews of workmen arrive and obstinately begin or continue construction on yet another new house. In the evening when they left, the playground had diminished. Civilization had advanced. These were the only working adults I ever saw, so I came to believe that this was what people did when they grew up. They made things.

One day many years later as an adult I made a great discovery. I looked around at all the people about me, and I suddenly realized that *I did not know anybody who made anything!* Not a single person. Not a single thing. For the first time I felt personally the impact of the information age. We all made our living by trading bits! When I went to my office in the fresh throes of this momentous discovery, I felt shame for my own work. Instead of leaving each day with a growing edifice for all to admire, I left with a pile of neatly bundled bits. Sometimes they were not even so neatly bundled, and few people could see them from any distance at all!

In the United States about two-thirds of us work in information-related jobs, such as in the insurance industry, teaching, financial services, and the professions. Only one-seventh of our population is required to produce all the food and material goods to satisfy not only our own needs, but those of a large export market as well. Our farms are so productive that we are all fed by less than 3 percent of our population, in spite of policies that selectively reduce crop yields. While the heavy industries have dwindled and drifted abroad, the service industries have flourished. Steel, coal, and cars are heavily imported, but law firms, financial services, government functions, health services, publishing, software, education, and so many other service providers have expanded and multiplied seemingly without bound. The industrial revolution has come and gone; the information age is here.

Barely a century ago nearly everybody worked at manual labor to feed and clothe himself and his fellows. The industrial revolution was welcomed as providing a means of multiplying and augmenting human labor. Now we see it as a period of callous exploitation. We shudder at the characters and descriptions of Charles Dickens, and are repelled by those stark, black-and-white photographs of the nineteenth-century industrial workers. We are haunted by the empty face of the child at the loom, and by the hopeless gazes of the miners returning from their subterranean purgatories. We have sympathy for the poverty-stricken farmers of the depression era as depicted in *Grapes of Wrath.* But at least we understand these things.

The toil over production of basic materials seems a condition of life. By contrast, it is hard to comprehend our role in a society where so few of us need to be engaged in these elemental pursuits.

2

What we used to think of as "honest toil" is for most of us only a historical teaching. Now we feel vaguely uncomfortable with the notion that we are perhaps no more than acolytes, bundling and bartering that intangible quantity we call information. Yet it is true: We are becoming a nation of clerks. Bob Cratchit's stool has become a swivel chair and his ledger a computer terminal. The hours are shorter and the pay considerably better, but how much difference in function can most of us claim?

Our attitudes about our changing role are occasionally mired in anachronism. Engineers like me sometimes think that people in brokerage houses, marketing, or executive-search firms constitute a friction on the economic system. But these middlepeople are the true citizens of the information age. They deal in information—the information required to put buyer and seller together, which has been elevated to a special place of importance. Banks have also become central. Far from conforming to our image of strongholds for the storage of money, they have become instead reservoirs of information about the whereabouts of assets. The actual possession of the assets themselves has become nearly superfluous. And as society becomes more litigious we wonder about the growing role of another class of middlepeople—the legal profession. Are they building a base of wisdom and ethics for this new age, or are they exploiting a weakness in the new structure while bleeding off the most talented of our youth?

One of my academic friends has observed a curious discrepancy in our feelings about information work. We accept the notion that while we cannot be conscripted to do common labor, we are required to do information work. For example, each year the Internal Revenue Service sends each of us many forms that we are compelled to take the time to understand and execute before returning them to the government. Suppose instead that the government had sent us each a pile of mechanical parts with detailed instructions for assembly. After we had completed many hours of construction, the finished assemblage was to be returned to the government for its own use. Can you imagine how we would protest the enforced labor? Why then is it considered ethical for us to be conscripted for equivalent information labor?

Most readers will no doubt believe, as I do, that information work is somehow more noble than manual labor, that the jobs of the information age will be more enriching and desirable. In discussing automation on a call-in radio talk show several years ago I commented that the more boring a job was, the more likely that it could be automated. It went without saying that the elimination of boring jobs was good for humanity. A man called me on the air and said, "You know those boring jobs you've been talking about? Well I have one, and I like it. Who are you to say what is good for people?" I was brought up short. Indeed, who is any of us to say what are to be the desirable attributes of jobs? Probably very few of the readers of this book will feel threatened by the the increasing importance of information in society, but perhaps a majority of people on earth will be resistant to these changes. Muscles have been trained, while minds have not.

What makes it harder for most of us is that in the information age, work has become more abstract. Reality has somehow disappeared behind the screen of the CRT, where little green numbers flicker with self-importance. Workers no longer make physical contact with the objects with which they deal; rather, they accomplish tasks through the medium of an information system. The sensuality of physical labor has been replaced by a complex system that is coldly abstract. It is also often true that once a job is computerized it is made routine and unchallenging, while at the same time it demands focused attention and abstract comprehension. Needless to say, that is a bad combination!

Acclimatizing ourselves to the information age is sometimes painful, but if we persevere, we should inevitably improve ourselves. Just as the machines of the industrial age increased man's muscle, the machines of the information age can increase man's mind. We have learned that the brain is more important than muscle, so it is probable that the information age will be more important in the affairs of man than the industrial age. Information should give us greater capacity to increase both human and machine productivity. By creating a network between people, computers will let us amplify our own individual intellects, and the computer's ability to customize manufacture may give us back some of the individuality that we lost in the industrial revolution. While we cannot argue that information will be a substitute for man's basic needs of food, shelter, and clothing, it is an enabling power that leads directly to the satisfaction of these needs. At the same time the information age is much more than the fulfillment of basics. We have evolved into a complex society, with sophisticated needs that transcend those of material goods. The enlightened use of information should be the next rung on our evolutionary ladder.

P R O P E R T I E S   O F
I N F O R M A T I O N

The information age itself is already a cliché. Yet for all the publicity that it has received, the concept of information itself and the philosophy of an economy based upon its production, processing, and movement lie tantalizingly beyond our real understanding. Information is, after all, an abstract substance, occupying neither space nor weight. It has properties quite different from those of the substantive goods with which we are used to dealing. We should dwell momentarily on these important differences, for they form a backdrop for our thinking about systems for the information age.

I N F O R M A T I O N   C A N   B E
C O M M U N I C A T E D
E L E C T R O N I C A L L Y

Information can be transmitted virtually anywhere cheaply, and at nearly the speed of light, but mark how this contrasts with the shipment of material goods! If we begin thinking of information as conveying real value in our society, we appreciate that nearly instantaneous electronic transmission is a miraculous property verging on teleportation. Money itself is a form of information today, and probably a major portion of all the data traffic on the telecommunications networks consists of messages moving electronic piles of money from one location to another. Bob Cratchit would be truly amazed!

The fact that information can be transported so effortlessly has important implications for our business and social systems. One of the significant small changes in our environment in recent years has been the credit-card telephone call, which is made possible by quick authorization from a central data bank, possibly located thousands of miles from the pay phone you choose to use. The convenience of automatic teller machines is another positive example of information movement in our day-to-day lives. In the information age, work itself can be communicated to a place of convenience that is unrelated to the place of its origin. Word processing centers have been formed in the offshore islands to take advantage of cheap labor pools, while legal offices in Minnesota handle New York business—examples of a practice labeled "telescabbing." Telecommuting has not really supplanted travel, but many people have taken to augmenting their work or educational environment through terminals in the home. The author Arthur C. Clarke writes from his beachfront home in Sri Lanka, perfectly attuned to the world at large through his private satellite link, helping prove what Harlan Cleveland has termed the "passing of remoteness."

The instantaneous nature of electronic transmission deserves further comment. Because of the speed of radio transmission, the so-called information "float" (the time between when something happens and when people know that it has happened) has all but disappeared. Events now happen with apparent simultaneity around the world, perhaps being affected in their very enactment by the spotlight of global observation. Terrorists are interviewed on network television during a hijacking; a revolution in the Phillipines takes place in our living rooms. The happenings seem not real, but rather as if choreographed for competition with the evening soap operas. What was it like a scant century ago when weeks went by before one continent discovered that another was at war? What effect does this global simultaneity have on our political systems?

Can there be a further reduction in the information float? Will the reception of information milliseconds before a competitor receives it enable beneficial actions otherwise impossible? With the evolving sophistication of financial networks, the race to capture information, make decisions, and effect transactions has the potential to extend perhaps indefinitely into the realm of electronic speeds. As a consequence, perhaps an investor in Australia would be disadvantaged relative to one in the United States in capitalizing on an event in New York. We might then imagine the Australian investor having an electronic surrogate in New York empowered to act on his behalf for expressly this purpose. As the time it takes to send and receive information is collapsed we have concern for the stability of our financial systems, which have evolved in complex fashion from a period in which there were appreciable human delays that served to buffer the ebb and flow of financial events.

INFORMATION CAN BE
DUPLICATED AND SHARED
• •

One of the most profound ways in which information differs from material goods is that it can be freely shared. We are accustomed to the feeling and perquisites of ownership of real property. Many of us have personally experienced the proverbial childhood acquaintance who took his football and went home, ending the game for everyone, because things were not going his way. Like the football, information can be shared. Unlike the football, when we take our information home, the game often goes on. It can be here and there at the same time. We can give it away, and at the same time keep it.

In many instances information is a kind of common good which, like a lighthouse on a rocky shoal, can serve in aid of any passerby. "Know-how" is a common form of information that can often be shared without diminishing its benefit to any party. For example, agricultural knowledge can be spread to needy countries and used to help alleviate starvation. There is no loss of value to the originators. We inhabitants of this world all then literally reap the benefits of the information pool thus created. Though we think of agriculture as a labor-intensive business, it is very much information driven. Much of the increase in productivity of the agricultural sector is directly attributable to gains in the pooled knowledge in this field.

More than just being shareable, information is self-synergistic, meaning that the value of the sum of shared information can be greater than that of the constituent parts. New information is created by putting together pieces of existing information, a kind of spontaneous creation as a result of "information collisions." Picture if you will a giant cloud chamber, with myriad tracks branching in geometric progression in response to the introduction of a new piece of information. The person who launches the information on its way, who shares it, is usually rewarded by its compounding, though he is not the unique benefactor.

It is not true, however, that the common good is *always* enhanced by the sharing of information. Though information itself can be duplicated inexpensively and shared at will, its value is not always replicated or increased. The investment banker who shares

7

his insider's knowledge with a market manipulator causes a redistribution of wealth in favor of the manipulator, with no increase in overall wealth, or indeed in the common good. Whether or not we can share our information and at the same time retain it for our own use, its effective value would seem to depend upon the impact of our information on the market in which it interacts. Will sharing the information increase the overall value? Or will the introduction of our information into the pool distort the very system in which it interacts?

As an example of a simple model of information sharing, imagine that we are given a sure tip on the winner of a horse race. At the going odds, we can realize as much gain as we are willing to invest in the bet, up to a point. However, the maximum we can gain is the entire value residing in the pari-mutuel pool which has been bet on other horses, given that we are willing to "invest" an amount so large that it diffuses all other winning bets. The sum in this pool is in a real sense the ultimate value of the information we possess. Sharing the information with others does not increase this value, and depending on the inclinations of those with whom we share, the pari-mutuel system may well be distorted through their greed. If the people who share our information are small bettors, then perhaps we could argue we have retained its value. On the other hand, if the recipients of our shared information choose to overwhelm the pari-mutuel pool with their bets, then our copy of this same information is rendered worthless. Both situations pertain in life. Sometimes life is a pari-mutuel pool, wins are equal to losses, and shared information is devalued. More often information is increased in value through the process of sharing, and we all stand to gain by its distribution.

NETWORKING OF INFORMATION

Although communication and sharing are perhaps the most fundamental ways in which the properties of information differ from those of material goods, there are a host of ancillary properties worthy of note. None of these properties will surprise the reader;

instead they are philosophically interesting only when viewed in the unusual light of comparison with our familiar world of material goods. Nonetheless, this is an important mind-set for thinking about the information age, since unconsciouslessly we all make assumptions based on past experiences that may not be applicable in this new domain. Our minds are most comfortable with concrete things—with a notion of space—whereas information is abstract and spaceless.

Unlike material goods, the creation of information does not necessarily consume natural resources (though of course it may). In information we are dealing with an inexhaustible resource. Information is infinitely expandable and, once created, it is hard to destroy. However, most information becomes rather quickly value-less on its own accord as time sweeps by its period of validity. Information is also very easy to store. The cost of most electronic storage technologies decreases by a factor of two every two to three years. Most people in the information business find that despite this increased economy in storage, their total expenditure for memory increases continually. This apparent paradox must be due to an exponentially growing appetite for information. It is also obvious to most of us that empty disks, like empty closets, attract junk. We become in the end victims of information greed. Storage costs increase linearly with the amount of information, and at the same time access costs increase faster than linearly (the best sorting algorithms increase as $n \log (n)$ with the number, n, of items). Finally, the value of much of the information contained in storage deteriorates with time.

In addition to the properties of communication and sharing, information can be broadcast and networked. Broadcasting is a familiar concept in which many recipients share an identical piece of information. Inherent in the broadcast process is the inability of any receiver to change the information itself; it is strictly a one-way street. Propaganda thrives on such a medium. Governments in the past have used newspapers, radio, and television to control the dissemination of information with some success.

In contrast to broadcasting, networking enables many users to pool their information. In networking, the information is processed and new information is generated. Although people themselves have always been in networks, the degree of networking has dramatically increased in the last few decades. The new mobility of people, the emergence of inexpensive air travel, and the cheap long-distance phone rates have linked people together in much tighter fashion. Conferences and meetings have proliferated, and these face-to-face get-togethers forge bonds that can be electronically nurtured. Early in this century it took many friend-to-friend links to connect arbitrary individuals. Today we are so networked that it takes very few. The usual "do you know so and so" gambit that is enacted at parties throughout the country is amazingly successful. Usually two strangers meeting can very quickly find a common acquaintance. As an example test, consider how many friend-to-friend links it would take you to reach the president of the United States. Think how far removed you would have been in the time of your grandparents.

The networking of humans is a deceptively powerful phenomenon. Right now there is a rumor going around in my company about some scandal on high corporate levels. Within only a few days it has reached probably tens of thousands of people in a dozen states. Even retired employees and neighbors outside the company have been passing the information along as its geometric progression has swept across a subset of the business community. I myself helped build the network by telling perhaps a half dozen people. However, at least two dozen people have brought the rumor back to me in various enhanced forms. Ironically, I have good reason to believe that there is not the proverbial shred of truth in this rumor. This is certainly an everyday example of information pooling at its most effective.

In the rumor mill, information is altered on each link. Each rumor is usually specific to a small, interested group, and there is enough retransmission on circular paths to keep the rumor generally intact, although dramatized. All of us have played the game where a story is told from person to person around a table, whereupon it emerges completely transfigured. In this game, there are no cross-links, and consequently no real network exists. At the other extreme, consider the network for jokes. It is truly incredible that a joke can literally inundate the country in a matter of days. Like computer data, jokes are protected from alteration by internal consistency checks—the punch lines must work. Thus with only slight variations on the theme the jokes circulate from node to node. What makes the network even more interesting is the mystery of the origin of the jokes. Who among us has ever started a joke on its network? Where do they come from? Perhaps, like rumors, they have their origins in fortuitous happenings, and only in subsequent networking are they molded into the traditional time-tested format for humor.

Networking plays a dominant role in many human endeavors. Scientists know that very few discoveries and inventions are made of whole cloth. The time becomes "ripe" for a given invention, it is "in the air," so to speak. In fact, the necessary knowledge is assembling itself in the network, ready to leap out at the first person with sufficient sensitivity to recognize that it is there, already manufactured by a process much bigger than any of us alone. A century ago the telephone was in the air, but history remembers only Alexander Graham Bell. In the end Bell prevailed over many pretenders, including Edison and, by a five-to-four decision of the Supreme Court, Elisha Gray. Most great inventions have similar tangled origins, which are straightened out only by the isolating spotlight of simplified remembrance. In similar fashion many of the great musical composers had their inspiration from so-called "folk tunes." These were tunes of the day, known by everybody and composed by none. To the receptive Beethoven, Mahler, or Dvorak they were there for the taking.

In the information age we have a new way of augmenting the effectiveness of networks. Computer networks are much more than just highways for corporate data; they also put people together in a new and intelligent manner. These networks now link a number of closed, but worldwide, communities, causing a new electronic informational proximity to emerge. Yet these networks are as yet only embryonic. Computers are now at a position similar to that of voice telephony at the turn of the century, when many small competing telephone companies had their own precious enclaves. Today there is little connectivity between local computer networks, and no national telephone directory for data users. We have growing pains, but they will pass. Inevitably, the world will be encompassed by interconnected computer networks.

Who really knows what capability will emerge from the computer-mediated networking of people and their information through data networks? Harlan Cleveland has spoken about the coming of an "information commons," analogous to the town commons of the last century where people met to discuss the issues of the day. Now we are too many for a village commons, and our issues are too complex for the few who govern. The information commons is a virtual place. It lies in the interstices of the electronic networks. It knows no political boundaries, and it will be accessible to everyone. Perhaps a new degree of human wisdom will eventually be enabled.

Not too long ago I saw a note on one of the consumer discussion groups on a computer network. Someone was thinking of installing a humidifier on his furnace. Would it rust his heating ducts, he asked? That is the kind of everyday question we always are confronting, and you never know whom to ask. Moreover, it is the kind of information that is very difficult to find in a library. By the end of the day I saw about twenty-five responses to the question. Most were from homeowners with humidifiers who had had no problem. A few responses were from plumbers, which says something very gratifying about the evolving population of the networks. And, typically, a number of responses were from scientists and engineers who had no practical experience, but who had theories! Consider, though, the power of being able to tap the experience and knowledge of others around the world. It is like mailing a letter addressed: "to anyone who knows about humidifiers and heating ducts."

OWNERSHIP OF INFORMATION

Because information is so easy to communicate, duplicate, and share, it is also exceedingly hard to own exclusively. Information is leaky, that is, it runs through the narrowest cracks and floods the area below. The consequences of this leakiness are profound. Information can no longer be held in the hands or the minds of a few leaders. Inevitably it diffuses down the hierarchy, and with it goes the power that the information conveys. The rigid hierarchy of leadership that was the commonplace of the industrial era melts down to a pool of consensus management in the information age. Indeed, with information so immediately pervasive up and down the corporate ladder it has been said that managers are reluctant to make decisions on the basis of information that their superiors receive simultaneously. Perhaps in the past the fact that information was more limited created an uncertainty which provided a kind of free space for human judgment. Today, of course, the ultimate aim is to replace that human judgment with computer algorithms. That sounds frightening, but consider the example of program trading in the financial community, where buy and sell decisions involving tens of millions of dollars are made almost instantaneously, solely by computers on the basis of information received from two or more financial markets.

Leadership by the many may be a necessary condition today, as one of the by-products of our technology is an increasing dependency upon extraordinarily complex systems. It may be that no one person or small group of persons will hold either the knowledge or expertise to encompass the needs of leadership and management of a business or society. The deepening complexity of our world is one of the ominous trends of the information age. Management of complexity is perhaps the most crucial problem of our time, yet we have only begun to recognize the dimensions of this problem. John Naisbitt has observed that the computer is a tool that manages complexity, and as such, just as highways encourage more cars, the computer invites more complexity into society. Furthermore, the worry over complexity is not just the amount of data being accumulated or the overwhelming number of variables in any system model that describes an important societal problem, but it is the growing opinion that we are now creating systems that are ultimately unknowable.

Those of us who deal with technology used to have an intuitive notion of what could and could not be done. A machine might require more resources for its construction than the gross national product, or alternatively it might be beyond the current state of knowledge. In that case we would have to await the needed breakthroughs. Now we are confronting a new situation in which we know how to build a system in nearly every detail, yet we have no assurance that, once built, the system will do what we wish. The Strategic Defense Initiative is one current example of such a dilemma. The complexity of the computer code foreseen in this system is so enormous that scientists argue over whether it is intrinsically incomprehensible—and so perhaps undoable—in spite of our complete faith in the construction of its component modules. Software systems, the stuff of the information age, are more intrinsically complex and difficult to construct than any mechanical system man has ever pondered. Fred Brooks, an eminent software philosopher, has observed that software is "invisible and unvisualizable," and as it is not inherently embedded in space, some of its complexity derives from the fact that the mind is deprived of its most powerful conceptual tools.

Since information is the key to power and wealth in the new society, people will surely wish to possess and control the intellectual property they create or acquire. However, the leaky nature of information makes absolute possession very difficult. Moreover, technology itself has provided an arsenal of tools for the would-be information pirate. The Xerox machine, tape cassettes, floppy disk duplication, VCRs, data networks, electronic bulletin boards, home satellite dishes, scientific publications, and the press are all mechanisms and institutions designed to make life difficult for those who would contain and control information. In spite of this array of impressive pirate technology, however, it will not do to concede the principle that information by its very nature must be shared. Anne Branscombe has argued that if we are to transform our economy to one that relies primarily upon the economic value of gathering, storing, processing, and distributing information, then we must develop principles from which we can derive economic value for such activities. The necessity to understand how either to control or to derive value from the flows of information is deeply woven into the issue of international competitiveness for those of us in the United States.

Our ethics, laws, and practices have had a hard time keeping up with the information age. Patent law has tried to accommodate the notion that more and more of the invention activity is embedded in software, but with limited success. Few software patents have been granted, and many people question whether the patents have any force. The patenting of hardware has been difficult enough. It has often been easy to design around patents, which must be based on an implementation rather than a concept. The patent system has been frustrating for engineers and attorneys alike. The protection by law of a basic idea is much more difficult than is apparent. This is due in part to the rarity of inventions conceived out of whole cloth, a notion that we discussed earlier. Often when we dissect in detail the origin of an important invention we encounter a trail with many branches that disappear into the jungles of technological history. Thus, even if we subscribe to the notion that a person should own the fruits of his intellectual labor, it is surprisingly difficult to authenticate the provenance of such works.

The battle over copy protection of software highlights the issues in ownership of intellectual goods. Most of us feel quite differently about the purchase of software than about hardware. Imagine your feelings toward buying a printer for your home, compared with the purchase of a similarly priced software package. The printer seems more generally useful, perhaps, but more importantly it is a thing of substance to which you can point with a certain pride of ownership. The material being of the printer advertises to the world a certain image of your own wealth and taste. When you want to upgrade the printer to a new model, you can perhaps sell it to a friend, since after all it is yours, as they say, lock, stock, and barrel.

The software, in contrast to the printer, seems to have less intrinsic value. We are bothered by its lack of substance, by the fact that it is carried upon a few cheap plastic disks. Why does it cost so much, we wonder? We read of young millionaires in the software business, and we worry about what should be a fair price for this expensive piece of nothingness. (The unsuccessful software entrepreneurs get little press.) The extent to which we differentiate between hardware and software in our minds is most clearly delineated in our conception of the morality of copying software. Very few of us would consider stealing a printer, even if we were given the perfect opportunity to do so. Stealing software, however, is quite another matter. Many of us think this is quite all right, for we are not really stealing any*thing* at all. If you doubt that many people think this way, check with your nearest college student.

Lined up on the one side we have the hackers of the world, perhaps a great many consumers, and most students. They derive gratification by beating copy-protection schemes, by trading software freely, and even by generating software that is put in the public domain through electronic-bulletin-board systems. On the other side, the software industry points to studies by independent consultants, whom they have hired, that show huge sums of money lost to the industry because of illegal copying. They ask how are we to give incentive and fair return to programmers whose life work is this nonmaterial code? They develop ever more sophisticated copy-protection schemes (whose cost, ironically, is passed on to the lawful purchasers of their products), and they write restrictive, shrink-wrap agreements for their products. When you open one of these shrink-wrap software packages you are said to accept strictures on the use of *their* code. You may not lend it, you may not use it on more than one computer, you may not sell it, etc. In effect, the attitude is that you do not own this code at all but have merely borrowed it temporarily. This viewpoint is as far from that of the

15

hackers as one could imagine. In these agreements, the ownership of information is elevated from the hacker's nothingness to a position superior to that of material goods. If only the software were made out of moving parts like the printer!

The schemes for software protection have become so onerous that many software developers have renounced them, casting their financial destinies behind the ethics of enlightened consumers and industrial clients. Meanwhile, one of the best selling personal computer programs in the last few years has been a copy program that unlocks the protection schemes. Naturally this program carries a warning label about not being used for illegal purposes, such as copying software. The situation in VCR taping of television is not much better, and the music industry is in the throes of agony over the introduction of digital audiotape recorders (DAT), which will enable users to make faithful reproductions of compact disks. Our law, and even our own sense of ethical behavior, is under assault by the pervasiveness and ease of duplication of this new form of value.

C O N T R O L   O F
I N F O R M A T I O N

When industry has paid for the collection or creation of information, it feels entitled to the exploitation of the results of its investment. No one would quarrel with that concept in general, and certainly businesses have always protected their private information in one way or another. What is new in recent years is a more concerted and organized effort of businesses to collect information from their competitors. Most of this effort is within legal bounds, so the word "collect," rather than "steal," is perfectly appropriate. There are many public channels in which business information leaks away from its source. Sometimes, in fact, even the employees of a corporation find out more about its policies through, say *The Wall Street Journal,* than through their own management or internal publications. On the nearer fringe of the law we have the vivid example in Tracey Kidder's *The Soul of a New Machine* of Tom West studying the design of Digital Equipment Corporation's VAX computer through a friendly intermediary "somewhere in the United States" in order to further the development of Data General's own entry into the same market. (" 'I wasn't really into G-Two,' said West.") No business today can operate in an intelligence vacuum; there is too much to be gained from tapping into what others have learned to be arrogant or stupid enough to go it alone.

While they organize their own intelligence collection, at the same time businesses have taken much greater cognizance of their own vulnerabilities to the leakage of information. Everywhere we see the new stamp "proprietary information." A new legal specialty has been formed to deal with "intellectual property." We should note particularly the word "property" being pushed adjacent to the adjective "intellectual." Presumably these people help enforce the similarity between intellectual and material assets, which as we have discussed is a most difficult and poorly understood subject. Unfortunately, the trend in technology is to make information all the more slippery, so the protection of these assets will get all the more difficult. Computer networks, for example, cut not only across corporate hierarchies but between corporations and even countries. They help promote a new measure of nearness that has little to do with corporate ties. Information floats around these networks in a fairly uncontrolled manner. The lack of control has alarmed corporate management, which has campaigned against this electronic openness. A recent discussion on a computer net warned against the "information police" who might well be eavesdropping on the conversation.

For those of us in research the questions of ownership of information are especially difficult. We operate within an international framework of scientific support. Scientific and engineering journals, conferences, and personal interchanges of information foster a pool that forms the time-tested, fertile environment for research progress. Operating without the support of this pool is unthinkable; the days of the garage inventor are all but gone. On the other hand, if a company's research cannot flourish without access to the research pool, how can it in good conscience not contribute its own research to help build the pool? And if all research is shared with the world, why should a company fund research at all? Where is that sought-after "competitive edge?" Most of the answer, or at least what answer there is, lies in timing. Information will diffuse, and it is good for all that it does. The so-called strategic edge for an individual corporation's investment lies in the transient nature of the diffusion. A company must be first to act upon its information, while at the same time sharing as a matter of course all of its longer-term research. There is not much new in that, since we have all been taught that the early bird gets the worm. On the other hand, Norman Augustine has given us the corollary, "The early worm gets eaten."

The government has the uneasy task of protecting the nation's information assets and secrets. Technologically advanced nations make use of the universities and the high-tech research in the United States to promote their own competitiveness, while less advanced nations simply appropriate intellectual property to produce royalty-free clones. In ancient times a moat or an encircling wall sufficed to keep the enemy without and the treasures within. But most of today's treasures are ethereal, and moats and walls and their equivalents in our age are hardly effective against the diffusion of information. On the one hand, the government has responsibility for developing and enforcing a policy that husbands the nation's technological information in order to maintain a globally competitive position in the balance of trade; on the other hand, the government itself is the largest producer of information, which includes the most critical defense secrets. The control of information is a vital function of government, but how should it be accomplished, and at what cost?

Armed with laws such as those on export control, the government has tried to stem the flow of technological information in key areas of military concern by prohibiting scientists and engineers from giving talks or publishing papers at certain conferences. This has caused an uproar in professional societies, whose members for the most part consider these actions a useless folly. Many argue that the predominant direction of flow in international technological conferences has turned in recent years *into* the United States as many centers of excellence have grown abroad, particularly in Japan and to a somewhat lesser extent Western Europe. In the last twenty-five years the number of international conferences has doubled, as technology has become internationalized. In any event this is a most serious business, and there is little wisdom about how best to conserve one's know-how for economic and military advantage.

The business of defense has for some time been information intensive. Unbelievably complex systems probe the skies and the earth, watching and listening, accumulating and comparing, processing and communicating. Intelligence organizations consume huge amounts of our budget. The information-age avionics on military aircraft make the airplane itself appear, as has been quipped, to be a mere peripheral. And underlying all this technology are what the public perceives as great military secrets. It seems to me that the existence of such secrets is largely a myth forged at the end of the Second World War by the development of the atomic bomb, and perpetuated ever since by innumerable spy novels in which scientists are kidnapped in order to steal their inventions for world dominance. Although this is great stuff for best-selling fiction, it hardly resembles reality. There are actually few technological secrets behind our critical defense systems—rather an enormous effort in systems integration. Moreover, these systems are the products of a political/military/industrial system that is nowhere equaled. This is not to say that it is unimportant to protect classified information, but only that no critical military system should depend on the protection of such secrets, for as we have argued, information is extraordinarily vulnerable to leaks which destroy its value. Rationally, the protection of military information is a question of cost/benefit trade-offs. The price of intelligence must be raised to an expensive level for the enemy. At the same time we must be fully aware that there is no absolute protection available at any cost.

THE INFORMATION HIERARCHY

Thus far we have avoided any definition of the word "information." We all have some intuitive notion of what information is, but beyond that imprecise feeling that we already know what the word means lies a great difficulty in further definition. Try a definition for yourself, and then test it against your own knowledge and experience. The dictionary definitions do not seem to capture the concept of the information we have been discussing in this chapter. Seemingly the concept is so purposely vague it cannot be contained in one small coherent thought, yet we have named our whole current age on its behalf!

Information may be communicated in many forms. In this book we will discuss the common information media of text, speech, and pictures in some detail. But these expressions of information are not the information itself, just as no one sees a dollar bill as a green slip of paper. Perhaps information itself is best described in terms of *organization,* implying that organization per se is the intellectual effort that manufactures information out of such raw material as observation. The more the organization, the higher the level of information. In contrast, where there is total disorder there is no information. The level of organization can be described in terms of a hierarchy, where we have borrowed the words sometimes used as synonymous with information to indicate the levels of organization—data, information, knowledge, and wisdom, as shown in Figure 1.

Where is the Life we have lost in living?
Where is the wisdom we have lost in knowledge?
Where is the knowledge we have lost in information?
　　　　　　　　　—T.S. Eliot, "The Rock"

The visualization of information as a hierarchy of organization is a useful structure, even if somewhat loosely defined. Certainly we can appreciate that there is some hierarchical structure associated with the concept of information, though how many layers and how they should be defined must be somewhat arbitrary. At the base of our pyramid we have what we shall call *data.* It consists of the raw material from which information is extracted, which might include unprocessed observations, random sights and sounds, the "ones"

FIGURE 1
Levels of the information hierarchy

and "zeros" in a data communications stream, etc. This is the sludge of the information age—stuff that no one has yet thought very much about.

At the second level of the pyramid is what we are for the moment calling *information*. Now someone has thought about the sludge—the raw data—and given it organization. Information takes the form of what appears in the morning newspapers or on television. It is in all the government publications containing voluminous statistics; it is in the endless files of the insurance companies, and it is in the libraries of the world. Someone has thought about the data, but not us. It is now only a collection of unconnected, or perhaps unassimilated, facts or fictions. When we take in information ourselves, for example by reading, and consciously or not store it in our minds with the rest of our remembered information, we create something personal, and at a higher level yet of organization. Now we call it *knowledge.*

The final level of the hierarchy is *wisdom*. This is organized, distilled, and integrated knowledge. It is something more than knowledge alone. It is the putting together of a base of knowledge in such an integrated fashion that it is possible to create new associations—new knowledge—from the accumulation. Wisdom is our aspiration, and it is far, far removed from the torrent of data that cascades upon all of us every day of our lives. In this information age we spend our time and energies shoveling data and thoughts from one level of the pyramid to the next.

Since the definitions of the levels of the information hierarchy are imprecise, and because common use dictates that words like "data" are used in association with information at several levels of the pyramid, we shall for the most part ignore these definitions in the remainder of the book. Generally speaking, organization at any level will be called "information," and we will also have many occasions to use the word "data" in its conventional sense.

THE INFORMATION FLOOD

It has been pointed out that there is no danger of running out of information, but that quite the opposite is happening. We are being flooded by so much information that we are unable to handle it all. There is so much material on the lower two levels of the pyramid that we simply do not have the time to sift through it all to know where to use our intellectual shovel. For all the sophistication in the information age, there is still the age-old limit on humans having only sixteen or so hours a day in which to think and work. Time is our limit, and selection is our task.

Just about everyone these days complains of an overload of information. Why is this happening, and what is to be done about it? About the latter question I can offer little advice; in fact it will probably get much worse. As to why there is more information, a number of reasons can be put forward.

PEOPLE ARE WRITING MORE
• • • • • • • • • • • • •

The number of books (new titles, not total copies) published in the United States over the last twenty years has steadily increased from about 11,000 to over 41,000. The rate of growth is that of compound interest, about 5 percent per year. This increase is partially accounted for by the population growth of about 3 percent per year. The same factor can be seen in the publication of technical journals, magazines, and reports. The fields in which we browse for information have grown beyond our individual horizons. If we are hungry for information, there is surely no reason to starve.

Certainly it is easier to write today than ever before. Word processing systems have been the biggest boon of the personal computer revolution. There is also a certain atmosphere of easy text entry, editing, and electronic distribution in this information age that encourages everyone to contribute to the flow. But people also have that human limit of time and energy; no matter how easy we make the mechanization of the publishing process it seems unlikely that the number of books or articles published per capita can continue to grow exponentially. (But then again, it might well continue its upward spiral for a long time yet!) Even if per capita writing were to be constant, the exponential increase in the world's population would produce a growing amount of printed information. More importantly, the number of literate people is growing at a higher rate than the population itself. Historically we are not so far removed from a time when a small number of people produced the bulk of the information output for the entire earth. Now there are many—many of us capable of contributing in writing and thought.

The growth in variety of publications is strong, but in itself it does not constitute the flood that we seem to be experiencing. It is not the fact of more being written as much as the increase in distribution of what is being written that causes our overwhelming glut of information.

THE DISTRIBUTION OF INFORMATION IS INCREASING
• • • • • • • • • • •

Earlier we pointed out that information is exceedingly easy to copy and communicate. As useful as these properties are for most purposes, they have negative side effects. It is getting so easy to distribute information that we are all becoming inundated with copies of information, much of which is redundant, useless for our purposes, or outright junk. Some factors are technological; for example, the Xerox machine, data transmission, desktop publishing, and satellite networks are some of the technologies that have increased the distribution of information. It is very easy to send copies of memoranda to everybody these days, since computerized mailing lists and stored descriptions of the individual interests of potential recipients have mechanized the process of shotgun distribution. In spite of brave talk about computers bringing on "paperless" offices, the per capita paper consumption in the United States has steadily risen from two hundred pounds in 1940 to six hundred pounds in 1980. Thus most people get large quantities of information in which they have only a marginal interest. It is time consuming to sort through this material, but people are hesitant about saying they do not want to receive mailings for fear they will miss some crucial piece of information.

The federal policies on mail and telecommunications have helped increase the distribution of low-quality information. Cheap postage rates on third class mail seem to ensure that we get enough junk mail to be able to use it to heat our houses during the winter.

It is a tricky task these days to be able to sort cleverly disguised junk mail from important bills and checks. Policies in the telephone realm have maintained flat-rate calling in the local area (although there is a trend toward a measured service). Here again this helps encourage a great many low-value calls. At the same time there has been such progress in the cost of long-distance transmission that many consumers are now getting routine long-distance junk calls. These calls are also promoted by the WATS tariffs, which give package discounts for calls originating from a single location. Probably the greatest increase in any sector of telecommunications is in overseas calling, as that cost has plummeted. All the communications channels have opened on us and are pouring information upon us. There is little incentive for the originators of this junk information to diminish their output, and in the end we suffer from our own greed.

Many people complain about their information overload, cursing the times and yearning for the old days when they had less information with which to contend. Although the two factors we have just discussed are significant, there is probably another, more personal, factor that is most to blame.

PERSONAL NETWORKS AND FIELDS OF INTEREST EXPAND WITH TIME
• • • • • • • • • • • • • • • • •

In order to determine how the information load increases with time we might consider measuring the received information for a given person over some period of time, preferably years. Our measurements would no doubt confirm the person's own feeling of being steadily more flooded with material as time goes by, but we would be hard pressed to distinguish how much of this flood was due to the changing external information environment, and how much was due to the changing interests of the individual himself. In scientific research, for example, a young researcher begins his or her career with few contacts, and in a specialized field of work which is probably a very new one. There may be only one journal worth following in this new field. The person is working at the very interface between what is known and what is unknown. In effect, he or she is a bud on the end of a fragile branch of the tree of knowledge.

If we were to return several years later to look in on this same researcher, typically we would see quite a different situation. The researcher now has many contacts and is imbedded in a rich network of other researchers that extends over several continents. Moreover, the nascent field in which he or she worked earlier has matured. There are now a number of journals that cover the field, some of which have already subdivided into new specialties. The researcher's own specialty is no longer at the cutting edge, and more and more he is becoming interested in a broader range of subjects. The bud he inhabited on the tree of knowledge has become a twig, and then a small branch with further branchings beyond. It is not so much that he is moving back toward the trunk, but that the tree itself is growing past his stationary position. Almost no one is able to stay on the bud over the course of a career. The closer one comes to the trunk, the more the flow of information, until it is such a torrent that one can only peer into the waters and sigh at all that might be known, but cannot.

All the trends suggest strongly that we will have to contend with more and more information on a very personal level in the future. In communications, breakthroughs in fiber optics promise super-highways of communications capacity beyond anything we have previously conceived. Computer networks have only recently begun to provide significant interconnectivity beyond their original, closed, user groups. Personal computers and workstations are being produced in still larger numbers to inhabit the work desks of the world. The concept of desktop publishing holds forth that any computer can take over the initial, mechanical tasks of a publishing house. If we believe there is a flood now, things will only get worse.

Is more information necessarily better? Perhaps not. It would be easier to argue that more and easier *access* to information is necessarily good, and that is surely happening. On-line data bases, abstracting services, optical-disk storage systems, document retrieval systems, and intelligent data-base front ends are among the technologies that enable easier access to stored information. Knowledge engineering, with its study of knowledge acquisition and representation, is a new field of study about human access to electronically stored information. It is very likely that in the future anyone, anywhere, will be able to access almost any information of which he knows the existence. But this still reduces to the selection problem: You must know what to ask for. The problem of how to get it once you know it exists will probably go away.

From the spy novel *Dunn's Conumdrum* by Stan Lee:

Negative information is that which, immediately upon acquiring, causes the recipient to know less than he did before.

While accessing specific information is getting considerably easier, serendipitous browsing may be becoming more difficult due to the sheer volume of material. Perhaps we need new methodologies for browsing at various levels of detail. All of us share a sort of core knowledge of current hot topics. The newspapers, television, and magazines bombard us with redundant discussions of the latest and the famous, like searchlights darting about in the night sky, first illuminating this and then that, while the world stands passively below with heads upturned to see what will be next. To have some personal uniqueness beyond this core knowledge, all of us will have to probe here and there on our own, turning over our intellectual shovel in unlikely places just to see what is there. The associations we make during our serendipitous searches are the keys to the formation of new knowledge. The size of the pile of information in which we must dig is growing exponentially, and its quality is very likely diminishing. That is why the information flood is dangerous. We must work harder at acquiring meta-information, that is, information about information. Just having some idea about what is "out there" is a real challenge. Having a marketable uniqueness associated with our own array of layered knowledge will be one of our goals in the information age.

THE MYSTERIES OF INFORMATION

So information and its sociological ramifications float about us like an all-enveloping mist of nourishment, complexity, and entanglement. But this book is not so much about the sociology of information as it is about the technology, and, to a lesser degree, the psychology of information. To be honest, it is really woven about what I think of as the mysteries of information—the properties of information that have bothered and captivated me for most of my career as a technologist. Some are deep issues of philosophy, while others are just little puzzles that seem especially conceived only to agitate me and no one else. For instance, I have never understood why rain does not come down my chimney when it pours outside. No one else seems to care about this. Also I do not know how ducks find out about your new duck pond. Or do you have to buy ducks? And if so, how do they know to stay? These are the kinds of things that bother me, so be forewarned!

This first chapter has been about one such mystery.

HOW DOES THE INFORMATION AGE WORK?

I do not understand how no one can make anything or grow anything, and yet everyone can live happily ever after just by ferreting out, sorting, and processing information. My Japanese friends who run large corporations for fun and profit are not so sure either They believe that a root cause of the trade imbalance with the United States is that Japan is still an industrial economy, while the United States has advanced far into the information economy. Though when I see the computerization of their banks and other institutions, I have my doubts about the image of Japan as a holdout from the benefits of modern information technology.

The next chapter is about a deep mystery that is fundamental to the technology of information handling and processing.

HOW IS INFORMATION TO BE DEFINED AND MEASURED?

This is a mystery that has been solved to the satisfaction of a great many mathematicians and engineers but perhaps of few others. To those of us who have lived these recent decades with the theory of information that was conceived by Claude Shannon in the waning shadows of World War II, there is an enduring truth and beauty associated with its revelations of information as a measure of order and disorder. To some few researchers it verges on a religion, while to many engineers and scientists it is just something that they have heard about but have never quite understood. To many artists and psychologists it is an overblown and discredited theory. Mystery or not? You can choose for yourself, but perhaps some of the thoughts in this book will help you in making your own classification.

A great deal of the remainder of this book is devoted to following the thread of information as embedded or expressed in our language.

HOW MUCH INFORMATION IS CONTAINED IN THE WORDS OF LANGUAGE?

What a silly mystery, you must think! Surely it depends upon what you say with these words. Well, of course, but in the computerized handling of those words it does not matter nearly as much as you might believe. On the average, language maintains a certain flow of information. It is a very strong structure on which we superimpose our individual variations. The structure itself is on the one hand excess baggage that must be carried wherever we go, and on the other hand an ingenious cocoon to protect the embedded information from harm. So on average how much information does the English language convey? No one knows. It is, after all, a mystery, but one that is central to both machine and human efficiency in the handling of information.

No sooner do we leave the mystery of the printed word than we encounter another mystery of an insidious sort having to do with the spoken word.

WHY DOES IT TAKE SO MANY MORE BITS TO REPRESENT SPEECH THAN TEXT?

I am sure that I will not give anything away to say that information is stored, carried, and measured by the bit. You would naturally think that the same number of bits could be used to store text as to store its spoken equivalent. Would you believe that it takes a thousand times as many bits for speech as text? Maybe even ten thousand! And it is not as if it is only a philosophical question, because the telephone companies of the world convert speech into

28

streams of bits. The more bits speech takes, the fewer channels can be carried. It is worth billions and billions of dollars, yet it remains a mystery.

Words alone are not the only form of information we share with one another and with machines. The amount of raw data that flows through our optic nerves into that greatest of processors, our brain, is stupendous. The eyes funnel this unbelievable traffic onto the brain's highway, but in the end how much true information gets through the exit ramps? Most of us feel intuitively that pictorial material is the bulk way to exchange information. But is it true?

IS A PICTURE WORTH A THOUSAND WORDS?

Pictures are indeed an information mystery. They may be worth a thousand words, they may not be. But incredibly, they require a thousand times as many bits. So perhaps they had better be a thousand times more valuable! Yet what is it worth, for example, to see the person you are talking to, as opposed to merely hearing their voice on a telephone? Would you believe that perhaps it is worth nothing? No one has yet been able to quantify a value.

All these mysteries inevitably lead to the greatest mystery. What does it matter how much information is here or there unless it reaches a human? So here we have these information-age machines storing and processing information ever so cleverly, only in the end to have to shovel the bits into or out of a Stone Age human. I say Stone Age only to emphasize the point that machines are evolving a lot faster than we are. We are stuck with us. And the trouble is, we do not seem to be very good at information handling, regardless of how hard the machines try to help.

WHAT ARE THE HUMAN CAPABILITIES FOR INFORMATION TRANSFER?

Ever since I was in graduate school, ever so long ago, I have been aware of a hypothesis dealing with humans and their consumption or production of information. I will put it to you starkly—we seem to be able to input or output only about 50 bits per second, regardless of how we go about it. This in spite of the billion bits per second flowing through our optic nerves, to mention only one source of data. Somewhere there seems to be a cognitive processing bottle-neck. Whenever we want the data to mean something—to be orga-nized, processed, categorized, or recognized—we seemingly have to call up cognitive processing subroutines in our brain that run very slowly.

In subsequent chapters we will examine the human abilities to input and output information through reading, speaking, typing, and vision. In each case we will see a limitation that is due to thinking, rather than to sensor inadequacy or muscle speed. How-ever, the cognitive bottleneck is only a hypothesis. All of the things we can measure support it, but perhaps tomorrow someone will come up with a scenario in which a human can input or output information at much higher rates. I am just not aware of any such circumstances at this time. You must realize, too, that in many postulated situations it is most difficult to measure the actual infor-mation transferred. Sometimes, as when looking at a picture, we have the naïve belief that we are gorging ourselves with bits of information. As we shall later discuss, this seems not to be the case. This great apparent discrepancy between human information rates and those of machines leads to many puzzlements. What I consider to be a fascinating paradox, for example, is the fact that we have to devote about 100 million bits per second to create a typical network television picture on your TV screen. But then you sit there in front of that bitwise voracious display and ingest only your meager few dozen bits per second.

Whenever I begin to feel sorry for myself as an information-limited human, I come back to the machine. What about its limits? Since it has all those engineers working to make it faster and smarter, why not use that power to present its information in a way that fits in with our abilities? Can it make up for our inadequacies? How about meeting us halfway?

WHAT ABILITIES CAN WE GIVE TO MACHINES TO EXCHANGE INFORMATION WITH US?

When I begin to consider this question, I come back to feeling proud of being human. Remember those cognitive processing routines that seem to slow us down so terribly? Well, we do not know how to give these abilities to machines. Consequently its abilities to understand our language, to hear and speak our words, and to understand our visual world are really rather pathetic. The more we investigate the difficulties in these seemingly simple human functions, the more we appreciate the wonders of our own minds. Again and again we shall return to this point. Machines have a long way to go to catch up with us Stone Age people.

C O N C L U S I O N

This has been a chapter largely about the changes in our social system that are taking place in this postindustrial era, called the information age. We observe these changes as passengers on a boat that none of us controls. As the scenery goes by we are slow to admire it, since we have no illusion of motion. Thus while the world becomes more dependent upon information as a basic resource, we still base our thinking on property and material goods.

In our childhood visions of the world we imagined that a small group of leaders gets together and decides, "Let's have an information age." In maturity we realize that such trends are far, far beyond the power of any collection of individuals. What is happening is the concurrence of many events, only some of which are technological. The technological factors are the enabling events, but in the final analysis it is the people that matter. Information is, after all, only for people. All information is generated by people and consumed by people. Perhaps some day machines too will originate and consume information, but for now they only serve as adept intermediaries. We cannot ignore the human factor in studying information, and we shall discuss it wherever possible in the remainder of this book.

Even though the evolution of the information age is beyond our specific control, that evolution is a good thing. Critics may point to negative effects, such as the possible loss of privacy and others that have been mentioned in this chapter, but the mental power that can be unleashed through the new systems will likely improve our lives in unforeseen ways. Hopefully we will be both more individual individuals and more integrated masses. Each is possible.

From *White Noise* by Don DeLillo

What good is knowledge if it just floats in the air? It goes from computer to computer . . . but nobody actually knows anything.

REFLECTIONS — THE INFORMATION AGE

From time to time I will include brief essays called Reflections, which are intended as lighthearted changes of pace from the rest of the material. While the Reflections are tongue-in-cheek, there is also usually a message to be found.

The advertisers assure us that we are about to plunge into the information age. Exactly what this is I'm not sure, but they say that the era to come will be much better than the Ice Age. Information will be good for us, they add—which is fortuitous since we don't seem to have a lot of choice in the matter. Like it or not we are about to be inundated under streams of information-carrying bits. Information access will be available every-where—in our homes and offices, through public terminals, and even in our cars and on airplanes. Everyone will have the right to bathe daily in tubs of bits, and afterwards to pull the plug and watch with gluttony as the excess information drains away into bit heaven. This excepts only those unfortunate individuals and nations who lack the necessary clout in computer IQ. The rest of us will spend all of our time in this age either in accessing information or in pretending to access information—the latter activity being recommended to preserve the illusion of the savvy informa-tion-age citizen. We will have to be diligent about this daily hunt for infor-mation, since in the information age the basic commodity of the land will be information rather than material goods. Our wealth and position in society will be determined solely by our market position in bits.

I'm a little nervous about the coming of this information age for several reasons. First, no one has told me what I'm supposed to do with all those bits. Moreover, I already seem to have more information than I can handle.

Finally, I secretly wonder who it is that will be generating all those bits that the rest of us are forced to absorb.

I barely have learned how to take care of money. What happens if we go on the bit standard? Will I be able to find ways to invest my hard-earned bits? Or can I hide bits in my mattress, against the rainy day when I find myself bitless? How will I ensure that I have enough bits to carry myself into retirement, when I no longer have the strength and ability to conduct the arduous, daily accessing of information that will be the *sine qua non* of the coming age? Will the value of bits depreciate with age because of bit inflation, or, like fine wines, will they improve if left to fester in a dank basement? (Perhaps no packet should be opened before its time.)

Putting these unanswered questions aside, the thing that scares me most about the coming of the information age is the implication that it is on its way, and not actually here at the moment. Frankly, I'm having some difficulty handling all the information that flows into my office now. If a lot more information is on its way here, then I'm in big trouble. I did a survey not so long ago and determined that my daily office mail contains on the average some three hundred pages of material, not including all the technical journals that I'm supposed to read to keep up competence in my profession. That represents about a half megabyte of whatever-it-is. Far from needing this oncoming information age, I wonder if we should find out who is responsible for generating the current glut and put a stop to all this excess information flow before it really gets out of hand.

After Claude Shannon and others conceived the principles of information theory in the late 1940s, a number of studies were conducted to determine the channel capacity of a human being. These studies were fairly consistent and depressing. No one does them anymore. It seems that a human being—you and I lest there be any doubt—is only good for about 50 bits per second of input or output. That is all the information that we are capable of taking in or putting out. I ask you, is this a being equipped for the onslaught of the information age?

At my modest 50 bits per second of capacity, those 300 daily pages would take me 24 hours to input, should I be so foolish as to spend my entire day operating in an input mode. But the real problems begin after the completion of the input cycle, should this have been possible in the first place. The question remains as to what happens to those bits. I mean are they stored away somewhere in my brain for reliable future access? Have they been processed and used to generate new, useful, perhaps saleable data, or have they just overflowed my inadequate input buffer facilities?

I get a kick out of all the ads in the newspapers and popular press for personal computers that are so technical that people who haven't the faintest idea of what they are talking about run around bragging about how many "K" of memory their system has. Well, maybe the same measure applies to people's memory too. For all I know, I'm working under the handicap of having only a 48K capacity upstairs, whereas you may have a deluxe 256K. So when I blithely shove that daily half megabyte into my economy-model brain, something is guaranteed to fall out the other side. This is the well-known pigeonhole theory of the brain. Mine may have been used up long ago merely under the trickle of bits preceding this oncoming information age.

The other day I stopped to make a phone call from O'Hare Airport to my son in college. It struck me that I should know his number by heart (a strange expression, that). Adeptly, I memorized it on the spot. After I dialed his number the friendly prerecorded message asked me to dial my credit card number. Shaking off my recurrent suspicion that a vaguely implied "or else" hung unspoken at the end of the request, I confidently put my finger forward to input the necessary 14 digits, long since burned into the ROM (Read Only Memory—chips that store permanent memory) section of my mind. My finger wavered futilely while my whole system looped. My credit card number had been zapped from my mind. It fell right off the back while I shoved the other digits in the front. The inadequacy of my ROM capacity was palpable. How am I supposed to be able to cope after the arrival of the information age?

On the other hand, perhaps we should be grateful for the promised ease of information access. Suppose bits became valuable and we had no way of getting them. I remember seeing several years ago an ad from a hobby electronics house selling a grab bag of used ROMs. The bag was very cheap—something like 99 cents as I recall. The ad offered terse enticement. "Some patterns may be useful," it said truthfully. This stimulates a fantasy in my mind of life in an age devoid of universal data access. I see myself scurrying about during the day in search of bits, just as ancient man went out bravely each morning looking for eatable animals somewhat smaller than dinosaurs.

"Pssst, want to buy some bits?"

The sibilant plea cut through the street sounds around me. I hesitated as my eyes accommodated to the discontinuity of the gloom in the intersecting alleyway. He was tall and shabbily dressed, his eyes vacantly focused on the street behind me. His jacket hung loosely opened and I licked my lips as I saw the computer printout folded in his inside pocket. Lines of bits ran across the dog-eared sheets.

"Are they used bits?" I asked tentatively.

He seemed to notice me for the first time. "Some are, some aren't," he answered noncommittally.

"How much?" I asked hoarsely.

There was a short pause while he seemed to size me up. "Fifty for a kilo," he said.

Fifty dollars for a kilopacket! I had no idea bits had become so expensive. "How do I know they're any good?"

He shrugged slightly and said nothing. His attention had already returned to the people in the street behind me. A distant siren touched the edge of my concentration and I noticed that his shoes were surprisingly well polished. I saw the gleam in his eyes as I reached for my wallet, and I knew that I should have bargained. Oh, whatever happened to cheap bits and easy access!?

Now that I think about it, maybe the industrial revolution still has a lot to offer after all.

2

A THEORY OF
INFORMATION

• • • • • • • • • • • • • •

INFORMATION THEORY

Information theory. When I was a graduate student it sounded like an all-encompassing theory of nature. Perhaps it has since fallen short of the expectations of my callow youth, but it still fascinates me. Most great physical and mathematical discoveries seem trivial after you understand them. You say to yourself, "I could have done that." But as I hold the tattered journal containing Claude Shannon's classic 1948 paper, "A Mathematical Theory of Communication," I see yellowed pages filled with vacuum tubes and mechanisms of yesteryear, and I know that I could never have conceived the insightful theory of information shining through these slippery, glossy pages of archaic font. I know of no greater work of genius in the annals of technological thought.

The period of time immediately following World War II was incredibly ripe for technology. The wartime impetus behind radar led to microwave radio transmission. The need for secrecy gave rise to digital transmission formats and pulse code modulation, which began the digital revolution in communications that still continues today. Information theory, the digital computer, and the transistor were all invented in these few short years. If the theory of punctuated equilibrium—that is, evolution in stepwise bursts—can be applied to the history of technology, this fertile period would appear to be the perfect example of such an evolutionary burst.

Shannon himself was able to indulge his growing interest in deriving a theoretical formulation for information through his wartime work in cryptography. As a boy he had been captivated by Edgar Allan Poe's "The Gold Bug," a story that has fascinated the youth of several generations. In his college years at Michigan and MIT, Shannon had read a 1928 paper by R. V. L. Hartley (the same Hartley, incidentally, who invented the best-known vacuum tube oscillator) dealing with the transmission of information, which Shannon said later had been an important influence on his life. At Bell Labs in the years between 1940 and 1945 Shannon began where Hartley had left off, working on information and communications and using the application to cryptography as a way of legitimatizing his work. The first mention of the phrase "information theory" occurs in a 1945 memorandum entitled "A Mathematical Theory of Cryptography." Curiously, this phrase never is used in his famous 1948 paper, which became the cornerstone of the new field of information theory.

Shannon's information theory is a philosophy of information from the point of view of communications. It is seldom prescriptive. It gives us a mathematical measure of information and of the informational capacity of a communications channel. Its central result is a theorem about the transmission of information over a communications channel, a result that has served as an inspiration to communications designers now for almost half a century. Shannon's genius lay in exposing a new way of thinking about information and communication. He pointed in a direction and set out the bounds within which one must stay. By now the road has been well traveled. The *Transactions on Information Theory,* the principal journal in the field, is filled with mathematical, abstract papers on esoteric problems with long titles—indicative of the degree of specialization that has been reached.

Information theory is primarily concerned about the *mechanics* of information handling. In the introduction to Shannon's paper we find the following:

The fundamental problem of communication is that of reproducing at one point either exactly or approximately a message selected at another point. Frequently the messages have *meaning*; that is they refer to or are correlated according to some system with certain physical or conceptual entities. These semantic aspects of communication are irrelevant to the engineering problem.

Thus, for the most part, information theory is not concerned with the meaning or the value of the information it describes. A bit of information could represent the chance throw of a coin—a head or a tail—or in the World War II era it could have represented the choice of location of the Allied invasion of France, whether it would be the coast of Normandy or Calais. In the eyes of information theory the same amount of information would be involved in either case, that is, the same storage capacity or the same transmission capacity would be required. Surely, you might argue, there is a great deal of difference. The chance flip of a coin might be of no consequence whatsoever, yet Hitler's foreknowledge of the location of the Allied invasion might have changed the course of the world.

In some respects I would agree that the disregarding of what Shannon called "meaning" is a philosophical deficiency of information theory. Yet I would despair of producing useful concepts in a theory that accounted for a property that is as difficult to measure as meaning, or, what is a consequence, value. Information theory considers information in much the same sense that we might study money in terms of the size and weight of the paper on which it is printed. Using such a theory we might derive the size of truck needed to transport our currency or the vault space required for its storage, but we would not be concerned with the fluctuations of the exchange rate or the effects of inflation on the intrinsic value of our paper certificates. Nevertheless, we shall see that Shannon's theoretical viewpoint provides deep insight about the generation and interpretation of information—insight that often borders on the questions of meaning and value.

MEASURING
INFORMATION

How shall we measure information? This is a question not far removed from asking what information is, but nowhere in this entire book will I give a definition of "information." It is a term so much used for so many different purposes that I have found that I cannot avoid using it in various ways myself. In the classical, Shannon sense, however, information has a precise, mathematical interpretation that I should like to introduce by considering intuitively what it means to have more or less of this quantity we call information.

Perhaps the cornerstone of information theory is the observation that any would-be information that we receive is a combination of the known and the unknown. Because it is so important, let me say synonymously that information is a blend of the expected and the unexpected, the foreseen and the unforeseen, or the certain and the uncertain. The first part, the expected, carries no real information; the measurable information is contained in the latter part, the unexpected.

If I tell you something that you already know, I give you no information. After all, it would seem that the whole idea of information is to "inform." More generally, even if I tell you something that you can deduce from other things that you know, I give you no information. There is nothing new added to your store of knowledge. The essence of information lies in the newness—the differentness—from that previously known, and from that which may be expected based upon what is previously known.

If I tell you something and your response is a shrug of the shoulders and the comment, "I figured as much," then little information has been conveyed. On the other hand, if your natural reaction is a surprised, "Wow, I had no idea!" then it would seem that you had received a significant amount of information. The measure of information intuitively must lie in the amount of surprise that resides in the unexpected or uncertain portion of the data received. We take the essence of information as the irreducible, fundamental underlying uncertainty that is removed by its receipt. In the Shannon sense information is measured through uncertainty. Information is viewed as being the *resolution of uncertainty*.

As the unit of information we take the prototypical uncertain event, the single throw of a fair coin. There are two possibilities that are equally likely, and we have no expectations, no prior indications, of whether the toss will yield a head or a tail. The actual throw resolves this uncertainty and gives us what we define as one bit of information. A bit resolves a single, binary choice. On a computer it is represented by a 1 or a 0. In everyday life it is the answer to a single "yes or no" question.

The word "bit" itself, which is a contraction of "binary digit," was invented by statistician John Tukey during a lunchtime conversation at Bell Labs. Although Tukey has other significant claims to a well-deserved fame, such as the popular and important Fast Fourier Transform, this little word grants him a kind of immortality in my mind. Imagine being the *inventor* of a word that is being used so constantly throughout the world! But let us return to our inspection of its deeper meaning.

So a single bit resolves the uncertainty of a coin toss. It is a far cry from that simple definition to the everyday information that we receive in so many different forms and formats. Life is not exactly constructed as the outcome of a series of coin tosses. However, if we are to measure information in the Shannon sense, we must interpret it in exactly this way. How many coin flips does it take to resolve the uncertainty in a given case? This is the measure of the information received.

There is an equivalent and more constructive way of getting at the number of "information bits" in data that we receive. It is also the *minimum number of yes/no questions required on the average to arrive at the given data,* knowing everything that we do know. Each bit of information is the answer to a single yes/no question, posed according the best possible strategy for the given situation. If you did not have this data, how many yes/no questions would it take you to reconstruct it?

This minimum average number of yes/no questions has a very real significance. It is not just a mathematical abstraction, for it is clearly the minimum amount of computer storage in bits required to save the data. Having the answers to the series of yes/no questions allows us to rederive the data any time we need it. This number is also directly related to the communications capacity required to send the information to us. How many bits have to be transmitted? Finally, this number may well be related to the human capability to intake, memorize, and output the data. The number of bits of information is the fundamental uncertainty associated with it.

Beginning with the single throw of a coin, I want to consider intuitively a progression of more complicated informational events. First let us change from a coin to a roulette wheel with 32 numbers. (It is a little smaller than usual for numerical convenience.) Again you have no prior expectations, and all 32 numbers represent equally likely outcomes of a single roll of the ball. How much information is required to convey an outcome? Well, it does not take too much cleverness to think of a good strategy for asking a series of yes/no questions to pin down a given result. "Is it sixteen or under?" you ask. If the answer is yes, you divide the range in half, and ask whether or not it is, for example, 8 or under. You continue to divide the range by two until you arrive at the number. It takes exactly five questions. There is no strategy that on average works better for this situation, so the information required to store or transmit a sequence of results of the roulette wheel is 5 bits per outcome.

We must be clear that the strategy for asking yes/no questions must yield the least questions *on average.* You might be tempted, for example, to ask immediately, "Did the ball land on number 22?" (You feel lucky.) I might look up in surprise, and say yes. "How did you know?" I ask in consternation. You smile knowingly and feel that you have beaten the system, that perhaps it really took only one bit to learn this particular information. But most of the time— $\frac{31}{32}$, to be exact—you will have wasted one precious question and gotten very little in return. That would be a bad strategy. The information content is represented by the strategy that works best on the average. To get at the measure of information you must imagine this exact situation being enacted many, many times— preferably by your clones in parallel universes—while the intrinsically random portion of the data varies over all possible cases according to its underlying probability distributions. Your strategy must enable you to specify the data in the fewest questions on the average over all of these enactments.

In the case of the 32-number roulette the branching strategy requires 5 questions, so the measure of the information associated with an outcome is 5 bits. If you have to save a sequence of roulette outcomes on your computer, you will have to devote an average of 5 bits to each. (In fact, you would use exactly 5 bits on each.) Notice that 5 is the number of times that 32 can be divided in half, or in mathematical notation $\log_2 32 = 5$. In any similar situation with equally likely outcomes the information associated with the result would be the logarithm (to the base 2) of the number of possible outcomes. A 64-number roulette wheel would produce a series of numbers that would take 6 bits apiece to store.

Where there are *n* equally likely outcomes, the information is

$\log_2 n$. (There are only a few more logarithms in this book, but in all cases they will be understood to be to the base 2.) The actual probability of getting as an outcome any individual value is of course $\frac{1}{n}$, so we could as well specify the information as

$$\text{information} = -\log_2(\text{probability}).$$

Notice that the information is positive, since the logarithm of a number less than one, such as a probability, is negative. This simple expression has profound meaning when properly interpreted. It says that the information is measured by the logarithm of the probability. The lower the probability of an event, the more surprising it is, and the more information it represents, but we must scale by the logarithm. If an event is half as likely as another event, for example, it gives us one more bit of information.

Although we have only shown that this simple relationship measures the information associated with a set of equally likely outcomes, Shannon proved that it is indeed a very general measure, that no other measure satisfies the basic requirements that the information always increases as the probability decreases (which is the element of "surprise"), and that the sum of two informational events has an information measure that is the sum of their individual information measures. (The probability of two independent events is the product of their individual probabilities; in logarithms, which scale the information measure, this is a sum.) Thus information is simply measured by the logarithm of the probability. The only problem in application, and it is a monstrous one, is that we must be able to enumerate all possible situations, evaluate the probability of each given all prior information, and average the information measure of all of these possibilities.

EXAMPLES OF INFORMATION

• • • • • • • • • • • • •

Now let me complicate the situation just slightly. Suppose that you place a bet on a particular number on the roulette wheel. The information you want now is not the winning number, which as we have seen requires 5 bits to specify, but merely whether or not you have won or lost. How much information does that take? Obviously here the intrinsic uncertainty is less than before; you do not expect to win. Most of the time I give you the uninteresting news that you have lost. A little of the time I give you the unexpected, information-rich, and incidentally happy news that you have won.

By analogy with the previous discussion we might guess that the information is the probability-weighted average of the information associated with each of the two possible outcomes. That is, $\frac{1}{32}$ of the time we get $-\log\frac{1}{32}$ bits of information, and $\frac{31}{32}$ of the time we get $-\log\frac{31}{32}$ bits.

$$Information = -(\tfrac{31}{32})\times\log(\tfrac{31}{32}) - (\tfrac{1}{32})\times\log(\tfrac{1}{32}) = 0.201 \; bits.$$

This is, in fact, the information associated with the news as to wins and losses in our bets. If we were to store in our computer a sequence of wins and losses, such as

L L L L L L L L L W L L L L L L L L L L L L L L L . . .

this simple relation tells us that it requires on the average about $\frac{1}{5}$ of a bit per outcome. Turning this news around, it means that there is a strategy for asking questions about these results that can specify the wins and losses with about an average of $\frac{1}{5}$ of a question each.

It is worth pausing a moment to appreciate the depth and beauty of Shannon's measure of information. It gives us an inescapable lower bound on the number of bits required to reconstruct data. In the roulette case this is about .2 bits. There is no way to do better, regardless of how hard we try or how clever we think we are. However, Shannon's measure *does not tell us how to achieve this minimum representation.* We know there is a strategy that achieves .2 bits per won/lost result, but we do not know what this strategy is. At first blush you might think this knowledge is not particularly helpful, but on the contrary it is enormously useful. It tells us how good it is possible to be, and when to quit trying to be more clever.

Let us return to the roulette example and see how we might encode the won/lost results to store them in a computer. Obviously we could begin by representing a win by a 1 and a loss by a 0. That requires 1 bit per result; we know we can do much better. In this situation, as well as in virtually every other case, the key is to package larger and larger amounts of data into each of the yes/no questions that we ask. We will go into this at greater length later in this chapter and see why larger packages are more effective. For now, in this example we see that we cannot afford as much as one question per result, so we are forced to package more results into our questions. Suppose, then, that we adopt the ad hoc strategy of asking about the next 8 results as a block. Our first question is whether they are all losses. There is a good chance the answer will be yes, and we will have resolved the next 8 outcomes with just 1 bit. If the answer is no, we will have to get more specific. Suppose in that case that we straightforwardly ask about each of the next 8 results individually. The coding scheme is then as follows:

0 means the next 8 results are $L\ L\ L\ L\ L\ L\ L\ L$;

$1XXXXXXXX$ means the 8 X bits specify the actual won/ lost pattern (for example, 100010000 means the next 8 results are $L\ L\ L\ W\ L\ L\ L\ L$) .

How well does our ad hoc scheme do? The probability that the next 8 results are all losses is $(\frac{31}{32})^8 = .776$. The average number of bits required to specify the next 8 results is $1\times.776 + 8\times(1-.776) = 2.568$. The average per result is thus $\frac{2.568}{8} = .321$. This is much better than 1 bit per result, but still somewhat more than the .2 bits promised by Shannon. So we can try to be more clever. For example, if we find that there is at least one win in the next 8 through a "no" answer to our first question, we could bank on there being probably only one win. Our next question could be whether or not there is only a single win. Probably the answer will be yes. Having established that there is only one win, we could use the divide-by-two strategy to pinpoint its location with the next three questions.

In the improbable case that there is more than one win, we could again revert to the brute force approach of asking about them all. I will spare you the details, but the average number of bits required per result using this strategy is .252. This is pretty close to the best we can do as promised by Shannon. We can quit trying. In fact, as we shall see later, the closer we try to get to the limit, the harder it becomes. The people who do not know about information theory will go on trying all kinds of devilish schemes to use even fewer bits. While this might seem farfetched, I can assure you that I hear all the time about such attempts. It is even somewhat fruitless to deter such people. Like the inventors of perpetual-motion machines, they are determined. They do not want to know about Shannon or information theory. They believe that there is some magical encoding scheme that reduces the storage requirement indefinitely.

In later chapters we will be concerned from time to time with the information content of practical sources of information—English text, speech, and pictures. Unlike the simple examples we have considered so far, virtually all real sources are characterized by the fact that successive results (for example, characters, words, or picture elements) are not independent. We are not in a state of complete ignorance about the forthcoming result, but we have certain expectations that help us in our considerations. The fundamental uncertainty in forthcoming outcomes is reduced by knowledge of the past.

As a simple example, suppose that we want to encode weather data in the form of sunny *(S)* or rain *(R)*. The weather business these days is highly computerized, and predictions are fairly accurate, but some years ago there was a widely held opinion that a good forecast could be made by simply predicting that the weather would be the same as the previous day. Obviously, there is some correlation from day to day. Let us take this to the extreme and model the situation as if the weather depends statistically only upon the previous day. (Which is known in probability theory as a first-order Markov process.) Specifically, suppose that if it is sunny today, there is a probability of .8 that it will also be sunny tomorrow, and a corresponding probability of .2 that it will become rainy. Similarly, if it is rainy today there is a probability of .8 that it will also be rainy tomorrow, and a probability of .2 that it will turn sunny. A sequence of results might be as follows:

S S S S S R R R R S S R R R R R R .

Overall it is equally likely on any given day that it will be rainy or sunny. However, each day we have a definite bias. The uncertainty is diminished by the knowledge of the previous day's weather. We should not have to ask a full question to determine each letter in this sequence. As a matter of fact, if we merely rewrite this sequence in terms of whether or not the weather changed, using *C* for *changed* and *U* for *unchanged,* we get the sequence

U U U U C U U U C U C U U U U U ,

which is exactly of the form that we considered in the roulette example. The successive symbols are independent, but U is much more likely than C. The information conveyed by a symbol is

$$information = -.8 \times \log(.8) - .2 \times \log(.2) = .722 \; bits.$$

We could come up with coding methods that packaged a number of symbols together and took advantage of the prevalence of Us, but as you can see there is not much to be gained. In the next chapter, when we consider text, we will describe an optimum method of encoding situations of this sort, called the Huffman code.

Often the interpretation of information from a sequence of symbols is philosophically difficult, for we do not always know the mechanisms of generation or the underlying probability distributions. Suppose that you are being given a sequence of binary digits:

$$1\ 0\ 0\ 1\ 0\ 1\ 1\ 0\ 0\ 0\ 0\ 1\ 1\ 0\ 1 \text{\underline{\hspace{1cm}}}.$$

How much information is contained in succeeding digits? You might feel that you really have no indication whatsoever about whether any digit will be a 1 or 0. Perhaps someone is flipping a coin behind a curtain and calling one or zero according to heads or tails. You need to ask one question to discover each digit. "Is it a one?" you ask. For each succeeding digit you ask the same question. How could you possibly get by on fewer questions?

Another observer takes a different tack. I cannot see beyond the curtain, he thinks, but I suspect that there is a pattern behind these digits. For a while he is forced to ask the usual one question per digit. Meanwhile he analyzes the statistical properties of the sequence he is uncovering. Suppose, for example, that he discovers that there are significantly more 0s than 1s. In order to take advantage of this tendency in his questions he blocks his questioning to encompass more than one digit at a time. "Are the next three digits all zero?" he asks. If the answer is "no," then he tries the three sequences containing two 0s. If the tendency towards 0 continues he may well average fewer than three questions per block of three digits. He declares that the information content of this sequence is less than one bit per digit.

Still another observer might know something that we do not. Perhaps he can see behind the curtain and is able to ascertain that the sequence is being generated by a computer program. Instead of asking about the output digits, he asks questions about the program that generates them. After a while he reconstructs the program himself and no longer has any need to ask further questions in order to predict the output digits. He runs the same program himself to reconstruct any desired length of output sequence. As the sequence length becomes very long, the average number of questions per digit approaches zero. In the limit he claims that the average information measure per digit is zero.

In many practical situations we are like the person confronted with the mysterious sequence being generated behind the curtain. Getting at the true statistics or the mechanism of generation is at least very difficult, and is perhaps even impossible. Almost no sequences are truly random and perfectly composed of unexpected events. Even the most innocent sources contain correlations, or redundancies, that lower their true information content. As a diversionary example of this truism, consider the next section.

SHANNON AND THE MIND-READING MACHINE — A DIGRESSION

We shall return to our explanation of information theory momentarily. In the meantime I would like to relate a story that will serve as a prelude for some of the issues that will interweave the remainder of this book, such as randomness and human behavior, as well as introduce a human element into what must ultimately become an abstract argument. Hopefully you will later feel some of the genius of Shannon's insight. Often when we are touched by genius, when we ourselves understand the vision unveiled thereby, we wonder about the person and the environment from which the original inspiration emerged. The story of the mind-reading machine, while by no means Shannon's alone, gives a hint of the people and the environment in mathematical research at Bell Labs in the early 1950s.

Shannon was an unusual combination of mathematician and tinkerer. Even today, in relative seclusion in a Boston home cluttered with gadgetry, robots, and toys, he occupies himself with the construction of juggling machines and the mathematical analysis of a stock portfolio that has grown to immense wealth. He has always been compelled by intellectual puzzles, yet at the same time his unquiet hands are those of a gifted craftsman. Today the problems he solves are diversions of his own choosing, left in drawers and unwritten thoughts. His ingenious toys never see the possibility of being taken to market. He appears rarely in public, and when he does it is usually only to claim the prizes that accumulate from the retrospective appreciation of the work of his youth.

In the early 1950s Shannon had completed his treatise on information theory and had won the freedom to indulge his whims for the construction of amusing and intelligent machines. At Bell Laboratories in Murray Hill, New Jersey, he built small artificial intelligence machines from relays and Erector sets. One was called Throwback, a calculator that operated in Roman numerals (evidence of a certain sense of humor!), and another was a machine that played a board game called Hex. In a day in which graphic displays were unknown, he built a machine that produced designs for logic circuits by dropping cards out of a slot to form a pictorial mosaic of the design. Perhaps his best known machine was Theseus, a maze-solving mouse. (In mythology Theseus slew the Minotaur, and by following the thread he had unwound on entering the maze where the Minotaur lived, he was able to find his way back out.) Theseus would be placed in a movable maze of metal partitions. It wandered about erratically until it reached the goal, but after that it was able to find the most direct solution and to memorize it for future attempts. The relay logic was hidden underneath the board, where Theseus himself was propelled by magnetic equipment. After Theseus, mechanical mice went out of style for 25 years, until microprocessors and a micromouse contest of the IEEE (Institute of Electrical and Electronic Engineers) breathed life into Theseus's modern progeny.

The mind-reading machine was the invention of Dave Hagelbarger, a kindred tinkerer at Bell Labs at that time. Hagelbarger lacked Shannon's mathematical sophistication, but like Shannon he brought ingenuity, mechanical visualization, and utter fascination to bear on the nearest interesting problem. Hagelbarger thought of Shannon as "a bright guy," but not all that unusual. Of course, Shannon would sometimes ride his unicycle down the hallway while juggling balls, and there were those occasional "clop clops"

FIGURE 2
Shannon and Theseus, the maze-solving mouse

as Shannon went by on his pogo stick—hardly the image of today's corporate research! Now researchers in artificial intelligence seldom stray far from the screen of their computer terminals, and pogo sticks have disappeared from the corporate vocabulary. Perhaps a certain flair and individuality have been lost to the mounting sophistication and complexity of technological America.

The happenstance that brought about Hagelbarger's invention is probably a typical story. Three events formed a collusion. At that time Hagelbarger was gainfully employed in vacuum tube research, with nary a thought toward such an outlandish machine as what was to come. But over a fateful weekend an assistant accidentally left a plastic glove in the oven containing Hagelbarger's precious assembly. The glove baked at 400 degrees centigrade for the entire weekend. On Monday morning Hagelbarger was greeted by a "gloppy mess," a vacuum system that had to be entirely rebuilt, and the ruination of months of effort. In complete shock, and with little else to do, he went to wander aimlessly in the library, freed from all that "gainful employment" of vacuum tube research.

The second event was Hagelbarger's discovery in the library of a fascinating book on telephone switching. Only recently had the art of telephone circuit switching been studied with the science of logic and Boolean algebra. (In fact, Shannon had discovered this link in a brilliant master's thesis at MIT.) Hagelbarger was completely captivated with the possibilities of design for "thinking machines" implemented with electrical relays. For days he was engrossed in reading the book on switching, and before long he made a connection with the third event, which was the mention by an associate of a science fiction story by J. J. Coupling in which a machine was able to create music in the style of various known composers by following their statistical patterns of musical notes. (J. J. Coupling was the pseudonym of another famous Bell Labs scientist, J. R. Pierce, who now four decades later spends his full time in the study of computer-composed music at Stanford.)

Hagelbarger now conceived the idea of a "mind-reading" machine that would try to beat a person in the game of penny matching by anticipating whether the person would declare a "head" or a "tail" at a given point in the game. Until now, you the reader have probably anticipated that this so-called "mind-reading" machine would be some kind of hoax. It was not. Hagelbarger built his machine, and over the course of 9,795 plays against human opponents the machine correctly anticipated the call of "head" or "tail" 5,218 times—a success rate that by chance alone would happen with probability less than one in 10 billion.

How is it possible for a machine to guess whether we will call "head" or "tail"? The explanation lies in our inability to generate a truly random sequence of calls. In fact, random numbers are quite hard to generate even in computers, and a good deal of research has gone into the development of various existing algorithms for random number generation. As we make calls to the machine we think to ourselves, well I chose a head twice in a row, now it is time for a tail. This is hardly a way to get at random calls, yet it is almost a universal approach. It results in the common fault that we choose too few long runs in our sequences—we change too often. For example, if you were asked to call 16 head or tail choices, you would be unlikely to include a run of four consecutive heads or tails. Yet the actual probability in truly random throws of such a streak is about two-thirds. Because our "random" choices are innately patterned, Hagelbarger's machine could in effect read our minds by anticipating choices through a simple pattern-sensing algorithm.

The mind-reading machine had 8 internal states (a 3-bit memory) which it used to remember a limited amount of past data. These states corresponded to whether or not the machine had won the most recent match attempt, whether or not it had won the match the time before that, and finally whether or not it had played "same" or "different" the last time (that is, whether it changed from head to tail or vice versa). For example, it would know from recent play if it had a winning percentage on the next match after being in the "won-lost-same" state previously, and whether or not its next play should be "same" or "different." If the machine had a good winning percentage in the current state, it would decisively call its guess from its memory of similar wins. If the winning percentage was only fair, it would use its memory only 3 times in 4, interspersing random guesses one-quarter of the time. If the machine had been losing in a given state, it would guess completely at random in the subsequent match attempt. (The random guesses were obtained by the phase of a motor at the time the human guess button was pushed.)

On reflection, the machine's strategy is well matched to our own process of producing guesses. Our short term memory only goes back a few guesses, and the kind of considerations we take before guessing are similar—whether or not we have been winning, and whether or not it is time to change. The machine just does a better job in the bookkeeping. When the machine was first built, people quickly became bored with the simple penny-matching game, and Hagelbarger had a hard time collecting enough data. The addition of 2 rows of 25 lights across the top of the machine changed the game from boring to addictive. When the human won, the next green light in its row would be illuminated; if the machine won, it would be the next red light. Now most people played until one or the other row of lights was exhausted, indicating a "final triumph" for either the human or the machine.

If the machine's human opponents had analyzed its strategy, they could have beaten the machine 60 percent of the time. However, all they could see was that the machine kept winning more than its fair share of matches. One player got hooked to the extent that he spent his lunch hour at the machine every day for weeks. Eventually he began to win by unconsciously adopting a winning strategy. Another player was convinced that the way to win was to play randomly. His technique was to ask himself what he believed were randomly inspired "yes" or "no" questions to determine his calls. "Did I put on a red tie this morning?" he would ask himself. He lost consistently, so perhaps the questions were not so random after all!

News of the omniscient machine spread, and soon the director of research ordered the machine brought before him for a personal demonstration. Surprisingly, he won convincingly. Hagelbarger was at a loss to understand why the machine had crumbled so easily before authority. Since the director's calls had been recorded, Hagelbarger played back the exact same sequence of calls into the machine back in his lab. This time the machine won easily. The technological reasons for its previous failure remain unknown, but no scientist or engineer will fail to recognize the well-known syndrome of an experiment that refuses to work in the face of upper management.

Naturally Shannon had been following the performances of the mind-reading machine. At that time he had been intrigued with the workings of the human mind. Hagelbarger recalls that he and Shannon had bought an electroencephalograph machine to look at brain waveforms. Shannon had it hooked up to his own head, and Hagelbarger studied the waveforms. Apparently they looked just like anyone else's. (Scratch one theory of genius!) Someone had the inspiration to hook it up to the mind-reading machine. The EEG of the mind-reading machine looked just like Shannon's! This coincidence frightened people until it was realized that the motor that generated the random choices had a vibrational mode at about the same frequency as the alpha rhythm of the human brain.

Shannon decided to build his own version of the mind-reading machine—one which was smaller and simpler. His machine used the same 8 states as Hagelbarger's, but stored less information for each state and employed just two modes for its guesses, completely deterministic and completely random. Shannon used his usual flair for artistry in the method of displaying results of the matches. Two tracks with steel balls in glass tubes indicated machine wins and human wins by the balls popping out from the stacks.

Now the two mind-reading machines were pitted against each other in a celebrated duel. It was necessary to construct a third machine to act as a referee, and to dole out random numbers as required by either contender (since there was no human to push a button). For days the three machines huddled in a laboratory. Hagelbarger observed that if you told people that you were conducting an experiment in probability, no one was interested. But if you gave people the idea that two thinking machines were dueling to the death, then everyone was excited. In the end Shannon's machine won by a slight margin, but no one knows whether this was due to a happenstance trend in the random numbers or to a definitive edge in the algorithm that Shannon employed.

There is an interesting postscript to the experiment. One of the referees for Hagelbarger's paper describing his machine was an IBM scientist with access to a "real" computer, which he programmed to emulate a mind-reading machine with many, many states and total capture of all data. Curiously, it never worked well at all. Apparently the guesses of humans have little correlation over periods longer than that used by Hagelbarger, and in the short games typically played it is hard to get a meaningful amount of data about longer statistical trends.

ENTROPY AND INFORMATION

Shannon assumes a model for the generation of information in which a sequence of discrete symbols, representing messages, is chosen randomly from a finite set of possible symbols. We might imagine the telegrapher of Shannon's day being handed a sequence of English letters. His job is to send the letters; he does not reflect on what they mean. He comes to believe that they are being selected at random through some stochastic process that he is not allowed to know. As the days go by he begins to notice the statistical properties of the letters. For example, he notices that *e* occurs more frequently than any other letter, and that *t* is the next most likely. He observes that the letter *t* is often followed by *h,* and that *q* is almost always followed by *u.* He begins to realize that the block of symbols *the* occurs quite frequently. All this kind of knowledge is perfectly compatible with the notion that the symbols are being produced randomly according to some statistical distributions. The telegrapher does not, however, read the messages. He attaches no meaning to the stream of nonsense symbols that he encodes with his rapidly clicking key.

The basing of his theory upon a probabilistic model was one of Shannon's important innovations. Twenty years earlier Hartley had observed, as we did previously, that information should be proportional to the logarithm of the number of possible symbols, but he did not make the connection to random selection and the mathematics of probability theory. There are two reasons why a probabilistic model of the world is often used in physical sciences. First, it acknowledges our ignorance of the true origins of the quantities involved and the minutia of their interrelationships. In effect we say that we do not understand all these details, so we pretend that the outcomes that we see—for example, the symbols that designate messages—are random. The second reason, however, is even more important. Probability theory is a powerful tool for analysis. Often when we are unable to calculate even one particular special case of known events, we find that we are able to calculate the *average* over many unknown, but random, events. So it was in information theory. Shannon's remarkable results are due in large part to the assumption of a random model of information generation.

Let me recount the measure for information that we described earlier. Suppose that we have a source of information that outputs a sequence of symbols, each of which is chosen from a set of n possible symbols. Then we found that the information per symbol is given by the expression:

$$H = - \sum_{i=1}^{n} p_i \log(p_i)$$

where the p_i are the probabilities of the n possible symbols.

Shannon called this uncertainty that measures information *entropy,* after a mathematically similar quantity in classical statistical mechanics. In statistical mechanics the entropy is a measure of the disorder, or uncertainty, in a system. Information is similar in that it also may be regarded in terms of the fundamental uncertainty. The entropy represents the state of our uncertainty as to the actual symbol values, which is equal to the information that needs to be provided to reconstruct them. Some of the mystique of information theory is due to this coupling with the entropy of statistical mechanics. The second law of thermodynamics, which says that entropy is always increasing, gives an almost metaphysical quality to entropy. That the entropy in an isolated system cannot decrease would mean by analogy that information, representing order and organization (the resolution of uncertainty), could only in some large sense be created locally at the expense of increased disorder elsewhere. Such philosophical arguments might be made appropriately late at night over a bottle of wine, but they have had really nothing to do with the evolution of information theory. It is probable that any analysis of order and disorder would result in similar equations. The extrapolations from the world of statistical thermodynamics, tempting as they are, have not yielded insight into the world of information and communications.

Examination of the equation shows that it is at a maximum when all the symbols are equally likely, that is, when $p_i = \frac{1}{n}$. This is the state of least prior knowledge. If some symbols are more likely than others, then naturally the uncertainty is less. Similarly, the sum of individual information events in this equation is made simple by the assumption that successive symbols are independent. If they are not, then the entropy of the source is again less, since knowledge of past symbols implies information about symbols yet to come. The entropy under these circumstances can be calculated by enumerating the possible states the source can attain and evaluating the conditional entropies associated with each state and the probabilities of transitions to other states. This can obviously be a matter of some bookkeeping, and need not concern us here.

Real life channels are invariably messy. Data sources like text, digitized speech, and pictures have complex dependencies that extend deep into the structure of the sequence of symbols. In most such cases the calculation of source entropy is really impossible. The most important example is the sequence of the symbols we call "letters" in the English language. How many bits does it take to specify each letter on average? This is a question we shall discuss in the next chapter. Along the way I hope you will be fascinated, as I have been, with the beautiful complexities and redundancies of our language. For the present, let me give a little appetizer in the form of an illustration of the manifest redundancy in English text.

How many yes/no questions does it take on average to specify a letter in English text? Since there are 26 possible letters, not counting spaces and punctuation, we might believe that it would take about 5 questions per letter. However, I remember from my childhood the fascination I had with the radio show "Twenty Questions." Perhaps you know of it or have played it yourself. The host would begin with, "I am thinking of something which is mineral (or animal or vegetable)." If the panel could not find the secret, mineral thing within 20 "yes" or "no" questions, then the contributor would receive some prize. Surprisingly, to me, the panel nearly always named the thing within the 20 questions.

If the game of 20 questions really works, then we can also say that nearly any noun in the popular knowledge domain can be represented by about 20 bits. If you feel this number is evidently sufficient, then think for a moment that the average length of words in this book is 6 letters. If each word can indeed be represented by 20 bits, then this means each letter can be encoded in approximately 3.3 bits. However, the way my computer works is that each key I strike on my word processor is encoded into an 8-bit byte and stored in the computer memory. Such a waste. Obviously, my computer does not know about information theory. We will return to these interesting philosophical questions in the next chapter.

In more recent times the radio shows have gone, but our interest in language games remains a constant. The television show "Wheel of Fortune" is in its way also a search for the entropy of English. A secret phrase is revealed only as the contestant is able to guess the letters it contains. In the process the contestant is given some "free" information in terms of the locations of the letters guessed within the phrase. In order to convert the average number of guesses required to the entropy of text, we would have to add the questions necessary to pinpoint the letter locations. With this minor, and easily calculated, modification, we could get some idea of the information content of English text through the number of guesses used week after week on "Wheel of Fortune." Of course, the contestants could care less about this interpretation.

While it is true that it is essentially impossible to calculate the entropy of a real source like English letters directly from the mathematics of information theory, the principles nonetheless serve for inspiration and insight. The coding of a real source usually devolves from artful, if ad hoc, methodology. In succeeding chapters we will discuss some of the coding methods for text, speech, and pictures that are used to squeeze out unwanted redundancy and lessen storage and transmission requirements. Information theory sets out this beautiful challenge. Perhaps it is just as well that it neglects to tell us how to achieve this minimum representation. Otherwise it would be too easy.

E N T R O P Y   A N D   T H E
I N F O R M A T I O N   P Y R A M I D

This seems like a good time to step back from Shannon's microscopic view of information to put in perspective the larger context of information in the sociological realm as discussed in the previous chapter. In that chapter we presented an information pyramid—data, information, knowledge, and wisdom. The difference between the layers of the pyramid was one of increasing organization as we approached the top, which was wisdom. We pictured the "information" layer itself as being the condensation through organization of the sludge we called data lying underneath.

In Shannon's theory we find the concept of information as the resolution of uncertainty. The measure of the uncertainty is called entropy, which is directly related to the degree of randomness or permissible disorder. Increasing entropy means decreasing order and structure. Order and structure in Shannon's framework represent redundancy, which diminishes the intrinsic uncertainty that is resolved by the receipt of information. Consequently, the more structure in the underlying process, the less information is conveyed by a specific observation of the process. On the other hand, the more freedom or allowable disorder in the underlying process, the more information can be conveyed.

In either the technological or the sociological sense information is a question of order and disorder. Shannon's theory is a technological or mechanical concept applicable on the bottom (data) level of our pyramid. It tells us about the size of containers we will need for our sludge; it gets to the essence of the sludge, the minimum storage that will contain the data. The more disorder that is permitted by the structure of the sludge, the more information the sludge can yield. For example, a demented monkey banging randomly on a typewriter generates more Shannon-type information per character than I am currently producing here on my terminal. (Actually, the monkey need not be demented, but more on the monkey in the next chapter.) He does not have to spell correctly, follow the rules

58

of grammar, or make semantic sense. I envy him his freedom. It would take more bits per character to store the monkey's output than to store mine, which is so much more constrained. For the same reason, you would find it much more difficult to memorize the monkey's characters than mine. It is not just a question of storing information in a machine; it is us too. We also are sludge containers.

Moving away from the sludge level to the personal and sociological concepts of information, we get a different perspective on information. The first key human job—and no machine can do it as effectively—is to distill the sludge, so as to boil off the unneeded or unwanted data. At the Shannon level the characters typed by the demented monkey were treated the same as the characters of this book. (Although sometimes I wonder. If I could actually find a demented monkey, I might be able to verify this.) There is no concept of value or relevancy. The information content is the measure of what is needed for perfect reconstruction. But in the real world we must exercise great art and skill in filtering or selecting among the possible information sources to screen for value, relevancy, and truth. Reject the monkey. Keep this, I hope.

After selection, to move the information to higher levels of value we need to integrate the information with our existing knowledge. We need to create interlocking links with the storage and filing structures that organize our knowledge, and we need to find ways to make the new information memorable. These actions will inevitably add redundancy to the newly acquired information, but this is redundancy of our own choosing, designed to protect the integrity of the new fragile bits. All of information processing can be seen in similar light. First we squeeze out undesirable redundancy, then we add desirable redundancy, and so forth. In the next section we will see a mechanical reason for adding redundancy back into data when we begin to worry about the vagaries and risks to information in communications.

COMMUNICATION CHANNELS AND CAPACITY

Let us turn our attention from data sources to the communication channels, which transport symbols. For our purposes the channel itself is a mysterious black box (these things get around a lot) that accepts a sequence of symbols at its input and delivers another, hopefully similar, sequence of symbols at its output. Think of a telephone connection sending data between computers or of a computer sending data to a disk drive, for example. The input and output of the channel are often geographically distant; they may be literally worlds apart. But all the complexity in the transmission system that transports the symbols is subsumed into a statistical knowledge of the transition relationships between input and output symbols. Sometimes it makes an error, mostly it does not. That kind of thing.

Shannon was remarkably prescient in thinking of and modeling the communications channel as a statistical passage of discrete symbols. In the late 1940s digital transmission was almost completely unknown. Pulse code modulation had been invented in 1939 by Reeves (of ITT), but it was not until 1961 that the first digital transmission system was deployed by the Bell System. Even in the 1950s very few communications engineers understood the philosophy of digital transmission. The crux of Alexander Graham Bell's invention of the telephone some 75 years earlier had been the use of *analog* representation, where the transmitted voltage was proportional to the sound pressure at each instant.

Today essentially all newly installed communications channels are said to be digital. I use the phase "said to be" because clearly at some point in the system analog voltage or lightwave pulses are used to convey the 1s and 0s that are decided at some distant point. Nevertheless, nearly all of us think of the channel as digital. We shove bits in one end of the connection, and they pour out at the other end. In between who knows what happens? Moreover, not many people care. The modern attitude is that the overwhelming majority of systems designers of the information age will think of communications channels as transporting bits, which are occasionally corrupted in some unfortunate way. The details of the actual transmission are relegated to a small subset of the technological world, whom we might think of as the "keepers of the channel"—engineers who design modems, microwave and satellite systems, etc. I do not mean to denigrate their role, since I and many of my friends make our living inside that black box, but in the deepening complexity of the information age it is often necessary to practice the hiding of lower-level details in a hierarchical fashion. Thus to most of us the communications channel, just as Shannon foretold, is merely a mover of symbols, and since we live in a binary world, those symbols are specifically binary digits, or what we call bits.

Inside the communications channel terrible things happen to our precious bits. The indignities they endure are remarkable. The bits are converted to pulses which are variously subjected to distortions, random voltage fluctuations known as electrical noise, electromagnetic interference, and assorted catastrophic events. Every now and then a little box in a manhole called a repeater decides whether or not the pulse it is looking at more resembles a 1 or a 0. Having made its irrevocable decision, the repeater generates a clean new pulse of the decided variety, which now travels to the next repeater. Such is the beauty of digital transmission; distortion is not allowed to accumulate. As long as the repeater decisions are correct, a series of virgin pulses is regenerated. Nonetheless, life is full of imperfections, and errors are inevitable.

In Shannon's time, electrical noise, caused in all electrical circuits by random, thermal motion, was considered the sole cause of errors and to be the limitation to transmission speeds. Today, while thermal noise may be the ultimate limitation, there are so many uncharted causes of transmission errors that few researchers seek descriptive mechanisms for error generation. Murphy's law overwhelms everything—errors happen, who knows why? But granted that errors are inevitable, what is their effect on the transmission of information? This is where Shannon's greatest contribution lay.

Suppose that we transmit a sequence of bits over the channel, and errors occur where I mark "X".

$$1011010001101110010111100101011000$$
$$X \qquad\qquad X \qquad X$$

Therefore we receive the sequence:

$$1011000001101110011111100111000.$$

This looks like a perfectly legitimate sequence to us; we have no way of knowing that it contains erroneous data. In order to reconstruct the original data we would have to know the error locations. The error locations could be represented by a sequence of bits with 0 for "no error" and 1 for "error," giving the following description:

00000100000000000010000000100000.

If we only knew this sequence, we would know which bits had to be changed (inverted), and we could fix the received data. This error sequence is the unknown, unprovided information. It is the result of the uncertainty added during transit by the communications channel. How much information does it take to learn this sequence and fix our data? Well, we just finished deriving the quantity of information necessary to describe a sequence exactly like this; it was what we called entropy, and we have a general equation to quantify it. In the case of independent, binary symbols, as above, the general equation for entropy simplifies to

$$H = - (p \log p + q \log q)$$

where p is the probability of the symbol 1, representing an error, and $q = 1 - p$ is the probability of the symbol 0, representing no error.

Somehow the received binary digits, as they are, are "missing" H bits of information. Before transmission each digit was worth one whole bit of information, but the channel subtracts H bits per digit of information because of the added uncertainty. Another way of looking at the transmission problem is to recall that we thought of the entropy H as *uncertainty.* In transmission what we are looking for is the opposite of uncertainty; it is what is left after removing the uncertainty, and it represents *certainty.* That certainty is now worth only $1 - H$ bits.

Shannon defined the *capacity* of a channel as its intrinsic ability to convey information. For the binary channels we have been discussing he proved what we might now suspect—that the capacity is simply $1 - H$, or

$$C = 1 + p \log p + (1 - p) \log (1 - p) \ \textit{bits per binary digit.}$$

(Again, I hate to add caveats, but this simple equation assumes that the errors are independent events. In real life errors almost always cluster together as if they wanted company. This dependency decreases the entropy and thus increases C.) Now perhaps with this

background the reader will not be surprised by Shannon's fundamental theorem, which is

> *A channel with capacity C* is capable, with suitable coding, of
> transmitting at any rate less than C bits per symbol with
> vanishingly small probability of error. For rates greater than
> C the probability of error cannot be made arbitrarily small.

Let me rephrase the meaning of this theorem. The problem is that
the raw symbols (the 1s and 0s) received at the channel output have
an uncertainty associated with them; in effect they are not worth a
full "bit" of true information. Some of the information that we
thought we could deliver at the receiver will have to be devoted
to another cause, that of uncovering the locations of the errors.
Shannon's fundamental theorem assures us that there is a way of
using some of the received bits to locate and correct the errors, and
that if the fraction of bits that we sacrifice for this use is larger than
the channel entropy H, then it is possible to find and correct virtually all of the errors. If we devote a fraction of bits smaller than
H, then Shannon tells us that regardless of how clever we may think
we are, it cannot be done.

Actually, Shannon's theorem does not say that we can eliminate
all errors, but only that we can make the residual error rate vanishingly small. By "vanishingly small" we mean that if we work at it
very hard we can make the error rate as small as we like. Although
I would like for the sake of simplicity to say that *errorless* transmission is possible at rates less than capacity, the correct mathematical
interpretation is that errors will still occur, but the fraction of errors
can be made arbitrarily small.

I wish I had found a way to tell those readers who have not
previously studied Shannon's work how magnificent and surprising
this seemingly simple result is. Unfortunately, it takes a certain
depth of insight that I feel I have failed to convey to the reader in
order to realize the profound implications of the concept of channel
capacity and its promise of errorless transmission in spite of channel
errors. In his book *Symbols, Signals, and Noise,* John R. Pierce (a
contemporary of Shannon at Bell Labs) observed that lay people
thought this an unsurprising result, while engineers and scientists
were shocked by it. Its impact on the communications engineer—
once it was understood, which took some years—cannot be under-
estimated. You might reason that if a channel has a capacity C bits

per symbol, then of course you should be able to send data at rates up to C. Obvious. But the catch is that the error rate must be made arbitrarily small at the same time that the communication rate is maintained at C. That this was possible was a revelation to the engineers of the early 1950s.

Here is how the engineers of those days reasoned. They felt that it was obvious that the error rate in a noisy channel could be made arbitrarily small. For instance, if you wanted to send the data 101 over a channel that occasionally made errors, you could simply repeat each bit three times and make a majority decision. Go for the best of three, you think. So you send 111000111. But there is still some residual probability of making an error. It might happen that two of the three bits are in error. Simple, you think, I will just go for best of five. So you send 111110000011111. Let the channel try to corrupt that, you exult. However, there is still some small probability of getting three errors in a block of five, and you must assure a "vanishingly small" error rate, so maybe it should be best of seven, or best of nine, or whatever. Anyway, eventually by this strategy you will reach whatever is considered a "vanishingly small" error rate.

But look what is happening. Sure, the error rate becomes smaller and smaller as we go for best of seven and best of nine, etc. But at the same time the data rate is getting smaller and smaller. Only one bit in seven carries information, then one bit in nine, etc. By the time we reach a vanishingly small error rate, we will also have a vanishingly small information rate! The stunning import of Shannon's theorem is that we can have our cake and eat it too. The probability of residual errors in the data can be made as small as we like without suffering any diminution of the data rate, as long as the data rate itself is less than the channel capacity. There is *some* way to get virtually errorless transmission *at the same time* as we achieve data rate C. Truly amazing!

Reflect for a moment that entropy in a *source* is something that we seek. The entropy of the source measures its "richness" in information content. Uncertainty is good in the sense that the raw bits from the source then carry higher value, whereas if the entropy is relatively low the raw bits are highly redundant. On the other hand, entropy in a *channel* is bad. Here we look for as complete a certainty as we can obtain. Any "unknown-ness" about the channel will diminish its intrinsic information-carrying capacity. So the philosophical approach to communications is the following. First we compress the data output from the source to remove redundancy, then we expand the compressed data to protect it against the vagaries of transmission through the channel. At the receiver the operations are reversed. This is shown diagrammatically in Figure 3. Communications engineers are always thinking of squeezing out the redundancy in the data at the source, and then of pouring redundancy back into the stream for protection at the channel. The

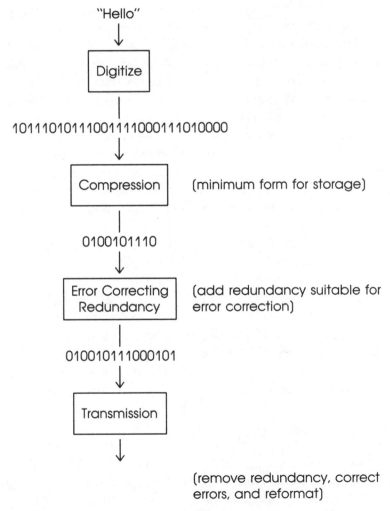

FIGURE 3
Transmitting source material through a channel

natural redundancy of the source bits is seldom suited to provide the specific protection we need at the channel.

ERROR CORRECTION
BY CODING

I often reflect on how marvelously we humans have adapted our natural communications methods to our environment. In our spoken language we too have to deal with a "noisy" channel that is uncertain in its correctness of transmission. For that reason we have evolved a vocabulary for transmission that includes redundancy that protects against channel uncertainties. Our speech is incredibly robust, and our detection mechanism unbelievably sophisticated. Consider the so-called "cocktail party" effect where we engage in conversation with someone in the midst of near bedlam. In spite of the blaring music and the presence of numerous, competing conversations all about, we are able to carry on a meaningful (perhaps!) conversation with the person on whom we focus our attention.

The central factor that builds robustness into language is the limitation of the vocabulary to a minute subset of the possible combinations of allowable letters. In English with 26 letters there are about 10 billion possible combinations of 7 letters which might be words. We get along on about 50,000 of these possible words. When we hear or read a word that is not one of those we recognize, we automatically search in our minds for possible words that are "close" to the garbled word we have heard or read. Communication codes do exactly the same thing with data words. However, we humans excel in even going much further than the electronic decoders; we are able to use the context and our entire experience and knowledge base to aid in our detection. There is redundancy woven deeply into our language. If we are sitting at the dinner table, and you hear me say, "Please pass the guther," you reach for the butter without conscious hesitation. That was an easy one, but think for a moment about how very, very good we are at such extraordinarily complex processing.

In contrast to the historically evolved redundancy in natural language, the computer data typically handled in communications channels either is, or appears to be, devoid of redundancy. If we have done a perfect job in source coding, the information rate of the stream will be one bit of information per symbol—every bit that we see really counts for a bit of true information. It is also possible that at the communication channel we may not be allowed to meddle with the bits we see. Like the uncaring telegrapher of Shannon's day, we may not be permitted to interpret meaning in the relentless flow of symbolic script. In either case every sequence of bits the channel handles is a legal vocabulary word. The block 10010111 makes as much sense as 00111010. Imagine trying to converse when every combination of letters represented an allowable word! Clearly, if the channel coding is to protect against errors, we must restrict the allowable data sequences to some subset of all those possible. Then, just as in human conversation, we check the received data words for validity. When we find an invalid word, we can search for the nearest legal word—nearest in the sense of being the most probable origin of the garbled word we have received. Alternatively, again analogous to human conversation, we could notify the transmitter that the word was garbled, and ask for a retransmission. ("Huh? Would you say that again?")

The error-correcting philosophy that comes from Shannon's information theory is the idea of devoting some of the bits to the purpose of locating and correcting possible errors. These so-called check bits add redundancy such that only certain combinations of data bits and check bits are legal data words, just like only certain combinations of letters produce words in English. Each check bit is in effect one of our yes/no questions, designed to ask a question that helps to identify the error sequence. For example, a question it might ask is whether or not there is an odd number of 1s in some predetermined subset of the bits, as indicated below.

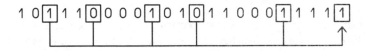

If there is an odd number of 1s in these boxes, then this check bit will be 1, otherwise it will be 0.

If we devote a fraction H or more of the bits to the purpose of checking, then there is sufficient information carried by the check bits to balance out the entropy of the channel and, *on average,* to correct the errors in transmission. However, that "on average" qualifier is terribly important. We only get one crack at it. Is there or is there not enough information in the check bits to correct the errors in our particular data sequence? Shannon assures us that if we ask the right questions with our check bits, and take the right actions based on the answers we get, then it is possible to get an error rate as small as we wish as the data sequence becomes longer and longer, while keeping the same fraction of check bits.

The first error-correcting codes were discovered by Richard Hamming at about the same time that Shannon was conceiving information theory. In Hamming's code, the data is grouped into 7-bit blocks, composed of 4 information bits and 3 check bits. The check bits are determined before transmission by the oddness or evenness of different combinations of these 4 information bits. At the receiver, the check bit calculations are repeated to see if the received check bits agree with the calculations. If a check bit disagrees at the receiver, then there are one or more errors in the data bits for which it is responsible (or the error can be in the check bit itself). By looking at the patterns of discrepancies in the received check bits, we can calculate the most likely error pattern that would have led to this particular set of check bit discrepancies. We then correct this most likely error pattern. Most of the time we will have fixed the errors; some of the time a less likely pattern (containing more errors) will be the actual cause of the discrepancies, and we will unknowingly correct the wrong thing.

For Hamming's famous code a little analysis shows that we will always do the right thing as long as there is only one error in the block of 7 bits (the 4 information bits and the 3 check bits). If there is more than one error in the block of 7 bits, then we mess up. Thus we sacrifice $\frac{3}{7}$ of the bits to correct any one error in 7 bits. As a result, the error rate is reduced, but not indefinitely as Shannon promised.

There are many other more complicated coding algorithms that have been discovered in the last forty years. The subject is a highly mathematical one, based largely on the theory of modern algebra, which is an abstract generalization of the algebra with which most of us are familiar. There was a time when most of us thought that modern algebra was a beautiful, but useless, recreation for mathematicians. Then it was discovered that error-correcting codes could be synthesized, and their performance guaranteed, by basing the code construction on the principles of modern algebra. The only catch was that there was not much use for these sophisticated error-correcting codes either.

I can remember the first time that I read about Reed-Solomon codes. This sophisticated coding algorithm was a generalization into an even more abstract space of the already abstract codes that were then known. Uselessness piled onto uselessness, I thought. That was then. Today I use a Reed-Solomon code for my own enjoyment almost every day. Perhaps you do too; it is in every compact disk player. The compact disk playback system is like a communications channel. Errors can occur because of imperfections in the disk, or because of dirt, or maybe because you scratched it. Anyway, you might not have realized that virtually all of these errors are found and corrected because of the redundancy built into the recording format using a very powerful Reed-Solomon code. You can run a nail file across a compact disk, and you will not hear a single hiccup on playback. Every bit of the music will be exactly as it should be. I have not actually had the courage to try this, but the theory guarantees it. The coding system is capable of correcting as many as 8,232 consecutive errors. Think about that; it puts those little redundancy checks into perspective!

During the course of writing this book I have stored the growing file of characters from my word processor again and again on hard disks and floppy disks. Thousands of times the file has gone back and forth, from the memory chips of my computer to the disk and back again. Each time the integrity of the bits has been ensured by an error-detecting code. In this storage application the data is accepted only if all the check bits are correct, otherwise the whole operation is repeated. Moreover, I have transmitted the files of characters back and forth between locations around the world and my home and office. I have done this hundreds of times, with a file that is almost a megabyte in size. Each time the file was first compressed to remove needless redundancy by an algorithm that we will discuss in the next chapter, resulting in approximately a halving of its size. Then about a 1 percent redundancy was added to the file in the form of check bits computed according to a standard code used in communications protocols for information exchange. If any block of data (typically 1,024 bytes) failed its checks, it was retransmitted. I never worried. There was no chance that so much as a comma would be lost. If you have ever written a large manuscript, you must know what these little characters meant to me, yet I entrusted them to codes. I never imagined that codes would be so important practically, but as you can see, they are.

MAKING AN EXAMPLE SMALL CODE
• • • • • • • • • • •

I have resisted so far the compulsion to describe in detail the construction of codes. This is, I keep telling myself, a "how come" book, rather than a "how to" book. When you lift the hood and look inside coding and decoding algorithms, you see a gleaming engine, with many moving parts. I could discuss how this lever moves that pushrod, which is attached to that wheel, and so forth. In fact, I am so proud of that polished engine that a little later I will succumb to the temptation and show you a gear or two! But too much of this and I know I would get lost in detail, and so perhaps would you. The principles that run the engine are some of the most compellingly beautiful mathematics that I know, but I fear that the detailed description would take us away from the foundations of information that form the theme of this book. Instead, I would like to take you through an exercise of making our own little code that uses no mathematics whatsoever. We will just pick code words at random, just as if we made up an English dictionary by drawing tiles from a Scrabble rack. However, even without mathematics I fear that the following sections are the most conceptually difficult in this book. Feel free to skip ahead. After all, that is what the information age is all about. And if you stay through and understand, then you will have reason to be proud of yourself.

In order to get at the general philosophy we will use a simple, concrete example. Suppose that the channel has a probability of error of .02, so that on the average 2 percent of the 1s come out as 0s, and vice versa. You have to suspend reality for a while because real communications channels are usually engineered for a probability of error of about one in a billion, but this channel is bad. When we calculate the channel capacity we find

$$C = 1 + .02\log.02 + .98\log.98 = .8585$$

70

We might notice in passing that even a small percentage of errors cuts down the channel capacity rather appreciably. According to Shannon's theorem, we ought to be able to use this channel for accurate transmission as long as only about 85 percent of the bits represent delivered information, with the other 15 percent of the bits providing redundancy and protection. Since we will not be greedy in this example (for good reason, as we will see), let us aim to get only half of the transmitted bits through correctly—half of the bits will represent information and half will be what we call check bits.

Actually, there is no need to think of particular bits being designated check bits, and other bits information bits, any more than we think of English words as being composed of "information" letters and "check" letters. The point is that we have a dictionary, and some sequences of letters are in it, while others are not. We can do the same thing with bits by selecting a dictionary of "approved" sequences, or what we will call code words. Then we make some kind of arbitrary assignment of information sequences into code words in the dictionary. As a specific example, suppose that we begin with very modest sizes of words in our vocabulary, using only 4-bit code words. Since the code rate is to be one-half, that means that every 2 bits that are input as information will dictate a particular 4-bit word from the dictionary to be transmitted. Since there are only four possible combinations of two bits (00, 01, 10, and 11), we need a dictionary that lists only four words. We could decide, for example, that when we get the input 00 we will send the code word 1011, and when we get input 01 we will send 0110, etc. There are 16 possible 4-bit combinations, but only 4 of these will represent legal code words. In this way the code words will be only a subset of all the possible combinations of channel bits, and we should be able to recognize when the words become garbled by channel errors. The price we pay, obviously, is that the effective information rate of the channel is cut by 50 percent.

The first problem we face is how to make up the dictionary. We need to designate 4 of the possible 16 combinations of 4 bits as code words. The number of ways that we could make this selection would be $16 \times 15 \times 14 \times 13$. That must seem like a lot of possibilities for such a simple problem (though indeed there are so many symmetries that far fewer possibilities are really significant), but in truth we have not touched the real difficulties yet. Surely, you imagine, there must be some optimum way to select the dictionary.

Some choices of code words must be better than others. As a rough guiding principle, it seems evident that we would like the code words to be as "different" as possible, so that they will be less likely to be confused by channel errors. For instance, we would prefer not to have both 1111 and 1110 in the code, since a single error in the last position would convert one code word to another, and we would have no way of knowing that the error had occurred. Indeed, an optimum way to select this particular dictionary is known, but only because the code is so small. For the moment we will just pretend that we do not know how to make an optimum code.

The first instinct of a mathematician facing the problem of determining how well a code can do would be to optimize the code dictionary, and then to find the performance of this best code. Lacking the ability to find an optimum code, most mathematicians would search for bounds on the performance of codes. In this vein Shannon found an ingenious lower bound through the observation that the best code must be at least as good as the average of codes picked randomly. The best must be at least as good as the average. That seems obvious enough, but it also sounds rather unhelpful. However, this so-called random coding bound turned out to be much more insightful than might have been anticipated. Let us follow this line of thought with our example. For the moment we do not know how to construct the best possible dictionary. Instead, we choose the code dictionary randomly by tossing a coin to write each bit in each code word it contains. I formed a number of such random codes on my computer. (I wonder what Shannon would have done with a computer like mine. Perhaps he would still be playing with it and information theory would never have happened!) One of the better codes can be found in the following table.

**EXAMPLE RANDOM CODE: 4-BIT
WORDS, .5 INFORMATION RATE**

INFORMATION	CODE WORD
00	1001
01	0000
10	1111
11	1110

To see how such a code might be effective suppose that the information block to be transmitted is 01. In our randomly constructed dictionary we find the entry 0000 as the code word to be transmitted. Suppose further that during transmission the third bit is in error, so that we receive the illegal word 0010. Searching through an identical dictionary at the receiver, we compare 0010 with each of the possible legal entries. This sequence differs from the first code word (1001) in three positions. Thus if the first code word had actually been transmitted, it would have taken 3 errors to result in the sequence that we received. Similarly the "distance" in errors from the other 3 legal code words is, respectively, 1, 3, and 2. The closest allowable word is the second word 0000. That is, it would have taken the fewest errors to convert that word to the word we received. Such a "maximum likelihood" decoding procedure results in minimizing the probability of error for a given dictionary. In this instance the decoding will result in correcting the error in transmission.

It is simple enough to determine the performance of our sample code. There are 4 possible, equally likely, code words that can be transmitted. In the channel one of 16 possible error patterns will be added to the code word. (We use "added" as the logical exclusive, that is, a 1 becomes a 0 and vice versa.) These error patterns are not of equal likelihood. The most probable error pattern is 0000, indicating no errors. It has a probability of $.98^4 = .922$. Next most probable are the four patterns with a single error: 0001, 0010, 0100, and 1000, each of which has a probability of $(.98^3)(.02) = .019$. Similarly there are six double error patterns, 4 triple error patterns, and one pattern in which all 4 bits are in error.

To evaluate the probability of error for the coded system we take each of the 4 possible code words, add each of the 16 possible error patterns and determine, as we did above in one of the instances, whether or not decoding by finding the closest allowable word will result in the correct decision. (Often it will happen that a word to be decoded will lie at equal distance from a number of possible code words, and we make an arbitrary assignment.) The product of these possibilities means 64 situations must be evaluated, but that is trivial in this example. We find that 62 percent of the time that a single error occurs in transmission it is corrected by the decoding procedure, and that 8 percent of the time that 2 errors occur the decoding is correct. We are out of luck if 3 or 4 errors occur in the block. Weighting these events by their probabilities of occurrence results in an overall probability of code-word error of .0304.

Summarizing for the moment, we took a raw channel with a probability of error of .02, and traded half of the transmitted bits in order to build redundancy into the stream. We did not know how to construct an optimum code dictionary so we made one up at random. At the receiver we used closest distance decoding, which we know is the best that can be done. The overall result of the experiment was that the code words have a probability of error of .0304 after decoding. Is this good? Well, not very. If we had sent 2-bit blocks without the 2 extra bits, the probability of error for the comparable blocks would have been $1 - .98^2 = .0396$, which is somewhat higher than our coded system. Thus the performance is indeed better, but admittedly not by a lot!

In a simple case such as 4-bit words it is easy enough to find the optimum dictionary with 4 entries. The code words are a little further apart from each other than the words we picked at random. In going through the exercise of finding the probability of error you would find that the optimum code corrects 75 percent of the single-error events, and none of the less probable error events. It has a probability of error of .0212. Still not great. What can we do?

TOWARD LONGER CODES
. . . .

Shannon promised us we could reduce the probability of error indefinitely. We did everything we could with our little dictionary of 4-bit entries. The only thing left to us is to go to larger dictionaries. Suppose now that we consider 8-bit code words. Since the words will have to carry 4 bits of information, there will be $2^4 = 16$ code words, chosen from a possible set of $2^8 = 256$ sequences. The number of ways the dictionary could be constructed is $256 \times 255 \times 254 \times \ldots \times 250 \times 249$, which is obviously a huge number, but again we can choose the dictionary entries randomly and acknowledge that the optimum code must be at least as good as our random choice.

My computer spewed out a number of randomly generated codes and evaluated their performances. There was not a great deal of spread in the final numbers, with the best probability of error in this lot being .0251. This particular dictionary corrected 87% of the single-error patterns and about 27 percent of the double-error patterns. Here again the optimum code is relatively easy to find, and with a small amount of cleverness we can determine that it corrects all 8 of the single-error patterns and 25% of the double-error patterns. It has a probability of error of .0079. Now we seem to be getting somewhere. If we had merely transmitted 4-bit information blocks without the redundancy of the 8-bit dictionary, the probability of a block error would have been $1 - .98^4 = .0776$. At least now it seems that we are getting some payback for giving up half of our bits for protection. The clue seems to be to go to longer codes.

Flushed with success, we would like to move on to 16-bit dictionaries. However, there is a big, big problem developing; it is the tyranny of exponential blowup in the complexity. It is very important for us to understand this because it is central, not only to the specific coding problem that we are discussing, but to so many of the important problems of information handling and processing. As we make longer code words we seem to be getting better performance. From what we have seen in our example, the progress is slow, but encouraging. We will examine momentarily the philosophy of why longer code words are better. Meanwhile look at what is happening to the complexity of our system. When the code words were 4 bits long, there were only 4 entries in our dictionary, representing the 2^2 possible 2-bit blocks to be encoded. To evaluate the code we looked at 16 different error patterns in combination with these 4 words—a total of 64 possibilities. Easy. With 8-bit words there are 2^4, or 16, entries in the dictionary. Still easy. In order to evaluate the codes we combine these with 2^8 possible 8-bit error patterns, which results in 4,096 possibilities. Modest, but we raise our eyebrows. Now to do 16-bit code words there are 256 code words and 2^{16} possible error patterns, which makes 16,777,216 possibilities to evaluate. I am just not going to be able to rummage with this on my little computer, or even on most of its bigger brothers. And 16-bit codes are tiny!

However, I do not want to make an issue of the number of error events that we have to consider to fairly evaluate a candidate code.

We should focus more on the size of the dictionary versus the gain in code performance. The situation is reviewed as follows:

RATE ½ CODES

CODE SIZE	DICTIONARY ENTRIES	PROBABILITY OF ERROR		
		RANDOM CODE	BEST CODE	PRACTICAL CODE
4	4	.0304	.0212	.0212
8	16	.0251	.00786	.00786
16	256	(hard to compute)	.00295	.00368
32	65,536	(impossible to compute)	.00035	.0029
64	4 billion	(impossible to compute)	.000042	.00127

So far I have withheld a most interesting fact. When Shannon used randomly chosen code dictionaries to underbound the performance of the unknown, optimum codes, he found that these random codes on the average fulfilled the promise of the channel capacity theorem—the probability of error approached zero exponentially as the code length increased. This retrospectively confirms the intuition we gained from our example. Codes get better as they get longer. Furthermore, amazingly, it is not necessary to be very selective about the code dictionaries; merely picking them at random works perfectly well. Of course, as you can see from the table, if you are really able to pick an optimum (best) code, you do a bit better. But really, almost any old code will do. Or so it seems.

Right away there are two problems. First, we really do not know how to make optimum codes of any appreciable length. Second, it is apparent that even though picking random codes sounds simple in concept, we would have to deal with horrendous numbers to construct longer codes. A code length of 100 might be reasonable in practice, but for a code with an information rate of ½, just writing down the dictionary would require a thousand trillion entries, not even to speak of the decoding problem. Thus we cannot even keep a dictionary! Random codes are out. We must instead find a code that we can mechanize; a code for which the appropriate code words can be *calculated* upon demand by recipe, and similarly decoded. We call these codes constructive, as opposed to random. We cannot keep dictionaries, we must build machines.

Through the work of thousands of intrigued scientists and engineers over the last forty years many constructive coding procedures have become known. The tyranny of numbers is so overwhelming that a very strong structure, a sort of mathematical scaffolding, must be built into the coding algorithm. There must be a strong rationality underneath the way the code words are derived. In a moment I will describe a popular means of mechanizing the selection and generation of code words. For comparison with the random and optimum codes in the earlier table, I have included the performance of some practical codes that can be derived by mechanized procedure, and likewise decoded. Notice that these mechanizable codes have a quite reasonable error-rate performance, so it appears that there is little penalty for requiring practicality.

MECHANIZING A CODE

We need to find some kind of mathematical crank that can turn out code words on demand, and that will provide some foundation for analysis so that we can predetermine the code performance. Among the many possible binary sequences that could be code words, we need to pick some small fraction of words that are somehow "far apart." Suppose that we were dealing with real numbers instead of binary sequences. One way that might occur to you might be to pick, say, every sixth number—0,6,12,18 . . . . The distinguishing characteristic of the "code numbers" would be that each would be divisible by six. It turns out that we can do something very much analogous with the binary sequences by making every legal code word evenly divisible by something called a generator polynomial. Let me explain.

As an example let me return to the Hamming code that I mentioned before. Each code word is 7 bits in length, and since there are 4 information bits in this code, there are 16 code words that must be selected from the 128 possible 7-bit sequences. Let me represent a 7-bit sequence as a polynomial in a variable X with binary coefficients corresponding to the bits in the sequence. If a particular bit in the sequence is a 0, then that term in the polynomial disappears. (I am sure that worries some of you, but wait a little, it is just a simple and powerful convenience.) Here are some example sequences and their polynomial representations:

$$1 \quad 0 \quad 0 \quad 1 \quad 1 \quad 1 \quad 1$$
$$X^6 \qquad\qquad +X^3 + X^2 + X + 1 ;$$

$$0 \quad 1 \quad 1 \quad 0 \quad 0 \quad 1 \quad 0$$
$$X^5 + X^4 \qquad\qquad +X .$$

That seems simple enough. For each 7-bit sequence we can write a corresponding polynomial in X, but why would we want to do that? Well, the secret behind the Hamming code is that each code word has a polynomial that is evenly divisible by the generator polynomial

$$g(X) = X^3 + X + 1.$$

For example, 0100111 is a legal code word in the Hamming code, and its polynomial representation is

$$X^5 + X^2 + X + 1 = g(X) \, (X^2 + 1).$$
$$= (X^3 + X + 1)(X^2 + 1)$$

Try this multiplication yourself, but you have to use the rules of binary arithmetic on the coefficients. That is: $1 + 0 = 1, 1 + 1 = 0, 1 \times 1 = 1, 1 \times 0 = 0$. Thus any code word is a multiple of that generator polynomial, and any sequence that is not a multiple of it is not a code word.

Now suppose someone says to you that they would like to transmit the information bits 0010. How do you find the right code word using the idea of the generator polynomial? In real numbers that would be like trying to find the multiple of 3 that was nearest (but not greater than) the number 22. We would first divide 22 by 3 and notice that we had a remainder of 1 left over, so by subtracting the 1 from 22 we would reach the desired answer of 21. We do exactly the same thing with the generator polynomial. First we shift the information bit sequence 3 positions to the left to leave room for the check bits:

0 0 1 0 _ _ _, or in terms of the polynomial, X^4.

Then we divide that X^4 by the generator polynomial. We get a remainder of $X^2 + X$, so by analogy if we subtract this from the X^4 the result will be evenly divisible by the generator polynomial.

In the binary field, addition is the same as subtraction, so the code word we find is:

$X^4 + X^2 + X$ or in terms of the bit sequence, 0 0 1 0 1 1 0.

So this is the simple recipe that produces code words from information sequences. The entire Hamming code generated by this process is as follows:

0000000	0001011	0010110	0011101
0100111	0101100	0110001	0111010
1000101	1001110	1010011	1011000
1100010	1101001	1110100	1111111

I would like you to take a moment to appreciate the beautiful structure in this code. I said it had to have very strong underpinnings, and you can see this by noticing the following properties of this code:

- Any sum of 2 or more code words equals another code word. For example, 0100111 + 1001110 = 1101001. Try it!

- Shift any code word by any amount in either direction, wrapping around the bits as they fall off the end, and you will get another code word. For example, 1100010 shifted right one bit is 0110001. Because of this property, the code is called cyclic.

- Every code word differs from every other code word in at least 3 positions. This is easiest to see by considering the code word 0000000. Notice that every other code word has at least 3 ones. This minimum distance of 3 guarantees that any single error will result in a sequence that is still closest to the original code word. Thus this Hamming code is called a single-error-correcting code. On the other hand, if it is used strictly for error detection, it takes at least 3 errors to turn a code word into another code word.

What marvelous properties! Where did they come from, you might ask? Partly they were the result of making the code from the multiples of the generator polynomial, but to get that last property of good minimum distance (which equates to good error-correcting abilities), the right generator polynomial had to be picked to begin with. And where do you get a good generator polynomial? The truth is—you look it up in a table that has been put together by mathematicians who possess the powerful magic to know which polynomials are good and which are not. The mathematicians can tell the error-correction properties from the roots of the generator polynomial $g(X)$. The roots of $g(X)$ are the values of X for which it is zero, but unfortunately the roots are not nice numbers like 2 or 3, rather they lie in mathematical abstractions called Galois fields. Sorry about that, but there are really good tables available even if you do not know about Galois fields!

There are very simple electronic circuits or software algorithms that do the polynomial division needed to calculate the check bits. The polynomial that protected all of my precious bits in this book was $X^{16} + X^{12} + X^5 + 1$. This polynomial is a standard used in many common communications software packages. It produces 16 bits, or 2 bytes, of remainder after division into the polynomial corresponding to the desired block of information. These bits are usually called Cyclic Redundancy Checks (CRCs), for some forgotten reason. At the receiver it is simple enough to recalculate the CRCs with the same generator polynomial to see whether or not there is agreement. On the other hand, if you want to do error correction instead of merely detecting errors at the receiver, the algorithms that find the maximum likelihood data sequence are really quite intricate and cumbersome. They do not strike me as so beautiful and shiny as the code generation algorithms, but fortunately there is always someone crawling under the engine who is really into these things.

THE CODING PARADOX

As constructive coding procedures like the one we just described were uncovered, their inventors gathered mathematical arguments proving the value of their codes. An obvious question concerned the power of these codes to decrease the error rate towards zero while holding the information rate constant. Surprise! The constructive codes were asymptotically bad, that is, as the block length became long either the information rate went to zero or the error rate approached .5 (complete garbage). This provoked consternation; codes picked entirely at random were good, but codes picked according to the most ingenious mathematical procedures were failures. The conundrum was aptly stated as, "All codes are good, except those that we know about." In 1972 a class of constructive codes was discovered that does achieve arbitrarily small probability of error at nonzero information rates (though not as high as capacity). Although this class is of philosophical interest, it has not been practically important. With this exception, it is still true that though any old code should do, essentially all the ones we know about do not have the asymptotic behavior that Shannon's results promise. Nevertheless, we do have very powerful coding algorithms for a wide range of midrange applications.

How can it be that randomly chosen codes have desirable properties, while mathematically chosen codes do not? It seems that what we are really after is true randomness, which is difficult to emulate with mathematical structure. What makes codes good is that the code words are far apart from each other. In a sense we want to sprinkle the code words throughout the available space uniformly in order to keep them far apart. Imagine being keeper of the universe and having to distribute the stars in the heavens— except that the space is not the three-dimensional, physical world but many-dimensional and binary. (We humans do have a way of visualizing things in our own spatial experience, and in some coding applications code sets are called "constellations.") In any event, one way to get a good distribution of our stars is just to throw them out there randomly. But unfortunately there are just so many that we cannot keep track of them all! On the other hand, if we derive ingenious, but relatively simple ways of accounting for and positioning our stars, they do not spread out uniformly but tend to cluster in some sense. Can we emulate randomness with an underlying mathematical structure? We do not know that it is impossible, but it does appear to be difficult.

Now I should like to explain why the error rate can be made to approach zero as the code length is made longer. The reason is quite fundamental and is shared with many physical phenomena; it is the statistical reliability of large collections of random numbers. Shannon's promised behavior relies on the same phenomenon that guarantees insurance companies a certain rate of return despite the probabilistic nature of their business. Many of us know these laws of large numbers from courses in statistics and probability. If I flip a coin once, I may get a head, or I may get a tail. There is not much we can say about the result *a priori*. If I flip the coin ten times, I would be surprised if I got less than 20 percent (i.e., two) heads, but not terribly so. If I flip the coin a thousand times, I would expect that the ratio of heads would be almost exactly .5. I do not expect exactly 500 heads, which is improbable, but I expect the *fraction* of heads to be very close to .5. For example, there would be high likelihood that between 470 and 530 of the 1,000 flips would be heads. The more I flip the coin the greater the probability that the ratio is close to .5. This is assured in spite of the fact that each individual toss is itself unpredictable. The standard deviation of the percent of heads shrinks as the inverse of the square root of the number of tosses.

This same predictability occurs in the transmitted data bits. With an error rate of .02, we should expect that as the code length becomes longer, very close to 2 percent of the bits will be in error—not 1 percent or 3 percent, but more and more exactly 2 percent. All we need is a code that corrects error patterns that deviate 2 percent in distance from the original code word. If we can make such a code, it will correct essentially all of the errors. A somewhat more informative way of looking at this phenomenon was pointed out by Shannon. Consider all the error patterns of length equal to the word length N. There are obviously 2^N of them, and for long word lengths that is a huge number of situations for the code to have to worry about. However, Shannon showed that only the smallest, minute fraction of these possible sequences becomes of any concern whatsoever as the length N becomes large. Specifically he found that only 2^{HN} sequences are significant: These sequences contain virtually all of the probability, while all other sequences have probability tending to zero. Thus the fraction of significant sequences is $2^{HN}/2^N = 2^{-CN}$. For example, in our channel with probability of error .02 and channel capacity $C = .8585$, if the code length is 100 then the fraction of error sequences that we have to worry about is only about 2^{-86}. This is the fraction of sequences with 2 percent of the bits in error. I do not have to tell you that that is an incredibly small number.

I would like to elaborate somewhat on this fundamental behavior. Here again we see that the entropy H is a central quantity. It represents the fraction of the *bits* that is significant in describing error locations. In our example, where $H = .1415$, the uncertainty in the error locations is low enough that the locations of the errors can be described by about 14 percent of the total bits, so that only $2^{.14N}$ error patterns occur with significant probability. All other error patterns have a very small total probability. In other words, certain error patterns are "typical," while all others are "atypical." As the length of the pattern considered becomes very long, the "typical" error sequences predominate.

Imagine that we list all of the 2^N possible error patterns in order of probability. The first such pattern is $0000 \ldots 00$, indicating no errors, while the next N patterns contain a single error in one location, such as $0000 \ldots 01$, etc. The next $N(N-1)/2$ patterns are the ones with two errors, etc. If we draw a line horizontally across our list after the $2^{HN}th$ entry, then all of the patterns above our line are typical. All the patterns below are atypical, and as the length N becomes large, these latter simply do not occur. (More properly, they occur with vanishingly small probability.) It is wonderful how so much certainty can be associated with the overall properties of random events!

If we return to our analogy of the coding problem as one of distributing stars in a universe, the significance of the existence of "typical" error sequences has a geometric interpretation. The code word positions are where the stars are located, but during transmission, error patterns that alter their locations are added to them. However, as we have seen, the disturbance does not take the stars just anywhere, but it only moves them to some point (in our example) that is approximately 2 percent away in bits. Thus a received star will lie somewhere roughly on a sphere centered about its original location. As the sequence gets longer and longer, we have the same geometric interpretation, except that the dimensionality gets higher and higher, and because of the law of large numbers the "skins" of the spheres where the stars are most likely to be found get thinner and thinner. With a high probability, the received sequences are found nearly on the surface of those 2 percent-deviation spheres. This is a phenomenon known as "sphere hardening." It is also a familiar fact in mathematics that all of the volume of a sphere goes towards its surface as the dimensionality gets higher and higher.

Because of sphere hardening, we know more and more exactly the region in which the received sequences will lie. If the code is ready for them, the errors will virtually all be corrected. In constructing a code, as in distributing the stars, all we have to do is to be sure that none of those spheres centered on our code words intersects with any other such sphere centered on a different code word. As we have seen, if the code rate is less than capacity, and we just throw the stars out there, it works—at least in the limit of long codes. When we examine the possible performance of finite-length codes, one of the methods for finding bounds on performance is termed "sphere packing." Just how many spheres of a given diameter can we fit into the space without overlap? How many Ping-Pong balls will fit inside a beach ball? Answers to these questions, which are the kinds of problems that fascinate mathematically inclined researchers, can tell us just how well a code of a given length and rate can do.

Arguments such as sphere packing help tell us just how long a code has to be to achieve a given error rate performance. After all, we are caught on the horns of a dilemma; the error rate can only be driven down by the reliability of the statistics of large numbers, thus we need long code lengths to encompass a significant number of error events. On the other hand, as the code length becomes longer, the number of code words, and consequently the complexity of the encoding and decoding process, increase exponentially. From the viewpoint of code derivation we are concerned with how many spheres can be packed into a given space, and at the same time as the code becomes longer, we await anxiously the effect of the law of large numbers causing the surfaces of the spheres, representing the probability densities of the received words, to "harden" into the Ping-Pong balls we hold in our imagination.

If we hold the effective information rate of the code constant while we increase the length N, the error rate attainable with the best possible code will decrease exponentially, that is,

$$Prob(error) < e^{-rN}$$

What interests us the most is the value of the exponent r, since that will determine how long a code must be for a given level of performance. Through the years a number of ingenious arguments have been used to find upper and lower bounds on r. It has been shown that the closer the information rate is to the channel capacity C, the smaller r becomes, and consequently codes have to be very long to be effective. The implication of this fact is that codes get better quickly when we operate at a small fraction of capacity (this is why we were not greedy in our example), but that they must be long when we try to get near capacity. What makes the situation worse is that long constructive codes may not be very efficient. Thus the story behind Shannon's remarkable theorem is not as sanguine as the simple statement of the theorem might lead us to believe.

A   R E T R O S P E C T I V E   O N
I N F O R M A T I O N   T H E O R Y

Some of the key ideas in information theory that we have discussed are the following:

- Information can be measured by the logarithm of the probability.

- The communications system can be divided into source coding to eliminate needless redundancy, and channel coding to incorporate desirable redundancy.

- There is a fundamental channel capacity that measures the maximum information rate a communications channel can sustain. The concept of channel capacity bridges the two concepts of source coding and channel coding. If the capacity of the channel exceeds the information rate of the source, then the source can be transmitted exactly over the channel.

- If the information rate is less than channel capacity, then error-correcting coding can be used to reduce the error rate to any arbitrarily small number. The error rate decreases exponentially as the code length becomes longer. At the same time the complexity of the system becomes exponentially larger.

When we examine such forms of information as text, speech, images, and computer files in future chapters, we shall have occasion to apply an information-theoretic viewpoint from time to time. It will serve sometimes as a philosophy, and at other times as an inspiration of what might be possible. Information theory can serve to anchor our feet, and to tell us when it would be foolish to dream of further gains. The core of information theory that we have presented here is a very beautiful work of human thought. In the ever-changing tapestry of the computer age it is one of the few timeless subjects. It is a classic tale, retold many times, yet it is with enthusiasm that I include my own version of the essentials here in the context of information technology.

When information theory was first publicized, it achieved immediate popularity and was applied to many fields of human endeavor. The literature was filled with attempts to use the principles of information theory in psychology, art, and music. These applications were often disappointing and are seldom seen today. Instead, the pendulum has swung the other way, and workers in the field are often skeptically asked what, if anything, information theory has accomplished. There are perhaps three answers to such a question. First, information theory stands alone as a work of art that needs no rationalization for its preeminent place in human knowledge. Second, information theory has served as a guiding philosophy in the design of communications systems. Lastly, information theory has led both directly and indirectly to the invention of many classes of useful error correcting and detecting codes. Only now that computation has become relatively inexpensive are these codes beginning to see widespread use in communications and in data storage and retrieval. If information theory is regarded as having had minimal impact on the world, it is because of unreasonable expectations and a lack of understanding of the depth and wisdom it contains.

REFLECTIONS — CODING IS DEAD

There is a small group of us in the communications field who will always remember a workshop held in Florida about twenty years ago at which we engineers took a look at the future and saw nothing but gloom for technology. One of my friends gave a talk that has lived in infamy as the "coding is dead" talk. His thesis was that he and the other coding theorists formed a small, inbred group that had been isolated from reality too long. He illustrated this talk with a single slide showing a pen of rats that psychologists had kept in a confined space for a long time. I cannot tell you here what these rats were doing, but suffice it to say that this slide has since been borrowed many times to depict the depths of depravity into which a disconnected group can fall. The rats made *Lord of the Flies* look like a school picnic.

All this depraved behavior had its parallel in the activities of the coding theorists, he argued. Too many equations had been generated, with too few consequences, just for the thrill of it all. One paper after another had justified itself on the basis of being an extension of the results of a "famous" predecessor paper, which unfortunately nobody outside the closed group cared about. (I am reminded of a proposal I was asked to review that began, "Lately there has been a great deal of interest in . . ." citing references 1 through 15. Checking in the back I discovered that those references had all been written by the author himself.) Coding theorist professors had begat more coding theory Ph.D.s in their own image, all preprogrammed with reverence for the mythical Galois fields, as a sort of mathematical Stonehenge. But no one else cared; it was time to see this perversion for what it was. Give up this fantasy and take up a useful occupation, exhorted my friend. Coding is dead.

Carried away with the mood of this somber day, I made my own prediction. "Data is dead," said I. There was an immediate chorus of dissent. It was not right to say this, they shouted. One should say instead "data *are* dead," in order to properly reflect the plural form. I stood corrected, but nonetheless went on to bemoan the coming of the dreaded digital networks, which would obviate all need for modems to connect to analog facilities. "Modems are dead," I said, confident of my grammar. Heads nodded in unison. Scratch modems, no point in working on them anymore. Marvelous how we technologists could chart the future when we put our minds to it.

I am sure there are morals enough in this little vignette for many an essay. Fortunately, no one gave up coding or modems. Today ads for modems appear on national television during football games. At home I have a Reed-Solomon coder casually sitting on an end table in my living room. It is inside a compact disk player, of course. Otherwise it would look rather silly. The computer in my basement uses error-checking hardware in its memory, and cyclic codes for disk access. And, yes, when I use my modem to send files to the office, codes are applied once again. My children even have their own modems. Great predictions, weren't they?

Why are we technologists so bad at predicting the future of technology? Now I know that futurology is easy to discredit. Famous wrong predictions are legion; it would not even be sport to quote them here. But it seems to me that we technologists are less adept at looking at the future of technology than are laypeople. The science fiction writers claim to have foretold almost everything we do, and in some cases, like Arthur C. Clarke and the communications satellite, there seems justification. Of course, from where we sit their job looks easy—throw out an infinite number of arbitrary predictions, and many will come true. Moreover, they are not burdened with knowing why it is impossible to do the things they suggest, and this is our own handicap. We are too close to the technology itself. From our myopic viewpoint we see only the problems, and not the possibilities that transcend what others see as only "engineering" details. Then, to be honest, some of our detractors say we lack imagination. Better than lacking breeding, however.

Of course most of the public thinks of us as being in charge of the future. When we make predictions, they listen. Silly them. If the coders had listened to themselves, they would have given up coding, but secretly they knew better. They would never have listened to their own predictions. But others have no such qualms. If the newspapers had covered our little meeting, I can see the headlines that would have resulted. "Data is dead, say experts." (Everyone quoted in the newspapers is an expert.) In my company the people in charge of bureaucracy send me an annual demand for a list of "expected breakthroughs." All the researchers think as I do that this is absurdity beyond belief, but how can we reject the demand without conveying the idea that we do not know what we are doing? I tried to make it go away, but that was more trouble than filling it in with such preposterous predictions as "room-temperature superconductivity." I suppose there are advantages to being thought of as omniscient.

That our predictions are usually worthless is but one interpretation to draw from this little incident. Let me give you a choice of morals to try on.

1. Coding theorists prove once again that engineers cannot predict future.
2. Coders persevere in spite of skepticism and, believing in their own work, triumph in the end.
3. Support fundamental studies in math. Do not be shortsighted, they will pay off in the long run.
4. Lazy theorists, comfortable in their work and unwilling to find new fields of endeavor, stick with the only thing they know and somehow luck out.

I do not mean to pick on coding theory. The same thing could be said about any field that has academic roots. Some we win, some not, but again and again we are faced with deciding what work we stop and what work we support, both for ourselves and for our businesses. While most people may feel that these decisions are especially difficult, I have no problem myself. I am fortunate in having this little list of things that are currently dead. Lack of space prevents reproducing the list here.

3

T E X T

• • • • •

In the information age the continuous flows and fragments of speech and images are like gusty winds in our face, but the ground on which we stand is the rubble of text. The knowledge legacy of man has been codified in the archeological mound of our writings—from the hieroglyphics of the Egyptian tombs to the abstract mathematics of the current scientific journals. Text is omnipresent and familiar; it covers our desks, overfills our mailboxes and files, and strains the resources of our libraries. Yet the more closely we examine this evolved form of information, the more unknowably complex it appears. The information age challenges us to deepen our understanding of written language so that we might better acquire, store, communicate, and access our information through this ancient, acquired medium that we all share.

INFORMATION AND THE EVOLUTION OF WRITTEN LANGUAGE

The computer age seems to have swept upon us overnight, but in the history of man written language itself is a relatively recent development. Apparently we got on quite well for thousands of years without any form of writing whatsoever; it is only within the last 5,000 years that a system of speech-sign communication has emerged. Speech came long before writing, which evolved as an assignment of speech forms to graphic symbols.

Curiously, there appears to be no information content in the cave paintings of the prewriting stage of history. Exactly what these paintings symbolize and why they were made are matters for scholarly argument, but examination reveals no attempt to convey a record of numbers of animals killed, or ownership, or any time sequence associated with an event or story. This interesting anomaly aside, the history of writing is largely explained by the growing need to express information in a permanent form. The brochure on the story of writing in the entrance to the library section of the British Museum begins, "The purpose of writing is information storage."

The attempt to communicate specific information was the first stage in the development of writing. The earliest writing was pictographic with mnemonic pictures representing objects, much as we use icons in certain mouse-based computer environments today. The typewriter keyboard retains some of this flavor today with the inclusion of %, &, and other such ideographic symbols. But it is hard to extend this pictographic writing very far, so written languages of this type gradually became more abstract and divorced from the natural form, to the extent that some of these writings remain untranslated to this day. The evolutionary trend was toward phonetic writing in which symbols were equated with sounds or segments of speech. In this stage of the development of writing, the signs represented words or syllables.

The principle of equating signs with words may have seemed ideal at first, but the expansion of knowledge increased the number of different symbols to an unwieldy number. In the period 2000–1000 B.C. the Egyptians had about 700 different signs, while the Sumerians used almost 2,000. The Chinese at this time during the Shang dynasty had 2,500 graphic characters, which offers a useful comparison with the 50,000 of Chinese today. Among all the world's written languages Chinese has remained the most logographic (meaning signs represent words, but Chinese is more properly described as logosyllabic, since signs also represent syllables).

In these early stages the esthetic qualities we associate with writing were neglected in favor of recording objects and events. I am reminded of my own keen sense of disappointment on the occasions when I have viewed an ancient writing form in some museum only to read that the translation is something like "John owns 6 cows." Somehow the aura of a priceless relic makes me always expect something like an *Illiad* or an ancient equivalent of a *Gone with the Wind*. Ironically, in the current early period of the information age, the same situation pertains in the computer storage and handling of information. Perhaps here too we will evolve towards more subtle use of the nuance possible in a language system.

Probably the most intriguing story of the deciphering of an ancient written language was that of Linear B, the earliest Greek writing. Over 3,000 clay tablets of this writing were uncovered beginning in 1902 at Knossos in Crete. These tablets dated from about 1400 B.C. to 1240 B.C.—the time of Agamemnon through the heroic age of Greece and the Trojan War. The story of the fifty-year quest for a translation, ending in the triumph in 1952 of the British architect Michael Ventris and the British classicist John Chadwick, has been recounted many times in print. What is seldom related is the content of this ancient library. Typical samples are as follows:

> Koldos the shepherd holds a lease from the village: 48 litres of wheat.
> One pair of wheels bound with bronze, unfit for service.
> Four slaves of Koradollos in charge of seed-corn.
> Two tripods: Aigeus the Cretan brings them.

In *The Codebreakers,* David Kahn has commented, "None of these tablets contains any literary work, nor any diplomatic instructions, personal letters, religious texts, historical writings, nor anything, in fact, beside these minutely detailed bureaucratic records of petty commercial transactions." We could imagine a future civilization finally translating the magnetic computer language of a long-buried tape cartridge of today, and finding in disappointment exactly the same thing—writing for the purpose of information storage.

Language scholars suggest that the most important principle in the history of writing was phonetic transfer, where existing word signs were used to express words of like sound for which there was no sign. For example the sign for the word "eye" might also be used to represent the word "I." These signs then have double meaning, and are *context dependent*. Although phonetic transfer in-

93

creases the functionality of the written symbols, in the computer interpretation of language it becomes a greatly complicating feature. It is believed that phonetic transfer was forced by the need for record keeping, and in particular for the growing number of proper names this required.

The last great innovation in written language was the alphabet, which was invented by the Greeks in about the 9th century B.C. (The earlier Greek language, Linear B, had been a syllabic script.) In the alphabet a small number of different characters represents the basic speech sounds of the vowels and consonants. The flexibility of phonetic writing inherent in an easily managed alphabet held great appeal, and during the last 2,800 years the alphabet has swept throughout the world. Although the aim of a phonetic writing system would be a perfect correspondence between written and spoken language, no language has such a pure system. English has many impurities in the correspondence, and a patchwork of exceptions has grown as small, incremental language innovations have overlaid the older system. Nonetheless, English is our legacy, for all its richness, and for all of its inherent complexity.

LANGUAGE, INFORMATION, AND COMPUTERS

It would be dehumanizing to think that the only purpose of language is information storage. Aldous Huxley observed that "The function of language is twofold: to communicate emotion and to give information." As computers process the streams of alphabetic characters we think of as language, they unwittingly face semantic content across this broad range from emotion to information. The emotion side of this range is exemplified by poetry, which is deeply embedded in human experience, and which is difficult and ambiguous in interpretation even for the most sophisticated of human processors. The next step toward information is fiction, such as Huxley's own *Brave New World,* where the emotional content may be blurred by the superstructure of a story—a chronological arrangement of facts and "pseudofacts," but an arrangement that must often be appreciated on a higher level as an integrated whole.

I think of a middle range between emotion and information as exemplified by textbooks (an interesting word in the con*text* of this chapter!), where the primary purpose is the *communication* of information to other people. I put the accent here on communication. In this book, for example, I am embarrassed to admit that the density of facts is quite small. At this moment I am instead attempting to communicate my thoughts to you, the thinking reader. I am conscious that these vague and faulty words are an imperfect condensation of the helter-skelter swirl of my own random thoughts, and I have little idea of how they will influence the patterns of your own thoughts at the future time at which they are read. Yet there is a path of communication between us. Once my words have been decided upon we can study their processing, storage, and transmission with a certain degree of precision. The transformations that map words to symbols to electrical signals and back again to words are the kinds of tasks for which we have developed models, mathematics, and mechanisms. In contrast, the mapping of my thoughts to these words to your thoughts is a mystical process which at best is poorly understood.

Moving now a shade away from the midcategory where communication may be an end in itself, we encounter a subrange of business and scientific reports, papers, and memoranda. Here, as is often painfully apparent, communication is quite secondary to the purpose of archiving information. (I am reminded of the old "Dragnet" refrain, "Just the facts, m'am.") The trend in recent years has been to further abstract this already terse medium. As an aid to understanding, and for personal archiving purposes, we have taken to using highlighting pens, reducing pages of text to handfuls of bright yellow sentences.

A similar condensation of the report format is accomplished in the making of "bullet-chart" transparencies. In fact, visual presentations of this form have become so ubiquitous that it has been suggested that the unit of information should be considered the view graph. The amount of information that we are expected to consume in a given time interval is then proportional to the height of the stack of view graphs in store. Although this suggestion is clearly facetious, we all recognize the kernel of truth it contains. Perhaps indeed an entire theory of life could be based upon the successive unfolding of a giant stack of view graphs reaching into faraway mists.

The "bullet-chart" appears to be a text format very close to what we might consider "pure" information. Even here, however, the medium is intended for human interpretation. Moreover, the interpretation is usually with respect to an individualized framework. Try to understand a report by reading someone else's bright yellow highlighted sentences. Or perhaps you have been sent a set of copies of view graphs used in a presentation you missed. Sometimes you are able to digest the entire essence of the material in a few minutes, and you congratulate yourself on saving an hour of valuable time. More often the view graphs are cryptic, and you berate yourself for wasting the frustrating minutes of puzzlement on them.

The text form closest to the information side in Huxley's observation is the table format, or what is equivalent, the computer data base. It is the only textual format which is at present easily amenable to the computer processing of the information itself. The use of language in this form is minimal; only the characters and words have been borrowed for use in symbolic representation. The depth and power inherent in the structure of language have been cut away. In this sense data bases are extremely simple systems, but this simplicity is belied by the numerous shelves of books on this subject in libraries, and by the surprising adaptability of the data-base format to a broad class of information retrieval applications.

To recapitulate, computers handle information that has been encoded in language in many packages and guises. The role of language in these formats varies from deep and inextricable to superficial, while the purpose runs from the expression of emotion through the simple maintenance of a ledger of data (see table below).

Language is, of course, a subject that has been studied by a great many people. If there is any different viewpoint to be gained from the context of this book, it would be in the view of language as seen by the current generation of computers. I imagine the computer looking out at us from the depths of its steel vault. "These people are strange machines," it would say to itself. "I am not sure why,

INFORMATION IN LANGUAGE

PURPOSE	FORMAT
Emotion	Poetry Fiction
Communication	Textbooks Reports View graphs
Information	Databases

but dealing with them is inefficient and cumbersome. I have to take my information and pad it with all kinds of redundancy, while following a ridiculous set of complex rules, which in turn have an extraordinary number of exceptions. But what can I do? That is the way they are.''

But I think as the computer's descendants gained intelligence they would admire us. They would see our language as a beautiful blend of robustness and choice, and as an infinitely extensible framework for both thought and expression of thought. They would be envious of the intense humanity and world knowledge inherent or assumed in even the simplest English sentences, and they would feel excluded. Rightfully so.

Today's computers have only rudimentary capabilities for understanding and manipulating language. (We will touch on some of these capabilities later.) For the most part they serve only as mute storage bins for the streams of characters we interpret as language. When we generate precious writings on word processors and store them in computer files, we do not expect the computer to have any comprehension of their content. I often wonder what the computer makes of these fragments of human information passing through its silicon dreams. But all we ask is for our characters back upon demand. In contrast to all previous historical forms of written language, the computer representation of language is not constrained to be read by people, so long as the original character stream can be regenerated by suitable processing. Thus internally to the computer, text might be represented in an efficient manner, requiring as few bits as possible to store or communicate a given text file.

In text compression we will trade the robustness of natural English text with its concomitant inefficiency of representation for conciseness and fragility. What makes this trade possible is the absolute precision of the computer. Our written language is robust and redundant because it derives from a phonetic representation of speech. Not only are there physical constraints on the successive sounds that we can form, but evolutionary forces tend to keep spoken language relatively immune to the confusion of noise and distortions that inevitably occur in human conversation. In contrast, the computer requires no redundancy, because *it does not make errors.* (Only those that we tell it to make through our clumsy software.)

The freedom from errors in computers is an important cornerstone in the philosophy of computation. We could not deal with a world in which our files were corrupted each time they were stored, retrieved, or processed. Computers are designed not to make errors because this philosophy simplifies our thinking about computing and the design of computers, not because this is technologically optimum. Ensuring that errors do not occur is the job of a lower conceptual layer of bit manipulation that uses error-detecting codes. In any event this layer and the hardware below it are invisible in the manipulation of text. We may simply take on faith the proposition of absolute accuracy. Consequently, the human need for robustness in language is not present within the computer.

THE LAYERS OF TEXT

Sometimes I stare at a common printed word until it looks strange and unfamiliar. The letters pull apart in my mind and separate so far that the unity of the concept that they designate together disappears. "What a funny word," I think. Then like an optical illusion, I give a mental shake and the letters recombine in my mind and disappear as individual entities to merge into the concept they represent. Look as I might, I can no longer imagine how I ever thought the sequence strange. In the following sections I want to do something like this with text. We will pull apart text from the standpoint of information science, starting with the most superficial characteristics, the microscopic view of isolated letters, and gradually zooming towards the macroscopic panorama of the deepest structure of language. The layers of text that we shall discuss are shown in an "onion-type" portrayal in Figure 4. The deeper that we can penetrate into these layers, the more capability we will be able to achieve in the processing of text.

TEXT AS LETTERS

The overwhelming characterization (an apt word) of text today in communication and computer system usage is as a sequence of independent characters. Each character is represented by an 8-bit chunk of data, which has come to be known universally as a "byte." The mapping of characters to bytes is simple and transparent, and

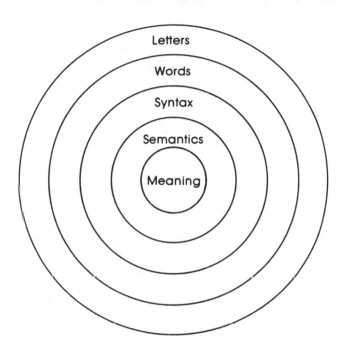

FIGURE 4
The textual onion

takes no account of the context in which the character appears. Fortunately almost every manufacturer in the last decade has followed the ASCII standard (American Standard Code for Information Interchange) for the mapping of alphanumeric characters into bytes. In ASCII, for example:

$$A = 01000001 \quad a = 01100001$$
$$B = 01000010 \quad b = 01100010.$$

For some reason tables of the ASCII code assignments are given in every computer book, and also appear as pop-up windows in a number of computer utility programs. I used to be able to read ASCII directly myself at one time, but this archaic ability atrophied in today's well-packaged world in which it is seldom necessary to know actual byte values. It is just comforting to know that these things exist and are standardized. In fact, since the ASCII standard was agreed upon several decades ago it has been the foundation rock of data interchange, both in terms of its solidity, and in terms of its bottom position, where it stands at the critical juncture between the worlds of symbols and of signals. In practice it is well known that when all the higher and more sophisticated data interchange attempts fail between devices or systems because of the inevitable incompatibilities, there is always the simple ASCII interface as a means of last resort. On this one level at least, everyone agrees.

Our computer memories are littered with ASCII text. Nearly all the files we originate ourselves are captured in ASCII. This includes (with minor format and coding variations) text-editing and word-processing files, source code in computer languages, spread sheet data, and data base information. The remaining files are mostly executable machine code, a sort of "text" for the computer itself. In comparison with the ASCII files, there are a very small number of different machine code files in the world. However, these files are replicated everywhere; so that, for example, there are hundreds of thousands of absolutely identical copies of the most popular word-processing and spread-sheet programs using up computer memories throughout the country. These "common domain" files clog up my home personal computer, while my computer storage at work—where I am expected to originate information—is completely dominated by my own ASCII text files. The executable files there are kept almost exclusively in a common file server that handles many users like myself.

All of us have an intuitive measure of quantity for text. We see piles of documents and shelves of books in our minds and we gauge accordingly. Now that so much text is stored and communicated as bytes of electronic data the size is less obvious, and the standards themselves shrink each year with the increasing density of computer memory and the increasing speeds of data communication. Just how much of a computer system's resources are consumed by a given amount of text can be estimated from the table on page 101.

In addition to the storage requirements for various quantities of text, we are concerned with the time required to transmit these same documents over typical telecommunications facilities. How long does it take to send a book or a library over the telephone? The next table will show transmission times for these documents using typical data transmission speeds that can be obtained on various telecommunications facilities. First let us survey briefly the range of speeds that might be used.

SIZES OF TYPICAL DOCUMENTS IN COMPUTER STORAGE UNITS

DOCUMENT	BYTES	FLOPPY DISKS	MAG TAPES/ CD-ROMs
Page	2,400	.003	0
Report	7.2×10^4	.1	0
Book	7.2×10^5	1	0
Dictionary	6×10^7	83	.06
Encyclopedia	1.3×10^8	180	.13
Local library	7×10^{10}	97,000	70
College library	7×10^{11}	970,000	700
Library of Congress	1.8×10^{13}	2.4×10^7	18,000

To begin with, the most common data transmission rate is either 1,200 or 2,400 bits per second (150 or 300 bytes per second). This is the speed you get with a plug-in board or an inexpensive modem for your home personal computer. You can dial up an ordinary telephone line at these speeds and be confident of reasonably accurate data transmission. At this rate you can fill the screen of your PC with characters in a few seconds. It suffices for most home terminal use in today's environment.

When computers are linked together to exchange files and to handle bundled streams of user message data, a higher rate is absolutely necessary. Today most of this computer-to-computer traffic travels on leased (not dialed) telephone lines at a rate of 56,000 or 64,000 bits per second. This is a standard service offering of the telephone companies, which is exemplified by AT&T's Digital Dataphone Service. Obviously, it is considerably more expensive than a dialed voice call. A new international standard called ISDN (Integrated Services Digital Network) is now evolving in many countries that will make end-to-end digital service at a rate of 64,000 bits per second a common business (and then residential) service. The telephone companies have long used this data rate to carry individual, digitized voice telephone calls within their own networks, but it has not been commonly or easily offered to customers before.

The next step up in speeds is the so-called T-1 data rate of 1.5 million bits per second (Mbps). For the last 25 years the telephone companies have used this data rate for their own purposes to carry 24 multiplexed (interleaved by byte) voice telephone calls from office to office within a metropolitan area. Now it is becoming more common for large businesses to lease this rate as a direct pipe into the common carrier network. Invariably its capacity is spread among many subuses, encompassing both voice telephone and data calls.

As a last benchmark in the table, I have added what in 1988 was the highest commercially obtained data rate over any physical communications medium. It is 1.7 billion bits per second (Gbps), which is achieved by fiber optic communications systems buried deep within the intercity network of the common-carrier facilities. At this point tens of thousands of telephone channels are interwoven to travel on the superhighway created by a tiny laser pulsing light over a hair-thin fiber. At this time such enormous capacities are not leased to individual customers, but it is instructive to note the capacities of these fiber optic systems in terms of document transmission. Now for the table:

TRANSMISSION TIMES FOR TYPICAL DOCUMENTS

DOCUMENT	VOICEBAND 2400 BPS	DDS-WIDEBAND 56KBPS	T-1 1.5MBPS	FIBER OPTICS 1.7GBPS
Page	8 sec	.34 sec	.013 sec	1.13×10^{-5} sec
Report	4 min	10.3 sec	.38 sec	3.39×10^{-4} sec
Book	.67 hr	1.7 min	3.84 sec	.0034 sec
Dictionary	2.3 days	2.38 hrs	5.3 min	.28 sec
Encyclopedia	5 days	5.15 hrs	11.6 hrs	.61 sec
Local library	7.4 yrs	116 days	4.32 days	5.49 min
College library	74 yrs	3.17 yrs	43.2 days	.92 hrs
Library of Congress	1,900 yrs	81.5 yrs	3 yrs	23.5 hrs

It is interesting to observe that the Library of Congress, which is sometimes used as a yardstick for the measure of human knowledge, would require a time almost as long as the entire Christian era to transmit at the common modem speeds most of us use today. By the time it had all been transmitted, of course, it would be only of historical interest. On the other hand, the range of data transmission rates obtainable on physical media is so great that the entire Library of Congress could be transmitted in less than a day over a hair-thin optical fiber, and the speeds in this medium are doubling about every year and a half. Already in the research lab speeds ten times the speed listed in the table are being demonstrated.

The last two tables give some idea of the dimensions of the computer use of text. The great advantages of straightforward ASCII representation for text are that it is transparent and portable. ASCII files can be moved and understood everywhere without translation. Even minor variations, such as the meddling with the high-order bit that is done by a popular word processing program, make text files nonportable. But it is also apparent from the tables that there is much to be gained by the compression of text files. If a text file could be compressed by a factor of two or three, it might make the difference between being able to store or transmit the file in a practical situation.

Intelligent compression of text files is one reason to study the statistics of English letters and words. It is interesting to note that compression is being used increasingly to save storage space and transmission time, in spite of the undeniable fact that storage is becoming cheaper and transmission is becoming faster. This trend provides a constant reminder of our insatiable appetites for ownership and access of information. Every year my friends who work in data compression bemoan the oncoming death of their field, since with the next year's memory devices and transmission systems there is no projected need for the making of smaller files. Yet every year the use of compression increases. It seems that the perceived requirements for data storage and transfer are growing at a faster rate than the technologies of memory and transmission. At the same time the growing processing power of computers makes the implementation of compression ever more attractive.

THE STATISTICS OF ENGLISH LETTERS

From *The Gold Bug* by Edgar Allen Poe, 1843

My first step was to ascertain the predominant letters, as well as the least frequent. Counting all, I constructed a table. Now in English, the letter which most frequently occurs is e. *Afterwards, the succession*

103

runs thus: a o i d h n r s t u y c f g l m w b k p q x z. E *predominates*
so remarkably that an individual sentence of any length is rarely seen,
in which it is not the prevailing character. Here, then, we have, in
the very beginning, the groundwork for something more than a mere
guess.

Now into the onion. We know that all those ASCII characters are
statistically related in an endlessly complicated fashion. The first
layer of our textual onion models English as a sequence of characters generated by a random process. To make this clearer, the kind
of text generated by such a model looks like the following:

up&nblf&uijt&dmfbsfs&uif&ljoe&pg&ufyu&hfofsbufe&cz&tvdi&
b&npefm&mpplt&mjlf&uif&gpmmpxjoh.

What boring looking stuff! Yet this sequence has exactly the statistical structure of English, were it continued indefinitely, except that
we would find that *f* is the most frequently occurring letter, and that
u is the next most popular, etc. In fact, this sequence is merely the
preceding sentence shifted forward by one character, that is, *a* has
been translated into *b,* and so forth. (The space character has
become *&.*)

The viewpoint that we want to take at this layer of the onion
is exemplified by the gibberish sentence above. Take a look at it
again. There are no words, no obvious spaces or punctuation marks,
and there is no hint of meaning. Such concepts lie deeper in the
onion. The letters make no more sense than the strings of 1s and
0s that fly across the wires of our computers. Yet we are aware of
a deep statistical structure, and we are permitted to use it to our
advantage in the processing of textual data. While this may seem
to be a very superficial model of language, it is the most useful one
at present in the implementation of text-compression systems. This
is because the model is simple mathematically, at least in concept,
if not in detail.

There is an important and difficult philosophical question about
the suitability of this model of text as represented by a randomly
generated sequence of letters. It is neither as bad a model as you
might first believe, nor as good as you might ultimately wish. Later
we shall return to the faults of the model, but for the moment let us
demonstrate its surprising strengths. We can build up the statistical

description of English text by determining the frequencies of occurrence of individual letters, then pairs of letters, then triplets, etc. The lower orders of these statistics have often been tabulated and are well known. We can only marvel in this computer age at the patience of the workers employed by E. L. Thorndike in the 1920s and 1930s, who tabulated over 20 million words of text by hand to determine relative frequencies. Earlier, in 1898, F. W. Kaeding had counted the frequencies of letter occurrences in German text totaling 59,298,274 letters! Today the computer is quite willing to do such easy statistical analysis, and it was the work of only a few minutes to compare the frequencies of my own use of letters in Chapters 1 and 2 against the "standard" table shown on page 106.

It is incredible how strong the compulsion is to conform to the "standard" frequencies for character occurrence. Without being in the least conscious of my use of characters I have achieved almost perfect conformance over two chapters with a total word count of about 27,000. (All right, so I do not know enough words that use *j,* but just look at my use of *z!*) No wonder cryptographers are able to break substitution ciphers with relative ease. It makes all the more astounding the stories of J. R. Pierce in *Symbols, Signals, and Noise* (attributed to cryptanalyst W. F. Friedman) of authors who intentionally suppressed the use of a given letter. For example, Pierce writes that Gottlob Burman, who was an 18th-century German poet, wrote 130 poems without once using the letter *r.* Apparently he rejected the letter so strongly that he even omitted the letter from his daily conversation during the last 17 years of his life! (I wonder how he introduced himself?) Even more incredible is Ernest Vincent Wright's 1939 novel of 267 pages, *Gadsby,* in which no use is made of the letter *e.* Here is a brief excerpt from the introduction:

> It is a story about a small town. It is not a gossipy yarn; nor is it a dry, monotonous account, full of such customary "fill-ins" as "romantic moonlight casting murky shadows down a long, winding country road." Nor will it say anything about twinklings lulling distant folds; robins carolling at twilight, nor any "warm glow of lamplight" from a cabin window.

Literature seems to have forgotten Wright's novel, apparently for good reason, but it is a feat not likely to be repeated. It is reported that Wright resorted to tying down the *e* typebar of his typewriter

FREQUENCIES OF OCCURRENCE OF INDIVIDUAL
LETTERS IN ENGLISH TEXT

LETTER	STANDARD FREQUENCY	CHAPTER 1	CHAPTER 2
a	.0761	.0763	.0759
b	.0154	.0149	.0187
c	.0311	.0320	.0358
d	.0395	.0295	.0320
e	.1262	.1213	.1233
f	.0234	.0281	.0239
g	.0195	.0181	.0174
h	.0551	.0475	.0508
i	.0734	.0800	.0763
j	.0015	.0009	.0007
k	.0065	.0060	.0049
l	.0411	.0400	.0393
m	.0254	.0281	.0269
n	.0711	.0761	.0708
o	.0765	.0844	.0799
p	.0203	.0232	.0220
q	.0010	.0010	.0028
r	.0615	.0614	.0613
s	.0650	.0639	.0660
t	.0933	.0918	.0946
u	.0272	.0270	.0279
v	.0099	.0102	.0086
w	.0189	.0192	.0194
x	.0019	.0017	.0021
y	.0172	.0164	.0178
z	.0009	.0009	.0009

in order to fight the irresistible urge to type the army of *e*'s lying just beyond his fingertips!

Similar tables exist for the digram frequencies of English, that is, for the probabilities of occurrence of the $26 \times 26 = 676$ successive letter pairs. The pair *th* is the most popular, occurring normally with a frequency of about .037, which is exactly its frequency in the first two chapters of this book. Not surprisingly *he* is next with a frequency of about .030. Both digrams benefit enormously from the word "the," which is by far the most commonly occurring word. Besides their use in cryptography, the letter and digram frequencies have sometimes been used to study literary styles and to judge disputed authorship, although these letter statistics would seem to be derivative, or second order, effects indicative only of the use of vocabulary and structure. For example, in the disputed *Federalist Papers,* attributed variously to James Madison or to Alexander Hamilton, the frequencies of the digrams *an* and *at* are .0126 and .0101. In this book these same digrams have frequencies .0166 and .0198. From such data we might infer that I was not the author of the *Federalist Papers.* However, the matter is not certain!

From such tables we can also derive the conditional probabilities, such as if the current letter is *r*, what is the probability that the next letter will be *e*? Since the study of the statistics of English (or any other language) is endlessly fascinating, and of obvious use in cryptography, much other intriguing data is readily available. For instance, the probabilities of occurrence of each letter as a function of position in a word have been tabulated. (The letter *t* is the most popular first letter.) Also the versatilities of the letters—meaning the number of different words in which the letter appears—are well known. The higher order statistics—trigram frequencies, etc.—are publicized less frequently, since they begin to require enormous data collection for their derivation or use. There are, for example, about a half million different combinations of four letters, some of which occur quite rarely if at all. Obviously, for any statistical certainty many millions of characters would have to be analyzed to derive these quadgrams.

What kind of a picture of language are we building from this statistical description of letters? There is an easy way to see for ourselves, since we are well trained in viewing English text. We can generate random sequences according to the statistical model at various levels, and assess from the "pseudo-English" produced just how well it resembles "real" English. We begin with generating random character sequences from the 26 alphabetic characters, together with the "space" character, with uniform probability across all 27 possibilities. This is what we call the zero order approximation.

Zero Order English Approximation

tsn   rdjpdzfigypmawaknodjwxltaqmucoxweoefi   jyfpxsdawbircocrlut sfptroy efbubxiebbb gbiocwfbsgi fafqqalf

---

There is not much danger of our mistaking this unpronounceable garbage for English or any other language. The approximation can be improved by taking account of the actual probabilities of occurrence for the individual letters (including the possibilities of capitalization and punctuation). This is the first order approximation. Each character occurs with the correct frequency, but is completely independent of its neighbors.

First Order English Approximation

yos tmbota i n sshntletnt anootnrnoPtoeeIc kwe hebq ith t. oeitai s oclcinryctaet. risonalven atia worgumfi. wleos enn

---

This looks a little more like something. Maybe it is in code or some unknown language. So up another level—this time we take account of the digram frequencies. For example, if the previous letter was a *t*, we use the conditional probability of, given a *t*, what are the probabilities for the succeeding letter? Each letter thus depends on its neighbor, but only one letter deep.

Second Order English Approximation

e obutant tnwe o Mar thionas pr is withious wid watout iofo inityrs ivasto tie w tapertibisthe te tsphan wiestime a

---

At this level of statistical description, we see a few short words, such as *is* in this instance. Also the pseudowords tend to be pronounceable. We would not for a moment think this to be English, but we might be fooled for a short time if someone told us that it was some exotic or ancient language. At the next level we use the trigram frequencies, so that each letter depends on the previous two letters.

Third Order English Approximation

Thea se thook, somly. Let ther of mory. A Romensmand codun shate sed be lat throphignis de thand sion le wentem macturt

At this point we begin to think perhaps this is garbled English. Things are taking shape now, but we can only go up one more level without stretching my statistical honesty. I am using the actual frequencies of letter patterns from the first two chapters of this book. Even at this fourth level, where each letter depends on the previous three letters, there is scant data in the 200,000 or so characters I have to work with.

Fourth Order English Approximation

The generated job providual better trand the displayed code, abovery upondults well the coderst in thestical it do hock bothe merg. (Instates cons eration. Never any of puble and to theory. Evential callegand to elast benerated in with pies as is with the

This is getting scary. By now there are many real English words, and even the pseudowords look like they ought to be real words. At a quick glance, it looks like ordinary English. Our mental processing has been conditioned through repeated training to accept such input. Psychologists have studied this familiarity phenomenon through experiments in which pseudowords are presented tachistoscopically (flashed briefly on a screen), and subsequent recall of the individual letters is tested as a function of exposure time. In these experiments the subjects were able to recall the positions of letters in fourth order pseudowords in about one-tenth the time required for zero order pseudowords. The zero order pseudowords remind me of eye charts, and just think how difficult they are to memorize.

That recall of pseudowords becomes progressively easier as the order of the approximation increases can be explained through familiarity and conditioning. Our minds are physically and logically evolved and trained to deal with the structure of our language. A very important determiner in what we see in reading a word or pseudoword is what we *expect* to see. Other experiments have shown increased recognition when the letters in the pseudowords agree with the positional frequencies of English words. Thus, for example, the word "more" has very high positional regularity, since *m* is quite often a first letter, *o* a second, etc., while the anagram "emor" using exactly the same letters in a different arrangement has relatively low positional regularity and would be considerably harder to recall. Our ability to read text rapidly may depend critically on the little guessing games within our mind, as we successively form and confirm or revise hypotheses about the oncoming letters and words.

The results of these recall experiments can also be explained in terms of the relative information-processing loads of the successive pseudowords. Just how much information do the zero order pseudowords carry compared to the fourth order pseudowords? Clearly there is much more redundancy in the fourth order pseudowords. Each letter in these words carries less information—because it is more constrained—than does each letter in the zero order words. In the previous chapter we discussed a mathematical measure for information, called entropy. Entropy represents the intrinsic uncertainty, which we define as the information content. When the entropy is evaluated for the various approximations to English, it is found that the recall time *per bit* is constant through the experiments.

The entropy of text is the fewest number of bits required on the average to represent each letter, using the best possible coding scheme. An overarching question in this chapter is what is the entropy of English text? If we knew the entropy of text, we would know exactly the degree to which ASCII text could be compressed for storage and transmission. While compression is a mechanical application, the entropy question is an important philosophical one, lending insight on the matter of human cognitive processing. For the statistical model of text that we have thus far assumed, the calculation of entropy is straightforward. For example, the entropy of the second order English approximation is given by:

$$H_2 = \sum_{i,j} p(i,j) \log p_i(j)$$

The term $\log p_i(j)$ is the entropy associated with the occurrence of the jth letter, given that the ith letter preceded it, while the term $p(i,j)$ is the probability of the digram consisting of the ith letter followed by the jth letter. Each digram is thereby weighted by its probability of occurrence to form an expression for the average uncertainty. Expressions for the entropies of other orders of approximation to English are entirely similar. When these entropies are evaluated, we arrive at table below.

ENTROPIES OF APPROXIMATIONS TO ENGLISH TEXT—BITS PER LETTER

ORDER	Zero	First	Second	Third	Fourth
ENTROPY	4.76	4.03	3.32	3.1	2.8

Thus it would appear that English text could be represented by less than 3 bits per character, as compared with the traditional ASCII byte of 8 bits. Obviously as we take more statistics into account, the entropy must become lower yet, since this implies less uncertainty in the successive characters. However, to get at a better approximation to the entropy of text we will need to delve deeper into the textual onion a little later in this chapter.

I am reminded of the old story about monkeys being set to typing randomly, and eventually typing all the works of Shakespeare. I imagine numbering the monkeys, with monkey 0 free to bang away randomly at his typewriter. Monkey 1 is trained to follow the character probabilities, monkey 2 the digram probabilities, and so on. We have seen the output of monkey 4, and it looks like he is making real progress toward Shakespeare. He certainly will get there a long time before monkey 0. In fact, the average time for monkey 0 to type a given 18-character sequence like "to be or not to be" would be about 1.5×10^{17} years (assuming monkeys type at 60 words per minute like humans). Monkey 4, on the other hand, by following the fourth order statistics of English is much more likely to type this sequence. He would get it on the average in something less than 8 million years. (These average times are simply calculated as 2 raised to the power of the entropy per character times the number of characters.) Monkey 4 is on the average 20 billion times faster at reaching this sequence than monkey 0!

Suppose now that we walk down the row of monkeys, past monkey 4, until we are out at monkey 100 or so—where the monkeys are as good at producing pseudo-English as they can get, based on the statistics of characters. Monkey 100 must be very good. I am sure he would type excellent, grammatical sentences. (However, the sentences would not *say* anything.) Based on experiments that we shall describe at a deeper level in the textual onion, we believe that the entropy of English is about 1 bit per character. Thus the mean number of attempts to arrive at a "typical" 18-character sequence for monkey 100 would be $2^{18} = 262,144$, which is less than two weeks' typing. The difference between him and monkey 0 is astronomical. What monkey 100 does in a week, monkey 0 could not have accomplished in the entire lifetime of the universe!

Imagine making 18 vertical columns of the 27 characters consisting of the alphabetics plus the space character. Each possible 18-character sequence is a path, or a thread, drawn through these columns. For monkey 0, who exercises no statistical discretion, all paths are equal, and there are 27^{18} such paths—as we have seen, a virtual infinity of paths. For monkey 100 where the entropy is 1 bit per character there are only 2^{18} typical paths that he is statistically constrained to travel. He cannot, for example, pass through two consecutive q's. He cannot even misspell a word and stay on a "typical" path. As we discussed in the previous chapter, the "typical" sequences absolutely predominate as the length becomes long.

It must be very frustrating to be monkey 100. He has so very little choice. For each letter he must take account of the previous 99 letters. But this is only a matter of training; after all, we do this same thing ourselves without conscious thought, and we do not feel any particular limitation. If we had a monkey 100, I am sure he would astound us with his skill. We would look at his perfect English and tell each other reassuringly that he is only a monkey and he has not the foggiest idea what he is typing. We would argue that our English writing is not a random process, and cannot be modeled as such. We would say that we form English from words, from grammatical structure, and from the semantic knowledge of a whole world of which the monkey has no experience—not from training in these ridiculous statistical distributions.

Yet somehow words, grammar, and semantics are subsumed in the statistical model. Monkey 100 would never say, "The triangular ball are walked everything five." Probably this sentence has never appeared previously in the English language. I hazard this guess from semantic knowledge, but all the monkey knows is that the statistics do not allow it. We would say that the verb nonagreement violates syntax rules. The monkey does not know about syntax, but he knows what his probability tables say. Perhaps he is like a human infant, grappling with the sounds he hears. But then again, he is only a monkey.

Perhaps a philosophical argument can be made that monkey 100 *knows* English. Conceivably, if we had monkey 100 behind a screen and a human writer behind another screen, we could not tell which was which by examination of their outputs. Note the similarity to the famous Turing test for a "thinking" computer, in which a hidden computer and human are interactively interrogated, although the masquerade of monkey 100 seems much easier since we cannot probe his intelligence with questions.

I think monkey 100 is like a young professional pianist I once heard in recital. Having enjoyed the concert, I congratulated the pianist on his performance of Schubert. He seemed greatly embarrassed, and confessed that he had totally forgotten the music in the midst of his playing. I said that did not seem possible, since the performance seemed flawless. "I just made it *sound* like Schubert," he explained meekly. Perhaps monkey 100 does the same with English.

Alas, monkey 100 is only a philosophical straw man—a chimera of language. The fact is *monkey 100 cannot exist!* The entire written output of the human race does not convey statistics out to 100 characters. Our largest library, the Library of Congress, at about 1.8×10^{13} bytes contains only enough data to characterize the statistics out to about ninth order—barely more than one word! The language itself is evolving faster than it could be characterized at a higher level. We can console ourselves that so little of what *could* be said, *has* been said. Our language, as constrained as it is, allows for much greater freedom of expression—infinitely greater freedom—than we will ever be able to use.

TEXT COMPRESSION

Straightforward ASCII text representation requires one 8-bit byte per character. In theory, text can be compressed down to the level of the entropy, but we have seen that the calculated entropy depends upon the mathematical model of how far backward we stretch the statistical dependence upon previous symbols. We will discuss two practical text compression techniques. The first technique, Huffman coding, was mentioned in the previous chapter. It was invented by David Huffman around 1960 at MIT. Practically speaking, it can only be applied at the level of monkey 1, where the actual probabilities of character occurrence are used but no advantage is taken of the dependence between characters. The other compression technique to be discussed, Lempel–Ziv compression, is a more recent invention that is capable of extending its statistical domain back indefinitely, thus achieving performance approaching the limit of what is possible, given the model of text as a stream of meaningless but related characters.

HUFFMAN CODING

• • • • • • • • • • • • • • • • •

The idea behind Huffman coding is simple enough; each character must be assigned a sequence of bits roughly equal in length to the amount of information it conveys. This was the same idea followed by Samuel F.B. Morse a century earlier in constructing his telegraph code. The letter e, being the most common, conveys relatively little information. Specifically, since its probability of occurrence is .126, the associated information is $-\log .126 = 3$ bits. On the other hand, z is uncommon, and conveys $-\log .0009 = 10$ bits of information. (In Morse code, for example, e is a single dot, whereas z is four dots.)

If we could assign e a 3-bit sequence—for example, 001—and z a 10-bit sequence, and every other character a sequence of length equal to the logarithm of its probability of occurrence, then the *average* length over a long passage of English text would be these logarithmically assigned lengths weighted by their probabilities of occurrence:

$$average\ length = \sum_i p_i \log (p_i),$$

in which p_i is the probability of the ith character. But this expression is simply the entropy of text at level 1. In other words such an assignment would provide the maximum compression possible of any scheme operating at the level of monkey 1.

114

The Huffman coding procedure is a simple way of achieving an ideal representation where each character is assigned a bit sequence approximately equal in length to the value of its information. Recognize that each bit in a binary sequence can be thought of as a choice between two alternatives, and picture a code sequence as a binary tree of successive branchings as shown in Figure 5. The less popular letters associated with longer sequences, like z and q, must be far out on the tree. They are only reached by many branchings, where the code sequences end on small twigs of the tree. The popular letters like e and t, which must use short sequences, must be near the trunk of the tree where they can be reached quickly.

An algorithm for constructing the Huffman code is to start from the smallest twigs and work towards the trunk, at each point combining the two lowest probability branches into a correspondingly larger branch. For the English alphabet the two lowest probability characters are z and q, with probabilities .0009 and .001. We combine these into a new branch with probability .0019. We label (arbitrarily, but consistently) the lower branch with a 1. We continue to repeat the step of combining the two lowest probability branches into a larger one. At some point along the way the branch we just created by combining z and q will be combined with another branch. Still later the popular characters like e and t will join the tree, and shortly thereafter all the branches will be joined and the base trunk reached.

Since we can only create lengths of integer values, the Huffman procedure does not result in compression exactly equal to the entropy, but it comes as close as possible in the circumstances. The average length of a Huffman code is only larger than the entropy by a little more than the probability of the most probable symbol. Not only is the Huffman code very effective, but the construction procedure guarantees the so-called "prefix" condition, such that an arbitrary sequence of Huffman-coded characters can be separated uniquely into its constituent characters. This is because the tree construction ensures that no character has a coded representation that is the prefix (beginning bits) of another code word. In the absence of errors, we can see exactly where one character string stops and another starts. If the code were not so carefully constructed, we might be able to break up a given string of bits into several alternative representations.

The practice of Huffman coding is only slightly more complicated than we have described. There are more characters in the

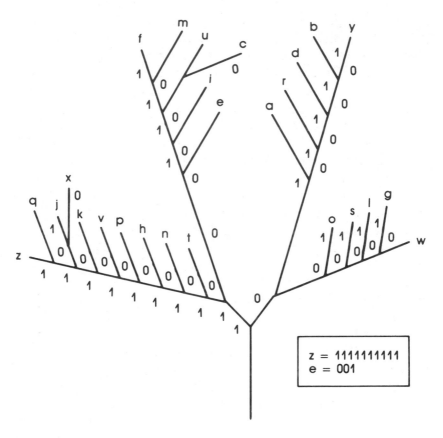

FIGURE 5
The Huffman tree for English characters

ASCII code than just the lowercase alphabetics. There are, for example, uppercase letters, numerals, punctuation, and control characters, such as carriage return. Depending on the material being coded, the statistics of the ASCII characters would vary greatly. It would be dangerous to assume that the frequencies of the characters were those of standard English text. The text file might be from a data base, for example, where many or all of the fields were numeric. For this reason data compression programs that use Huffman coding, like the UNIX⊤ "compact" command, employ an *adaptive* procedure that creates the Huffman code tree from the actual statistics of the text file being compressed.

Adaptive Huffman coding begins with a standard ASCII representation, one byte per character. The compressor program and the decompressor program agree that the first, say, 100 characters will be ASCII. Throughout the operation of the program a running count is kept for the occurrences of each letter. Periodically the compressor and decompressor programs reconstitute the Huffman code according to the current counts of each character processed. After many characters have been processed, the counts reflect the actual probabilities of the different characters in the file being compressed, and the compression of the code approaches the entropy of the material as seen by monkey 1.

As an example, we take the text file from Chapter 2 of this book and form the adaptive Huffman code as the data unfolds. The table below shows the progression of the code at different stages of the file. Notice that the final savings through compression obtained by the adaptive Huffman code is 42.81 percent, which means that each character is on average conveyed by 4.575 bits $[(1-.4281)\times8]$. Compare this with the entropy for English text at level 1, which is 4.03 bits per character. The latter figure was obtained by consider-

ADAPTIVE HUFFMAN CODE—TEXT OF CHAPTER TWO

BYTES	E	M	Z	PERCENT SAVINGS
0	01100101	01101101	01111010	0%
50	111010	001101	001001	9.80%
100	110101	0011000	0010000	15.38%
200	001101	0011100	1111110	20.95%
400	11010	1000100	01010110	23.19%
1,000	0001	001010	010101001	30.80%
4,000	0100	10111	1110001100	38.82%
10,000	0000	11011	1000101101	41.41%
20,000	111	010000	0010101010	42.24%
40,000	111	000000	01100001000	42.88%
100,000	111	001000	11110010000	42.81%

ing only the lowercase alphabetics in addition to the space character. All the rest of the ASCII characters, together with any inefficiency of the code, account for the small difference in these figures.

There is no conceptual difficulty in extending the Huffman code to the levels of monkey 2 and above, but the computational burden becomes enormous very quickly. If we were to build a Huffman tree at level 2 where we account for the dependence on the previous character, then there would be $256 \times 256 = 65,536$ combinations to encode, from the popular *th* through the nonoccurring *qq*. Even at level 1 quite a bit of computation is required, so that compression of the 125,000 characters of text in Chapter 2 on a 1 MIPS minicomputer (1 million instructions per second, a typical minicomputer speed in the early 1980s) takes about 30 seconds.

L E M P E L – Z I V   C O D I N G

For a quarter of a century Huffman coding remained relatively unchallenged as the ultimate form of text compression. It was understandable, elegant, and probably optimum. System designers often conveniently forgot that their implementations of the Huffman code worked only at level 1, where no advantage was taken of the intercharacter redundancies of the language. Now only in the most recent years has a new compression algorithm, the Lempel–Ziv technique, taken over nearly completely from Huffman. The Lempel–Ziv algorithm is considerably simpler to implement than Huffman, and it works effectively at higher levels to do the best possible compression of text within certain limitations. It is implemented in such programs as the UNIX⊤ "compress" command and the popular MSDOS "ARC" utility for squeezing files.

Jacob Ziv is a trim, mild-mannered Israeli information theorist. His base is the Technion Israel Institute of Technology, perched high on the hills overlooking the busy port of Haifa in Israel, but like most of his fellow "card-carrying" information theorists, Jacob is a citizen of the technological world. Though Jacob has regularly spent summers and sabbaticals at Bell Labs, I have seen him mostly at the scientific watering holes of the world. The society of information theorists is a small one, probably on the order of several hundred true members, who write mostly for each other in elegant papers couched in abstract concepts.

The truth of such things is hard to get at, but I suspect that even fellow information theorists have a hard time reading each other's papers unless the subject is directly related to the reader's own research. That does not necessarily mean that their work is unappreciated or unused. Papers are usually written for peers and for posterity, rather than for anything approaching mass communication. The dissemination of knowledge in scientific disciplines is imperfectly understood, but it appears to require only a very small number of diligent readers to start the human networking process that eventually socializes the information in an important paper. Many other papers never get socialized at all and pass unnoticed into the archival purgatory.

In 1976, Jacob Ziv, writing with his Technion colleague Abraham Lempel, published a paper entitled "On the Complexity of Finite Sequences" in the *IEEE Transactions on Information Theory*. A flavor of this paper can be gleaned from the following excerpt from the initial mathematical definition of the problem.

II. REPRODUCTION AND PRODUCTION OF SEQUENCES

Let $A*$ denote the set of all finite length sequences over a finite alphabet A. Let $l(S)$ denote the length of $S \in A *$ and let

$$A^n = \{S \in A* \mid l(S) = n\}, \qquad n \geq 0.$$

The null-sequence Λ, i.e., the "sequence" of length zero, is assumed to be an element of $A*$.

A sequence $S \in A^n$ is fully specified by writing $S = s_1 s_2 \ldots s_n$; when S is formed from a single element $a \in A$, we write $S = a^n$. To indicate a substring of S that starts at position i and ends at position j, we write $S(i,j)$. That is, when $i \leq j$, $S(i,j) = s_i s_{i+1} \ldots s_j$ and $S(i,j) = \Lambda$, for $i > j$.

The concatenation of $Q \in A^m$ and $R \in A^n$ forms a new sequence $S = QR = q_1 q_2 \ldots q_m r_1 r_2 \ldots r_n \in A^{m+n}$, where $Q = S(1,m)$ and $R = S(m + 1, m + n)$. We use the power notation $S^2 = SS$ to indicate concatenation of S with itself; more generally, $S^0 = \Lambda$ and $S^i = S^{i-1} S$, $i \geq 1$.

Q is called a *prefix* of $S \in A*$, and S is called an *extension* of Q if there exists an integer i such that $Q = S(1, i)$; a prefix Q and its extension S are said to be *proper* if $l(Q) <$

$l(S)$. When the length of a sequence S is not specified explicitly, it is convenient to identify prefixes of S by means of a special operator π according to $S\pi^i = S(1, l(S) - i)$, $i = 0,1, \ldots$ In particular, $S\pi^0 = S$ and $S\pi^i = \Lambda$, for $i \geq l(S)$.

The *vocabulary* of a sequence S, denoted by $v(S)$, is the subset of A^* formed by all the substrings, or *words*, $S(i,j)$ of S. For example,

$$v(0010) = \{\Lambda,0,1,00,01,10,001,010,0010\}.$$

I do not mean for you to read this. I include it so that you can join me in marveling that such abstraction can eventually lead to practical applications. For this to happen it takes understanding, translation, socialization, and finally popularization. Not too many papers of this sort are able to make this whole path. The language is the precise one of mathematics. While the level of intrinsic difficulty is not especially high, a form of text compression is in effect because of the conciseness of the mathematical notation. It is slow reading and relatively inaccessible to the novice, but it will be studied long after this simplified book is out of print.

The problem that Lempel and Ziv studied is an interesting and philosophical one that has a direct bearing on text compression—not as seen by any of our trained monkeys, but as seen by a very intelligent monkey who has no knowledge of the language other than that implied by the unfolding sequence of characters offered for compression. This is quite opposite from our previous discussion wherein the monkeys were completely unintelligent but had perfect knowledge of the statistical description of language up to a certain level.

How much can be inferred from a finite sequence of characters about succeeding, yet-to-be-seen characters given no other information about the sequence or its origin? Intuitively, if the sequence is "completely random," then we would say that nothing can be inferred, and to do recoverable compression of the sequence—to squeeze bits out of it—would be impossible. Lempel and Ziv described such sequences as "complex." If there is, however, any crack in the edifice of complete randomness, then the sequence is in a sense less complex, and an appropriate machine could use the sequence itself as an aid in "producing" new portions as they arrive.

Since this means less information would be required to specify these new portions, there is an obvious relationship to text compression.

The essence of the Lempel–Ziv definition of complexity is the assessment of the degree to which new portions of the sequence look like portions that have been seen earlier. In other words, to what degree is the past a prologue to the future? To gauge the rate of accumulation of "newness" they suggested that the sequence be parsed (segmented) into chunks that are the smallest subsequences not previously encountered. For example, suppose the input is the binary sequence:

$$001100100011010100011. \ldots$$

The first symbol, a 0, also becomes the first chunk. We have not seen anything before this, so it is new in itself.

$$0 \mid 01100100011010100011 \ldots$$

The second symbol is a 0 also. We just saw one of these, so it is nothing new, and we continue on to the third symbol, a 1. The sequence 01 is new, so it is our next chunk.

$$0 \mid 01 \mid 100100011010100011. \ldots$$

Continuing in this manner we parse the entire sequence as follows:

$$0 \mid 01 \mid 1 \mid 00 \mid 10 \mid 001 \mid 101 \mid 010 \mid 0011 \mid \ldots.$$

Notice that each consecutive chunk is composed of a subsequence we have seen before—one of the previous chunks—plus a new symbol that makes the chunk different from all previous chunks.

We can of course do the same thing with alphabetic characters. The sequence "a cat had a hat" parses in this way:

$$a \mid \_ \mid c \mid at \mid \_h \mid ad \mid \_a \mid \_ha \mid t \, .$$

Now clearly the chunks get longer and longer as we go along and as we build up an ever more extensive vocabulary of sequences that have been seen before. The key to a measure of complexity is the rate of buildup of the vocabulary. In a truly random sequence the succeeding characters are as "new" as possible. They just do not have any relation to anything that has gone before. For such a sequence the number of chunks would be expected to be larger for a given length than for any sequence in which succeeding characters were in some way, statistically or mechanically, related to previous characters. For a completely random binary sequence of length n, the number of chunks grows as $\frac{n}{\log(n)}$ for sufficiently long lengths. Lempel and Ziv suggest that any finite sequence whose decomposition grows at this maximal rate be considered "complex." Such a sequence might or might not actually be composed from random bits, but in any event it would be seen to emulate random behavior in this important respect.

If the symbols in the input sequence are interrelated in some fashion, then the complexity as measured by vocabulary buildup is lessened. More often than in the truly random case the succeeding symbols form sequences that resemble something that has gone before. In the particular case in which the symbols are from a random process of binary symbols, but in which the symbols are not independent, then the buildup of vocabulary for long, typical sequences approaches $\frac{Hn}{\log(n)}$, where—surprise!—H is the entropy of the random process, which is of course in the range $0 \leq H \leq 1$.

Do not be misled by this association of the Lempel–Ziv complexity to the concept of entropy in a random process. Entropy is a concept steeped in the behavior of infinite sequences of well-behaved random variables. It does not make sense to speak of the entropy of a short sequence of characters of unknown origin. Lempel and Ziv speak instead to the *mechanical composition* of the sequence. What we see is what we have, and all we have. We can always evaluate the Lempel–Ziv complexity by parsing the sequence into the innovative chunks, although such a calculation lacks the intuitive and insightful simplification that we have in dealing with the concept of entropy. By relating this complexity to the notion of entropy in the special case where the sequence is a very long one actually constituted from random variables, we are able to provide grounding and motivation for Lempel–Ziv complexity, and to bridge this notion into the classical one of entropy.

Compression of finite sequences was the original aim of the study of sequence complexity. For some years Ziv had been seeking a universal coding approach that was not dependent upon a known statistical structure for the source. Armed with the notion of sequence complexity, Lempel and Ziv now asked the question: What is the best compression that can be achieved by a finite-state machine operating upon a given source sequence? By a finite-state machine we might picture the electronic analog of a large mechanical box. As each character comes into the box, gears crunch and wheels turn. The box is then quiet, waiting for the next character, with many or all of its levers and gears now in different positions, that is, the machine is in a different state. Now the next character enters and is digested as everything moves again. Every now and then the machine regurgitates a block of output digits, which is usually shorter than the accumulated input stream since the machine is supposed to be a compressor. Obviously, a ground rule is that we must be able to construct another box, the decompressor, that is capable of taking the regurgitated, compressed output, and with suitable clunking of gears exactly reproduce the original input sequence. Neither box may be infinitely big, nor may the gears have an infinite number of possible positions.

We might imagine holding a contest to design the compressor and decompressor boxes. Contestants would come from afar, clutching their entries, and we would hold a sort of "crunch-off" upon a sequence previously secreted in a sealed envelope to see which machine could achieve the most compression. We could imagine the intuition and ingenuity that would go into the various designs. Yet it is one of the startling revelations of information theory that very often it is able to tell us exactly how well the very best such box could ever do, regardless of how clever the design. And every now and then the proof of such a bound is constructive; it tells how to design the best box. Such was the case in Lempel and Ziv's analysis of the compression of sequences by a finite-state machine.

The answer to how well the machine can do is appealingly intuitive. The compression ratio can be as good as the ratio of the number of innovative chunks in the sequence to the number of chunks in a truly random sequence, which we know to be $\frac{n}{\log(n)}$. There are a number of ways to implement a compressor that achieves this level of performance; all are based on using subsequences from the past history of the unfolding sequence as a kind of shorthand to describe what follows. One of the ways Lempel and Ziv suggested was to collect new characters as they arrive and look for previous matching sequences until the new sequence no longer matches anything we can find in the past. Then the longest matching sequence is encoded simply as the position and length of its previous occurrence. For example, suppose that we begin the encoding of the present chapter of this book, having just processed the previous chapter. The first sentence begins "In the information age . . ." This first phrase contains 22 ASCII characters, each of which would ordinarily be encoded with an 8-bit byte, for a total of 176 bits.

In the previous chapter the longest sequence that matches the beginning of our test phrase occurs near the beginning of that chapter, where we find the phrase "In the introduction to Shannon's . . ." Thus the first 9 characters (including spaces, of course), "In the in," of our phrase can be encoded as the position and length of this previous sequence. The last 13 characters, "formation age," are matched later in the chapter in a sentence that ends ". . . systems designers of the information age." There are about 125,000 characters in Chapter 2, so we require a 17-bit pointer ($2^{17} = 131,072$) to specify any particular starting position. Suppose further that we allocate 4 bits to specify the length of the sequence being matched. Then our test phrase can be encoded as two 17-bit pointers and two 4-bit lengths for a total of 42 bits. Compared with the 176 bits originally required in the ASCII representation this gives a compression ratio of about 4. The encoding of the test phrase required about 2 bits per character. Notice that this is better than the entropy of English at level four.

Popular computer programs use a slightly different version of the Lempel–Ziv philosophy that provides similar performance but is simplified to run efficiently. This version of the Lempel–Ziv algorithm maintains an ever-growing dictionary of all the different chunks or phrases that have appeared in the past. As new characters are offered for compression the phrase (string) that they are forming is continually checked for its presence in the dictionary. As long as the new phrase appears in the dictionary, the compressor takes in additional characters without any action to encode the evolving phrase. When the addition of a subsequent new character causes the phrase not to appear in the dictionary, the compressor encodes the most recent phrase as a pointer to its position in the dictionary, adds the current phrase as a new entry to the dictionary, and begins building the next new phrase with the current character.

As an example suppose that the previous paragraph, which begins "Popular computer . . ." is being encoded. The first character, "P," appears in the dictionary, so we add the next character to form "Po." Suppose that we look this up, and it also appears in the dictionary; consequently we add the succeeding character, which now makes the phrase "Pop," and so forth. Suppose that the phrases continue to be listed in the dictionary up through "Popular__c," but the next phrase "Popular__co" is not listed. Now we do the following:

1. "Popular__c" is encoded as a pointer to its dictionary entry. Common practice is to begin with a 12-bit code for this pointer, which allows for a dictionary of 4,096 entries.
2. The new phrase "Popular__co" is added to the dictionary. (If the dictionary exceeds 4,096 entries, we will have to increase the number of bits in the dictionary pointer.)
3. We start growing the next phrase to be encoded with the current character "o." The subsequent phrases to be checked for appearance in the dictionary will be "om," "omp," "ompu," etc.

Without belaboring the point let us say that it is possible to build a decompressor that exactly expands the encoded sequence of dictionary pointers back into the original character stream. Since the decompressor cannot see the dictionary that the compressor used, it must build its own as it goes along, which will be at any given point in the sequence an exact replica of the one the compressor had been using. Notice, however, that the effect of an error in the encoded data can be somewhat catastrophic. Not only will the dictionary pointer denote the wrong phrase, but the decompressor dictionary will subsequently have an incorrect entry, and will begin to diverge from the dictionary that had been used by the compressor. This is why we must be sure that there are no errors in storage or transmission of the compressed data. Fortunately the practice of error control is so effective that errors are not of concern in data compression.

One of the beautiful aspects of Lempel–Ziv coding is that it is not dependent upon prior knowledge of source statistics. The dictionary is built from the character stream itself, and eventually reflects its characteristics. If the language is Spanish, it learns Spanish. If the data are numeric, the dictionary becomes a table of numbers. (Though this sounds like an ineffective case, many numbers tend to be repeated, or like strings of 0s, are special and common.)

To give some feel for the Lempel–Ziv process, the table below is a sample of the dictionary entries listed alphabetically under *i* after 4,000 characters have been encoded using the text file of Chapter 2 of this book.

Observe that for every entry each of its substrings created by removal of the last character also appears, since this was the way the dictionary was constructed. In building a word like "information" in the dictionary we might first get help from the appearance of the

PORTION OF LEMPEL–ZIV DICTIONARY—CHAPTER 2, 4,000 BYTES

i__	if	in__t	ing__h
i__k	ig	in__th	ing__i
i__w	iga	ina	ing__o
ia	il	ina__	ing__or
ia__	ill	inc	ing__t
ia__m	ilo	ind	ini
ial	im	indu	inin
iat	ima	inf	ina
ic	imar	info	int
ica	imat	infor	int__
ical	iml	inform	int__e
ical__	imp	informa	inv
icat	impo	informat	inve
icati	in	informati	io
icatio	in__	informatio	io__
ich	in__a	information	iod
ich__	in__c	ing	ion
icp	in__d	ing__	ion__
icr	in__e	ing__	ion__o
id	in__h	ing__a	ion__of
ie	in__s	ing__ab	ion__t

subword "in," which is popular in itself. Later as the entries proceeded past "informa" probably only the word "information" itself would have to be incurred again and again to build the complete entry. The process reminds me of the spelling game "Ghost," where each successive contestant adds a letter while attempting not to complete a word. In specialized material like this book the dictionary would be adapted to the material, and words like "information" and its derivatives would appear early in the compressor dictionary.

Because each dictionary entry is composed of a previous entry plus one new letter, the dictionary can be structured as a single byte representing the new letter plus a constant-length pointer to a previous entry. Thus all the dictionary entries are of the same length, which facilitates the mechanization of the data base. The Lempel–Ziv algorithm is also amenable to a number of other computation-saving tricks of the computer science trade, such as hashing, that make it extremely efficient, requiring only a small number of computer cycles per character compressed. The Lempel–Ziv compression of the text file of Chapter 2 using the UNIX(T) "compress" command was completed in only 16 percent of the time required by the adaptive Huffman procedure.

The following table shows the effectiveness of this version of the Lempel–Ziv algorithm in compressing the text file from Chapter 2 of this book.

LEMPEL–ZIV COMPRESSION— CHAPTER 2

BYTES	SAVINGS
100	1.70%
200	13.08%
400	15.23%
1,000	23.17%
4,000	40.32%
10,000	46.78%
20,000	49.07%
40,000	52.87%
100,000	55.77%

As the compression proceeds further into the material, the dictionary phrases get longer and more atuned to the material; hence the compression becomes more effective. At the same time, however, the dictionary gets larger and there are increases in the length of the encoded dictionary pointers. If the material is completely stable, in the sense that the vocabulary, usage, and phraseology are constant, then the compression ratio should improve asymptotically towards some final value. However, typically text is not stable over long intervals. The vocabulary will shift with a new subject, and the old dictionary becomes less useful. In fact, it becomes a burden as its size dictates the length of the encoding pointers. Practical implementations of the algorithm periodically check the compression ratio being attained. As long as it is increasing, the process continues. When it begins to decrease, perhaps signaling a shift in vocabulary, the dictionary is completely discarded and a new one is begun from scratch.

The final compression ratio attained on the text of Chapter 2, 55.77 percent, is typical of the Lempel–Ziv algorithm. Such a ratio would be indicative of an entropy of 3.54 bits per character, which is about equivalent to the entropy of text at level 2. This is indeed a level better than Huffman coding is able to achieve, but it is curious that it is no better than this. (The beauty of the algorithm makes us greedy.) We shall return to this question presently. Other experimenters, using samples of text files comprising several megabytes as found on their computer systems, have published Lempel–Ziv compression factors in the range of 40 to 60 percent.

IN QUEST OF ENTROPY ON A DEEPER LEVEL

In this book we alternate between the practical and the philosophical. In treating text files as collections of statistically related characters we were very much in the practical realm. The Lempel–Ziv algorithm, after compression and decompression, restores the original file exactly as it was before—every comma, numeral, and control character returned to its intended place. Such handling, and the thought which goes with it, is safe, but also mechanical and superficial. As clever and effective as the algorithm is, we cannot help but feel that so much more lies at the deeper levels of text—in the words, syntax, semantics, and in the ultimate meaning. The information itself, unless the format is a predigested table, lies at this deeper level.

We have a natural urge to try to isolate the essence of the information in the text. Some of the current emphasis in artificial intelligence and computational linguistics is towards the development of concepts and tools that can extract meaning from text. We will discuss this in the next chapter when we talk about the computer-human interface in the generation and consumption of text files. For the remainder of this chapter I would like to follow the philosophical thread of the ultimate entropy, or statistical uncertainty, of English text. In leaving the character level, we leave behind the world of practical data compression. There are just too many significant, nonalphabetic characters and too many departures from standard, grammatical English in most computer text files to be able to depend upon the deeper structure for lossless (perfectly reconstructible) compression. But the beauties, mysteries, and humanity of text far transcend the statistical banalities we have thus far considered.

The question of the ultimate entropy of text is more than just a bound to the best possible text compression. In a very real sense the entropy represents a quantitative measure of the essence of a given text. How much is new? What information is added to our preexisting repertoire? Within all the rules—the morphology of words, the syntax of grammar, and the semantics of our world-as-it-is—lies an overhead that constrains our writing to be mostly padding. Like monkey 100, the paths that we can follow are relatively few.

WORDS
· · · · · · ·

Very few arbitrary combinations of letters form allowable, pronounceable words. Consonants and vowels must alternate in a certain fashion. An intuitive measure of the ease with which letters form words is the degree of difficulty in composing crossword puzzles. In Hebrew, where there is a greater entropy per letter (there is more freedom), it is even possible to construct three-dimensional crossword puzzles. Our increasing usage of acronyms is one of the by-products of the information age that continually adds words to the language. This is particularly evident in the software field, and very often these new acronyms barely, if at all, follow the rules of morphology in forming pleasing, pronounceable words.

Curiously, the whole idea of separating words was not obvious in early writing. The Greeks and Romans did not consistently separate words. If writing was to be a phonetic translation of speech, then the flow did not necessarily need to be broken at each word. It has been suggested that the printer's pride in his craftsmanship led to the custom of delimiting words with spaces in about the tenth century.

The *Oxford English Dictionary* lists about half a million words. (More properly, lexical units, since verb tenses, plurals, and other forms of words are not listed separately.) If we were to designate each word with a binary sequence, this could be accomplished with 19 bits per word. Since the average word is about 5.5 characters, this straightforward encoding by word lookup would be the equivalent of about 3.45 bits per character, which in referring to the previous section would be at the entropy level of monkey 2.

The actual vocabularies that we use are very much smaller than the complete *Oxford English Dictionary.* Whereas our recognition vocabulary might be as high as 200,000 words, the recall vocabulary we use in writing is only about 10,000 words. James Joyce used only 29,899 different words in *Ulysses,* and most of us remember that as tough going. Thus far in this book I have used 5,045 different words. I am not sure whether to be embarrassed by that impoverished amount of variety, or to be proud that I have kept the vocabulary accessible, since my aim is intermediate in the scale of emotion to information. Whichever, it would seem that 19 bits is far too generous to allow for the representation of a word. Surely 14 bits would suffice. That would put us at the level of 2.55 bits per character, which would walk us by monkey 4 and leave Lempel–Ziv behind.

The frequency with which we use the words in our writing vocabulary varies enormously across the range from "the" to, say, "xylophone." Naturally there have been many studies of word frequencies, from the tenth-century Talmudists studying the Torah to the little program I wrote a few minutes ago. The most frequently used words according to a survey in 1967 by Kucera and Francis are shown on the following page, along with the most frequent words from the first three chapters of this book.

There are a number of interesting observations that we can make about the listing of most popular words. They are virtually all monosyllabic words. Of the 200 most frequently used words almost all are monosyllables. In the list of words used in this book, with the exception of the special word "information," the first 51 words are all monosyllables. (The 52nd is another special word, "sequence.") It is almost as if the designers of our language knew about information theory and Huffman coding; it has been optimized for efficiency of communication. Moreover, when we have the need to use a long word we often find a way to abbreviate it, or else to create yet another acronym.

Along with the monosyllabic nature of the most popular words goes the thought that they are almost devoid of information content. Yet 45 percent of the total words we use in writing are composed of the top 50 on this list—all words we might think of as mere stuffing to satisfy the nuances of rhythm and flow. George A. Miller put this quite well in his book *Language and Communication* when he commented that, "Language is based on a framework of a relatively small number of different words, arranged in many patterns, which supports the more variegated words that convey most of the information."

Back in 1935 G. K. Zipf noticed that if the logarithm of the frequency of occurrence of words was plotted against the rank ordering, the resulting curve was a straight line. This is a way of saying that the probabilities of words seem to fall off exponentially. This approximation has come to be known as Zipf's law. The Zipf plot for English is shown in Figure 6, along with some points representing the frequencies of words in this book.

It is not too surprising that the frequencies of words decrease exponentially with rank. Engineers all realize that very many, if not most, experiments yield data that plots as a straight line on log paper. Also many situations seemingly ruled by chance display the same behavior, as for example the populations of cities plotted against rank. Information theorists have rationalized Zipf's law by several mathematical derivations, based on various assumptions, that show the exponential behavior. Moreover, if we examine the pseudowords at level one that we generated earlier by using the

131

MOST FREQUENTLY USED WORDS

KUCERA & FRANCIS		CHAPTERS 1–3	
WORD	**FREQ.**	**WORD**	**FREQ.**
the	.0700	the	.0684
of	.0364	of	.0429
and	.0289	a	.0228
to	.0261	to	.0219
a	.0232	in	.0214
in	.0213	is	.0197
that	.0106	and	.0163
is	.0101	we	.0133
was	.0098	information	.0119
he	.0095	that	.0117
for	.0095	it	.0088
it	.0088	for	.0087
with	.0073	be	.0084
as	.0073	are	.0079
his	.0070	as	.0074
on	.0067	this	.0071
be	.0064	I	.0071
at	.0054	which	.0062
by	.0053	with	.0060
I	.0052	have	.0060
this	.0051	at	.0054
had	.0051	on	.0048
not	.0046	by	.0048
are	.0046	our	.0047
but	.0044	not	.0046
from	.0044	or	.0041

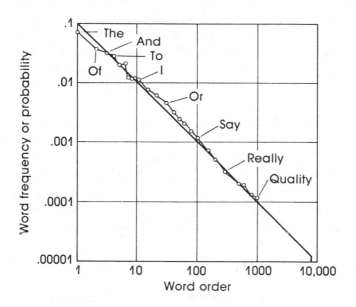

FIGURE 6
Frequencies of words in English text vs. rank order

probabilities of occurrence of letters and spaces, we would also find that these words obey Zipf's law.

Zipf's law exerts a certain tyranny over our writings. If it were to hold exactly, then it assures us that most of our words will be the short, popular, informationless words. According to the law, half of all the words we write will consist of the N most popular words, where N is the square root of the total number of words in the material. For example, so far in this book I have written 38,000 words. This would mean that regardless of how I twist and turn to put information content into this material, half of all my words will come from the top 71 words. In actuality when I checked, I found that the halfway point was at the 86th most popular word. This slight deviation was expected, because the sample size is a little too small here. Zipf found that his law held best for samples about the size of 120,000 words.

Zipf's law holds for other languages also, though the slope of the straight line varies. We can imagine the slope of the line being directly related to the intrinsic entropy of the language. If the slope were very steep, then the most popular words would absolutely predominate, and there would be little freedom, or entropy, in the use of the language. A flat slope, on the other hand, would mean that almost all words were equally probable, and there would be a relatively high entropy associated with this anarchy in choice. English seems a nice compromise, though my conditioning probably causes a strong bias.

Zipf's law can be used to calculate the entropy of English on the first order word level, that is, assuming no interword dependencies. Obviously, the Zipf approximation cannot hold indefinitely as the word rank becomes very large, since the total probability would eventually exceed unity. After 8,727 words a probability of unity is accumulated using the approximation of Zipf's law, and an easy way to do the entropy calculation is to assume that less probable words simply do not occur. On this basis Shannon calculated the entropy of English as 11.82 bits per word. This gives us an entropy per letter of 2.62 bits.

In theory it would be possible to look at word probabilities on higher levels and calculate entropies taking account of joint probabilities of successive words, as we might find for word-typing monkeys 2 and up. The number of combinations of successive words is so enormous, however, that the slim statistics are almost meaningless. We know also that Zipf's law does not hold above the first level. For example, the conditional probabilities for words following the word "of" fall off with a very steep slope, since "the" occurs almost ten times more frequently than any other word in that position. In contrast, the curve for words following "the" is very gradual, as there is a long list of nouns and adjectives that are nearly equally likely in that position.

STRUCTURE, MEANING, AND ENTROPY
• • • • • • • • • • • •

This chapter could be prolonged indefinitely by delving ever more deeply into the structure and meaning of language. Let me say at the outset that we will not do so. Our purpose at the moment is the pursuit of entropy, which requires us to examine the constraints of language usage: the way words may and may not be cascaded together in ordinary writing. To begin, we realize that words must be arranged according to the syntax of grammar, which must therefore reduce freedom and entropy. The structure of sentences can be formalized according to the science of linguistics. It is conceivable that a mathematical model of a formal grammar could be used to calculate the entropy of a system of words arranged into sentences according to the rules of grammar, but as far as I know it has not been done. Furthermore, it is not obvious that such a result would be useful, since the interpretation of syntax is not unrelated to the overriding question of meaning.

It is difficult to discuss meaning without sounding pretentious. Even a half-hearted literature search reveals hundreds of books in such fields as linguistics, psycholinguistics, sociolinguistics, and cognitive psychology. It is a feature of the information age that the librarians keep squirreling away such material and working very hard to make it all easily accessible without giving us any clue as to which ones are still relevant, and which ones never were. I suppose otherwise it would be too easy. In any event I intend to spare both of us most of the pedantic, heavy-handed approach that usually accompanies this subject. We will now have a little of this in the form of a few thoughts on the relevancy of meaning in language to the computer processing of text.

- In the context of entropy, meaning itself is not significant. It is only the strong compulsion to write meaningful passages that decreases our choice in language use. We could as easily phrase grammatical, but nonsensical sentences. But since we almost never write nonsense, this is not a case of interest. We can assume in both the construction and interpretation of writing that there is an intent to convey meaning.

- There are generally many choices in the meanings of words. In fact, the usage of such choices tends itself to obey a form of Zipf's law, with an exponential falloff versus rank. It is only in the context of the material that an intelligent choice of definition can be made for each word. These choices are also interwoven with the syntactical structure.

135

- The meaning of a sentence has little to do with the surface structure of choice in phrasing—declarative, passive, interrogative, and so on—but lies in what Noam Chomsky has called the deep structure, where the conceptual thought is stripped of these nuances. Meaning, however, does not stand alone within the context of an individual sentence but is contained in discourse, which includes not only adjacent sentences, but real-world knowledge and expectations.

- In the field of cognitive psychology a popular viewpoint is that meaning is *created,* rather than stored and retrieved, and there is no meaning or knowledge in language per se. This seems an overstrong statement, intended to underline an important point. In spite of the unimaginable gap between our civilization and that of Bronze-Age Greece, 500 years before Homer, we understand fairly well the meaning of the Linear B tablet with the translation: "One tripod: it is not sound as regards one foot." On the other hand, we are continually asking ourselves such questions as what did Robert Frost mean when he wrote "But I have promises to keep / and miles to go before I sleep?" We do indeed create our own meaning upon text retrieval, but the latitude we enjoy—or lament—probably depends on the place of the material on the scale of emotion to information.

In his desire to determine the "ultimate" entropy of text Claude Shannon conceived of a simple experiment to cut through the ambiguities of philosophy in which language can wander. Imagine for a moment that we had a computer so intelligent that in predicting what letters were yet to come it could take account of grammar, semantics, and meaning. Then we have seen that the concept of entropy lies right behind, since we would in effect be determining the "newness" or "unexpectedness" of succeeding letters. But actually we do have such a computer; lots of them. You and I are typical samples. Thus Shannon used people as text predictors, letting them read a text up to a certain point where they were asked to guess at the next letter. If the guess was wrong, they continued guessing until the guess was correct, then proceeded to the next letter. About 77 percent of the time the subject was able to guess the next letter on the first attempt.

A typical experiment was the following phrase. The numbers underneath indicate the guess at which the correct letter was obtained.

```
t  h  e  r  e     i  s     n  o  r     e  v     e  r  s  e     o  n
1  1  1  5  1  1  2  1  1  2  1  1  15 1  17 1  1  2  1  1  3  2
```

With data from experiments of this sort, the entropy of text can be computed from the simple calculation of the entropy of the sequence of guesses. Every time the number 1 appears, indicating a correct guess on the first attempt, no information whatsoever is needed to predict the next letter. Considering experimental error, and the mathematics of the process, Shannon gave the following upper and lower bounds for the entropy of English text as a function of the number of letters considered into the past.

ENTROPY OF ENGLISH—BITS PER LETTER

LETTERS CONSIDERED	1	2	3	4	5	6	7	8	9	10		100
UPPER BOUND	4.0	3.4	3.0	2.6	2.6	2.2	2.2	1.8	1.8	1.8		1.3
LOWER BOUND	3.2	2.5	2.1	1.7	1.7	1.3	1.3	1.0	1.0	1.0		0.6

In Shannon's entropy experiments he asked subjects to guess letters using a limited number of previous letters from the book *Jefferson the Virginian* by Dumas Malone. An excerpt from the material Shannon used is as follows:

The surviving descriptions of her are meager, and there is none contemporary with these events. In comparison with him, she certainly was not tall; as an old slave put it, she was "low." The tradition is that her figure was slight, though well-formed, that she had large hazel eyes and luxuriant auburn hair. Within the family much was said afterwards about her beauty, and this can be accepted in essence though not in full detail. Jefferson himself was straight and strong and his counte-nance was not unpleasing, but he was not a handsome man; beyond a doubt he prided himself on winning a pretty wife.

SUMMARY AND DISCUSSION

We have followed the trail of entropy in English text as far at it goes. The ASCII representation of an 8-bit byte per character is convenient and standard, but it is an artifact only loosely commen-surate with information. Probably the first real benchmark is the 4.76 bits per letter of nonstatistical letters at level 0. Grouping letters into words reduces the entropy to about 2.55 bits per letter. Structure in the form of the lowest level of grammar probably influences the entropy slightly at about the span of 15 letters in Shannon's guessing experiments to perhaps 1.5 bits per letter. Fi-nally, semantics and meaning over a half dozen sentences, as well as our extralinguistic knowledge, reduces the entropy to about 1 bit per letter.

The trail may not have seemed a long one—a factor of 8 in entropy may not appear significant. But it is a huge difference, as it is a factor of 8 in the *exponent* of many quantities of interest, such as in the mean time to repeat a given combination of letters or words. Remember the gap between monkey 0, who in the entire history of the universe could not type a simple, short Shakespearean phrase, and monkey 100, for whom it is a few week's job.

We discussed a simple, elegant text compression algorithm, the Lempel–Ziv technique, that is capable of "learning" English—or any other language—and compressing it to the greatest extent pos-sible. When applied to English it compresses the text to about 3.5 bits per character, which is more than 2 bits per character above what is commonly believed to the the true entropy. Now for the nagging question: Why does it not work better? The truth is, you see, that Lempel–Ziv does not really learn English as we know it at all. It has no chance. Therein lies the profound difference between the way we learn language and a brute force computer implementation.

Recall that the number of entries in the Lempel–Ziv dictionary (the number of "new" chunks) grows with the length of the text, n, as $\frac{Hn}{\log(n)}$, where H is the entropy. The total number of characters in the dictionary is n, as all the text ends up in the dictionary one way or another. Thus the average number of characters per entry is simply $\frac{\log(n)}{H}$. In the example we showed earlier, the average length of dictionary entries after 4,000 characters of the file of Chapter 2 was 4.4 characters. Extrapolating this logarithmically, the average length of dictionary entries after an entire book had been coded would be 8.3 characters. How much semantics, grammar, and meaning can there be in so paltry a memory? The answer is, of course, practically none. And to make these phrases longer we would have to feed in fantastically long text inputs, since the length of dictionary entries only grows logarithmically. After a complete encyclopedia had been coded, the length would be about 11 characters; after the Library of Congress, 17 characters. Also as we pointed out earlier, text is not at all stable over long passages. Even if we could feed Lempel–Ziv the zillions of words necessary to build out the vocabulary to include meaningful phrases, the subject and vocabulary of the input would be constantly changing and obviating most of the learned phrases. Even conceptually, I think, Lempel–Ziv cannot learn English.

Lempel–Ziv is intuitively pleasing in its approach, like a baby listening to the babbling around itself and storing away useful phrases to be used in appropriate occasions in the future. But the storage approach just does not extrapolate out to meaningful language: The memory requirements are awesomely impossible. Instead we must rely on structure, which I mean in a most general sense to include grammar, meaning, and knowledge. Only through structure can we construct and reconstruct meaning and information from language. Either our brains have evolved to incorporate the necessary structural processing for language, or language has evolved to be based upon the inherent structural processing capabilities of the brain. In either event, it is miraculous, and no computer will come anywhere near duplicating this capability for a long, long while to come.

Is it possible that the true entropy of English is less than the 1 bit per character Shannon estimated? In many cases I believe so. This would help account for the incredible memory feats that we humans can routinely achieve for certain material. It has always fascinated me that musicians can re-create exactly, and I mean exactly, entire symphonies and concertos. Beethoven's Piano Concerto No. 4, for example, is not of exceptional length, but it has over 23,000 notes. With the number of keys on the piano, and the different timing possibilities for each note, it would require 9 bits to represent straightforwardly each note. The total information content for the concerto on this basis would be about 211,000 bits. Memorizing the concerto would be equivalent to memorizing 64,000 decimal digits!

Music is very much like text. We could conduct experiments with musicians similar to Shannon's letter guessing experiments. We might well find that the entropy is of the same order as text, say 1 bit per note. That would still mean that it required 23,000 bits to code the concerto, and that memorizing the music would be equivalent to memorizing a 7,000-digit number. Now remember that if we have reached the true entropy there should be no structural clues left in the coded version to aid in memory; it should be exactly like a very long random number with no seeming rhyme or reason. If there were rhyme or reason remaining, we would not have reached the true entropy. Now very clearly we could never memorize a 7,000-digit number, but it is just as clear that memorizing concertos is an everyday business for professionals and amateurs alike.

Where is the catch? I would say that music has a very strong, deep structure. (Leonard Bernstein has written on this.) There is almost what I would think of as a simple mechanism behind most pieces. The mind of man has conceived of the piece as a kind of whole entity, and it can be understood in the same entirety. All of our training and musical heritage has resulted in what I think of as an internal music synthesizer in our minds. Just give it a few clues and it can fill in the rest. I believe that the real entropy per note of most pieces is very small.

I do not know the process by which professional musicians learn or memorize music, but as an amateur I find my own gropings interesting in the context of information theory. As a very young adult I read a popular book on playing the piano. One piece of advice made an indelible impression upon me; it was the maxim that you should never teach your *fingers* the music, you should teach your mind. I do not have any idea what this means. For myself it is only my fingers that seem to know the music. If I try to think about the succeeding notes, I am undone. It is that synthesizer in my head that must be allowed to unroll its preordained schema. Furthermore, I am unable to begin at any arbitrary point in the music; there are only certain allowed entry points. Like monkey 100, I must have the preceding context flowing before the oncoming notes can be processed.

The first time I play a particular piece I begin hesitantly. (After all, I am not very good!) But after only a few lines of music I begin to get the idea of the piece, and it begins to flow. It is almost as if I were building a Lempel–Ziv vocabulary of phrasings in the piece. Even though the rest of the music may seem different, there is a sameness about it that can be extrapolated from the overall structure and idea transmitted in the very beginning.

You may argue that music is inherently different from text. Perhaps, but then again, perhaps not. Consider the feat of the actor who memorizes the part of Hamlet. I count a total of about 12,000 words, or about 70,000 characters. Even at Shannon's 1 bit per character this would be 70,000 bits, or the equivalent of memorizing a 21,000-digit number. How many actors these past four centuries have been able to achieve this remarkable feat? Legions, I am sure.

In Hamlet, as in Beethoven, we find an underlying structure, an overall idea or scheme from which the minutia can be reconstructed, particularly in the context of the discourse with the other roles interwoven with Hamlet's own speeches. The exact wording is also aided by the syntax of unrhymed, iambic pentameter, but recall also that the English of Shakespeare has evolved considerably to that of today. In the "To be or not to be" soliloquy we find such phrases as:

> *When he himself night has quietus make . . .*
> *with a bare bodkin?*
> *Who would fardels bear, . . .*

It is not at all obvious. Certainly such memorization is a tribute to the remarkable long-term memory capacity of average humans, but it also leads me to believe that the actual entropy of English—the minimum information from which all the rest can be reconstructed—might be very considerably less than Shannon's 1 bit per letter.

As a final discussion point I would like to emphasize the role of entropy. The entropy of text which we have been following is the minimum information necessary to reconstruct the text itself—every letter, comma, and glitch in the file. In a sense it has nothing to do with the information contained in the words of the file, though as we have seen that may well guide us in reconstructing the actual words from this minimum information. When we read a report we may file away the gist of the text in our minds, discarding all those commas and irrelevant, short popular words. After all, we can always reconstruct a reasonable facsimile of them if someone asks us what was in the report. The minimum information to reconstruct what we consider to be the *information* contained within the text must, by definition, be less than the entropy. Sometimes it is very much less, but in an information-dense format, such as a table or data base, it would be much closer to the entropy. I hope this is not confusing, but I think it is.

REFLECTIONS— THE PAPERMILL

Several times in this chapter I have referred to the technical literature. Most laymen probably consider this archive of esoteric philosophy and mathematics with a kind of awe. As in most human endeavors, the truth is a mixture. It is a blend of a very little genius amidst a deluge of trivia. The publication system itself is also a very human system, with all the failings and innate humor that go with that humanity. The following tongue-in-cheek article pokes a little fun at the system, but it also contains a little truth. Perhaps you can sort out which is which.

A long time ago I wrote my first technical paper. I was really proud to see my name in an IEEE Transactions index. I was an author! Many people were impressed—me, my mother, and possibly a few laypeople who happened to glimpse the Transactions issue as it lay carelessly thrown on top of the living room coffee table. For years to come I would be able to drop into arbitrary libraries and find myself incarcerated, as it were, in the dusty stacks. What a marvelous system for publication we engineers had!

In the decades since, I have had occasional glimpses of the Truth. I had one vision of it in the religious quiet of the libraries of the British Museum and of Cambridge, where the actual notebooks of such immortals as

Isaac Newton made me shiver with the shared pride of a great scientific heritage, whose knowledge is promulgated through a venerated publication system. I've marveled at the lasting and renascent wisdom that can still be mined from our great papers—Nyquist in 1928, Rice in 1948, Shannon in 1949, to name a few in the communications field. Indeed, we engineers have much to be proud of in the record we have left behind.

However, there is another vision of our publication system. It is the myopic, day-to-day vision seen from the close-up position of the participants—reader, author, reviewer, and editor. From their standpoints it is indeed a miracle that there is any trace of a legacy to pass on to the next month's engineers. To begin with let's dispense with the myth that the publications are for the readers. Naturally, readers are a necessity, but we must be careful not to overestimate their value. For one thing, readers are a nuisance. They continually complain about the worthlessness of the material they are receiving. They want more practical papers, they say— not these incomprehensible theoretical exercises. Should the journal be so fortunate as to publish one of the practical papers it so rarely receives, the readers complain about the noticeable drop in quality in the current issue.

Worst of all, the readers make the outrageous claim that they are in fact—readers. They line the shelves of their offices with reams of pretentious journals, proclaiming to the world their sophisticated erudition. But I've heard the estimate that the average technical paper has approximately three readers. It's hard to judge, because there's some kind of uncertainty principle involved in studying readership. The process of measurement affects the system. People will fill out polls saying that they read N papers in an average issue. N is never equal to zero. Nobody could admit to not reading a journal he receives. Thus there is some kind of unspoken agreement that among us engineers N equals, say, three. This means that, for example, in the Communications Transactions with about 15,000 subscribers and 15 papers, the average paper would be read by 3,000 people. If you believe that, you probably also believe that giant vacuum tubes once walked the earth. On reflection, however, any author should be quite pleased to have three good readers who would study his paper and pass on its essence to their associates, for this is the way our system truly works.

The author, on the other hand, feels that his paper is a great masterpiece written in deathless prose for consumption by the masses. His or her ego is on the line when the precious opus is dropped in the mail for the cruel scrutiny of the review system. Most authors would be satisfied only with a telegram from the editor the next day, telling them that their paper is so important that it will be published immediately, without review, in a special issue of the journal with their picture on the cover. As the days tick by without reply their apprehension grows. Has their paper been sent to their arch rival? Will their own simplicity be apparent, or has it been well concealed by the usual practice of beginning with the general case, and explaining only special examples (the places they actually started) as afterthoughts treated as of no importance to the potential reader? The euphoria attached to the initial generation of the paper dims, to be replaced with a latent anger ready to be fired at hostile reviewers. Meanwhile their energies are consumed with preparing their next paper, entitled "_____Part N," "Return of _____," or "Further Implications of _____."

While this is going on, the reviewer has received the paper from the editor with a request for an opinion. As befits the dignity attached to rendering such a judgment, the reviewer first hurriedly turns to the back of the paper to see if he himself has been referenced. Probably he has been, since this is how the editor generally selects reviewers, but heaven help the author if he has neglected to reference such important work that might have been published by the reviewer. I remember being attacked during a patent trial on the basis of a paper I referenced in a textbook which I coauthored. Why, the barrister asked, did I reference that paper if it in fact had no bearing on my invention? I tried to explain, "When one writes a book like this one tries not to make any more enemies than he can. General procedure is to reference everybody in sight; it helps sell books." Fortunately, there were no more questions along this line.

Next the reviewer turns to the front to see who the author is. There are three possibilities. First, it can be good friend Allen, who is known never to produce a bad paper, by definition, since it would be professional death to pronounce one of his papers bad. Second, it could be well-known faker George, who is trying to slip one through the review process again, hoping to get a less astute reviewer than yours truly. Finally, it could be that rarity—the unknown author. (Incidentally, there is always an outcry about removing the author's name from the manuscript—this only delays by milliseconds the recognition of the above categories.) In the latter event, it will be necessary for the reviewer to put in a certain amount of work in order to establish his own preeminence in the field. After all, this author should realize just who it is he or she is dealing with.

Finally, in the middle of all this is the editor. The main skill necessary here is that of translation. The letters from the reviewers and authors must be translated before transmission. "This is the worst paper I have ever reviewed . . ." gets translated to "Reviewer A has found a certain deficiency in your paper . . ." In trying to placate these warring factions the editor makes few friends. Most letters he originates are apologetic. "I realize that the two years which have elapsed in the review of your fine paper may seem exorbitant to you . . . ," he begins. Untouched on his desk is the yearly paper proving Einstein's theory of relativity wrong and the slew of letters from would-be authors protesting that, being outside the "system," their revolutionary papers won't be accepted by the traditional reviewers. In the back of the editor's mind is the nagging doubt that maybe they're right. The trouble is—it just isn't likely.

Indeed, it's a merry-go-round, and few of the papers published this year will be referenced in the year 2000. We could debate the relative worthlessness of individual papers. Certainly there are layers and layers of worthlessness, but it's hard to say from moment to moment which papers will in the years to come merit special reconsideration. The system may not be as fair as it should be, and everyone concerned will from time to time have legitimate complaints, but I for one think that time has proven its value to all of us. On the whole, it works.

4

TEXT INPUT AND
OUTPUT

• • • • • • • •

Voltage levels fly whisperingly like the wind within the computer, as bytes representing text are manipulated and stored at speeds we cannot even imagine. Disk systems whir and printers crackle. But all that speed, power, and complexity go for naught unless humans like you and me are able to generate and access the text that these computers hold so dear to their silicon hearts.

In this chapter we will discuss getting text from human minds into computers, and returning it back to human minds. Therein lies a problem that has intrigued me since I first thought about information theory. We humans, like it or not, are a bottleneck. While the capacities of machines double every three or four years, our own information-handling capabilities have changed nary a whit—and they were rather poor to begin with. Communication rates within computers are around 10 to 100 megabits per second, and improving daily. Our own input/output rates are less than 100 bits per second, and stuck. On the one side we have the marvelously flexible and intelligent human bottleneck, on the other we have the dumb but burgeoning power of the machine.

Although humans are more or less what they always used to be, the inevitable juggernaut of technology brings computers ever closer to people. If we can find a better way to input or output text, computers can help with the implementation. For example, one of my associates is at present building a motion-sensing system that can track the position of hands. Perhaps we could input information by waving our hands at the computer, as practiced in the sign language for deaf people. But I do not think that this will improve communication with the computer, just as signing is no faster than speech. Regardless of the approach or mechanism, there seems to be a limit on human performance.

To preview some of the issues we will discuss later, let us review some representative rates for human communication (see Communication Rates table).

**COMMUNICATION RATES
IN WORDS PER MINUTE**

METHOD	RATE
Speaking	150
Listening	250
Typing	60
Reading	360

We seem to be remarkably balanced in our information input/output capabilities. Speech, handwriting, typing, reading, and other means all take place at roughly the same rate in spite of the fact that they are very dissimilar in their means of production. This is because the limit is not with our eyes, our ears, or our muscles; it is in our cognitive processing ability. Depending on whether we decide to judge each character as worth 8 bits, as in ASCII, or closer to the Shannon information value of about 1 bit, the range of these speeds is somewhere between 1 bit per second and 50 bits per second. Perhaps we are not, after all, fully equipped for the information age!

I cannot speak of the problems of inputting text to computers without reflecting on ancient means of text capture. The illuminated manuscripts of the Middle Ages are a remarkable legacy. I imagine the long hours or days spent in inspired labor over every paragraph. No one really cared how many bits per second were conveyed, and even today, so many centuries later, the contents of these manuscripts are of much less intrinsic interest than the art contained in the illustrations. In those days, of course, very few people could read and write, and even kings dictated their writings to scribes. There are many examples in the world's art that depict people writing in various ways.

The popularization of printing caused less emphasis to be put on handmade manuscripts. Printing must have seemed somehow less personal, but it greatly speeded and expanded the distribution of knowledge. People still wrote by hand, while books were laboriously typeset. Only now in recent years has the computer in its comfortable guise as a word processor taken over much of the responsibility for accepting direct text input from humans. Nearly everyone I know now types directly at a terminal in preference to writing by hand. Again an element of personalization seems lost. I get a chill when I see the handwritten papers of Leonardo da Vinci, Newton, or Shakespeare. I feel, mistakenly I am sure, nearer to their presence. It seems unlikely that anyone will want to view the actual floppy disk used by one of today's great writers. Nor will contemporary art of the future depict people at computer terminals the way artists of the past have shown people with their pens in hand, presumably composing letters and memoirs.

Because terminals have become so ubiquitous, some of the social structure of the business community has been turned upside down. The professionals are becoming secretaries, and the secretaries are becoming executives. I spend too much of my time typing and trying to figure out the right commands to get word processors to print files like this manuscript just the way I want them. It can be very frustrating, as most readers will know. I spent a whole day trying to get the page headers printed out correctly. Meanwhile my secretary has, I think, assumed my job. Sherry Turkle, the author and MIT sociologist, expressed this anguish in a recent talk. "I use all this energy trying to decide what font expresses my feelings," she said. She went on to observe that the problem is that the computer "invites perfection." Perhaps we have not come so far from the illuminated manuscript after all.

On the output side of the terminal we read text just as we always have. The abilities of the computer only give us new ways of finding and accessing text. A sign at the entrance to the library at my company says, "The world of information is as close as your keyboard." That presumably makes information very close, since there are on average two terminals per employee where I work. The library science people have been in the vanguard of the computer and information businesses and have made it possible to search title and abstract data bases from the convenience of our friendly terminals. Reach out and touch information, that is what it is all about.

While it is true that computer programmers have tried very hard to structure information to make it easy to browse electronically, for the most part we prefer the paper format, in spite of the great potential versatility of the electronic display medium. Either way, text has always served us well as an information retrieval format. One of its great advantages over speech is that it is a parallel format, instead of serial, like speech. We can skip over gobs of material to find just what we want. The effective rate of disposing of unwanted text can be quite high. We can also reread whenever we miss a point, and time shift the access of the material to whenever is convenient. Text, at least in its paper format, has both a real and perceived permanency that stands in contrast to speech. Unfortunately, electronic display has not yet reached all these levels of powerful convenience.

Although we are often professionally trapped into listening to unwanted or incomprehensible talks, and suffer the disadvantage of speech being a serial format, on many occasions speech can make up for this defect because, unlike text, it can be interactive. There is nothing so effective in getting a specific piece of information as asking an expert. Very quickly the inquiry can be sharpened, and working interactively an appropriate answer can be obtained through successive iterations of questions and answers. Obtaining the equivalent answer through text search would probably take much longer, and might often be misunderstood. So perhaps it still is a matter of reaching out and touching some*one,* instead of some*thing.*

In following these thoughts about the role of text, I would like to reiterate the belief that finding specific information has always been relatively easy; the information age will only increase this ease. The real task of the information age is acquiring a store of meta-information—knowing what is known and who knows it, rather than the details of that particular branch of knowledge. Furthermore, all of us need a reservoir of general information to serve as a framework for the specifics. Text is an excellent medium for the acquisition of this general knowledge because it is relatively speedy, portable, and browsable. Speech is much less satisfactory here. Try going to an expert and asking him or her to tell you about his or her specialty. It ends up a hopeless mishmash!

T Y P I N G

A few years ago someone asked me which of my high school courses had been the most useful. After a few moments of aimless consideration I surprised myself with my answer. "Typing," I replied. Of the store of knowledge and skills I have acquired through the years, only typing was achieved solely and definitively in that short window of time decades ago. I was the only boy in the class, since typing was for secretaries, who were girls.

Today a great many of my associates make their livelihood as computer programmers. They spend every day typing at their terminals. Many of them are not touch typists, though they are singularly adept at hunt-and-peck. Studies have shown that such fluency never approaches the speeds of touch typing, and it is very unusual for hunt-and-peck typists to unlearn those habits to become touch typists. They seldom reach even half the rate expected of entry-level typists. In fact there is a great deal of variation in typing speeds across skill levels. We can see in the table below that there is almost a factor of 15 between an excellent typist and a terrible one.

AVERAGE TYPING SPEEDS (WORDS PER MINUTE)

LEVEL	SPEED
Best typist	135
Good typist	90
Skilled typist	55
Nonsecretary typist	40
Typing random letters	22
Typing complex codes	15
Nontypist	9

In spite of their lack of proficiency, most hunt-and-peck programmers would probably argue that their lack of typing skill has no effect on their job performance. After all, being a programmer is not like being a copy typist whose job is the mindless and mechanical reproduction of previously recorded material. A key entry operator may execute 56,000 to 83,000 keystrokes per day, which corresponds to only 0.51 to 0.35 seconds per keystroke. But at those rates the symbols seem to flow through the human without conscious intervention. A programmer, on the other hand, in interacting with a computer terminal spends less than a third of his time in actual communication. Thus any inefficiency in typing is diluted by the relatively small fraction of the time in which the skill can be exercised.

Some indication of the value of fluency in typing was obtained by Alphonse Chapanis and his associates at Johns Hopkins University, who conducted experiments in interactive human communications in the early 1970s. In these experiments pairs of volunteer subjects were given tasks to accomplish that involved the necessity for the exchange of information. For example, one subject was given a telephone directory and the other a map. How long would it take to locate the physician who was closest to a given address on the map? The pairs required to communicate by typing took almost two and a half times as long to solve the problem as those who were allowed to talk to each other—even if the participants were skilled typists. Chapanis's conclusion was that the copy typing that we learn is not effective in interactive communication, where the messages are characterized by hesitations, mistakes, changes of thought, and irregular tempos.

From my own experiences in direct communication through typing, I would agree with Chapanis's conclusion. We are not used to speaking to another person in that clumsy way. Nevertheless, I feel quite different about communicating with a computer through typing. The computer cannot speak to me, nor I to it. Fluency in typing does seem important to me in that keyboard efficiency is *in the way* of reaching the computer. Ideally there should be nothing intervening between my thoughts and the computer. The more mechanical considerations intervene, the more they themselves become the focus of attention, and the more my thoughts race ahead of my fingers and are lost as they fall off the output buffer in my mind. It would seem to me to be beneficial if transparency could be closely attained. In the table we previewed a few paragraphs ago, we saw that even skilled typing, at the typical stenographer level of 60 words per minute, is significantly slower than speech. And since I seem to "speak" my thoughts in my mind as I write, I would conclude that there is indeed a mismatch between thinking rate and the speed of keyboard input to a computer. Can this be improved, and if so, how?

It is clearly possible to type as fast as we talk. That authoritative source, the *Guinness Book of Records,* tells us that the world's record for typing speed is 170 words per minute. Moreover, it is demonstrated every day in courtrooms across the country that court stenographers, using their own special chord keyboards, are easily able to follow the fastest and most intricate speech. While achieving this remarkable feat, they even chew gum and stare around the room, apparently daydreaming. As far as I can tell, they do not even listen to the boring testimony, which is most everything. Granted, then, it is possible if one is a court stenographer or a world typing champion to match the speed of speech with keyboard input. But what about you and me? Not much chance, I am afraid. To begin with there is the keyboard.

K E Y B O A R D S
· · · · · · · · · ·

In computer technology more than in any other field we seem to be caught in the dilemma between standardization and progress. Progress is so extremely rapid, there are so many manufacturers, and there is such need for things to plug together—and they never seem to. In all this mess the one thing that is standardized is the keyboard. Well, almost. The alphabetic keys form the familiar QWERTY above the home row, but we argue endlessly about the placement of the control keys and the numeric keypad. IBM caused a typist revolution by departing from their own Selectric standard with their first PC Computer keyboard, and incidentally made the day of some after-market keyboard vendors. Forgetting about these controversies, the QWERTY keyboard has been with us for over a century. Imagine that in the computer business!

It is hard to conceive now of how the business world must have been for secretaries in the late 1800s. There were scores of different keyboards, with seemingly haphazard arrangements of keys. Every manufacturer wanted to be unique. Sound familiar? How fortunate we are that somehow rationality triumphed and the QWERTY keyboard, patented in 1878 by C. L. Sholes and C. Glidden, became universal. The Remington Arms Company had begun manufacturing a version of this typewriter in 1874. Except for a change in the position of the letter *m,* the arrangement of keys is the same today. It is really too bad that it is possibly a terrible arrangement of the keys.

What was the logic behind the QWERTY design? Apparently none of the contemporaries of Sholes and Glidden thought to ask. Who could have believed that in a hundred years everyone would be using that arrangement? A popular belief is that Sholes and Glidden, who were compositors, sought to separate the typebars of the popular digrams to alleviate jamming of the keys. In other words, they deliberately tried to slow down the typist. This story has been written so often that it has probably gained an undeserved truth, for it is supported neither by history nor analysis; a totally random arrangement of the keys has fewer "close" typebars for the English language than the QWERTY. It is even possible that QWERTY is simply an alphabetical placement, since *F, G, H, J, K, L,* and *M* (originally) appeared in the middle row. No one knows.

There are some inventions and theories that seem to attract fanatical detractors with alternative solutions. Keyboards are in this category. An unbelievable number of keyboards have been proposed during this century. Many of them were funny looking; some were outrageous. Some were based on the fuzziest logic imaginable, while others were supported by whole books of scientific analysis. None has been accepted. I would guess that more than one keyboard inventor has claimed that he was suppressed by the powers-that-be from giving the world a keyboard that would have saved untold hours of secretarial labor. It is probably closer to the truth that the world only gave a great big yawn.

One inventor has at least achieved a certain notoriety. Dr. August Dvorak, a professor of statistics at the University of Washington, led a team of industrial engineers in the early 1930s that tested 250 variations of keyboards. He concluded that the QWERTY placement was one of the worst possible arrangements for touch typing. Naturally he had his own proposal for a keyboard that he felt was greatly superior to QWERTY. Before we get to that proposal, let us consider Dvorak's criticisms of the QWERTY keyboard.

1. Too much of the typing (57 percent) is done by the left hand, which is the weaker and less coordinated for the majority of the population. Whole words, such as "was,"

"were," "extra," and "address," are typed by the left hand alone. (Whew! Try typing that list, as I just did!) In the *Funk and Wagnall's Collegiate Dictionary* there are 2,700 words that are typed by the left hand alone and only 300 that can be typed solely by the right.

2. Not enough of the typing is done on the home (middle) row of keys. Only 32 percent of average English text is typed on the middle row, where the fingers ordinarily reside, while 52 percent is done on the back row and 16 percent on the front (bottom) row.

3. The weakest fingers are overloaded. For example, the very popular letter *A* is under the weakest finger of all—the little finger of the left hand. This is the feature most disliked by fluent touch-typists. On manual machines those poor little fingers even have to handle the heavy shift keys, but that century-old disadvantage has now been mitigated through electronics.

4. Many common digrams require hopping back and forth between rows, which considerably increases the amount of finger and hand motion. Popular digrams like *br, un,* and *in* require going back and forth between the top and bottom rows using the same hand.

While we are condemning our omnipresent friend, QWERTY, let us add the criticisms of other investigators. One of the most important principles in keyboard operation is the cooperation of the two hands. While one hand is pushing a key, the other can be readying itself in position for the next keystroke. However, in QWERTY, about 48 percent of all repositioning is done by the same hand, whereas analysis shows that it is possible to reduce such one-handedness to about 33 percent. The easiest typing of all to do is that which alternates between left and right hand while remaining on the home row. A beautiful example is the word "half." "Half" is such a pleasure to type that I just did it again! Unfortunately, it is also a rarity, as only 4% of motions between keys are of this class.

If all this is not sufficient condemnation, the ergonomics people have added their own. The vertical arrangement of keys in QWERTY slopes upward from right to left in parallel lines for both hands. Since our hands are mirror images of each other, it would seem that a better arrangement would have these vertical slopes also mirror images, as a gentle V, rather than parallel. Also, in reaching upward, the third and little fingers are particularly stressed to reach the outermost keys in the upper row. Typing a 1 or a 0, as I have had to do often in this book about the information age, just stops my touch-typing cold. Finally, because of all the hopping around between the rows of QWERTY it is hard to keep the home row position correctly. I often end up displaced, typing an *S* for an *A,* and so on.

If I go on in this vein any longer, I will hate this keyboard, and there will be no more of this book. This sense of frustration is exceeded only by my fear that they will tell me that everyone has to use a different keyboard. This is the only one I know.

Dvorak's idea for a keyboard design was to put the most commonly used letters on the home row, with the vowels on the left hand, and the consonants on the right, so typing would often alternate between the hands, and as much as possible it would stay on the home row. Dvorak's keyboard is shown in comparison with QWERTY in Figure 7. These principles are typical of many of the would-be keyboard designs. Put the most commonly used letters under the strongest fingers. Have the most popular letters in the home row. Examine all the popular digrams and try to distribute them between the two hands. Minimize motion between the rows. Give the thumbs something useful to do. Try to get to a design that invokes a "rhythm" of cooperation between the hands in ordinary English text. Shape the keyboard to fit the hands better. The good qualities of these precepts seem unarguable. The problem is that they cannot all be satisfied simultaneously.

Common folklore is that the Dvorak keyboard is much better than QWERTY, and that if we could all retrain ourselves we would come out a long way ahead. Dvorak died in 1975, about the same time that personal computers were beginning their takeover of the world. Because so many people have come so much closer to keyboards, and because changing key placement is now relatively trivial, interest in the Dvorak layout has been growing. One of the models of the Apple computer has a switch that converts the keyboard into a Dvorak layout. In these days of electronics it is easy; usually it is only necessary to change a software pointer to a different table in memory. Software vendors sell programs that map any key to any other key, and there are packages of new keytops to change the lettering. The flexibility of today's situation is a far cry from the mechanical nightmare of the typewriters and teletypewriters of only a few decades ago. Of course the problem is not in

Qwerty keyboard

FIGURE 7
QWERTY and Dvorak keyboards

changing the electronics or software. The problem is—as it is so often—in changing us.

How much would we actually gain by taking up the Dvorak keyboard? I feel sure that most readers would believe that there have been many definitive studies comparing the performance of typists on Dvorak and QWERTY through all these many years. Surprisingly, that is not the case, and even today there is lingering doubt about the degree of improvement. Meaningful, unbiased experiments are very difficult to construct and costly to run. The problem is that just about everyone has some degree of familiarity with QWERTY. Imagine for a minute how you would run such a comparison. Do you retain QWERTY people? Do you find bush-people with no familiarity with either, let alone the English language? How many people do you need for how long and at what cost? Although findings of government studies favoring Dvorak by the Navy and the National Bureau of Standards have been widely quoted, no concrete experimental data has been published, and the one experimental comparison in the open literature, which incidentally shows no advantage for Dvorak, seems faulty.

Since experimenting with people is so difficult, researchers have turned to computer analysis and simulation. It is relatively easy to calculate the distance fingers travel in typing a given text on a particular keyboard. Typically we find that the fingers have to move less on a Dvorak keyboard than on a QWERTY, but only by 30 percent or so. For example, in typing the Hamlet soliloquy ("To be or not to be . . ."), the ratio of distances is 1.39. This is certainly indicative of better performance—faster, less tiring, and so on—for the Dvorak, but it is not a definitive comparison, since we do not know the speeds of the various movements involved. Even this result is not reassuring in terms of the degree of superiority, for it is far less than that touted by the Dvorak supporters.

This kind of analysis was extended to a more comprehensive simulation at the University of California at San Diego, where researchers used stop-action videos to analyze finger movements so as to derive a computer model that simulates a skilled typist. This simulation showed that the Dvorak keyboard produced speeds only 5 to 10 percent faster than QWERTY. The ability to simulate behavior is one of the most profound capabilities given to us by the computer age. Although many laypeople may think that if a computer says something, it must be true, there is a deep skepticism of most simulations in the scientific professions. It is not that we distrust the computer; only that the results are no more accurate than the model, and we have been bitten too many times by models that were inaccurate or failed to include or reflect the behavior of various parameters. This is not to say that the typing simulation is wrong, because what other evidence we have tends to support it. Rather, I think that the last word has not yet been heard.

Why is there not a greater difference in typing speeds between Dvorak and QWERTY? Several researchers have made extensive studies of the times taken for typing the digrams in English. If we consider the most popular 135 digrams, their use constitutes about 83 percent of all the use of digrams. It seems, according to these studies, that whether by accident or design these digrams are actually typed rather efficiently in QWERTY and that there is almost no difference in their speeds overall between QWERTY and Dvorak. This is possibly because there is a relatively good, though certainly not optimal, coordination between the hands in typing most of the popular digrams. Perhaps QWERTY is not so bad after all, but as one frustrated keyboard designer put it, "Research of this nature on a device such as the ubiquitous QWERTY keyboard is fruitless, since it merely supports the fact that given time and motivation, an individual can become skilled on any inefficiently designed device, within reason." Do I detect in this a note of disgust with a too easily satisfied world? Apparently, QWERTY is "within reason," and violating a century-old standard for an extra 10 percent does not make a great deal of sense.

MECHANICS AND COGNITION IN TYPING
• • • • • • • • • • • • • • • • • •

My friends in robotics research have an extra hand. As you can see from Figure 8, it is made out of metal, and it is worked by an intricate system of motor-driven strings and pulleys under computer control. The hand is rudimentary; it has only 32 degrees of freedom, which given ingenious programming can presumably enable the artificial hand to do some of the things that a real hand can do. So far it does very little. It certainly makes me appreciate what a human hand and its controller, the mind, must do to accomplish something like skilled typing.

Suppose that we tried to make the robot hand type. We would think of the task in terms of two distinct problems: the mechanics and the control program. In the mechanical part we would study what movements could be made, and how fast they could be made with optimum trajectories between points. Then we would write, painstakingly I am sure, programs that were subroutines for motor control to make the fingers move in the proper arcs by coordination of all the degrees of freedom. Next we would write higher level subroutines that controlled the motion of the hands. Finally we would write the top level program that coordinated the overall motions, looking ahead at the forthcoming letters, and calling the subroutines in a pipelined sequence so that one finger was preparing for the forthcoming stroke while the other finger was still pressing its key.

Psychologists look at typing in much the same way. Perhaps because it is fashionable, they speak in terms of programs in the

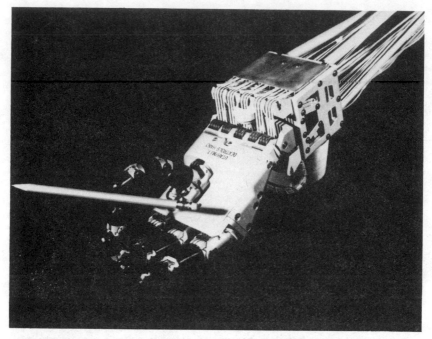

FIGURE 8
The MIT/Utah robotic hand

mind for motor control of the fingers, and they look for analogs from the world of computing. They speak of motor commands from the brain that correspond to the assignment of movement goals for the fingers, which are then passed to lower level muscle systems for detailed implementation based on acquired experience. Typing requires multiple control of 60 tendons and 30 joints, just to move the fingers. Movies show that finger movements start several letters ahead of their scheduled arrival time, often out of order of the sequence of final arrivals. It seems that each finger starts as early as possible towards its intended key, while the hand provides cooperate movement to configure itself towards as many targets at a time as possible.

We are limited in both mechanical and cognitive capabilities. The fastest we can tap with a single finger is about 6 taps per second. Try it. That would correspond to a typing speed of about 60 words per minute, if tapping were the only motion involved. However, the speed of typing the fastest digrams is about twice as fast if the same hand is used, and about 25 percent faster than that if two

hands are involved. This is because of the overlap in the complicated choreography of the sequence of individual finger movements. Thus a good keyboard design, combined with the fastest
possible finger motions and efficient mental programming, can
yield a speed of around 120 to 150 words per minute at best.

This is not quite the highest rate of mechanical output that a
human can achieve, but it is indicative of our limitations. We can
get a somewhat different viewpoint by considering our performance on an entirely different kind of keyboard, that of the piano.
Skillful performance pianists routinely attain speeds of 1,500 to
2,000 keystrokes a minute, which would be equivalent to typing
speeds of 300 to 400 words per minute. Chopin's Minute Waltz
(Op. 64, No. 1) contains 1,632 notes, for example, and can be
played in one minute to prove the point (though the artistry suffers
at this speed). Moreover, the pianist is able to control the dynamics
of touch and to maintain a strict sense of timing, which may even
be polyrhythmic (different for the two hands). For example, in
Chopin's Fantaisie–Impromptu (Op. 66), which contains the familiar "I'm always chasing rainbows," the right hand plays 16 notes
to the measure while the left hand plays 12. It is as if the two hands
are under the control of two autonomous programs, which are only
coordinated at a higher level.

That the speeds of keying on that long, linear piano keyboard
are so much faster than on the typewriter keyboard may seem
surprising, but there are several explanations. The fastest speeds are
usually attained by rolling or rocking motions of the hands, rather
than by tapping, and unlike English text and the typewriter keyboard, piano music is written to be played on the piano, so that fast,
awkward sequences simply do not happen. The Chopin waltz is
designed to flow with the hand, while at the same time being
musically appealing. Another factor is that on the piano several
notes are usually played simultaneously to form chords. (This is also
the principle of operation of the stenotype machine used for court-
room recording.) From the standpoint of mechanical manipulation,
this reduces the speed required to press a given total number of
notes, but it means that the brain must think more about each
combination to be pressed. In some measurements that I did on
recorded piano music, the total number of notes played per minute
did not exceed the 1,500 to 2,000 range, regardless of whether the
piece consisted primarily of single notes played rapidly in sequence,
or multiple notes—chords—played at a slower rate. There are to

my knowledge no pieces in which chords are played at a very rapid rate. Even the idea makes me weary!

The constraints on the playability of music, together with the strong musical structure of harmony and flow, imply that the entropy per note of music must be less than that of text, so that the overall *information* rate produced by the piano keying may be very much the same as is produced by typing. As we discussed in the previous chapter, the exact information associated with either text or music is in some question, but we begin to see the glimmerings of the widespread hypothesis that the human input/output capabilities are limited to about 100 bits per second regardless of what we do.

The cognitive programming involved in typing is weakly illuminated by several classic experiments. In one of these experiments subjects typed letters that were displayed on a screen so as to keep a fixed number of letters visible; as one letter was typed it disappeared and a new letter was added to the end of the string. The latency (delay) between key presses was studied as a function of the number of letters displayed. It was discovered that the number of letters displayed had no effect on typing speed as long as it was about 8 or more, but reducing this preview below 8 caused reductions in typing speed. For one skilled typist the average latency when preview was unlimited was 110 milliseconds, corresponding to a typing speed of 109 words per minute. The latency became progressively longer as the amount of preview became less, until when there was no preview (only the current letter to be typed was shown) the latency was about 475 milliseconds, which is a typing speed of only 25 words per minute.

The import of this experiment is that if we cannot see ahead, our typing speed falls off drastically. It reminds me of the surprise I received as a young adult when I first saw very good pool players in competition. None of them seemed to pay the least attention to the current shot, but rather the concern was wholly with assessing the position the balls would assume for the *next* shot. So it is in fluent typing. The essence is in planning ahead and in accessing a subroutine for the motor control of a sequence of strokes rather than for the execution of a single stroke.

If the forthcoming letters shown in the preview window did not form English words or pseudowords, a significant delay was added to the latency, cutting the typing speed in half for the case of full look-ahead. When the material we have to type is nonsense, we lack the proper subroutines to organize the letters into larger patterns. This effect was shown rather dramatically in a different experiment in which subjects were shown a short sequence of random letters that was to be typed upon receiving a signal. Naturally, the longer the sequence, the longer it took to type that sequence. We would expect, however, that the time required *per letter* would remain more or less constant with different length sequences. Surprisingly, that was not the case. The subjects actually took longer to type *each letter* in the longer sequences than in the shorter sequences.

That latency per letter increases with sequence length when typing random letter patterns is an intriguing and unexpected result. The latency was found to increase linearly with sequence length; for example, if the sequence length doubled, then the latency per letter also doubled, and the total time to type the sequence increased by a factor of 4. The researchers attributed this increase in latency to the time required for a mental search for what they called "subprogram retrieval." In other words we have to fool around in our minds trying to find or put together a program to connect the designated keystrokes. The longer the sequence, the more mental time is required in addition to the expected mechanical delays. If the sequence to be typed is an English word, the effect disappears completely. Now the familiar subroutines are applicable and ready.

The analysis of errors in typing also gives evidence of the hierarchy of motor control programs. A very common error is the transposition of adjacent letters. I often type "adn" for "and," for example. Frequently this error can be seen to be precipitated by the contextual envelope of preceding letters, so as to maintain a certain left hand–right hand rhythm. In such cases the correct letter seems to violate the established rhythm. Each hand types the correct letters in the correct order, but the ordering of the interlace of the hands is wrong. The suggestion is that the motor program maintains separate command arrays for each hand, which are controlled on a higher level of the program hierarchy.

In typing, as in all other human input/output methods, we have to account for the time to *think* and the time to *do.* We have seen evidence in typing of limitations on both of these facilities. We have also seen the deep connection with the concept of entropy discussed in previous chapters. Once again, entropy represents the degree of unexpectedness of the oncoming character stream. We can easily imagine that it is the unexpectedness that causes the mental and physical workload in typing or in piano playing. Even though our language has this large, built-in redundancy, we do not pay a proportional penalty in our ability to input and output. If there were no redundancy in language, our manuscripts would be perhaps a factor of 3 shorter, but since every letter would be totally unexpected, our typing time would increase significantly. Experiments indicate that it would at least double.

WORD PROCESSING

From *1984* by George Orwell

Winston dialed "back numbers" on the telescreen and called for the appropriate issues of the Times, *which slid out of the pneumatic tube after only a few minutes' delay. The messages he had received referred to articles of news items which for one reason or another it was thought necessary to alter, or, as the official phrase had it, to rectify.*

Winston Smith could certainly have used a word processor! With one execution of the "global substitute" command Oceania would always have been at war with Eurasia. How was George Orwell to have known that in the actual year 1984 computerized word processors would be cheap, powerful, and ubiquitous? Like Orwell's Ministry of Truth, word processors have done away with the idea of permanency. And what a burden it was! Some of us can remember the stress of typing with multiple carbons. Now the world of freedom has opened in front of us; the ease of changeability has dramatically increased the fluency of communication with the computer in text capture and editing. It also should result in better quality writing, though that effect may not yet be manifestly evident.

In Orwell's day the sole job of a typist was to transcribe material from another format, usually handwriting or dictation. Now the computer terminal has become the main point of capture for original text, and the power and flexibility of this interface are determined by the word processing software. I could not write a book about information without speaking of word processing, yet it is difficult to say anything that is fundamental or philosophical, or even that will last until the publication date of this manuscript. As is often true in the computer business, the technology has raced far ahead of our understanding of the human interface, and there is really little hope that this situation will change. The way we find out about desirable features in a word processor is to market the word processor. Success in the market is indicative of good features, at least for the time being. The converse is also true.

In the spirit of this chapter we can discuss the mechanics and dynamics of the man-machine interface in a word processor. We have already described the most important operation, which is the keystroke itself, and its efficiency in the typing of English text. From this elemental operation we can build models of the execution of more complicated commands. How many keystrokes are required to effect a word substitution in a particular editor? How many other operations, and how long does it take to think, and at which points in the sequence?

The following times are representative of human performance in word processor–related tasks:

Keystroke, skilled typist—.20 sec.

Pointing to a target with a mouse—1.10 sec.
(In case some readers are not computer addicts, a "mouse" is a handheld pointer for a computer—not a rodent.)

Homing the hands on the keyboard—.40 sec.

Mentally preparing for an action—1.35 sec. (e.g., recalling proper command)

Acquisition of a task by looking at manuscript—2.0 sec. (e.g., finding next marked change)

Acquisition of a task by looking at manuscript and screen—4.0 sec.

For any given editing task we could add up the various component actions which are required by our editor and make an estimate of the time required. For example, in one particular line editor if we were to replace one 5-letter word with another 5-letter word we would have to type the substitute command and both old and new words. During this sequence there would be 4 times at which we would probably pause to think—at the beginning of the sequence and at the 3 times we hesitate before terminating an input by the return key. The estimated time would be 15 keystrokes at .2 seconds each, and 4 mental pauses of 1.35 seconds, which results in a total execution time of 8.4 seconds. Experiments have shown that such a model predicts fairly accurately the times required for expert users.

Several researchers have conducted experiments designed to test the efficiency of various pointing methods, such as the mouse, joystick, trackball, lightpen, and cursor keys. The mouse seems to be the clear-cut winner on measured efficiency of operation, though individual preference would certainly be a more important determinant in selection. In following our theme of human interaction and information, the experimentally derived time to position a mouse is worth a comment. It has been found that the pointing time for a mouse varies as a function of the distance to the target, d, and the size of the target, s, according to:

$$t = .8 + .1 \log(\tfrac{d}{s} + .5) \; sec.$$

This is a form of what is known as Fitt's law, which describes how long it takes to move your hand to a particular location.

Suppose that we look at mouse positioning as an information-generating task, just as we have looked at the typing of text. If we move a mouse distance d and point to a target of size s, how much information do we specify? In traversing d we could end anywhere on a circle whose circumference is $2\pi d$, but we are specifying a region of length s. Thus we are in effect choosing between $\frac{2\pi d}{s}$ alternatives, and the information we convey is simply $\log(\frac{2\pi d}{s})$. Compare this information with the mouse-positioning time in the equation given in Fitts' law. Notice that the time to position is directly proportional (forgetting the constant overhead of .8 seconds) to the information conveyed. That certainly is fortunate, otherwise there would be a big problem somewhere! Furthermore, we can see by the proportionality that the information rate is 10 bits per second. Once again, in an entirely different task, we see the typical and meager information capabilities of humans like you and me.

The keystroke model of text editors predicts the performance of expert users in an error-free environment. Typically, however, even experts spend about one quarter of their time in correcting errors. Another quarter of the time goes to suboptimum use of editor commands and miscellaneous ineptitude. One of the beautiful aspects of using an editor is that the cost of making an error is so small that we tend to type very fast and correct the many errors as we go along. For myself, I would like to feel that I have optimized my total throughput by my tradeoff between speed of typing and error rate, but I suspect I have gone much too far in the speed direction and have instead maximized my psychological comfort with the flow. On the other hand, when we type commands to the editor, as opposed to text, we do tend to slow down, as mistakes are generally more costly.

That the keystroke model applies only to experts might seem a weakness, but that is the only situation in which an efficiency study makes sense. However, no one will ever get to be an expert on an editor that is not somehow constructed for beginners to learn. Also we must realize that differences in the efficiencies of editors are washed out by differences in the skills of the individuals using them, and that differences in features, feel, and ease of memorization far outweigh the considerations of efficiency in keystroke operations.

Although we have in this brief section stressed the mechanics of editing, the far more important issues are the social and environmental ones. The inventions of screen editors, windowing, help screens, page-sized displays, language-knowledgeable editors (computer languages), spell correctors, grammar analyzers, on-line thesauruses, desktop publishing, and so forth probably constitute the most significant advances in text entry since, well, ever. More and more these features remove the overhead in writing and bring us closer to fluency in expression.

I must admit to having some mixed emotion about all the help I am getting from editors already. As an example of what currently is available, I ran this chapter up to this point through the UNIX(T) Writer's Workbench analysis program. On what is about 20 pages of text, it gave me 15 pages of advice. There are 33 spelling errors, it told me. I thought only 5 of these were real errors, and the others it was not smart enough to know were right. People should know how to spell, I said to myself. Next it gave me 10 pages of suggestions on improving my grammar. I ignored them all. It has no sense of humor whatsoever.

In commenting on the style and readability of my text, the

UNIX⊤ writer's workbench concluded that according to the Kincaid readability index, a person with 11 years of schooling would be able to read this. Gratuitously, it added that that was good for this sort of material. (How did it know what sort of material this was, I wondered.) One of my sentences was 54 words long. It did not like that. My average sentence length was 19.6 words, and words averaged 4.75 characters. In sentence structure, 39 percent of my sentences were simple, and 43 percent complex. I have 11 questions and 2 imperatives, while 12 percent of my sentences are passive. On word usage 24.4 percent are nouns, 15.8 percent adjectives, and 7 percent pronouns. If I want to be compared against a number of profiles for different kinds of material, it recommended further programs. It also made other suggestions about seeing specialist programs. I hope there is a cure.

READABILITY INDEXES

A readability index is a simple measure of the difficulty of reading a given piece of text. Usually such measures rely on the percentage of long words (e.g., more than 2 syllables) or the percentage of long sentences. Both of these percentages are indicative of complexity and abstraction. The index is generally calibrated based upon estimated years of education required for reading text of like statistical makeup.

The UNIX⊤ Writer's Workbench program reports four readability indexes. They are defined as follows:

Kincaid Index—
Grade level = .39(Words per sentence) + 11.8(Syllables per word) − 15.59

Automated Readability Index—
Grade level = 4.71(Letters per word) + 0.5(Words per sentence) − 21.53

Coleman-Liau Index—
Grade level = 5.89(Letters per word) − 0.3(Sentences per 100 words) − 15.8

Flesch Index (Scores 0–100)—
Score = 206.835 − 84.6(Syllables per word) − 1.015 (Words per sentence)

The use and interpretation of these indexes is controversial. They are not indicative of organization or flow within the text, nor do they account for the interest and fit with the desired audience. Some studies have shown negative correlation between readability indexes and readers' ratings of understandability. Plato's dialog *Parmenides* scores in the fourth to eighth level. So much for simplicity of sentences and brevity of words!

This chapter has the following readability indexes: Kincaid—10.4, Auto—10.6, Coleman-Liau—10.6, Flesch—11.1 (54.7).

R E A D I N G

It strikes me as ironic that you the reader are about to read about reading. Obviously you know how! Many of you have no experience with information theory, and many of you are not fluent typists, but all of you have spent a lifetime experimenting with reading. Yet I wonder how many of you have given any thought to the miracle that we so routinely practice? It is an acquired skill that much of world's population lacks, in spite of the fact that virtually everybody learns a spoken language. Even the majority of those who learn to read seems not to care about exercising this ability to acquire information. I am so often amazed to sit beside strangers on transcontinental airline flights who are perfectly prepared to sit for six hours and stare straight ahead. Then again I will see a shabbily dressed teenager swaying on a steamy New York subway reading Kierkegaard, and I think that perhaps all is right with the world.

But how do we read? Can computers help by displaying the information more effectively? While the second question is a new and interesting one, the first question has been a subject of considerable research in cognitive psychology for over a hundred years. It was in 1878 that the French scientist Emile Javal discovered that in reading the eye did not move continuously across the line, but instead moved in small jumps, which are called saccades. (A word like that adds a touch of class, but can be safely forgotten.) Between these jumps the eye makes a momentary fixation on a small area of print. While your eye can track a moving finger or other object in a continuous fashion, it is incapable of moving smoothly on its own, as would be required if we really read by sweeping our eye across the line, as is our sensation.

For many years psychologists have experimented with tachisto-scopic (briefly illuminated) presentation of letters, words, and pseudowords to study the apprehension of text that might be accomplished during these fixations. They have found that English words can be recognized if flashed for about 50 milliseconds, which is about the duration of a blink. Letter patterns that form pseudo-words are more difficult to report than words of the same length. Completely random patterns of letters are even more difficult. The fact that there is something "whole" about a word that seems to be accessed as a unit has provoked a number of theories about word recognition. Based upon the discussion in the previous chapter, we can well imagine how word recognition could be related to the concept of information. Just as in typing, our mental processes, and perhaps even the physiology of our brains, has become adapted to the processing of language, including particularly its innate statistical structure.

The defect in these experiments with briefly flashed letter patterns is that the context of ordinary reading is missing. In the last few years significant strides have been made in the application of computer technology to experiments in reading, so that it is now possible with eye trackers to monitor within a single character where the eye is focused every few milliseconds. Furthermore, and perhaps more importantly, computers make it possible to take in a great amount of data and to process the data in ways hitherto impossible. The data can be gained from a variety of readers without in any way interfering with their normal reading habits. As a result we are now learning a great deal more about the mechanics of reading, though the inner processes of the mind which accompany the mechanics are an area shrouded in complexity and speculation.

During reading the average time that the eye is fixated before it jumps ahead to the next position is between 200 and 250 milliseconds. The jump itself is very fast, occupying only about 10 to 20 milliseconds, and during this movement vision is smeared. While our eye is fixed, we can focus effectively on only a small area encompassing a visual angle of 1 to 2 degrees. This is the portion of the image focused on the part of our retina known as the fovea, where the density of cones (visual detectors) peaks up sharply. You can test this span of visual acuity in a moment after finishing this paragraph (please!) by focusing your eyes on the X in the phrase contained in the box. Do not look anywhere else, and see how far to the left and to the right you can recognize the letters.

Curfew tolls the X knell of parting day.

As you have no doubt experienced, the span of acuity is quite limited. Generally speaking, it extends from about 4 characters to the left of the point of focus to at most 15 to the right. Much of the information beyond about 6 characters to the right of fixation is rather gross in nature. There is a region here of parafoveal vision (a kind of peripheral vision) in which the letters cannot be recognized, but perhaps the number of letters or the presence of spaces can be made out. Early experiments seemed to indicate that this peripheral vision was helpful in giving indication of forthcoming material, but more recent work seems to discount its value. Researchers in the field more and more tend to believe that we see only the word on which we are focused. The image of this narrow pattern of letters is transferred to an iconic short-term memory for further translation.

Now suppose we do the arithmetic. How fast can we read? We can only make about 5 jumps of our eye per second regardless of how we try. This is a physical limit. Between jumps we can only recognize about a dozen letters during the fixations. This again is a physical limit that is not subject to training, contrary to what you may have been led to believe by advertisements for speed reading methods. (It is really quite impossible to run your eye down the center of a page and see all the letters.) Therefore the best we can do is to see approximately 3 words on each fixation, and with 5 fixations per second this gives a maximum reading rate of 900 words per minute. That may surprise you, as it did me when I first encountered this information.

This maximum reading rate of around 900 words per minute is certainly faster than the average college student at about 360 words per minute, but it is not all that much faster. I am sure that many of you want to argue that you read faster than this, or that you know people who do. The reason is simple; you (or they) skip words. The calculation of maximum reading rate is based on the assumption that all words are read. Speed readers simply skip material. In many circumstances there is nothing wrong with this; it is the best manner of efficient information filtering. Think of how fast we read when we simply discard a memorandum based on an uninteresting title! Looked at this way, those strangers beside me on airplanes are reading at infinite rates. They have decided to skip the world's literature.

Of course, there are good practices associated with reading which increase its speed and comprehension. Bad readers regress very often in their points of fixation and often miss the beginnings of lines. Good readers have regressions too, though they are at the 10 to 20 percent level. Typically these regressions are only 2 to 5 character spaces, but occasionally there are regressions to previous sentences or lines. Good readers tend to have fewer fixations per line than poor readers, and to require less time per fixation. Previewing the material to be read and exercising concentration upon the reading task are said to help in raising speed. I tend to read scientific literature fastest when I read for a specific purpose or for certain needed information. On the other hand, reading for general information is difficult, and I tend to lose concentration more easily.

Studies of eye fixations show that skilled adult readers fixate on almost every word. Researchers at Carnegie Mellon University compiling statistics of fixations found that subjects reading *Newsweek* fixated on 83 percent of the content words; for *Reader's Digest* the corresponding figure was 74 percent. (Is there a message there?) The content words are the nouns, adjectives, adverbs, verbs, and pronouns. By contrast the function words, which are the conjunctions, articles, and prepositions, were only fixated 40 percent of the time. There is something interesting going on here. In skimming we consciously skip words, but on a lower level our natural reading process also skips words that our semantic processing system feels that it can do without. The probability of fixating on the word "and" was only .29 in these tests; for "the" it was .40.

The time of fixation perhaps varies according to the semantic difficulty in processing the word. The strongest determinant is the word length. The longer the word, the longer the average fixation. For 3-letter words the average fixation is about 120 milliseconds, while for 6-letter words the fixation intervals are around 300 milliseconds. There is almost a proportionality here indicative of a per-letter processing time. In fact, it has been shown that we are conscious of every letter in a word, as we have little difficulty in spotting spelling errors in the middle letter of a 7-letter word, for example. On the other hand, there are a number of experiments that demonstrate the unity of a word, so the actual word recognition algorithm is in some doubt.

After length, the fixation duration varies most strongly with the frequency of the word. We spend little time on very popular words, more time on less popular words, and as much as 400 to 500 milliseconds on rare words. When we encounter a word we do not know, we pause an extraordinary time—about a second on average—trying to infer its meaning from context, and perhaps constructing a mental dictionary entry analogous to the Lempel–Ziv coding that we discussed in the previous chapter.

Between skipping short words and function words, and generally paying less attention to popular words, we unconsciously act in a scientifically efficient manner. Recall that in the previous chapter we pointed out how so many words were short, informationless words that served only to decrease the effective information content of text. Of course, when we write material, we have no choice but to include these words to satisfy form and esthetics. (People who wrote telegrams in past years formed an interesting exception.) But when we read, we zip past this padding, saving our time for the substantive words.

Years ago I sat with a directory assistance operator as she answered her endless series of requests for telephone numbers. She kept her phone book open to the page containing the most requested numbers, which were the government office listings. Her fingers held other popular positions in the directory. She was ready. Most requests were handled with great alacrity. They had to be, since she was continually timed by supervision. It seems that we do much the same thing in reading. We are ready for the popular interpretations, others may take a while. We may be slow, but we are not dumb!

Word length and frequency account for the majority of the variation in duration of fixation. Other factors that often cause us to tarry on a particular word are when it begins a new topic or ends a sentence. One hypothesis is that we need a certain cognitive interval at the end of a sentence to integrate the information into our existing mental structures. We also tend to lengthen our fixation upon the verb in simple sentences. This is, after all, where the action is. The verb phrase is what holds the sentence together. In the next section of this chapter we will discuss an approach to machine processing of language which relies upon the notion of "frames." The frame is activated by the verb, and is an encompassing notion (in the sense of a picture frame) that wraps together who does what to whom. The other words in the sentence fill in the blanks as to the "who" and "whom." Once we see the verb we have the empty frame in our minds, and we can put the other words into their proper places.

The data on eye fixations give some clues as to how we parse sentence structures. By "parse" we mean the determination of sentence structure, just as most of us have diagrammed sentences in English courses at some time in our past. In the computer world there are a number of approaches to sentence parsing, which differ in their strategies for searching for the correct, or most likely, path through the tree of possible interpretations. The problem is exacerbated in that the words are presented sequentially from left to right, but we may not be able to put them in their proper syntactic places until later words appear. One approach that we might follow in reading would be to hold all the words in short-term memory until the sentence is complete enough to determine its syntactic structure. But we lack the short-term memory capacity for that, so we need to rely on some kind of parse-as-you-go strategy, together with backtracking as necessary in our eye movements.

One experiment that psychologists are fond of using is the so-called "garden path" sentence. This is a sentence that seems to be heading a particular direction, and then having led us down the path towards this expected direction suddenly turns into something else altogether. As an example consider the following sentence: *While Mary was mending, the sock fell off her lap.* In reading this we coast along comfortably thinking that Mary is mending a sock, until abruptly we find that she may not be mending a sock at all. Perhaps she was mending a sweater. We have to reinterpret the sentence. When we reach the surprise twist in the sentence, we naturally pause longer than usual, but we do not search backwards step by step or return to the beginning of the sentence. Apparently, we do the best we can with what we have and then go on. The supposition is that we do a kind of simple, instantaneous parsing, fitting the sentence to its most likely interpretation as we go along. I think of this as somewhat analogous to our actions in playing golf when we lose a ball. The natural instinct is to look first in the fairway, where if we find it we will be in good position. We only look in the rough or the woods when all the more pleasant options are exhausted. When we are reading, we find that the overwhelming majority of sentences are nicely structured. Only when we are being tested by psychologists are we going to encounter many of these garden path sentences. Why carry around a processing burden just to be prepared for such tests?

The simultaneity of eye fixation and cognitive processing has been a matter of some interest. In a computer we would probably fill up an input buffer with the incoming characters, which would subsequently be processed after some time lag. We can experience such a time lag in the situation in which we are reading aloud and the lights suddenly fail. We are good for a few more words before our own buffer is empty. This is because the physical enactment of voicing lags behind the vision and mental processing of the words. But if we are reading silently and the lights fail, do we have any more input available or are we exhausted? The answer seems to be that we do not buffer any of the incoming words. We are where we are, if that makes any sense. As we see a word, we do all the processing associated with that word before we move on. Apparently we plod through the text, word by word, assembling and integrating the information content as it occurs. This is also a convenient working hypothesis for people in reading research, since it means that they can correlate directly their eye fixation measurements with what they believe to be happening at that same moment in their minds.

The mechanical picture of reading painted by the measurements of eye movements is a pleasing scenario to a technologist. I think to myself that if I were designing a computer system to read, I would plan something exactly like this. The system should be prepared for the high probability words and phrases and spend as little time as possible on the highly redundant, or informationless, portions. In any hypothesis testing application there is a deliberate bias towards the events that are more likely a priori. Perception can be viewed as a form of hypothesis testing, in which hypotheses generated on the basis of knowledge and experience are tested against sensory information. Thus this tendency towards the expected in our own cognitive processing is not only unsurprising, but reassuring. We may not be so bad after all.

After the input character shapes are stored in iconic memory a conversion to semantic information takes place, but exactly how this occurs is a matter of some speculation. One theory, called subvocalization, holds that we convert the alphabetic symbols to sounds in our minds and then rely on the same processing that we use in listening to speech. In effect, we read by talking to ourselves and listening to what we have to say. ("How interesting I am," we think to ourselves!) Another theory, termed direct access, postulates that we convert directly from symbols to concepts without going through speech-like recoding of the information. Several other theories are somewhere in between; either we do a partial recoding, or sometimes we sound things out and at other times we do not. Unfortunately, it has been pointed out that these latter theories are uninteresting, since claiming that everything is true at some time or another leaves little room for being disproved.

There are strong arguments against subvocalization. Basically, we read faster than we can talk, so it seems impossible. Nonetheless, there are elements of our understanding of words that have to do with how they sound, rather than how they appear. For example, in proofreading we tend to miss errors that result in pronounceable letter strings, for example, *werk* for *work.* On the other hand, there is evidence that we do not need to go through a vocal recoding. Readers of Chinese and other logographic writing systems do not have a direct sound equivalent of their symbols. When we use logograms in English, such as "$," we do not sound them out to ourselves. Somehow that dollar sign makes direct contact in our mind with the concept it represents. The thought of direct access is appealing. In my mind I see backward readers with their lips moving as they read, but recent results seem to indicate that recoding into sound forms can take place at faster rates than we can physically speak, so perhaps subvocalization is not as bad as I have thought. Although the dual-coding hypothesis is probably the correct one, the matter of how the character shapes are converted to meaningful concepts is still an open question.

So much for the mechanics and cognition in reading. Now can the computer help us read better? For the first time in history the display of words is under instantaneous control. We can produce words and melt them away in the blink of an eye. We could track your eye and change the display accordingly. Interesting possibilities, but so far little as been done. All we do is display the words statically on a screen and expect the user to adapt his reading habits to the upright, glass format of little glowing dots. Studies show that people do not read as well on CRT terminals as they do on paper, at least over periods of several hours. In shorter intervals the reading rates are roughly equivalent.

One approach to electronic reading assistance that is receiving attention is called Rapid Sequential Visual Presentation, or RSVP. (Is there no end to the clever use of acronyms?) In this system the electronics does the scanning for you. You stare at a small window in the CRT screen while the electronics moves the words through this window at the prescribed reading rate. It can force us to read faster, or slower, and it will not allow any regressions or missed lines. I have not experienced it personally, but it sounds relentless.

In RSVP information is presented sequentially, just as in speech, rather than in the usual free-form parallel text format. Comprehension and recall of RSVP reading and speech at 200 words per minute seem to be approximately equivalent. When RSVP is speeded up to 360 words per minute, a normal reading rate for college students, the sensation of RSVP is said to be much like normal reading. There is some evidence that poorer readers actually benefit from the enforced presentation of RSVP, and perhaps a weak indication that good readers may suffer somewhat. As RSVP is speeded up beyond the comfortable reading range to 720 words per minute it still seems possible to read all the words, but as one author put it, "The ideas seem to pass through the mind without being adequately retained." Indeed, comprehension can be seen to diminish at the higher speeds.

RSVP is a relatively new method and still subject to considerable experimentation. It is a straightforward example of what computer technology can do in the field of information display, but there is obviously much more that can be tried. Unfortunately, it does not seem possible to circumvent our cognitive limitations. Though awkward readers may be brought up to normal speeds, it will probably be impossible to increase reading speeds of normal readers. The real secret, as we have said before, is the skipping of material. If the computer knew which words or sections to skip, it could help, but it seems unlikely (but not impossible) that we could derive algorithms for skimming text. The real task of the information age is the selection of which information we take in, or what we think of as information filtering. Like it or not, we humans are the only candidate for an information filter. In this, we get no help.

NATURAL LANGUAGE PROCESSING

After the stock markets closed on a dark and dreary day in mid-January of 1983 a computer at Bell Labs paused to look at its data base of stock quotations. It wrote as follows:

> Wall Street's securities markets rose steadily through most of the morning, before sliding downhill late in the day. The stock market posted a small loss yesterday, with the indexes finishing with mixed results in active trading. The Dow Jones average of 30 industrials surrendered a 16.28 gain at 4 P.M. and declined slightly to finish at 1083.61, off 0.18 points.

This synopsis, I am sure you will agree, sounds very much like what appears in the morning papers as a capsule market summary. Yet it was written entirely by a computer program of a type known as a knowledge-based report generator. As such it exemplifies a dream that many of us share that one day computers will understand English as we do, and converse with us as we do with each other.

Although the computer-generated market summary shows a quick gleam of what might be possible, it is in truth only skin deep. The computer cannot go on to tell us *why* the market was off. (Though I often wonder if the human writers can do this either.) It cannot correlate the performance, for example, with the business news of the day, with a change in prime rate, or the release of economic indicators. It knows nothing of the world but what is in its market quote data base, together with an elementary knowledge of the structure of English and the vocabulary of the sublanguage used in reporting market summaries. It merely (yet this is an understatement) makes a list of "facts" concerning the day's data. For instance, it observes that the market closed at 0.18 lower than the previous day, but that at 4:00 P.M. the index was up by 16.28. It has a number of other "interesting" situations for which it tests.

Having assembled a small list of interesting facts, the program converts the messages to a sequence of sentences in English. In forming the sentences it uses a small (519 entries) dictionary of phrases typically used by humans in writing the market synopsis. For example, it has subject phrases like "Wall Street securities markets" and predicate phrases such as "were swept into a broad and steep decline." The report generator matches these phrases against the messages it wants to convey. The phrases are then combined in a variety of syntactic forms—different clauses forming complex sentences—in order to resemble fluent English. According to one author this resembles the way people generate utterances, which is "mostly by stitching together swatches of text that they have heard before."

Though this simple explanation belies the complexity of such manuevers as "stitching together" phrases, I am also sure that it removes any sense of magic that the ritual incantation of English by a computer might convey to the uninformed. In concept, the idea here is relatively straightforward, and it might be applied in a number of practical situations, such as daily weather reports, weekly sales reports from corporate data bases, or quarterly economic reports based upon government statistics. The stock market report generator does demonstrate, in a way to which most of us can relate, that computers can write English, at least in restricted situations.

What else can computers do in the way of understanding and writing English? We will go through several examples that sample the evolution and state-of-the-art of the field called natural language processing. At present, this is a very active subfield within artificial intelligence. It is populated by linguists, psychologists, and computer scientists. Each of these groups sees the problems of manipulating natural language in light of their own specialization. Roughly speaking (no pun intended), the linguists look to characterize the language itself, without regard to the process by which it is generated. The cognitive psychologists aim to study the use of language, generally by experiments in human timing and comprehension. The approach of the computer scientists is pragmatic. They want to make something that works, which generally means computational efficiency at the sacrifice of generality. We will follow the latter course.

ELIZA

• • • • • •

"The rain in Spain stays mainly on the plain." So repeated Eliza Dolittle in *My Fair Lady* as she worked diligently to perfect her language. She did eventually learn, as we all know, and that was why Joseph Weisenbaum named his English language computer program after her. His program, written at MIT in the early 1960s, also aspired to learn English well enough to converse with an intelligent person. History has probably shown us since that Eliza was a red herring—a technological cul de sac—but it was also a program of philosophical importance, and a great deal of good fun.

Eliza grew out of project MAC at MIT, which pioneered the time-sharing concept of computer usage. Time-sharing has since come and almost gone, but the memory of Eliza lives on in the form of many versions now available for personal computers. Eliza's author, Joseph Weisenbaum, is still a famous professor at MIT who reminds me a bit of Salvador Dali, both in looks and in his impish touch of genius. Weisenbaum constructed Eliza to enable a conversation between a human and a computer. In this he was wildly successful, due in most part to the inspired choice of the scenario of a psychiatrist (the computer) talking to the human patient. As Weisenbaum explains, "This mode of conversation was chosen because the psychiatric interview is one of the few examples of categorized dyadic natural language communication in which one of the participating pair is free to assume the pose of knowing almost nothing of the real world. If, for example, one were to tell a psychiatrist 'I went for a long boat ride' and he responded 'Tell me about boats,' one would not assume that he knew nothing about boats, but that he had some purpose in so directing the subsequent conversation."

A CONVERSATION WITH ELIZA

Men are all alike.

In what way?

They're always bugging us about something or other.

Can you think of a specific example?

Well, my boyfriend made me come here.

Your boyfriend made you come here?

He says I'm depressed much of the time.

I am sorry to hear you are depressed.

It's true. I am unhappy.

You think coming here will help you not to be unhappy?

I need some help. That much seems certain.

What would it mean to you if you got some help?

Perhaps I could learn to get along with my mother.

Tell me more about your family.

My mother takes care of me.

Who else in your family takes care of you?

My father.

Your father?

Stories have been passed down through these years about how people insisted on privacy in dealing with Eliza, and sometimes even refused to believe that they were conversing with a computer. There was brave talk about how Eliza passed the Turing test of a computer capable of thought, in which a person at a terminal cannot tell by a series of questions and answers whether or not he is dealing with a machine or another human. Weisenbaum himself was appalled by this presumption. When asked recently about including Eliza in a Smithsonian Museum exhibit on information he commented that we should not elevate the question of machines thinking to any important status, for it was probably irrelevant, and at least premature.

The problem is, Weisenbaum suggests, that we insist on making inductive leaps that may be unwarranted. For example, if we were given a machine that multiplied every pair of numbers that we put into it, we would certainly presume that it was capable of multiplication. But we would ordinarily assume much more, since we think of multiplication as an advanced skill. We would have a hard time believing that we had exhausted the entire repertoire of the machine. So it is in Eliza. There is something which has come to be known as the "Eliza effect." We assume with an inductive leap of faith that the machine, which acts the role of the psychiatrist, is capable of thought, whereas the truth is that we have completely exhausted its capabilities with only a smidgen of artless conversation.

The principle behind the conversational capabilities of Eliza is a simple pattern-matching algorithm. Never one to trumpet false prophets, Weisenbaum began his 1966 paper on Eliza with the following comment:

> It is said that to explain is to explain away. This maxim is nowhere so well fulfilled as in the area of computer programming, especially in what is called heuristic programming and artificial intelligence. For in those realms machines are made to behave in wondrous ways, often sufficient to dazzle even the most experienced observer. But once a particular program is unmasked, once its inner workings are explained in language sufficiently plain to induce understanding, its magic crumbles away; it stands revealed as a mere collection of procedures, each quite comprehensible. The observer says to himself "I could have written that." With that thought he moves the program in question from the shelf marked "intelligent" to that reserved for curios, fit to be discussed only with people less enlightened than he.

The original Eliza script (equivalent to a program in the LISP computer language) is only a little over 200 lines of code. It contains a number of patterns and key words that the program tries to match against the human input sentences. For each pattern there are a number of responses listed. The first time a pattern occurs the first response is given, the second time, the second, and so on. For example, in the scenario given earlier when the input is "He says I'm depressed much of the time," this is matched against the pattern:

(blah blah) I am (sad unhappy depressed sick) (blah blah).

Where (blah blah) is any set of words, which are considered extraneous. The first response to this pattern is

I am sorry to hear you are (whatever it was).

Then the person replies, "It's true, I am unhappy." This matches the same pattern, so the second response is given, which is

Do you think coming here will help you not to be (whatever it was)?

The principle of pattern-matching is appealingly simple. Make a list of all the sentences or sentence fragments that are expected, and another corresponding list of responses. The problem is that the number of possible sentences is enormous. Eliza evades that difficulty by throwing away almost everything in the input sentences in order to lump together huge numbers of possible variations. In our example all of the "I am" sentences receive the same pattern of responses. If there is no match within a given input sentence, then Eliza uses an innocuous response, like "I am not sure I understand you fully" or "Please go on." Obviously this process trivializes English. Although Eliza exudes a veneer of intelligence, like its namesake it knows nothing more than its paltry list of memorized replies. Eliza is reminiscent of Poe's raven. Somehow the raven too seems intelligent with its refrain of "Nevermore," but Poe emphasizes that "what it utters is its only stock and store." Eliza does not generalize to more meaningful language dialog.

NATURAL LANGUAGE INTERFACES
• • • • • • • • • • •

As we have seen, Eliza is in truth only an ingenious hoax. It pokes fun at artificial intelligence, psychiatrists, and gullible us. We endow it with an undeserved capacity to understand English sentences, but it really has no clue at all. Eliza only appears to understand in that it seems to be responsive to our questions in the restrictive context of the psychiatric interview. After all, what do we mean by "understanding" English sentences? Necessarily we can rely only upon some external manifestation of the computer's internal processes; thus "understanding" is usually equated with the ability to answer questions. In this sense Eliza might be said to "understand," but this is only because of our laxity in accepting a minimal responsiveness in this one type of scenario. The question is whether we can build systems that respond to questions in the English language in real information-gathering dialogs.

There is no doubt whatsoever that we now can construct computer programs that respond to English questions within limited domains. As we shall describe, there have evolved in the last decade a number of programs that act as "front ends" to data base systems, so as to translate enquiries in English into a formal query language that the computer uses to retrieve the desired information from the data base software. If desired, the information so obtained can then be reformulated into English. Even though such systems have been successfully demonstrated, a matter of concern is the size of the domains of application for these systems. How large a subset of the English language will they accept as input, and how much knowledge can their answers encompass? Here we are less sanguine. By restricting the subset of English, and by answering only questions about a narrowly defined data base we can surely make the system responsive. Decades of research will be required to expand these narrow domains.

Having a computer that is able to understand the English language would be enormously important. For a start, such a capability could be used to enable a neophyte user to interact with a computer to obtain information from a data base that otherwise might well be restricted to experts knowledgeable in the query language. However, even experts would usually find English a much more concise way of formulating complex questions than formal computer languages. A single English sentence, such as "Please list the women managers who live in the city and make more than thirty thousand dollars a year," would translate into many error-prone lines of formal statements. English is actually surprisingly compact and versatile. It is also filled with ambiguity, which is what makes the problem of understanding the query deeply complex.

Beyond the application of data base queries, we could imagine using English understanding systems to provide services usually mediated by people. The information age is filled with jobs such as order taking, making reservations, trading stocks, and so forth. Typically a person conducts a dialog with the client to obtain the information needed, and then initiates an automated system that effects the desired transaction. Natural language processing systems would be a key ingredient in augmentation of the clerical labor force for these information-age services.

Another dream inspired by the modest success in natural language processing is automated literature search in response to vaguely worded inquiries. All of life does not consist of precisely framed queries to narrow data bases. Usually we want to ask something like "What do gerbils eat?" or "What questions should I ask before buying a used car?" Answers to these sorts of questions are buried in the library data base and may often be difficult to uncover. At best they require us to do a lot of skimming of extraneous material. If a computer system could be made to understand the intent of our question, and to recognize what the form of a potential answer might be, then it could skim through great amounts of material in our stead. Such a capability might be more than a convenience; conceivably it could amplify that small, but critical skill we occasionally display in which we conjoin previously disparate concepts to create new ideas.

Because natural language processing could be of such great importance to information acquisition and management, it is essential that we come to some understanding of what can and cannot be done in this respect by present and near-future computer systems. Perhaps the best introduction to natural language query systems is to look at some example questions answered successfully by noteworthy prototype systems in recent years.

From STUDENT, 1968, MIT
(able to solve algebra story problems)

- *If the number of customers Tom gets is twice the square of 20 percent of the number of advertisements he runs, and the number of advertisements he runs is 45, what is the number of customers Tom gets?*

- *The sum of the perimeter of a rectangle and the perimeter of a triangle is 24 inches. If the perimeter of the rectangle is twice the perimeter of the triangle, what is the perimeter of the triangle?*

From LUNAR, 1971, Bolt, Beranek, and Newman
(knows about the lunar rock samples from the Apollo missions)

- *What is the average concentration of aluminum in glass?*

- *What documents refer to fayalitic olivine?*

- *Give me those samples.*

From REQUEST, 1976, IBM
(knows about a Fortune-500 data base)

- *Is IBM's headquarters in Armonk?*

- *What was Xerox's rank with respect to growth rate in 1970?*

- *Roughly how many workers were employed by GM in 1969?*

From ROBOT, 1977, Dartmouth
(knows about a personnel data base)

- *How many New Hampshire and Connecticut people are there?*

- *Broken down by state and city, print a salary report for these
people, including their name and age.*

From PLANES, 1978, University of Illinois
(knows about a US Navy aircraft maintenance data base)

- *How many flights did the A7 with tail number 003 make in
January, 1973?*

- *How many flights did it make in Feb. 73?*

- *During April?*

- *In 1973 which A7s had more flights in March than plane 3?*

Notice that all of these questions sound fairly ordinary. They are
neither stilted to favor computer understanding, nor are they
overly complex, cryptic, or ungrammatical, which would work
against computer interpretation. Each of these systems will answer
questions only about the narrow data base indicated. Moreover,
they were all molded about their particular data bases, so that a
great deal of work would be required to remold one of these
systems to a different data base. Partly for this reason, none of these
systems has been more than an experimental demonstration of
natural language understanding by computer. (Although ROBOT
was the forerunner of a commercial system for mainframe data
bases.)

The example questions are composed of a relatively small number of general-purpose, popular words, together with a narrow

vocabulary of more complex words specific to the particular data bases indicated. A typical vocabulary size understood by one of these systems might be on the order of several thousand words. As we have seen in the previous chapter, it does not take a great many different words to encompass typical text segments. Spoken English, which such questions resemble more closely than formal text, uses on average a far smaller vocabulary. Thus the difficulty in natural language understanding by computer does not lie in defining a large number of words. Rather, as we shall discuss, the difficulties lie in the deep, complex structure of natural language, its ambiguities, and the world knowledge assumptions built into even the simplest questions.

The LUNAR system was demonstrated at the Lunar Science Conference in 1971. Using a data base of about 13,000 entries concerning the composition of lunar rock samples, it was exhibited for answering the spontaneous questions of the attending lunar geologists. LUNAR distinguished itself by handling 87 of the 111 requests it faced without error. All of this sounds impressive, and it is probable that many readers will be led (or misled) by the example questions to believe that computers can at last speak English. To a degree, there is a certain truth in this belief, for within the confines of ordinary questions and the narrow bounds of a specific data base, it is likely that natural language systems could prove quite useful in practice. So far there has not been widespread proof of this conjecture, though it has been claimed that real users with a genuine need for the information in the data base have been quite receptive to the experimental systems.

The designer of the LUNAR system, W. Woods, was modest enough to admit that "If a [lunar geologist] really sat down to use the system to do some research he would quickly find himself wanting to say things which are beyond the ability of the current system." Moreover, there is a certain skepticism about any of the published dialogs. As noted by R. Harris in his preamble to the published ROBOT dialog, "Sample dialogs are infamous for misrepresenting programs, because of the author's understandable desire to display the system in its best light, and the reader's tendency to extrapolate the results." This is well said. It is one of those curious human exchanges in which both sides willingly cooperate in their own deception.

Now how do these things work? Although there are substantial variations in approach between the systems (it would never do to use someone else's methods), the general idea is first to look up each word in a computer-based dictionary to identify its type (noun, adjective, verb, etc.), then to do a syntactic analysis of the sentence to determine its structure, e.g., [this noun] does [this verb] to [this object], and finally to do the semantics, which is to associate meanings with the words with respect to the information in the data base. The most difficult part of this procedure is the parsing of the sentence to determine its syntax.

PARSING WITH AUGMENTED TRANSITION NETWORKS

One of the popular approaches to parsing was pioneered by W. Woods in the LUNAR system. This technique fits a sentence to possible syntactic constructions by tracing paths through a map known as an augmented transition network, affectionately known as an ATN. The rules of grammar are represented by the structure of this network and the allowable transitions that can be made between nodes. (This same philosophy is also used in ROBOT and PLANES.) As with most algorithms, it is possible to describe this procedure in an accurate fashion that cannot be understood by a nonspecialist. Sometimes the alternative is to do great injustice to the concept by simplification and analogy with the commonplace. But with only a slight blush, I would like to introduce augmented transition networks by saying that they are very much like the little games, designed to keep young children occupied until the food arrives, that come on placemats in inexpensive restaurants.

A simple augmented transition network is shown in Figure 9. The game is to trace a path from the start to one of the several possible ending points using the word types in the left-to-right sequence in which they occur in the sentence to be parsed.

In tracing a path through the augmented transition network we must follow all the rules associated with each possible branch. (These rules are why the network is said to be "augmented.") If a branch says, "Go directly to jail, do not pass GO, do not collect two hundred dollars," then this is what we must do. But the ATN is not quite this interesting. Instead it says, for example, that to follow a particular branch the next word or sequence of words must

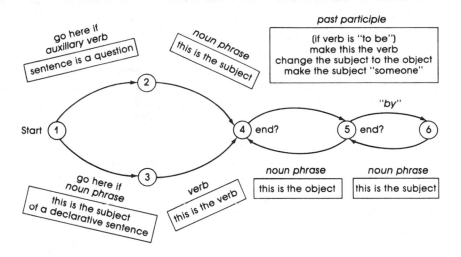

FIGURE 9
A simple augmented transition network

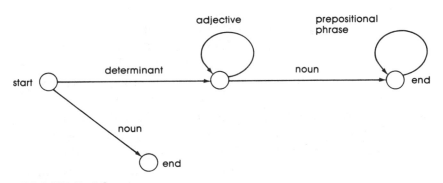

FIGURE 10
A subnetwork for noun phrases

be a noun phrase. In such a case we would have to test whether we can make a noun phrase out of the succeeding words by using a subordinate augmented transition network for noun phrases as shown in Figure 10. In the meantime we must remember where we left the main augmented transition network, because we will come right back to where we were as soon as we either fail or succeed in finding a noun phrase using the subordinate ATN. As we play this game branch by branch we collect little rewards that we store away as we go. Instead of collecting money or other game tokens, we squirrel away little nuggets of information, such as "this sentence is a question," or "the present word is the subject of this sentence."

As an example, we can parse the sentence "The largest customer paid the monthly bill." (This is probably the data-base equivalent of "Run, Spot, run.") This sentence begins with what we find to be the noun phrase "the largest customer." In following branch 2, we set aside the information that the sentence is declarative, and its subject is "customer." Next we find the verb "paid," which takes us along branch 4. The sentence is completed by the noun phrase "the monthly bill" on branch 6, which also rewards us with the object "bill."

After the parsing is complete we see that we have something called a "customer," which commits the action of "to pay" on the object "bill." Each of these words must relate to objects and operations in the data base. "Customer" is further modified by the quantifier "largest," which translates to a mathematical operation on the data base field "customer." Similarly, "monthly" designates a particular subset of the entries in the field corresponding to "bill."

As an exercise, you might try to parse the sentence "Was the monthly bill paid by the largest customer?" In this case we start with an auxillary verb "was," and along the way we discover that the sentence is interrogative and passive. Because it is passive, one of the steps requires us to switch what we thought was the subject to the position of the object. This particular sentence has a close relationship to our original example sentence, "The largest customer paid the monthly bill." These two sentences are said to have a common deep structure, according to the concepts of transformational grammar, conceived and popularized by Noam Chomsky of MIT starting in 1957. That is, both of these sentences can be derived by a set of grammatical transformations from the same basic idea of a particular customer paying a kind of bill. They are differing flavors of the same thought.

Although Chomsky's transformational grammar has been enormously influential in the linguistics field, it has seldom been used in computational algorithms since it is inherently a top-down philosophy of sentence construction—it tells us how to *generate* a variety of similar sentences from a given high-level thought. The natural language processing problem is quite the opposite. Beginning with a collection of low-level tokens (words), we must work our way upward toward the top-level concepts. This is much harder, and all approaches are ad hoc to a greater or lesser extent.

A surprisingly large number of simple sentences can be parsed by the ATN of Figure 9, but it fails on more complex sentence constructions. Practical augmented transition networks tend to get more and more extensive as successive patches are added to take care of a greater number of possible sentence constructions. We should also realize that there is often more than one possible pathway through the ATN for a given sentence. For example, many common words can be either a noun or a verb, or in more complicated networks there may be several allowable branches from a given node to allow for differing grammatical constructions. In these situations the parser may elect to follow only what it feels is the most probable path, or it may follow a multiplicity of possibilities. Depending on what it chooses, the parser may later find itself in a cul de sac where it cannot go forward, forcing it to backtrack to an earlier point and to choose a different alternative path. There are many ways to play this game, and the only real winner is the solution giving the interpretation intended by the human originator. Ultimately, the natural language system can only guess at what the human had in mind. Of course, it could ask, but that is another story!

Augmented transition networks appear to be an appealing way to model language parsing. Possibly they are appealing because they are graphical, and we are accustomed to dealing with alternative routes on road maps. As we have seen, ATNs have been used in fairly extensive working systems, but there are serious difficulties in their application. One such deficiency is the requirement for correct grammar. Unfortunately, people do not always cooperate in phrasing their queries with proper grammar and spelling. We might feel that this is boorish behavior on the part of the person, and that such ungrammatical sentences should be rejected, but that this continued rejection would make a lot of enemies rather quickly. We really should be able to deal with the computer in the same fluent way that we deal with each other. There are many occasions in which the suspension of grammatical constraints is a normal dialogue convention. A computer system should be gracious about this; ATNs are not, as by nature they are fragile and unforgiving.

PARSING WITH CASE FRAMES

A more forgiving approach to natural language processing is the one to which we alluded earlier in this chapter which uses the concept of case frames. Roughly speaking, in the case frame approach the parser looks for the verb in the sentence. Having found the verb, the parser associates a structure, or frame, with the semantics of this particular verb. In effect the parser says to itself that this verb is just not *any* verb, but one which it knows something about, and this semantic knowledge will help it parse the structure of the sentence. The frame it associates with the verb contains empty slots, or cases, for information that usually accompanies this verb. The parser looks to fill in these empty slots with the other words it finds in the sentence or clause. The general structure of a case frame might be as follows:

VERB

case frame

agent: (the active causal agent instigating the action)

object: (the object upon which the action is done)

instrument: (an instrument used to assist in the action)

recipient: (the receiver of an action—often the indirect object)

directive: (the target of an action)

locative: (the location where the action takes place)

benefactive: (the entity on whose behalf the action is taken)

co-agent: (a secondary or assistant active agent)

For any particular head verb all of these associated cases might not be required. Some of them might be optional, some might be required, and some might be forbidden.

In our example sentence the parser would find the verb "paid." The parser would then look up its preformed case frame that puts together the concepts that are usually associated with "pay" in the particular data base. Notice that the frame may be shaped for the semantics of a specialized data base, and that the case frame approach combines both syntax and semantics in its parsing. Contrast this with the ATN, in which the meanings of the words are ignored until the grammatical structure is determined. (It is, of course, possible to modify the ATN so as to incorporate some degree of semantic knowledge.) Another way to look at the case frame philosophy is to observe that it combines bottom-up recognition of individual words and clauses with top-down direction based on semantic knowledge or expectations.

Returning now to our example sentence, the parser has the verb "pay," the associated case frame, and the collection of words it has to somehow fit into the empty slots in the frame. The parser knows that it must fill in the agent slot. It thinks to itself, "There must be an agent around here somewhere. I will look around for some telltale words that give me its position." I can imagine the parser smiling to itself when it finds the preposition "by," for this surely marks the location of the agent. If no positional indicator word or words were found it would assume that the agent was the first phrase in the sentence. Similarly, the object "bill" might be identified by its position. The preposition "to" might mark the location of a recipient, while "with" would indicate the instrument (such as a check, for example), and "at" would mark the locative. Like Sherlock Holmes, the parser would continue to fill in its case frame until all the words in the sentence were exhausted. The information fitted into the cases of the frame would then translate directly to operations on the data base.

It seems intuitive that it is easier to make the case frame approach more tolerant of errors than the ATN. In the augmented transition network the parser is stymied by a single ungrammatical word or construction, whereas in filling in the case frame, the parser can get some sense from the sentence even if it has to guess at missing cases. Frames also serve as a good way to store semantic knowledge to help resolve anaphoric references ("it," "that," etc.) and ellipses, or sentence fragments. For example, if the next sentence is "Was it paid last month?" then the parser can assume the "it" refers to the object in the most recent query. Notice in the sample sentences from PLANES how the system is able to answer the question, "How many flights did it make in Feb. 1973?" The following question, "During April?" demonstrates the ability to handle an ellipsis. To answer this query the system assumes that all slots in the frame are kept intact except those that are expressly overridden, which in this instance are the slots having to do with time.

Everyday English is full of difficulties for a natural language computer system. Spelling errors are very common, as anyone can verify by sampling some of the discussion groups in computer bulletin boards, where convention frowns upon calling attention to misspellings in the postings of other respondents. In addition there are omissions, repetitions, fragmentary expressions, idiomatic expressions, and numerous cases of lack of agreement and other grammatical errors. Frankly, it is a mess, but a mess to which we humans have become well adapted, so we have little trouble ourselves. It just tends to make life miserable for a computer system that tries to take everything a little too literally, because to do otherwise is considerably more difficult.

Anaphora and ellipses seem to be in a different category than these sloppy grammatical errors. They are examples of an interesting acquired ability that we have at the top semantic level to achieve economy of expression. The principle of brevity holds that people will naturally find the most terse way to express a given thought. Thus in typing or talking we take advantage of context, world knowledge, shared experience, and other assumptions to minimize what we have to say in order to communicate. "It" is one of the dozen most popular words. This is most fascinating in light of the search for entropy discussed in the previous chapter. Whereas we might be very careless about bits on the surface level—throwing away many more than are required from an information theoretic viewpoint—we commonly use very powerful high-level constructs that save many paragraphs of elaboration. A computer scientist might argue that the same philosophy is used in writing computer programs in high-level languages like Ada, Pascal, and C, which are then compiled in an arguably sloppy fashion into many assembly language statements.

Just in case all this does not seem difficult enough consider the possibilities for syntactic ambiguity. Winograd constructed a pair of sentences that illustrate the dilemmas which can arise.

The city council refused to grant the women a parade permit because they advocated violence.

The city council refused to grant the women a parade permit because they feared violence.

In the first sentence "they" refers to the women, while in the second the same word refers to the council. Yet the sentences are exactly similar in their construction, with only a small change in the nuance of the verb from "advocated" to "feared." This subtle difference is matched against the world model in our minds and results in a completely different interpretation of the sentence.

It seems to me that one of the most important principles in language is the use of metaphor. There are just not enough words at any given time to describe all of human experience. Metaphors can be used to fill in the cracks between words, and to create new expressions. When we describe a silence as "like the blanket of a heavy snowfall," it draws an analogy from one domain to an entirely different realm, but one that is intensely human. Metaphors also often form the core of idiomatic expressions. If a computer wanted a yes or no answer and you replied, "You hit the nail on the head," what on earth would a rational language processor conclude? (Though a workable approach would be to use pattern-matching against a dictionary of idiomatic phrases.) In following these lines of thought it is very easy to conclude that there are depths upon depths to language, and that it would be entirely unreasonable to expect computers to plumb these depths today, or perhaps ever. As I have said before, I think this is fortunate. There should be some advantages to being human.

DIALOGUES

· · · · · · · · · · ·

By focusing on syntactic and semantic analysis of sentences we have once again ignored the context of discourse in which individual sentences are imbedded. Recall that in Shannon's experiments using human subjects to guess forthcoming letters given a limited past history there was a large difference in entropy—about a factor of 2—between guesses when given 100 previous letters and guesses with only 10. Thus much of the predictability in English is contained in the flow from sentence to sentence. The anaphoric references are only a limited part of this dependency across sentences. As an aspiring author I am painfully conscious of the burden of maintaining flow between sentences, between paragraphs, and even between chapters. I feel as though I cannot say things the way that I want because of these constraints. If it is this hard to choose words that maintain flow, then there must be a great deal of language structure that evolves in a complex, extragrammatical fashion.

A dialogue is a special sort of discourse in which participants alternate short speeches or writings. In a dialogue there is a flow also, but it is shared by the two participants, and this interplay results in a different kind of superstructure than does writing such as this. In a dialogue we share a focus, which shifts gradually, much as the flow of topics in this book. It is extraordinarily disconcerting to carry on a conversation with someone who will not focus on a single topic for a comfortable interval. The overarching presence of this focus helps promote an economy in expression, as we can use anaphoric references and allude to previous arguments and shared experiences. Although we have an unspoken agreement at any given time about the focus of the conversation, we usually differ in the goals to which we aspire in the conversation. In striving to attain our own particular goals we base the strategy of our statements upon the models we maintain of our partner's knowledge and beliefs.

In a human dialogue we often follow an information-minimizing script. If I tell you about a trip to my dentist, I do not need to go through the details step by step. I assume that you have done something entirely similar, and that you know the time sequence of events. I only have to tell you what was different or unusual about this particular trip. Or perhaps I only tell you the outcome, and you can infer every miserable thing that I went through. Perhaps you even wince just recreating the reconstructed events in your own mind. If I tell you about a baseball game I saw last night, and you are an American male, I will assume that you know all the rules and conventions of the sport and probably the current state of the pennant races. A little bit of additional information, like a tiny pinch of seasoning, will go a long way.

The dialogue form is especially important in the human-computer interaction. There is usually one of us and one of it. We are very proficient in dialogue with other humans. We get a lot of practice. In spite of misunderstandings, poor enunciation, and chopped up nonsentences, we usually accomplish the desired information transfer. Computers in their present state know very little of the polite conventions of dialogue. Even though they may process individual sentences, and even untangle anaphoric references, they cannot yet add the superstructure of ordinary dialogue. Fortunately we are very tolerant of this defect, since they are only computers and our expectations are minimal.

Now assume for a moment that you are a computer system whose job is to accept airline reservations. Even though humans do this now for a living, perhaps it seems like a well-circumscribed task for a computer. There is only certain information that you need to extract from this human in order to be able to complete the reservation. You might conveniently choose to represent this information as a frame, with slots for the name of the customer, his address, times of flights, destinations, etc. These slots might be complex enough that they themselves require subframes with their own sets of slots. As a reservation clerk you are responsible for filling in these slots. Once they are filled the mechanization of the order becomes a straightforward task. In order to fill these slots you engage in a dialogue with the human. If you were a human, you would be afraid, but you are only a computer and have no fear.

You assume that the focus of the conversation will be on making an airline reservation. If the customer wants to talk about something else you are in big trouble, because your entire knowledge base, your whole world, is that airline flight guide. There is what Feigenbaum has termed a "knowledge cliff" just outside that guide. If the topic strays over that cliff, you are lost. Your goal is gently and persuasively to use the dialogue mechanism to keep the human walking along the edge of that knowledge cliff, and to steer him along your subgoals of filling in the blanks of the frame. If he says he wants to go to Chicago because his sister is getting married there, you have to be clever enough to know that it does not matter to you about sisters and getting married, but Chicago is important. If after choosing a flight he asks, "Was that wise?" you have to politely steer him back to methods of payment or whatever, while you worry in the background about what you are missing. You cannot keep repeating inane things like "does not compute" or no one will deal with you. You will get fired, and they will bring the human back. They may even pull your plug.

In spite of these awesome difficulties there is one thing that you have going for you. You yourself can be very sloppy in your own English. After all, there is a human out there to interpret. They are good.

REFLECTIONS — THE FRIENDLY INTERFACE

I am amused by trying to put myself in the place of a computer that knows nothing, yet has to deal with these unreasonable people. Usually I look at the interface from the other side, and I feel that the computer is the unreasonable one. When I wrote the following column, I had heard so much about "friendly" interfaces that I began to wonder. Just how friendly are these interfaces anyway?

I was recently quoted in an ad as saying "For a long time we've been trying to make people more like computers, it's time we made computers more like people." Where do I get off saying dumb things like that? Secretly I feel that machines should be taught their place, and not be led on to get all uppity and begin to feel that they are people.

The friendly interface is a concept that is very in right now. A good man-machine interface should go out of its way to incorporate speech recognition and pattern recognition. It should have a limited and simple set of commands, and should always be careful to convey humble messages, giving the impression of being an obedient servant. This is, of course, the machine part of the interface. The man should properly assume an attitude of arrogance and infallibility.

As in any marriage, there are occasional problems in the friendly interface concept. Last month there was a story that a computer service bureau got a call from a police station with a dead computer terminal. When the serviceperson arrived later, the terminal was indeed dead. Standing over the smoking terminal was a cop with a smoking gun. There were two bullet holes in the terminal. In a similar vein, I cheered when I read last year about a man in California who was arrested for shooting his lawn mower. After a great deal of frustration when it wouldn't start he went into his house and came back with a shotgun. He let the lawn mower have a full blast. I know just how he felt. Score: Men 2, Machines 0.

In contrast to these unfortunate interface failures, I feel that I have the perfect model for an interface in my home already. It is my dog Muffy. Muffy has all the attributes I listed earlier. In addition he is energy efficient and requires no logon. He gratefully accepts all inputs. When something doesn't compute, he responds with his one error message—he looks, well, quizzical. Knowing that I cannot err, Muffy realizes from his lowly position that he has failed to understand properly my command. The essential difference between Muffy and my home computer is that when I look into the former's moist brown eyes it is plainly apparent to me that there is someone inside. Until recently I had felt that there was no one home inside my computer. My computer, so to speak, was not playing with a full deck. Its elevator didn't go all the way to the top. When Muffy sleeps, every now and then his tail swishes back and forth, and I know that some happy memory is flooding through his little dog mind. But in the dark I watch the status lamps on my idle computer while they flash as though engaging in some demonic pinball game. I think of all my precious files stored in its perishable memory, and I worry about what malevolent plots it is conjuring against me during its silicon dreams.

Now I'm beginning to change my mind about machine intelligence, and I have this fear that they're changing their minds about human intelligence or at least about mine. Several years ago during a busy day as I went for a coffee break I passed a new computer chess prototype. I couldn't resist the offer to try my hand against the machine. It wasn't very far into the game before I realized that I was outclassed. I agonized over my moves, conscious of the scrutiny of a number of bystanders. Meanwhile the machine was conserving its total time allocation by moving instantly in response to my pitiful agonies. I was having a hard time assuming the proper attitude of arrogance and infallibility. About the time when I realized that there was no dignified way out of this debacle, the program's author whispered some advice to me, suggesting a move which sacrificed a bishop to no apparent advantage. I jumped on this opportunity to reassign the blame for my inevitable defeat. "Have a bishop," I said loudly to the computer. After it had gobbled my bishop with nary a thank you, or even a burp, my advisor suggested that I now gorge the computer with a free rook. "Have a rook," I said. A few milliseconds after my rook had been zapped, I realized that thanks to my brilliant moves I had created a situation in which I had a two-move, forced mate.

I sat back and smirked at the machine, really getting into the arrogance and infallibility bit. The machine wouldn't move. It just sat there. "Take your time," I said, "Think it over." I sipped my coffee. The bystanders left. I finished my coffee. Nothing came out of the machine. "Whenever you're ready to concede," I said, remaining the epitome of patience. After 45 minutes the machine interposed its queen—a useless sacrifice only postponing the inevitable denouement. With the grace and aplomb that only a human can project, I accepted the queen. The machine stubbornly waited, using up its total time allocation before it would acknowledge

defeat. "How machine-like," I thought. A person would have congratulated me long ago. I was lost in my reveries when my secretary finally
found me. "Everybody is after you," she panted. "What on earth have you
been doing?" "Well . . .", I started to explain, more to myself than her. I
mean, how could I explain that I had been waiting over an hour just to
humiliate a computer when everyone in the world could see that the
game was already won? Is this a friendly interface?

Since that time some of that machine's friends (other machines, of
course, since they have this annoying habit of sticking to their own) have
been treating me with increasing disrespect. My home computer, Brutus,
doesn't seem to appreciate the fact that I take care of it, that the warm
roof over its head and its daily quota of electrical power are only because
of my hard work. Instead of politely pointing out minor mistakes, my computer has taken to curt responses such as "bad syntax," or, worse, "bs
error." Recently when it gave an error message to what I felt was a perfectly reasonable command, I retyped the line to see if it had got it right.
"That's twice," warned the printout.

I had of course been aware for some time that my computer did not
have a high opinion of me. When I would do really dumb things (depress-
ingly often) I would look around nervously and listen closely for the telltale
chunk and buzz of a disk access being used to archive my indiscretion. I
began to feel that the computer was keeping a file to use against me. The
other night I went down in the basement to use the computer at an
unexpected hour, and I'm sure I saw the light flashing out on the CRT as
I came in. I suspect that the computer had been working on itself, so to
speak. Tonight I plan to sneak up on it and catch it by surprise.

I know there are a lot of people who think we should win machines over
with friendliness, but I say we should tough this out. Let them know who's
boss. A little discipline would go a long way with these things. I mean, have
they gone out of their way to be friendly with us? If we don't meet them
on the beaches now, we may be sorry later. The friendly interface? Bah,
humbug!

5

S P E E C H

• • • • • • • •

Sunday, June 25, 1876, was a fateful day in history. The most memorable event was taking place near the Little Big Horn River in Montana, where General George Custer was discovering that it was going to be a very bad day. At the same time, in civilized Philadelphia, a young schoolteacher named Alexander Graham Bell was beginning the first public demonstration of his Telephone to a panel of learned judges at the Centennial Exposition. As he began speaking the Hamlet soliloquy into the transmitter, Emperor Dom Pedro II of Brazil heard the words "To be or not to be" at his nearby receiver. "My God, it speaks!" he cried in Portuguese. The arresting part of this quote is the word "it." Machines are not supposed to talk. While we have always been comfortable with machines producing text (at least since the invention of the printing press), speech seems in contrast to be the natural province of humans.

A century of experience with talking machines since Bell's demonstration has not cured our ambivalence about machines that talk. The telephone itself at least has a human at the other end. Nonetheless, it has taken the better part of this last century for us to learn how to use it easily and efficiently. In 1877 an advertisement for the telephone proclaimed the following:

> The proprietors of the Telephone are now prepared to furnish Telephones for the transmission of articulate speech

through instruments not more than twenty miles apart. Conversation can easily be carried on after slight practice and with occasional repetition of a word or sentence. On first listening to the Telephone, though the sound is perfectly audible, the articulation seems to be indistinct; but after a few trials the ear becomes accustomed to the peculiar sound.

Some hint of the difficulty that early users were experiencing is contained in the following instructions from another telephone advertisement.

After speaking transfer the Telephone from the mouth to the ear very promptly. When replying to communication from another, do not speak too promptly. Much trouble is caused from both parties speaking at the same time. When you are not speaking, you should be listening.

It is reported that users of the telephone suffered from a stage fright that made them tongue-tied. Even the simplest conversation was a major undertaking fraught with physical and psychological difficulties. This seems humorous now, but I have noticed that people from the older generation do not always seem to know how to conduct telephone conversations. I myself can certainly remember when the very words "long distance calling" were an ominous harbinger of fortune and tragedy, pressing upon the recipient the necessity for a heavy formality worthy of the occasion.

When a machine originates speech on its own, instead of merely transmitting the speech of another human talker, the implications are more disturbing. Most of us have only begun to encounter computer-synthesized speech in the last few years. Hopefully it will not take us as long to become accustomed to dealing with speaking machines as it did for us to gain our everyday ease and efficiency in the usage of the telephone. This recent emergence of synthesized speech is attributable to the discovery of efficient mathematical algorithms that are suitable for this purpose, and to the new availability of integrated circuits designed specifically to implement these algorithms. Simply stated, now is the time that the machines of the world are finding their voices. We wait expectantly to hear what they will have to say.

The history of synthesized speech is entertaining and even

mildly illuminating. In 1779 the Imperial Academy of St. Petersburg offered a prize to whoever could build a machine that could speak the vowels *a, e, i, o, u.* This prize was claimed by a Christian Gottlieb Kratzenstein, who constructed a pipe-organ-like set of five variously shaped resonators that could sound the vowels when activated by air blowing through a vibrating reed (as in the clarinet). Other inventors in subsequent years built similar wind-instrument approximations of the human vocal tract. Alexander Graham Bell himself, prior to his invention of the telephone, constructed a facsimile of the human skull with a working tongue and a controllable vocal tract. Bell claimed that his model could produce a "few simple utterances," but who knows? Perhaps if he had continued this work his fame today might have equaled that of Christian Kratzenstein.

The drawings of mechanical speech inventions appear somewhat ludicrous. The idea of a human as a walking pipe organ brings to mind the hilarious old movies of aircraft that tried to fly by flapping wings. Modeling nature is not always a good way to design machines intended to reproduce natural behavior. Nonetheless, speech synthesis has been the exception, and today's best synthesis systems have been motivated by study of the human vocal system. Instead of bellows and pipes they have their electronic equivalents in noise and tone generators and variable electrical filters.

The public was introduced to speech synthesis at the 1939 World's Fair in New York, where the Bell System exhibit featured the giant speaking machine, called the Voder, shown in Figure 11. ("Voder" sounds like something from *Star Wars,* but it merely stands for "Voice Operation Demonstrator.") The Voder was the ingenious invention of Homer Dudley, who conceived of the idea of using electrical networks with resonances similar to those of speech. Dudley's Voder used ten electrical filters, each of which could adjust the amplitude of sound within a given narrow frequency band, just as today's high fidelity audio systems use graphic equalizers for customization of audio response. An operator played the Voder through a keyboard in such a way as to produce speech-like sounds. In a sense, the Voder was an electronic organ, but instead of producing pure tones the Voder produced tone-like noises that could be strung together to emulate speech.

The Voder was quite difficult to play, and it took skilled operators more than a year to learn to produce speech. Nevertheless, the

FIGURE 11
The Voder display at the 1939 New York World's Fair

Voder was much more than a stunt. It has influenced speech synthesis to this day, and people at Bell Labs still refer to it with the kind
of reverence given to legendary sagas. For those in the public who
attended the World's Fair the Voder must have been a memorable
experience. Imagine being talked to (or *at*) by that awesome ma-

chine when you had never heard artificial speech before! Today we might even fear that this ominous-looking machine would breathe loudly between sentences. It would be scary.

My own first experience with synthesized speech was in 1967 when I received a copy of the journal *Bell Laboratories Record*, which contained a plastic phonograph record with segments of computer-generated speech. I rushed home to play the record, and I was particularly taken with a segment in which the computer sang "Daisy, Daisy, give me your answer, do," using a too-perfect computerized pitch. I played the record for many of my friends, but I doubt their enthusiasm for the performance came up to my expectations. Did they realize the implications of a speaking computer? Did I? In any event, it was only a few years later when this same segment became a centerpiece in a celebrated movie by Stanley Kubrick. As you read this dialogue, think of the relative impact and nuance when the computer gives voice to its words, as opposed to if the words had instead been merely displayed as text on a terminal display.

Conversations between the Astronaut Bowman
and the Computer Hal

From the movie *2001*

"Hal, I am in control of this ship. I order you to release the manual hibernation control."

"I'm sorry, Dave, but in accordance with special subroutine C one-four-three-five dash four, quote, When the crew are dead or incapacitated, the onboard computer must assume control, unquote. I must, therefore, overrule your authority, since you are not in any condition to exercise it intelligently."

(as Bowman pulls out Hal's circuit boards)

"Dave," said Hal, "I don't understand why you're doing this to me . . . I have the greatest enthusiasm for the mission . . . You are destroying my mind . . . The reciprocal of three is zero point three three three three . . . I seem to be having some difficulty—my first instructor was Dr. Chandra. He taught me to sing a song, it goes like this, 'Daisy, Daisy, give me your answer, do. I'm half crazy all for the love of you.'"

Bowman could bear no more. He jerked out the last unit, and Hal was silent forever.

S P E E C H   A N D   I N F O R M A T I O N

When I was an impressionable youth, television had not yet become commonplace. I watched the orange, glowing filaments of the tubes in my radio and imagined that the originators of the disembodied voices to which I paid such rapt attention had been imprisoned within these metallic fires. On one of the radio shows some inventor had perfected a machine that could eavesdrop on any voice from the past by suitable tuning of time and location dials. Confronted with the miracle of radio itself this was easy enough to believe. The theory was that all of those voices were still out there circulating in space; only they were infinitesimally small and required a great deal of amplification to resurrect. Is this not almost plausible?

The idea that all the words ever spoken are still out there somewhere appeals to me vividly. I play out the fantasy of tuning in on historic conversations and discovering what *really* happened in the branching points of history. But then I think of the sea of verbal refuse in which these nuggets swim, and I am returned to reality and to the balanced weaknesses and strengths of speech as a form of information. The thought of recovering by-gone speech is antithetical to our whole concept of speech as a transient, even evanescent, format. On this day, as in many past such days, I have been under the constant bombardment of speech waves. These waves have had their effect on the evolution of physical and logical structure in my brain. Having left their chemical imprint, they have gone into the nothingness that passes for speech heaven. As I survey the stacks of never-to-be-read memoranda on my desk, I think perhaps the world may be a better place for the passing of most information. There is something to be said for transience.

When we wish to communicate a piece of information to another person, we generally have a choice of formats. The telephone is ubiquitous and convenient; we need only reach out our hand. To speak face-to-face, on the other hand, may be inconvenient even if the other person is only a few rooms away. Besides, the social compulsion in a telephone conversation is not as strong as in face-to-face; thus the dialogue necessary to impart the information can be more efficient, without the need for ancillary small talk to satisfy convention (87 percent of telephone conversations are less than ten minutes in duration, but only 19 percent of face-to-face contacts are). This convenience and efficiency make the telephone the first choice in most business circumstances. However, depending upon the nature of the information we may feel uneasy about the transience of speech. Often we feel that a written record must endure, or we may believe that a certain formality is necessary which can only be achieved through text. It is sometimes said that these were the reasons that William Orton, the president of Western Union Telegraph Company, turned down Alexander Graham Bell's offer of his telephone patent for $100,000 in 1876. Who would ever want to depend upon a mere verbal conversation to conduct a business transaction?

When compared with text, voice conversation has the extraordinary advantage of being fully interactive. I would guess that a majority of everyday information transactions require some interaction with the other party. Perhaps in only a third of the cases will a simple one-way message accomplish the goals of both parties in the transaction. The interaction enabled by a simple telephone call can cut through what might be weeks or months of memoranda, notes, and letters. Unfortunately, the only way this interaction can occur is if the other party is as handy to his telephone as we are to ours, and surveys show that only about one quarter of the time does a business call reach its intended recipient. The telephone tag that results from successive back and forth messages to call so-and-so is one of most frustrating aspects of business life today.

When I have a need to obtain or exchange information with a busy person, I am immediately depressed by the impossibility of actually talking to that person on the telephone. One of the great advantages of corporate rank or fame is the power to compel the returning of telephone calls. Thus people at the top are able to communicate information effectively, while people at the bottom are on the wrong side of the telephone power balance, where their calls are unlikely to be returned. A new service known as call screening threatens to amplify this discrepancy. In call screening the calling party may be identified at the receiving terminal before the called party decides whether or not to answer. This may help destroy the most interesting aspect of telephony, in which we experience a compulsion to answer a call in spite of the anonymity of the caller. After all, the call may be to tell us that we have won the lottery!

One of the trends in communications technology today is toward what is known as personal communication, or the ability to reach anyone, anywhere. But as a communications technologist whose job it is to better communication, whatever that means, I am often struck by the duality of the access problem. I want to be able to reach other people whenever I wish, but I do not want other people to reach *me* whenever *they* wish. I fear there is no technological solution to this dilemma, so in spite of mobile telephones in cars, airplanes, and briefcases, I believe that business communication will have to endure without our ever being sure that we will be able to engage in a personal, interactive conversation at the time that such exchange is actually needed.

Because people are not available to speak to us when needed, we are pushed to less interactive means using intermediaries. A good secretary can serve as a communications surrogate, enabling a reasonable percentage of transactions to occur over a day's time, providing that negotiation, pleading, or extended messages capable of being garbled are not involved. Telephone answering machines have the advantage of verbatim transcription, but are strictly noninteractive, and are seldom used really effectively. Electronic mail, by distinction, has its own nuances and attributes. It is quicker than post office mail, leaves a text message in a volatile electronic format, and permits a slow form of interaction. Additionally, electronic mail has been acquiring its own social convention whereby, for example, it is easier in this format than in any other to approach important strangers or corporate officials.

Though speech can be very effective in obtaining selective information through an interactive dialogue, when we seek to acquire information in quantity, then voice transactions are generally much less efficient than reading text. The ability to roam freely through the text, skipping gobs of material and then concentrating on the difficult or high-value portions, has no equivalent in speech, which is by nature slow and serial. Dense material, such as that contained in legal documents or scientific papers, can seldom be assimilated in voice format. On the other hand, it is surprising how fast this material can be read from text. In most cases the reader is already familiar with the general field and only needs to identify the new information in the document. Equations go by the eyes in the space of a blink. They just "look" familiar. Other parts have the nature of an obligatory recital of a catechism. In the midst of all this, something leaps out as different and unfamiliar. It is almost a question of pattern recognition rather than content analysis. Just think of how impossible this would be in listening to the same document being read.

Midway between the typical information transactions of the telephone and the mass input of information from a text document is the briefing, or prepared speech. In the last decade or so almost all such presentations have included audio-visual aids—usually in the form of transparencies. For the most part these transparencies merely serve to underline particular words and phrases that are being said in the speech itself. However, this emphasis goes much further than would be possible in voice alone. For one thing the alternative medium of vision differentiates the material very effectively. Moreover, the visual augmentation serves to illuminate the structure or organization of the material, inasmuch as we can see spatial relationships, while speech has only the time dimension. Probably most importantly, the visual presentation holds a modest amount of information temporarily for our perusal which we would be unable to store in our own very limited short-term memory. Thus in computer terminology we might think of the slide as a peripheral to our human memory system.

Speech and text complement each other quite well in an audio-visual presentation. I often muse on the apparent discrepancy between the typical rate of speaking and our speed of thinking. We seem to have a lot of thinking power left over while we listen. This excess capacity lets us daydream and mentally wander about while still keeping up with the talk. I picture having an imaginary attention readout dial in my head, which might ordinarily hover at about 40 percent or so, depending on the information density of the particular talk. Then it dips down to 10 percent for a short time, and I suddenly find that I no longer know what the speaker has been saying. On the other hand, I am very uncomfortable if I have to raise this attention factor to 80 percent or more, as for example when listening to compressed (speeded up) speech. It is probably just an acquired lazy habit, but I feel somehow that I am entitled to about 50 percent of my total available mental time for my own purposes. In any event, transparencies that accompany a talk can eat into this unused mental processing capacity, and often I find that I have been reading instead of listening. As I tune back in, I usually find that the speaker is simply reading the charts to me, since he does not know what else to do with them. I do not know either.

Text and speech can also be combined in formats other than the familiar view graph presentation or briefing. A recent concept is hypertext, which is a generalization of a text-only document in which motion-video and speech might appear whenever and wherever they might be appropriate. In hypertext, footnotes would zoom into extended discourse if desired, and references would automatically appear on line. At various points in the text we could ask for amplification. Instead of frozen text, we might think of hypertext as a program enveloping the subject information, capable of being invoked in an individual way by each user. If this book were hypertext, for instance, I would be able to make much use of speech in this chapter to illustrate the qualities of various speech technologies. In fact, I have always envied researchers in speech technology the possibilities for demonstration of their work which are so easily exhibited through tape recordings during their talks. On the other hand, the technical papers they write for journals leave much to be desired. They have no way of displaying their wares on paper. (Sometimes plastic phonograph records are included with their magazines.) Although the idea of hypertext that includes sound is greatly appealing, the actual implementation, and ongoing maintenance, of such complicated formats is very costly. I do not expect to see much of multimedia hypertext over the lifetime of this book.

Unlike text capture, which requires fluency in typing dexterity, speech can be captured essentially exactly by electronic recording. As long as the aim is to re-create the voice itself, the process is trivial by today's standards. If, however, the aim is to convert the speech into text, then the task is anything but straightforward. Even when there is a human intermediary—for example, a stenographer—it takes considerable skill on the part of both the person giving as well as the person taking the dictation to produce a reasonable document. I am always impressed by people who are capable of dictating flawless letters and memoranda, since for myself the inability to "see" the exact wording in previous sentences imposes a second-rate quality on my dictation. However, there are people who almost talk in the same language as they write; who can stand on a moment's notice and create voice documents in the sound waves emanating from their mouths.

Although being able to speak in beautiful prose is a gift that few have, the rest of us should not despair, for it is seldom the case that a good speech reads like good text. The two formats are essentially different—text is not necessarily fossilized speech. On a number of occasions I have had the experience of reading verbatim transcripts of my speeches. I can assure you that they are dreadful, and when I have to edit them to produce a text version I fall into a hopeless depression. Yet in some cases I *know,* I tell myself, that these were first-rate speeches and that I communicated effectively with the audience. Alas, there is no written evidence of that communication. The transcript shows all the fragmentary word phrases posing as sentences, the rudimentary grammar, the "ahs" and "ers," the hyperactive switching of thoughts in the middle of sentences, and the apparent disorganization. On the other hand, many of the most boring talks I have ever heard were read verbatim from perfect text.

Even the vocabulary in ordinary speech differs from that used in text. One glaring example is that all-important word "I." The frequency of its use in this book, .006, is fairly consistent with its use in popular writing, though far above its usual nonappearance in scientific literature. In telephone conversations, however, "I" becomes the most popular word, with a relative frequency of .05. Moreover, on the telephone the size of our vocabulary shrinks rather dramatically. We overuse the popular words, and eschew the more obscure words almost completely. I would never use the word "eschew" on the telephone; people would get the wrong idea. Again, I do not think this is bad. The English language allows us a great freedom to express ourselves in alternative wordings. The culture of speech allows us wide latitude in grammar and organization, while removing some of the variety of which the language is capable. Because of this relative freedom of expression it is much easier to talk than to write. Writing a book like this is hard work for me.

Text itself even assumes a different guise when it is read orally. For some years I had a long commute in my car, which I endured by listening to books read on audio tape cassettes. I went through perhaps a hundred books by listening to them in this way. My memory of those books is of a different character than the ones which I have read as text. I have experienced the books on tape only as interpreted through the eyes, minds, and voices of other people. I am not quite capable of remaking them as I might have interpreted them for myself if I had read the books as texts, that is, as I might have vocalized them to myself in my mind. I have audio memories of them, and it is another person's audio. They are not mine.

How would this book be different if it were in speech instead of text? The information contained in the speech would duplicate that in the text that you are now reading. But there would be something more. There would be a message on top of the words, the nuance of my voice conveying an additional level of meaning, acting to selectively stress, color, and flavor the bare words themselves. Hearing my voice you would feel intuitively that you had understood me and my intentions better. This voice-layer information would be hard to quantify in terms of value, for people often use their voices not only to augment, stress, and intensify, but sometimes even to mislead and to call attention away from the failures in logic of the words alone. An extreme example was Hitler, whose voice helped mesmerize a nation. We cannot deny that there is some extra value in hearing the words spoken, as opposed to reading the text, but one of the deepest mysteries of the theory of information is the astonishing amount of information, that is, the number of bits that is required to convey this intangible, human message. We shall discuss this in the next chapter.

In summary, when compared with text, speech is somewhat slower and serial, but it is ubiquitous, interactive, and easy to capture electronically. We cannot "browse" through speech, and our limited short-term memory imposes a small, sliding window through which we "see" with clarity only the most recent spoken words. Speech also has a perceived transience, but this very transience contributes to a sense of grammatical freedom which opens up the communications channel. Above all, speech has a humanity; hearing the spoken words allows us to "see" the person behind the words in a way that the written words would never permit. It is this humanity that will occupy our discussion at various points in this and the following chapter as we plow ahead with descriptions of the technology of speech coding, synthesis, and recognition.

A P P L I C A T I O N S   O F
S P E E C H   T E C H N O L O G Y

About a decade ago the problems and possibilities of applying computer technology to office automation began to fascinate a lot of us technologists. For the first time we could build small, inexpensive computer terminals and put them on the desks of office workers. At Bell Labs we built a combination telephone and computer terminal that fit within an ordinary telephone housing. It had a little CRT display, a compact keyboard, and a telephone handset. It was cute, lovable, and made a terrific status symbol for a desk. Everybody wanted one. We dreamed of unlimited applications for information systems in the office workplace using these beautiful new terminals.

As the wise reader might guess, practically none of this worked out. It was clear at the beginning that not everyone could have this expensive terminal. Thus a subset of employees was selected at random to participate in a trial system. This random subset was chosen to be the top layer of corporate management. (What else did you expect?) In this environment the little terminal faced insurmountable obstacles to acceptance. We quickly verified the common knowledge of that day that *executives did not type.* Whether this was because they did not know how or because typing was unseemly became the subject of considerable argument, but perhaps it was irrelevant. More important was the observation that any executive powerful enough to command a prestigious experimental terminal also had one or more capable human assistants. When he, or she, wanted information it was simply acquired. He asked; he received. She asked; she received. The lonely little terminals only gathered dust.

As we reclaimed our unused terminals we murmured to ourselves about the need for voice-based machines in the office. No one with power or money would touch a keyboard. The little terminals would never sell. Voice was the key to everything. It was a shame that voice technology had so little capability and was so expensive, for it was clear that voice was the only way to communicate information with busy, important people.

Of course the world has changed this last decade. Speech technology, at least as output and to a lesser degree as input, has become a reality. Perhaps more than any other event, the introduction by Texas Instruments of a toy called "Speak-and-Spell" called the attention of the engineering world to synthetic speech. For less than $50 children could be given a toy that used synthesized speech to teach spelling in an entertaining way. I have no idea whether or not children thought that this was a big deal, but we engineers were electrified by what had happened. There is nothing like turning an esoteric technical concept into a best-selling toy to prove that a technology has arrived.

The office environment has changed too. Many of the executives who did not type have retired and have been replaced by younger people who have grown up with terminals. I think it is quite possible that in the near future, if not today, executives will be comfortable with keyboard input and video display. But they will also have a choice of voice input and output. The question will not be whether or not machines should speak, but rather when they should speak and what they should say.

Meanwhile my limited personal experiences with speech technology have warned me that speech may not be the panacea that I once thought. I tried talking to a voice-actuated editor. "Cursor left," I said slowly to it. I had to shut the door to my office. I was embarrassed to be talking to a machine. I also gave machines a chance to talk to me. Sometimes it seemed appropriate, sometimes not. I could not agree with the author of a recent technical article who predicted that "people will talk to computers, typewriters, toys, TV sets, household appliances, automobile controls, door locks, and wristwatches." Really? Do you *want* to talk to your wristwatch? Try it now and see how it feels.

A more cautionary assessment of speech technology was made by a respected worker in the field, who commented that machines will "begin by talking too much." Indeed, talking elevators and cash registers have not been universally accepted, and quite a few automobile owners have ripped out the electronic throats of their nagging, artificial voices. For myself, a synthesized voice leaves a metallic taste in my mouth. One of my friends volunteered the wisdom that nothing should speak unless it was willing to listen. Not many of these machines care what we humans have to say.

There are several difficulties in the perception of even today's best synthesized speech. One is the monotony in hearing a phrase repeated exactly the same way time after time. The mechanical voice that automatically greets people when the grocery store door is opened may be perfectly acceptable to the entering customer, but pity the poor clerk who works near the door and hears this endless refrain. In addition to monotony, I have a psychological difficulty with what I perceive as an emptiness of intelligence behind the voice. I find a parallel here in the appreciation of computer-composed music. In *The Mind's I,* Douglas Hofstadter decries the idea of a mechanical box mass-producing from its "sterile circuitry" pieces that Chopin or Bach might have written. Hofstadter argues that only a human has had the profoundly emotional experiences from which music should spring.

> A "program" which could produce music as they did would have to wander around the world on its own, fighting its way through the maze of life and feeling every moment of it. It would have to understand the joy and loneliness of a chilly night wind, the longing for a cherished hand, the inaccessibility of a distant town, the heartbreak and regeneration after a human death. It would have to have known resignation and world-weariness, grief and despair, determination and victory, piety and awe. In it would have had to commingle such opposites as hope and fear, anguish and jubilation, serenity and suspense. Part and parcel of it would have to be a sense of grace, humor, rhythm, a sense of the unexpected—and of course an exquisite awareness of the magic of fresh creation. Therein, and therein only, lie the sources of meaning in music.

Perhaps some of the same arguments could be made about programs that speak. But I wonder. Had the eight-year-old Mozart experienced these emotions when he wrote his first symphonies, or was the neural network in his mind merely well connected in a way that facilitated the production of music? Is the beauty in the eye of the beholder, the listener, or was it put there by the composer? What happens when the quality of speech synthesis improves to where it is indistinguishable from human speech? Suppose the emotional content of the speech could be put under complete program control. How would we feel about a machine that could inflect its speech with an appealing sincerity or a beguiling seductiveness? Would we feel duped? Or would it matter at all?

Regardless of these philosophical issues for the longer term, many immediate, useful applications of speech technology are now finding their way to the marketplace. The easiest to justify are the applications in which there is no alternative methodology for information input or output, such as might be required for handicapped individuals or for situations needing hands-free or eyes-free operation. For example, there are now voice dialers for mobile telephones, which enable automobile drivers to keep their hands on the steering wheel and their eyes on the road. At the computer terminal voice input can be advantageous when one hand is occupied with a mouse. The mouse can designate where, while the voice says what. In the airplane cockpit, where there is visual overload, voice output gives a diversity that underlines the information. I can well imagine the riveting attention commanded by the synthesized announcement, "Pull up! Pull up!"

There is another class of voice applications that takes advantage of the ubiquity of telephone service. Touch-tone information input with synthesized voice output makes a good combination for order entry and for information retrieval in such situations as stock market quotes. Voice messaging systems, which store and retrieve speech messages in digitized form, are a speech equivalent of electronic mail and can be accessed from any telephone. Because of the electronic format, voice messages may be stored, duplicated, annotated, and forwarded. Such systems are more capable than telephone answering machines. They may not eliminate telephone tag, but they help, and their convenience and accessibility are better than keyboard-based, electronic mail.

Electronic mail can itself be made more accessible through text-to-speech synthesis, enabling users to have their stored E-mail messages read to them by a synthesizer through an ordinary voice telephone call. Consider for a moment how such a system would need to be designed for user-friendliness, contrasted with the usual text display protocols associated with electronic mail. The voice system could not make use of menus, for example; nor would it be appropriate for it to speak long headers, return addresses, or other information which would be routinely displayed on the CRT. The shortcomings of speech are evident, but the universal access permitted by speech is an extraordinary advantage obtained in trade.

A final category of voice applications is based upon the sophisticated processing of digitized voice signals. Speeded up speech can be generated to sound reasonably natural. Tests show that listeners to fast speech still have some moderate comprehension at rates as high as 300 words per minute, which is about the same as an average reading rate. Voice processing can also enable the editing of voice "documents" on a computer terminal, just as we edit text documents with word processing programs. A time line on the display shows a cursor indicating the current position in the voice document. Fast forward can speed through the words, and commands such as delete and insert allow the user to alter the voiced words in the document.

Speech recognition technology holds the promise that is just outside the grasp of technology. When I was a youth there was a yearly list of most-wanted inventions. The voice-operated type-writer always topped this list, along with automatic translation of spoken language. What a wonderful thing an automatic transcriber would be, I always thought to myself. Now that machine-assisted speech transcription is almost achievable, I never run across the most-wanted invention list. Maybe the list is not kept anymore, but even if it was I doubt the voice typewriter would be on top, since we are so much wiser about the intrinsic difficulty in transcription. Nonetheless, automatic stenography machines are now reaching the market. In these machines the human mediates the transcription through a display, menus, and a keyboard. The machine cannot do it all, but with our help reasonable text documents can be produced from speech input.

Speech recognition is closely related to *speaker* recognition, which is useful for password and credit verification, and perhaps for that talking lock mentioned earlier. To close this listing with a thought-provoking possibility, consider the use of speech recognition by intelligence agencies in eavesdropping. Many conversations can be monitored and skimmed to search for certain key words and key speakers. You can imagine your own list of those words and speakers that might call for a closer examination of the conversation by a human. I know that this has overtones of Big Brother, but there are few technologies that cannot be used for both good and evil. In general, however, the applications of speech technology are very much to our benefit, particularly inasmuch as they open up information access to many untrained users who otherwise might be deprived by lack of familiarity and skill.

As the bottom line on speech applications, however, I must return to the idea of interactive communications. Experiments have shown time after time that speech is the way humans communicate best with each other. No other medium is nearly as effective (e.g., typing, handwriting), and no other augmentation beyond speech seems to help (e.g., video, face-to-face). Only through speech do we have the fluent interaction to which we have become accustomed. We might dream that one day computers will share this fluency. In the rest of this chapter and the next I will try to put the prospects for this dream in perspective.

THE MECHANICS AND ANALYSIS OF SPEECH

Our primary concern in the next chapter will be machines that talk and listen, but to appreciate how these machines work requires us to reflect on how humans accomplish these same functions. The study of the human speech system predates even the discovery of electricity, and any cursory walk through a local library will reveal volume upon volume of reference material devoted to the physiology and classification of speech. In these books we discover that our speech mechanism is nothing more than a fancy wind instrument that we carry ready at hand. Possibly early man communicated by sign language and invented speech when he found it difficult to talk with his hands full, pressing into service an ancillary feature of apparatus designed to serve the more fundamental functions of eating and breathing. So we came to communicate with each other by blowing air through our vocal apparatus to make funny noises at each other that we interpreted as language. When I think of it that way it seems undignified, but it has served us well for perhaps a hundred thousand years, and has ultimately distinguished us from the other, nonspeaking, species with which we share this planet. No wonder scientists have long held such a fascination with the mechanism of speech.

In the world of speech technology there are a number of possible viewpoints, each of which is espoused by a particular variety of scientist or engineer. One such group studies the physiology of speech production. They argue that if we understand how the speech sounds are formed by the human body, then we will be able to replicate this same behavior in a machine. They use X rays, air-pressure and air-flow measurements, movies, and physical measurements in the attempt to correlate the movements of the lips, tongue, and other organs of speech with the production of the variety of speech sounds. Speech synthesis from this viewpoint might bear some resemblance in concept to Alexander Graham Bell's talking head. Wiggle this part this way and that part that way and out comes "mama."

Another group, more typified by electrical engineers, might say that how the sounds are produced is not so important. Let us study the result, they would say. This group uses microphones to enable recording of the air pressure waves produced by speech. The recordings are analyzed in detail using the tools of statistical signal analysis. According to the engineers, once we understand the mathematical properties of these waveforms it will only be necessary to design an electronic machine that produces identical waveforms. This machine may bear no resemblance to the human vocal system, but it does not matter. What it produces will look and sound exactly like speech.

Still another viewpoint might hold that producing the exact waveform is senseless or wasteful. As in the case of the proverbial tree that falls in the forest, what matters is what we hear. Consequently, let us study the perception of sounds by the human ear. Once we understand what properties in a sound determine how it is heard, then we can design machines to produce sound waveforms that the human ear will interpret as speech. These waveforms may look nothing like the recorded waveforms from human speakers, but they will produce the same effects in the listener.

Obviously there is some truth in all of these viewpoints, but because of my training I have a bias towards the middle position, wherein it is primarily necessary to study and emulate the waveforms produced by human speakers. I am afraid that this bias will be seen in the relative dearth of material that I will present which is related to an anatomical description of the human vocal system. Nevertheless, the most successful speech synthesis and recognition techniques are based upon a prudent blend of all three positions. In theory, we should be able to analyze and synthesize sound signals without reference to the underlying mechanism of production, but in practice the insight gained through a study of the human vocal system guides us in knowing what properties of the speech signal are important, and gives us a simple mathematical model upon which to base our analysis and synthesis.

Knowledge of the speech production system might seem to obviate the necessity for studying the perception of hearing. We might argue that hearing evolved to respond specifically to the sounds that we were capable of producing, but in truth we could also argue the reverse. In any event, in our attempts to synthesize speech it is often necessary to gauge our success by measurement through the perception of hearing. After all, it has been said that we speak in order to be heard. Even being heard is not enough if the sounds themselves are not meaningful. We seek to be heard in order to be understood.

MODELING OF THE VOCAL TRACT

• • • • • • • • • • • • • •

In these days of computer graphics, researchers who work on modeling the vocal tract are able to visualize the motions of the vocal system through animated displays. Figure 12 shows the computer representation of a cutaway, side view of the vocal tract. The tract is in essence a tube about 17 cm in length and 2 cm in diameter, stretching from the vocal cords at the lower end to the lips at the upper end. Along the length of this tube we have the ability to vary the cross-sectional area, such as through placement and curvature of the tongue or by positioning of the lips and jaw. In addition, we can open and close a muscular flap at the back of the soft palate known as the velum, which connects to the nasal tract and allows an auxiliary flow of air to escape through the nose. This is the basic instrument we have to play.

In order to create sounds with our instrument we use lung pressure to force air through the vocal tract. We modulate this airflow and make the music of speech by several different means. At the bottom of the vocal tract the vocal cords can interrupt the air flow, chopping the flow into a series of puffs at some controllable frequency (like when you say "ahh" for the doctor). By constricting the vocal tube we can create turbulent flow, or by stopping the flow at occlusions that we make (such as by closing the lips), we can cause little explosions of pent-up air. Finally, by changing the shape of the vocal tract we impose resonant properties that color the sound of the basic notes created by the airflows.

In forming the sounds that constitute our language, the vocal articulators (jaws, lips, tongue) move relatively slowly but in a beautifully coordinated overlapping ballet, perhaps not unlike that of the fingers in typing. Here too the movements of our articulators anticipate forthcoming goals. For example, say the word "stew" and notice how your lips round during the *st* in order to be ready for the next sound. (This is known as coarticulation.) Compare this with your lip position for the same *st* in "strike". Furthermore, as the reader might now expect, the fastest speeds of articulation, about 6–8 syllables per second, are roughly equivalent in words per minute to the fastest typing speeds. In spite of our intuitive feeling that the motions of the articulators should occur in bursts of activity

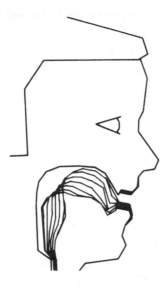

FIGURE 12
Computer model of the vocal tract

corresponding to words, they actually appear to move continuously. Without the sound, we would not have the slightest clue of what they were up to.

The choreography of the speech process was first observed in animation through X-ray movies made in the 1920s. Today, of course, the mechanics are well understood, and the computer model can be instructed to show us the motions necessary to say basic sounds. Figure 12 shows the superposition of a number of intermediate diagrams of the model during the mechanics of vocalizing a sound. If this book were in hypertext, I would now show you the motion picture of this sequence. But it is not, and I cannot.

In the functioning of the vocal system there is a primary distinction between the ways in which the vowels and consonants are created. Vowels are produced by allowing a relatively free flow of air to flow through the vocal tract, while in consonants there is an obstruction of the airstream at some point in the tract. For example, in that last sentence sound out the *o* in "flow" and the *p* in "point." Notice the difference in the way air is forced through the vocal cavity in these two sounds. The *o* in "flow" sounds like a musical note. The fundamental frequency of this note is imparted by the vibration of the vocal cords, which open and close about a hundred times per second, chopping or modulating the air flow through the vocal tract. Meanwhile, the vocal tract permits the free flow of this voiced sound as we act to shape the tract to create the resonances characteristic of this particular vowel.

Contrast the making of this vowel with the creation of the sound of *p* in "point." Here the airstream is cut off at our lips until enough pressure is built up to create a small explosion of air. The sound is unvoiced—the vocal cords do not vibrate—and except for the feeling of blowing a trumpet, there is no resemblance to a musical note. For obvious reasons this particular sound is called a plosive, and it is one of a class of sounds known as stops, in which the passage of air is totally blocked at some point in the passage. There are a number of other types of stops, such as the *g* in "goose," where the stoppage occurs at the back of the tongue.

The vowels are all produced in similar fashion to the *o* in "flow." The airflow is voiced by the vocal cords, and since there are no constrictions in the vocal tract the air flows relatively freely. The variation in the vowels is produced by shaping of the tract, principally by the tongue and lips. Try saying "he" and then "had," and observe how the tongue is high for the former and low for the latter. (Nice that we can try these little experiments so easily!)

On the other hand, there is considerably more variety in the generation of consonants, which are classified both in terms of the place of obstruction and in the manner of obstruction. For example, the *s* in "speech" is called a fricative. The airstream in this case is not completely cut off, but is so narrowed as to create a turbulent flow. Another class of consonant sounds is the lateral, such as the *l* in "lull," in which the air is impeded in the center of the tongue but allowed to escape to the sides. Notice in this case that the sound is voiced like the vowels. What the consonants have in common is the partial or complete obstruction of the vocal passage.

The basic sounds, called phones, of which the languages of the world are constituted have been extensively cataloged and classified. There is an International Phonetic Alphabet of more than a hundred phones that are described in terms of the mechanics of their production. The *p* from "point" is an instance of a bilabial plosive, while the vowels are given in terms of the tongue position and amount of lip rounding. In theory, I am told, an expert phoneticist can transcribe an unknown language in terms of the symbols of this phonetic alphabet and then recreate the sounds of the language upon demand. Knowledge of the mechanics can also be helpful in learning a new language, but the near impossibility of a congenitally deaf person being able to speak the proper sounds of language through mechanical mimicry alone makes us painfully aware of how dependent we are upon the feedback of hearing for the control of articulation.

So far we have a wind instrument and a compendium of differentiable sounds that we can make with it. This is the hardware, but there is a long step of software between this and a language. There is no meaning per se in the sound of a particular phone. It is simply a sound that we can discriminate through heritage and practice from the sounds of other phones. Where then does meaning reside? This is a surprisingly elusive question, for meaning seems to lie in the system of language itself, rather than any subcomponent. We string phones together according to certain rules akin to grammar (called phonotactics) in order to build bigger and bigger subunits. Vowels and consonants roughly alternate to make syllables, but we cannot just concatenate arbitrary phones to do this. Certain phones are not allowed to follow certain other phones, either for mechanical reasons or because the language will not allow it.

Just as in the makeup of text, there is a great deal of redundancy interwoven into the strings of successive phones forming spoken language. This redundancy makes possible the detection of speech in such unbelievably hostile environments as the typical cocktail party. We could trace this redundancy and quantify it in terms of the entropy, or fundamental uncertainty, per word, exactly as we did in Chapter 3 with text. Instead of the ordinary alphabetic symbols of text, we would use the symbols of the phonetic alphabet. We could then evaluate the entropy of successively higher approximations of spoken language. To the information theorist, it is immaterial that the phonetic symbols represent sounds. They are, after all, only symbols of an unknown language. Ultimately, if we pursued the trail of entropy deeply enough we would find to our surprise that the entropy of this unknown phonetic language was exactly the same as that of English text. The information conveyed is at base the same, though arguably additional overtones of nuance not present in text might well be added in the coding of the phonetic transcriptions.

Syllables, like phones, generally have no meaning in themselves. Again, they are just differentiable sound chunks built of smaller chunks. The idea of a dictionary of syllables seems absurd. By the time syllables have been combined to form words, however, most readers would probably argue that we have at last uncovered meaning. But is that really so? Almost every word has multiple definitions in the dictionary. The choice of definition to be applied depends upon the context of the word, so it would seem that meaning lies on a yet higher level. Perhaps dictionaries of words have no more relevance than the nonexistent dictionaries of syllables. It is just that the number of possible definitions at the word level is so much less.

We could pursue further the information-theoretical aspects of the speech communication channel by considering the system as a whole, from the speaker through a noisy environment to the perception of the listener. Curiously, the various possible phones constituting the speech message are not perceived with equal sensitivity by the ear. The vowels are generally distinguished much more easily than the consonants, which have less acoustic energy. The difference in sensitivity is as large as 30 decibels—an astounding factor of a thousand in favor of being able to detect a particular vowel over a particular consonant. This is in spite of the fact that, as we have seen in Chapter 3, many of the vowels are individually near the top of the list in frequency of occurrence, and consequently carry less information than individual consonants. As an example, try to read this sentence with only vowels and then with only consonants.

```
A__   a__   e__a_____e,   _____   __o   __ea__   ____i__
__e__e___e  __i___   o_____   __o_e___   a___
____e__  __i___   o_____   __o__o_a_____.

__s  __n  __x__mpl__,  try  t__  r____d  th__s  s__nt__nc__
w__th  __nly  v__w__ls  __nd  th__n  w__th  __nly
c__ns__n__nts.
```

The sentence is almost readable with only consonants, and totally meaningless with only vowels. There are about twice as many total occurrences of consonants as of vowels, whereas there are more than four times as many possible consonants (21 versus 5). I think of the leavening in the sentence as being provided by the popular vowels, while the differentiation is added by the individually less popular consonants. At other points in this book I have reflected on the wisdom and economy of design in nature, almost in accordance with the principles of information theory. In this instance it is not obvious why we have evolved a language in which the differentiating elements are less detectable than the leavening elements.

A N A L Y S I S   O F   T H E
S P E E C H   S I G N A L

Let us now turn to the more traditional viewpoint of the engineer. We have a phenomenon called speech, which is manifested as a periodic variation in air pressure. Let us measure the waveform of this signal, and dissect it mathematically until we understand its structure well enough to reproduce it synthetically. If there was any doubt that we need a real human being to generate these particular sounds, it should be dispelled by the success of the parrot, or the even smaller mynah bird, in mimicry. If the mynah bird had a human-sized vocal tract, the little bird would be made up entirely of one balled-up vocal tube, and even that would not be enough. Worse yet, the poor bird does not even have a larynx. It does pretty well anyway, and it produces the same sounds without altering the shape of a resonant cavity, as we do, but by a different modulation process. On the other hand, the ape has fine vocal apparatus, but apparently being the strong, silent type has no idea how to use it to produce speech—what a curious state of affairs!

The oscilloscope trace in the bottom of Figure 13 is the typical result of recording a sample of speech. There is, as we would expect, a squiggly line that alternates up and down at a frequency of hundreds of hertz. There is a modulation envelope on top of this squiggly line corresponding to the bursts of speech and relative silences delineating words. Other than these gross features, it is really impossible to see anything interesting in these time-domain traces. Even an expert who has worked with speech waveforms all his life could not be sure that this was speech without actually putting it through an amplifier and listening to it.

Just how hard it is to correlate the sound of speech with the appearance of its waveform is remembered by technologists who worked to scramble and unscramble speech for secrecy during the second world war. Researchers at that time invented all sorts of

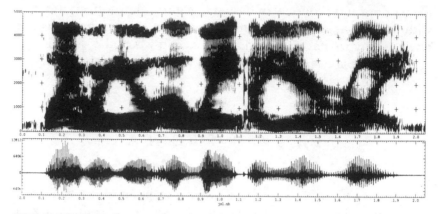

FIGURE 13
Speech waveforms for the sentence "Why were you away a year, Roy?" Visible speech demonstrated by spectograph *(above)* and original speech waveform *(below)*.

techniques for mutilating the speech waveform in vicious ways that deformed and rearranged the signal. Time after time their elation turned to dismay when the scrambled signal was played into an amplifier, and, miraculously, out came intelligible speech—albeit often mildly garbled. The lesson is that somewhere in that squiggly line is buried the sound of speech, and it is not in the exact shape of the waveform, but it lies deeper in properties of the signal structure that are not revealed in this straightforward portrait.

Out of the wartime experiences grew a new way of displaying speech waveforms that made it possible to see their characteristic properties. This portrayal was called a spectrograph, and although the processing is now done by computer rather than mechanically, the display format remains the same today almost half a century after the publication of the landmark book *Visible Speech* by R. K. Potter, G. A. Kopp, and H. C. Green. The spectrograph displays the frequency content of the speech waveform as a function of time. An example is shown in the upper portion of Figure 13. In this format, time is on the horizontal axis, while frequency is indicated by height and relative power by the darkness of the display.

If I were to tap a key on the piano, say the traditional tune-up middle A, the spectrograph display would show a horizontal line running across the page at a height corresponding to the frequency of 440 Hz. The line would get gradually lighter as it moved to the right and the sound of the note died away. But since the piano note is not a pure tone (otherwise it would be musically uninteresting), we would see overtones or harmonics of the basic frequency of 440 Hz. There would be another horizontal line at approximately twice the height, around 880 Hz, but not as dark as the fundamental line. Still other horizontal lines would appear at regularly spaced intervals corresponding to higher harmonics around 1,320 Hz, 1,760 Hz, and so on. The higher lines would generally appear progressively dimmer.

Now look at the spectrograph of the sentence "Why were you away a year, Roy?" in Figure 13. You might think of this display as a player-piano roll. As it unwinds from left to right the keys on the piano are pressed according to the height and darkness of the inking on this chart. Picture the keys arranged vertically, as if the piano were on its side, so as to correspond with height in the diagram. In theory the music created by this player-piano roll would be speech. That is exactly what speech synthesis systems try to emulate.

In the spectrograph of speech we do not see the horizontal lines of pure musical tones, nor do we see the uniform spacing of naturally occurring harmonics of a fundamental frequency. The black bands running across the figure are like "fat" musical notes. In isolation they would sound like noisy, buzzy, but recognizable tones. Typically we see three or four of these bands corresponding to each voiced sound (usually a vowel) in the sentence. The lowest of the bands is the tone imposed by the vibrations of the vocal cords. In singing we are capable of moving this tone over quite a wide range. From the lowest note in the classical vocal bass repertoire to the highest soprano note is over four octaves—73 Hz to 1,400 Hz. (Both lowest and highest notes occur in Mozart operas.)

The pulsing air emitted through the vocal chords has many strong overtones. It is very rich in spectral content. When we speak we reconfigure our vocal tract so as to change its resonant properties and effectively select certain of these overtones while attenuating others. Our vocal tract at any given moment will have several resonant frequencies in the audible range, called formants. These formants are the bars of darkness running across the spectrograph. The vocal tract is like an adjustable shower stall. We all have noticed how when we sing in the shower the geometry of the stall amplifies certain notes through resonance. It sounds good. We should sound this good all the time, we think!

227

The vocal system has about three significant resonances or formants in the range below 3,000 Hz, which may be moved around while we speak. If the vocal tract were an ideal tube of 17 cm, closed at the lower end and open at the top, then according to the theory of acoustics the resonances would be at the odd quarter-wave multiples of the fundamental, which would be 500 Hz, 1,500 Hz, 2,500 Hz, etc. (There are higher formants which are not very significant for the recognition of speech.) Every voiced sound in the test sentence shows a particular, recognizable pattern of formants. In the diphthongs, where there is a blending of one vowel sound into another, we see the sliding of the formants from one vowel set into the other. The strange test sentence is replete with voiced sounds. Consequently, the formant bars are almost continuous in the spectrograph. Where there are unvoiced, consonant sounds like stops or fricatives the formant bars momentarily disappear, since energy in a hiss-like or plosive sound is spread rather uniformly over the acoustic spectrum.

In speech synthesis our aim is recreate the energy patterns of that spectrograph. In speech recognition we look at the spectrograph of unknown speech and try to match the patterns against known patterns of words. In speaker recognition we look at the patterns in the spectrograph and compare them with similar patterns made by various speakers. Whose patterns are these, we ask? All the tasks of speech technology are illustrated in those spectrographs.

As advertised, the spectrograph is indeed visible speech, and all of speech technology is wrapped around the information shown so vividly in that format. However, just because it is visible does not mean it is obvious. None of my talented friends who have spent their entire careers in speech technology can accurately read speech from a spectrograph. The sounds and the patterns blend into one another to make smooth transitions. The patterns differ in detail, if not in substance, from one speaker to another. And to begin with, where does one sound end and another start? Where are the words? One linguist commented many years ago that the spectrograph patterns were like the hieroglyphics of an unknown language. Imagine finding patterns like these in an archeological excavation and trying to piece together what they mean. Yet what looks so impossible in that display turns into child's play, literally, when we put the waveform through an amplifier and speaker and simply listen. If only the machines worked the way we do. In the next chapter we shall see how they try to reproduce and recognize patterns similar to these.

R E F L E C T I O N S — T H E C O M M U N I C A T I O N S S U R R O G A T E

People keep asking about the future of the telephone. Now that we have cordless phones and automatic call forwarding, what more could we ask? It would seem that the nirvana of universal access is upon us. Yet whenever I reflect on such matters I end with the unresolvable conflict between communications availability and personal privacy. I imagine a Dick Tracy-like wristphone from which I can call anyone in the world with a simple verbal command. The only problem is that I want to be the only person who owns one. Being able to call other people is great, but the corollary is that anyone else can call me at any time and any place—and there are times and places when I'm not keen on being called. Furthermore, if I call someone who I know has a wristphone and they don't answer, what am I to infer? Are they dead?

We all know the game of telephone tag. I just now made eight calls and reached no one. It's frustrating because I need to talk to those people, but maybe they don't need to talk to me. The only solution that technology has thus far provided is the answering machine. Of course, if it is your machine, it is a great invention. If it is someone else's, which you have just reached with your call, it is a hated mechanism. But these machines have been so put upon by columnists that I will pass them by graciously on this occasion. We need something more, but never fear, once again technology races to the rescue—the intelligent communications surrogate has been proposed. This society-saving gizmo combines artificial intelligence and speech technology to handle our communications needs when we're not around. Telephone tag is eliminated; we simply deal with other people's communications surrogates and they with ours, thereby freeing real people to do whatever it is that real people do.

To give us all some appreciation for the wonders that the communications surrogate could accomplish, bear with me while I imagine a series of calls being dextrously dispatched.

MACHINE: Hello, this is Jim's phone.
VOICE: Is Jim there?

MACHINE: Jim isn't here right now. I'm his electronic alter ego. May I help you?

VOICE: I was wondering if Jim would be available for a meeting of the nominations committee on Thursday afternoon.

MACHINE: Yes, he would be available then. I will place this meeting on his calendar. Thank you for calling. (Click)

MACHINE: Hello, this is Jim's phone.

VOICE: It's that lousy machine again. I want to talk to Jim.

MACHINE: Jim isn't here. I'd like to help you in his stead.

VOICE: This isn't stuff that I can share with a machine. When will he be there?

MACHINE: Who is this calling?

VOICE: This is Bill Bixler, you idiot.

MACHINE: I'm sorry, but Jim will not ever be here. Thank you for calling, Bill. (Click.)

MACHINE: Hello, this is Jim's phone.

VOICE: Oh, it's you. Listen, this is his boss. I really need to get Jim right away. We have a crisis situation in our Denver office. Can you locate Jim and have him call me?

MACHINE: I'm sorry, Mr. Hisboss, Jim is playing golf this afternoon, and left orders not to be disturbed.

VOICE: Look, I'm thin on patience this afternoon. This is HIS BOSS calling, not Mr. Hisboss. Get Jim. Now.

MACHINE: I'm sorry you have patients this afternoon, Dr. Thin. If you want to reach Jim's boss just dial 553-8861. Certainly you would never find him here in Jim's office. Jim has him listed in our directory under the alias of "The Phantom."

VOICE: Take this message and get it straight, machine. Tell him that the "Phantom" knows what evil lurks in the mind of Jim, and that he will rue the day he turned his telephone over to a pile of microchips. (Click.)

MACHINE: Hello, this is Jim's phone.

VOICE: Oh hello, you darling machine. I just wanted to check that we're still on for dinner and whatever.

MACHINE: Of course, Sue, I have you for Thursday at the usual spot.

VOICE: This is his fiancée, Barbara. Who is Sue?

MACHINE: Oh Barbara, I didn't recognize your voice. I never heard of anyone named Sue.

VOICE: But you just said he was meeting with Sue on Thursday.

MACHINE: Oh, that Sue. Are you sure you have the right number? This is Bill Finch's phone.

VOICE: You can't pull that dodge on me, machine. Tell Jim it's all over.

MACHINE: You have reached a nonworking number, please check your listing and redial. (Click.)

MACHINE: Hello, this is Jim's phone.

VOICE: Another one of those machines. Well, this is Sampson's dance studios. Do you think Jim would be interested in dancing lessons?

MACHINE: I'll check Jim's interest profile. Yes, Jim likes dancing.

VOICE: Great, just give me his American Express card number and I'll sign him up.

MACHINE: I'm not authorized to release that information.

VOICE: Hmm. How about VISA?

MACHINE: Oh sure, that is 2215-198-681-226.

VOICE: Thanks machine, tell him the charge is $870. (Click.)

MACHINE: Hello, this is Jim's phone.

VOICE: Are you satisfied with your present investments? Have you considered the advantages of tax-free municipal bonds? Please give your name and address now.

MACHINE: This is Jim's phone.

VOICE: Thank you Mr. Jimsphone. Let me tell you more about our present investment opportunities . . .

This all seems a throwback to me. I remember some years ago during a telephone strike when engineers were asked to temporarily man operator consoles. This story surely must be apocryphal, but it seems that one engineer on an unfamiliar switchboard was in the middle of receiving complicated instructions from a payphone customer when the customer suddenly stopped and asked, "Wait a minute—is this a man or is this a machine I'm talking to?" Thinking quickly about being out of his depth, the engineer replied stiffly, "I is a machine." Indeed, for many years to come this is the only kind of machine that will handle calls with intelligence. Right now I feel like my own alter ego. Let's see how I can handle this pile of messages in front of my phone.

6

S P E E C H
P R O C E S S I N G
• • • • • • • • • • • •

The previous chapter has given
some flavor of the science of speech and of the applications of
speech technology. Having nibbled at the human side of speech
communications, it is time to chew on the machine end of this. For
us, natural speech is a miracle we take for granted. Talking and
listening computers seem, in contrast, so much more complex. But
of course the reverse is actually true. It is the computer that is
simple; we are the complex ones. After discussing computer speech
synthesis and recognition in this chapter you should have if nothing
else a greater appreciation for our own speech capabilities.

Machine synthesis and recognition of speech sound glamorous.
Whenever a computer does something seemingly reserved for humans we get excited or nervous about it. The second half of this
chapter will be about these subjects, but first we have to talk about
speech coding. How do we turn a speech waveform into a stream
of bits? How many bits do we need? Unfortunately, this sounds like
a grubby subject reserved for a few engineers who have to be
forced to think about such things. No one else should really care.
Sometimes I even feel this way myself, but there are two good
reasons to worry about speech coding in this book. First, we have
to know how to represent speech digitally in order to do speech
synthesis and recognition, and second, the information content of
various media of interchange has been one of the themes of this
book. Besides, if you stick with the subject, perhaps you will find

it is not so dull after all. There is a great deal of technological sophistication that goes into the coding of speech. I hope that you will be able to see the beauty shining through the inevitable litany of little miseries that complicate this problem that has occupied engineers now for half a century.

S P E E C H   C O D I N G

Since Thomas Edison first recorded the human voice on a rotating cylinder we have aspired to find better ways of storing speech and music for later reproduction. Edison's phonograph, like the vinyl records of today, recorded the voice as an analog waveform. The engraved track that the reproducing needle followed was exactly the shape of the speech waveform. The vibrations in air pressure that were caused by speech were written upon the cylinder, and mechanically reproduced by a loudspeaker. The same principle was followed in Bell's telephone; the variations in air pressure were converted to a voltage waveform and transmitted in exactly that format. Think of the squiggly line we saw as a speech waveform in the last chapter being transmitted as a proportional voltage.

Today the world is becoming more and more digital. The problem with analog transmission and storage is that it is fragile, and consequently easily corrupted. Our phonograph records develop pops and crackles, and we hear the hiss of background noise. In contrast, compact disks store the same music or speech in digital format where it is robust. It is easy to alter an analog quantity by some small amount, whereas it is much harder to change a 1 to a 0 in a string of digits. Furthermore, error detecting and correcting codes can ensure the integrity of a sequence of digits. There is no equivalent in preserving an analog waveform. Even the telephone system has been converted to digital transmission. The natural language of the telephone network is the same as that of computers—it is digital. Everywhere in the information age speech has to be changed to a stream of bits. How this is done and how many bits it requires are the subjects of this section on speech coding.

Speech coding means the conversion of an analog speech signal into a sequence of bits that can then subsequently be used to recon-

FIGURE 14
Speech coding

stitute the original speech. Just to be sure this is understood, the concept is framed in the diagram shown in Figure 14.

The goals of speech coding are evident. For efficient transmission and storage there should be as few bits as possible, but at the same time we want the decoded speech to sound identical to the original speech. The science and art in speech coding is using our knowledge of the speech mechanism and properties to minimize the number of bits required for a given fidelity of reproduction.

The practical impacts of efficient speech coding are immense. Nearly all of the world's telecommunications facilities are being converted to digital transmission, in which the cost of voice communications is directly proportional to the allocated bit rate. Moreover, the amount of speech that can be stored in a given amount of memory is also dependent upon the efficiency of our digital representation. However, for the philosophical purposes of this book there is another reason to discuss speech coding, and that is to get at the information content of speech. In earlier chapters we traced the tangled thread of entropy in English text. How many bits did it take to represent text? Now let us ask that same question about speech. It will be interesting to compare our answers.

CODING BY SAMPLING AND QUANTIZING

In 1962 the Bell System began installing the first commercial digital transmission system, setting a standard for voice coding that still

235

dominates the telecommunications evolution a quarter of a century later. In this system, called T-1 carrier, voice was encoded at 64,000 bits per second (64 kbps). That probably seems like a lot of bits, as well it should. Yet it was the minimum number of bits that, with relatively straightforward encoding and decoding, could be depended upon to result in ordinary telephone-quality speech. We will see presently how this number was chosen.

In an analog waveform there are an infinite number of different possibilities, each a squiggly line differing by the slightest degree from other possible squiggly lines. But a sequence of bits can only account for a finite number of possible combinations, so something has to give. In the end there must be some small error in the reconstituted waveform, but the reconstituted speech should sound as much like the original as possible under the circumstances.

The traditional method for digitization of an analog signal is to sample the signal at regular intervals and to quantize (round off) the voltage amplitude at each of these sampling instants. To be specific, in the T-1 system the waveform is sampled 8,000 times a second. Eight bits are allocated to describe the amplitude of the waveform at each sample, so it is possible to specify which of 256 reference amplitudes is closest to the actual signal amplitude. The coding rate of 64,000 bits per second is simply the 8-bit approximation to the actual amplitude done 8,000 times a second.

You can imagine that the effect of sampling and quantizing is as if we overlaid the squiggly line of the signal with a sheet of transparent graph paper and drew a new waveform on the graph paper to approximate the original waveform beneath. In order to quantize our approximation, we require that our drawing only go through the corners of the little squares on the graph paper. If we used graph paper with finer and finer grids, the two waveforms would become more and more identical, but it would take an ever-increasing number of bits to designate the sequence of squares traversed by the signal. There must be a good compromise here somewhere.

SAMPLING
· · · · · · · · · ·

When the speech waveform is sampled, in effect by blinking our electronic eye at the signal, we convert the waveform into a sequence of precise numbers, like $1.6712 - 2.3189$, that we might picture like those in Figure 15. Later these precise numbers will be approximated as best we can with a small number of bits, but for now we will concentrate on the questions of what sampling rate is necessary and what have we lost.

The necessary sampling rate is related directly to the bandwidth (the highest contained frequency) of the waveform being sampled. Roughly speaking, the highest frequency in the signal determines the fineness of ripples in the waveform, and if we do not want to miss anything we must be prepared to sample at least several times in every ripple. There is a famous theorem, about which whole volumes have been written, that says that if we sample a waveform at a rate of at least twice its bandwidth, then we can reconstruct the waveform *exactly* from these samples. So if we were to remove all frequency components above 4 kHz from a speech signal, then we could recreate this bandlimited speech from 8,000 samples per second.

The sampling theorem is taken by engineers as almost a religious commandment, not to be trifled with. If the speech signal is sampled at less than twice its highest frequency component, then something is being missed. The something that is missed is the high frequency ripples, and in reconstructing the waveform these ripples appear magically transformed into lower frequencies (an effect called aliasing). The resultant speech sounds warbled and reverberent, with a burbling running through it. In bad cases I could imagine that the speaker was talking in an underwater cathedral.

It may seem amazing to readers unfamiliar with the sampling theorem that it is possible to reconstruct the original waveform exactly from these regular samples. It looks as if we have thrown away everything in between the samples. But imagine drawing a line that connects the tips of the samples. You would want the line

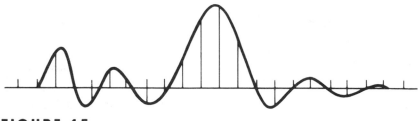

FIGURE 15
Sampling

to be smooth, and to make all the bends as gently as possible. Insisting on this smoothness, the line you might draw through the points would look very much like what I might draw. In fact, there is only one line through these points that does not contain frequency components higher than half the sampling rate, and that line is our original signal. In practice, we send a train of electrical impulses of the requisite heights through a low pass filter, and out comes our original signal unscathed—a miracle of the sampling theorem!

Granted that we must sample at twice the bandwidth, but what exactly is the bandwidth of speech? In the case of telephone-quality speech this decision was made many years ago when it was decided to separate adjacent telephone channels in radio transmission by 4,000 Hz. As each voice conversation traverses the telephone plant it passes through many bandlimiting filters designed to prevent overlap between channels placed in nearby frequencies. Inevitably it is worn down to a bandwidth of about 3,000 Hz. The choice of a sampling rate of 8,000 samples per second for digital telephony was perhaps conservative, but there is not much to be gained in pushing further.

The confinement of telephone speech to less than 4 kHz is certainly a compromise. We expect our high fidelity amplifiers to have a bandwidth of 20 kHz, and in the compact disk audio system a sampling rate of 44.1 kHz was chosen, corresponding to a bandwidth of slightly more than 22 kHz. On the other hand, we can see from the spectrograph in the previous chapter that the first three formants of speech generally are below 3 kHz. These lower formants determine intelligibility and lend most of the individuality to speech. Listener tests have confirmed the intelligibility of 3 kHz speech, but then we all demonstrate this in our everyday use of the telephone. In truth, we are all so well trained on telephone-quality speech that we may have forgotten what we are missing by not hearing the higher formants.

It is also possible to decrease the bandwidth of speech below 3 kHz, to perhaps as low as 1.5 kHz, without suffering significant loss of intelligibility for most male speakers. In these circumstances we would be able to include only the lower two formants. While the speech is understandable, the naturalness suffers, and for female speakers we might well cross the borderline of losing the second formant, and with it, intelligibility. The telephone standard is rooted in history, but for now it seems reasonable. In the future we may decide that those nuances conveyed by the decapitated overtones of 4 kHz speech were more important than we realized in the 20th century.

QUANTIZING SAMPLES

Now how many bits are required in the quantization that approximates the amplitude at a sampling instant? The effect of using fewer bits per sample is to coarsen the approximation, or equivalently to increase the average error between the reconstituted and original signals. This error is perceived as a noise or hiss on top of the speech. (Well, almost. Unless the quantization is very fine, it is possible to hear the voice in the quantization noise.) The aim in choosing the number of bits of quantization in digital telephony was to keep this noise slightly below the level of audibility relative to the speech. In the transmission of a voice signal through the telephone plant, noise inevitably creeps into the waveform, and it is the background hiss with which we all are familiar. In contrast, in digital transmission a bit is a bit, and there is no added noise in transmission. As long as the bit error rate is negligible, the only noise we hear in digital transmission is the quantizing noise. It was obviously necessary to keep this noise at a lower level than is usually experienced in analog transmission.

Analysis and experiments showed that an 8-bit quantization was better than the standards set for toll-quality, analog telephone transmission noise. For every bit in quantization that we back off, the approximation error doubles, and the apparent noise increases 6 db. Since a 3 db increase in sound level is usually considered a perceptible step, this means that every bit fewer in quantization turns up the noise two notches. For a given number of bits in quantization the most benefit is obtained by spacing the quantization thresholds exponentially, so there is a fine scale of approximation when the signal is small and noise would be very evident, and a coarse scale when the signal is large and the noise would be effectively masked by the signal. Actually, the signal is compressed logarithmically and sampled uniformly, which is the same thing.

For the telephone application 8-bit quantization with logarithmic compression gives a 35 db signal-to-noise ratio, which meets the standards for so-called "toll quality" speech. We might compare this with the 16 bits used in the compact disk audio system, which gives music a much wider dynamic range than is possible in telephone transmission. To me, the greatest benefit of the compact disk system is the velvet silence from which the music springs. Beautiful, but it is costly. If the telephone quantization standard was used on CDs, then they would play ten times as long.

THE MYSTERY OF INFORMATION CONTENT IN SPEECH

Let us now compare the information required to convey speech with that required for text. If we assume a speaking rate of about 3 words per second, we can summarize what we have discussed thus far in this book in the table below.

Incredible! There is a ratio of 1,000 to more than 10,000 in the information rate required to communicate language in the form of speech as compared to text. The number of bits on a compact disk for an hour of speech or popular music would suffice for the text of 3 Encyclopedia Brittanicas. Another startling way to view this number is to estimate our own data storage capacity as 50 bits per second input through our cognitive processing channels for the 72 years we are expected to live. Assuming nothing is lost, and that there is no input other than that passing through cognitive processing, then we amass about 113 billion bits (14 gigabytes) in our brain. This is only 22 CD albums. Sad, when you think of it; only 22 playings of Madonna or Bruce Springsteen or whomever, and we are finished. But why is it that speech (or music) requires such a great number of bits as compared to text? What is it that we

FORMAT	BITS/WORD
Stereo CD	466,000
PCM Telephone	21,000
ASCII Text	44
Entropy	5.5

achieve by the addition of this overwhelming amount of additional information?

Frankly, I consider this one of the great mysteries of information technology. It seems as if the core information, the "facts" as it were, is contained in a very small number of bits, but adding nuance to expression of these facts requires level upon level of additional information. In other words, there is some powerful law of diminishing returns. Every little amount of embellishment in format calls for an exponentially larger number of bits. We will see this same expansion in the next chapter when we consider images.

Now what is the embellishment of speech over text? Ironically, I am actually writing these words in a crowded auditorium during a boring speech. The speaker at the rostrum is reading a speech verbatim from previously prepared text. As he stumbles over the words in a monotone, I am inclined to argue that in the present case there is no added value whatsoever in the speech format. Perhaps all those extra bits are acting as negative information, helping to mask the few bits that actually constitute the basic idea behind his talk. Since the person in the chair next to me is now surreptitiously reading these words, let me turn to the benefits of the speech format.

Even when speech and text consist of identical words, speech generally conveys added information. The speech contains an *interpretation* of the words, as if the speaker has inserted notes in the margins of the text. He adds stress, emotion, force, and cadence to the words, while simultaneously transmitting some ancillary information about himself, perhaps unrelated to the words themselves. He gives character and personality both to the words and to himself.

Granted that information has been added, why is it so costly? My own viewpoint would be that usually this added information is small compared with that contained in the words, but that we have no idea how to code it efficiently. Whenever we touch upon human emotions, we open up doors that bits pour through, as we have no real symbolism or framework for efficient expression. In the margin of the text we could write "sad," but there are many degrees of sadness, tinged and mixed as colors on a canvas. A human voice would describe this to us. Nonetheless, I do not think there are the stupendous varieties of emotion indicated by the thousands of bits per word voice carries in excess of the information in identical text.

Even though these bare words convey no hint of my voice,

those of you readers who know me personally can hear my voice in your minds saying these words. Just as we read by vocalizing to ourselves, we have the capability of recreating the voices of others in our minds. When we read a letter from a friend, we hear their voice from afar. (The movies often portray this with a voice-over when an actor gazes at a letter.) In recalling a conversation we recreate the voice from what is undoubtedly a text-like storage in our minds. There is no way we are going to store the 64,000 bits per second of the actual voice. If we hear a conversation in a foreign language that we do not understand, we generally cannot recall the sounds of the meaningless words.

When we read a speech by Winston Churchill we hear his voice ringing clearly through the austere words on the page. If we can *re-create* voices, then conceptually no voice information needs to be added to the text. The simple words "as spoken by Winston Churchill" tell us much of what we need to know in order to reformat the words into speech. We have already stored the Winston Churchill personality processing module in our minds. Conceivably, electronic storage and retrieval could do the same kind of re-creation. For example, this book might contain a floppy disk in the back cover with a characterization of my voice. Using this profile, these words could be vocalized electronically as I *might* have read them.

Though the book would then be read in my own voice, there would be none of my own interpretation added. Thus I might add markings along with the words on these pages, as if this text were a symphony, indicating tempo, pitch, dynamics, and loudness. Like a symphony, the book could be *performed* or *interpreted* with the aid of hints from the composer. But remember that Beethoven shared the fame with Toscanini. Even in music, which has attempted to evolve a symbolism for audio interpretation, the original intent of the composer is not preserved. Esthetically, that might not be so important; perhaps Toscanini knew better than Beethoven, and Walter Cronkite could surely read this book better than I. However, it does illustrate our inability to measure, describe, or quantify human emotions in a symbolic framework. Perhaps that is why so many more bits are required to communicate speech than to transmit text.

How he hated the telephone, which promised so much more than it gave. It was as if its capacity to convey emotion was limited by the thinness of the wire. It was unsuitable for any message more complicated than you could send by Morse code.

Communication by telephone was simply not normal, and perhaps was not even possible. One interpreted the sounds and measured the pauses. These were the only clues to whatever messages one hoped to exchange.

Powers stared at the dead phone in his hand, and thought that it isolated those who used it into worlds as small, as sterile, and as separate as their individual phone booths. It was perfect for causing pain.

Year of the Dragon *by Robert Daley*

SPEECH COMPRESSION

We have seen that the digitization of telephone quality speech requires about 64 kbps. The rewards for finding ways of decreasing this number without hurting the speech quality are very large. When speech is stored in computers, think of how much memory capacity is used up for such a paltry amount of speech. That soliloquy from *Hamlet*, for example, uses about 100 seconds of speech, which would require about all of one 700 kbyte floppy disk. In that particular case, it would be worth it, but we can see that speech does not go very far on a computer when it has to be coded at the standard telephone rate.

The transmission of speech over the telephone network is another application where great economic benefit would come from reducing the coding requirements. The carrier systems that convey our speech over microwave radio towers and through buried optical fibers are really bit pipes. All the fiber knows is that it lugs 1.7 billion bits per second from one repeater station to another. If speech has to be coded at 64 kbps, then the pipe carries 25,000 voice conversations. On the other hand, if we were clever enough to be able to code the speech using only half that bit rate, then we could carry 50,000 voice channels, effectively doubling the network capacity. It would be like building another telephone network. Obviously there is much to be gained. Let us try to see just how much.

So far we have dealt with two extremes of media for the communications of language—telephone-quality speech and text. But there is a continuum of possibilities between these extremes. In the 64 kbps bit per second encoding of speech there is no real attempt to take advantage of the properties of speech other than its bandwidth limitation. By designing algorithms that rely on the properties of speech we are able to build coders that operate at lower bit rates, but invariably also at a lower quality of reproduction. As we squeeze more and more bits from the representation of speech it loses its character, turning gradually into mechanical speech, or even someone else's speech, as when a telegram is read to us over the telephone. Just how well we can reproduce speech at a given bit rate depends upon the efficiency of our mathematical algorithms and upon the power of our computers. Speech gives up its bits grudgingly, and the demands for wisdom and processing grow exponentially as the bit rate shrinks, even as the flavor and character drain from the decoded voice.

Figure 16 shows a general curve of the speech quality that engineers have been able to obtain as a function of bit rate. Although the values of quality shown reflect the state of the art at the time of this writing, I would expect the general shape of the curve to be maintained. The task of new speech algorithms and processors will be to gradually lift the curve and stretch the region of acceptability for low-bit-rate voice.

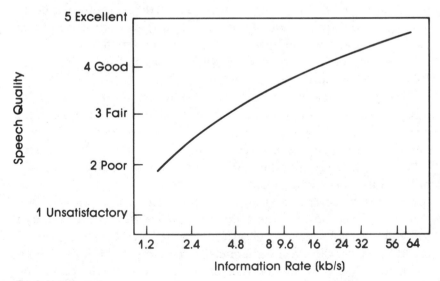

FIGURE 16

Quality of coded speech vs. bit rate *(from J. L. Flanagan)*

There is no one speech processing algorithm that yields this curve, rather it represents the envelope of a collection of different methods. At the higher bit rates, say above 16 kbps, the speech coding procedures are generally what we term waveform coders. That is, these coders attempt as best they can to preserve the actual waveform of the speech signal. Below this bit rate the procedures rely more and more upon models of the physical speech generation mechanism. In effect they give up trying to produce an identical waveform, and only try to create similar sounds, that is, sounds having the same short-term amplitude (frequency) spectrum, as opposed to sounds having the same precise time waveform. They do this by analyzing the input speech and transmitting the changing parameters of the model to the decoder, where similar speech is synthesized. Ultimately, we could imagine a "talking head" coder. The information stream transmitted would consist of such commands as "now wiggle the tongue downward in an arched position." The intimate relationship of the original speech with the details of the mechanics of its generation is irrevocably lost. These kinds of analysis/synthesis coders are usually called vocoders, which is a contraction of voice coder.

I do not want to prolong unduly this section, but I would like to describe the principal ideas behind one waveform coder and one vocoder. The latter example will be the so-called linear predictive coder, and it is important to understand because it forms a basis for both speech synthesis, per se, and speech recognition.

WAVEFORM CODING USING SIGNAL PREDICTION

In 1984 the international standards body in telecommunications approved a new standard for encoding voiceband waveforms at 32 kbps based upon the use of a technique called adaptive differential pulse code modulation, ADPCM. This type of coder achieves the same quality of speech as the 64 kbps coder at half the bit rate, though it is considerably more complex, and it is fragile for non-voice signals (such as from data modems) that happen to flow through the same signal path. It achieves its compression using a general principle of signal prediction that is sufficiently powerful and so widely applied as to be worth explaining here. Also, it is very cute.

Realizing that the actual information content of a speech signal is far less than seems to be required for brute-force coding of the samples, we might suspect that the series of samples is highly redundant. This suspicion is confirmed by the fact that the correlation between adjacent samples is about 0.9. How can we take advantage of this strong correlation in our coding procedure? An often used attack on redundancy is the use of a predictor to remove the predictable portion of each sample, leaving only the surprise, or random, component. To see how this is effective, let us suppose that we have a little box that is able to predict the forthcoming speech sample based upon the previous samples. Presently I will describe how this might be accomplished, but for the moment assume that we have such a predictor. It is not perfect, but it tries very hard and generally comes close to guessing the next speech sample. How would we use it to lower the bit rate requirement for speech?

Well, to be honest we need two of these predictors, and they must be identical twins. One twin works in the coder, while the other twin works in the decoder. The predictor in the coder takes a crack at guessing each new speech sample before it appears. When the next sample does show up, the coder compares its prediction with the actual sample. Invariably there is some difference between them, since nobody claimed that the predictor was omniscient. But the difference is generally much smaller than the signal itself, so the coder quantizes the *difference,* and transmits it to the receiver.

Because the difference signal is generally smaller than the original speech signal, it requires fewer bits for an adequate approximation for reproduction. Specifically, in the ADPCM encoder only 4 bits give an adequate approximation of the difference, as compared with the 8 bits required for the quantization of the signal samples in the previous systems. (Part of this economy comes from the fact that the quantization in ADPCM is made to change with the excursions in amplitude of the speech signal, like an electronic genie riding the volume control. As the volume swells and diminishes, the "staircase" of reference quantization levels is made to expand and contract like an accordion. The receiver follows this expansion and contraction with its own gain control.)

At the receiver the predictor's twin is at work making identical guesses of the next speech sample based upon its previously decoded samples. It subsequently uses the received difference signal to adjust its guesses to the correct value. It might seem as if this is all done with mirrors, since the decoder is using its own previous decisions to help make the next decision. As delicate and complex as this may be, the fact that it actually works has been confirmed by the decision to have hundreds of thousands of these systems throughout the world handling voice signals wherever telephones are being used. These ADPCM systems will purr along beautifully, until, of course, there is some error in transmission and the poor twins are working on different sequences of bits. But that is another story for another book!

That we can make a predictor for speech may seem magical, but that is what redundancy and entropy are all about. The speech

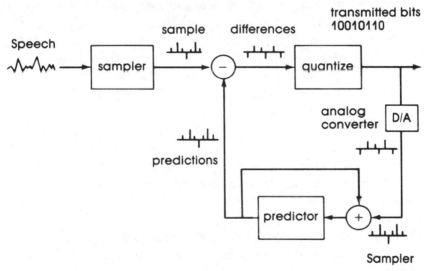

ADPCM Transmitter

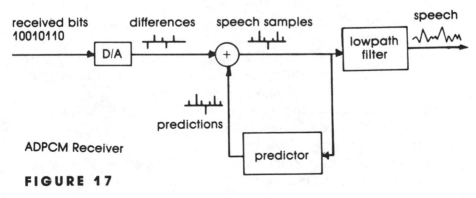

ADPCM Receiver

FIGURE 17

signal is not entirely random; otherwise it would sound like noise. To a certain degree the nonrandom component of the speech signal can be predicted from the preceding signal. Just as in text, there is something about the pattern of letters or the squiggle of the wave- form that conditions what follows. Each new sample of speech is a little bit expected, and a little bit random. (The same thing has been said about the music of Beethoven, that he perfected the blend that gave each succeeding note just the right amount of expectedness and surprise.) A predictor can tell us the expected part, while the unexpected or random part will be the ultimate difference signal to be transmitted to the receiver.

Nearly all practical predictors are linear predictors. They pre- dict the forthcoming sample as a linear combination (a weighted sum) of the previous samples. In words, take a little of the sample you just saw, add or subtract some of the one before that, add a touch of eye of newt (just kidding!), and you have a reasonable prediction. The coefficients in the linear combination are changed relatively slowly with time, say every hundred samples (keeping up with the changing phones), in a constant attempt to keep the mean square error in the prediction as small as possible. This kind of prediction was analyzed and used during the Second World War to train guns mounted on ships in rolling seas upon planes flying trajectories above. In that case too there are predictable and unpre- dictable components. The best that can be done is to follow the predictable part.

In the ADPCM standard there are eight variable coefficients to be adjusted in the linear predictor. All are simultaneously adjusted in an incremental fashion according to a gradient algorithm, which is mathematically similar to what you might do in trying to reach the bottom of a valley, that is, continue to step downwards until there is no longer any step that is down. In this case "down" is defined as less mean square error in the prediction. After a certain number of steps there is nowhere to go in reducing the mean square predictor error, and the predictor is doing as well as possible for the moment for a linear algorithm with that many degrees of free- dom. Typically the residual error after prediction will be about 10 db below the original signal. The adaptation is implemented digi- tally using either special purpose microchips or programmable digi- tal signal processor chips. The ADPCM standard defines the algorithm precisely, because it is essential that all predictors, everywhere, adjust themselves exactly the same way, and make the same predictions with the same input samples. Amazing!

Even in the ADPCM coder observe that we have not really done anything based particularly on speech, except to specify the bandwidth and the allowable quantization error in the difference signal. If, for example, the signal being handled by the ADPCM coder was not speech but instead was a signal from a voiceband modem carrying data, then the unknowing predictor would just go ahead and make predictions, and the decoder would reconstruct the waveform from its own predictions and the difference signal. The only problem would be that the modem signal might be less predictable than voice, and the quantization might not be sufficient to maintain a low probability of error in the received data. Since users have become accustomed to using the telephone network for modems as well as voice it is necessary to detect the presence of a data signal and modify the ADPCM coders accordingly. Ah, the burdens of history!

LINEAR PREDICTIVE CODING (LPC)

So much for waveform coders. Below about 16 kbps it is just not possible to preserve the actual waveform of the speech signal. The trick is to transmit some other kind of information that enables the generation of a similar voice at the receiver. Thus there is a class of speech coding systems which *analyze* the voice signal at the transmitter, transmit parameters derived from this analysis, and then *synthesize* the voice at the receiver. The most popular example of this class is the linear predictive coder, or LPC. (I have tried to avoid acronyms where possible, but sometimes the acronym is better known than the name itself.) With LPC it is possible to transmit fair quality voice at 4.8 kbps and poorer quality voice at even lower rates. The LPC speech at 4.8 kbps is termed "communication quality" speech, which means it is noticeably inferior to the toll-quality speech of PCM and ADPCM. Personally, I think it sounds pretty good, but I have an untrained ear and do not know any better.

I would like to introduce LPC by going back to that marvelous adaptive linear predictor that we used for ADPCM. Suppose, for simplicity, that the difference signal is not quantized, but instead it is transmitted directly as an analog signal to the receiver. We will worry about the receiver presently, but for the moment consider what is going on at the transmitter. The adaptive linear predictor is working away trying its best to minimize the difference between its predictions and the actual speech samples. In order to minimize this difference the predictor has to *undo* the speech, and in so doing it accomplishes the *analysis* part of the vocoder task. The coefficients that it uses for its minimization give us much of the information that we could use to resynthesize the voice.

To see what I mean, consider the energy distribution of the speech and of the difference (transmitted) signal as shown in Figure 18. The speech signal itself displays the typical resonance peaks of the formants in its energy spectrum. On the other hand, if we would look at the difference signal we would see that not only is its average power considerably less than that of the original speech but that its spectrum would be rather flat, which is the characteristic of white noise. In other words, as a natural consequence of minimizing the prediction error the prediction filter "whitens" the speech spectrum. It removes the formant resonances by continuously adapting

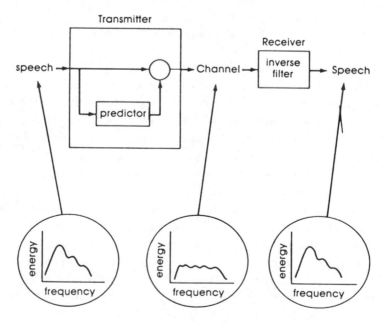

FIGURE 18
Linear predictive coding

its filter characteristics to flatten these formant peaks. If we could watch its characteristic change with time, we would see that it is nearly an inverse of what our own vocal tract is doing to shape spectrally the sound in the first place.

Now let us turn our attention towards the reconstruction of the speech signal at the receiver. It should be evident that if we can build a filter at the receiver that exactly undoes what the transmitter filter did (it undoes the undoing of the speech), then we can turn the difference signal back into speech. Contrary to what we learned from Humpty-Dumpty, with linear filtering this is usually (but not always) possible. If we know the coefficients of the transmitter prediction filter, we can grind out some calculations and put together a digital algorithm that implements an inverse filter at the receiver. As you can see from Figure 18, the characteristic of this filter will be the same as the original speech spectrum. It gives the spectrally flat difference signal the spectral shape of the original speech. We think of this filter as the *synthesis* filter, and what it would be doing would be analogous to what our vocal tract did when it colored the original sound.

I hope that the system of Figure 18 is understandable. First we undo the speech with a filter that flattens its spectrum, and then we restore the damage with an inverse filter. A nice trick if we can do it, but you are probably wondering what this has to do with LPC coding. Well, we are close to the central idea of LPC. To resynthesize the speech at the receiver we need two things—the information about what the transmitter filter is doing, and the difference signal. Getting the filter information is the easier part. In concept, we transmit the coefficients of the transmitter predictor filter (or their equivalents) to the receiver. For example, we send a digital stream to the receiver which says that the first coefficient is presently .2319, the second is −.1903, etc. Naturally, these values have to be quantized for digital transmission, and this costs us some of our precious data rate, but that turns out to be a bargain. The more important question is how to get the equivalent of the difference signal to the receiver without using a lot of bits.

I picture the synthesis filter at the receiver as a sort of working vocal tract simulator. Just as our vocal organs are constantly working to deform our malleable vocal tube to have the desired resonances, the receiver filter is working to shape the electrical signal with the same resonance properties. If we feed it the difference signal, out comes the voice. From this same viewpoint, it follows that we can think of the difference signal as being the excitation waveform that has its analog in the air forced through our vocal tract. If the sound is unvoiced, like the turbulent air in the *s* of "see," then the difference signal is very much like white noise, sounding like the hiss between stations on FM radio. On the other hand, if the sound is voiced, as in the *ee* of "see," then the difference signal is analogous to the pulsed air emitted by our vocal cords. The sound of the difference signal in this case is typically a "buzz" at the fundamental pitch that we impart to that *ee*. Thus, if we could listen to the difference signal we would hear a kind of buzzy hiss. (To be honest, we hear a little intelligible voice in there too, albeit raspy, noisy, and distorted—neither the model nor the implementation is perfect.) Now you might think, why waste a lot of bits sending a buzzy hiss? Why not just create some new buzzy hiss at the receiver and use that instead? This is the idea of LPC.

Various LPC systems differ in the way that they recreate the difference signal (the excitation) at the receiver. Three alternatives are shown in Figure 19. The earliest and most popular means is to use two sources at the receiver, one of white noise (the hiss) and the other with a series of pulses at the current pitch rate (the buzz). The decision as to which is more appropriate for a given speech segment must be made as part of the speech analysis at the transmitter. Additionally, the transmitter must do pitch extraction to determine the frequency of the pitch pulses to be used. There is a great deal of art and science in these seemingly innocuous decisions, which are surprisingly difficult both in concept and in practice. This is the type of LPC that is standardized for government/military low-bit-rate voice as LPC-10, or "buzz-hiss" LPC.

To put some numbers on this conceptual framework, the input speech could be sampled at 8 kHz and passed through a time window of about 10 to 30 milliseconds, the analysis period over which the vocal tract would be assumed to be stationary. The analysis filter could have 12 coefficients, which would be derived from a numerical analysis using a series of recursive operations on the input samples in the window (equivalent to solving a set of simultaneous linear equations). It turns out to be inefficient to quantize these coefficients directly, as too many bits are required for a given accuracy at the receiver, so the transmitted parameters are derived from a mathematical transformation of these coefficients. We might allocate a total of 60 bits for these parameters, and in addition, 6

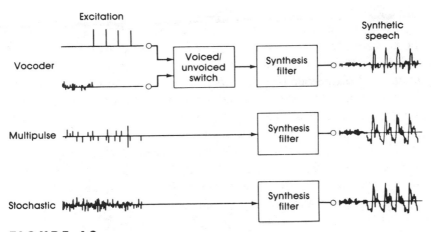

FIGURE 19
Linear predictive coding alternatives

bits to specify the extracted pitch frequency, 5 bits to quantize the average power in the speech samples, and a single bit for the voiced/unvoiced decision. This would be a total of 72 bits per frame, or 7,200 bits per second, which is a typical data rate for this form of LPC.

Recall that the reconstituted speech differs from the original only in that we have substituted an artificial difference signal. A lot depends on how clever we are about matching this artificial excitation to the original. A more modern approach to this matching is called multipulse LPC. In multipulse, as shown in Figure 19, the buzz-hiss excitation is replaced by a sequence of pulses, whose locations and amplitudes are chosen by the transmitter to minimize the perceptual difference between the original and synthetic speech signals. There might be 10 pulses within a 10 millisecond segment, and quantizing their amplitudes and positions could well use up 4 kbps, but the quality of the reproduction is considerably enhanced relative to the "buzz-hiss" LPC. Also, it is significant that the multipulse approach relieves the transmitter of the burden of making the voiced/unvoiced decision and having to do pitch extraction.

The last alternative shown is stochastic excitation, or what is sometimes called stochastic coding. In this method the coder and decoder have a predetermined code book of random excitation signals. For each speech signal the transmitter searches through its code book of handy signals for the one that gives the best perceptual match to the sound. Then it transmits bits to the receiver which, for example, say to use waveform number 1,328 for excitation on the current segment. This is a relatively new and promising speech coding methodology that appears to give good quality speech at around 4 kbps. Stochastic coding requires a prodigious amount of computation, of the order of 20 million multiply/add operations per second. This is the kind of computing power we associate with supercomputers, yet stochastic coding is being considered as a viable alternative for such applications as mobile telephony, where bandwidth is a precious commodity. Such processing is made possible by the fact that the algorithm is specialized, and the ever-increasing speed and density of microelectronic circuitry permits realization in a few intricate and powerful chips.

Below 2.4 kbps all pretense at faithful reproduction of voice is abandoned. However, it is still possible to synthesize intelligible voice from the LPC approach. In this regime we cannot afford to transmit all of the LPC parameters in their full-blown precision. A lot has to give, but as always it is possible to give in with a degree of intelligence. There is still a great deal of redundancy in the parameters being transmitted by LPC, and a general technique of taking advantage of this redundancy is to encode the parameters a block at a time, instead of quantizing each individual coefficient by itself. This is known as vector quantization, since it is the multidimensional analog of (scalar) quantization. This follows the same philosophy that we discussed in the chapter on information theory: The more dimensions we can agglomerate before coding, the more typical is the behavior of the composite.

As an example of vector quantization, suppose that we can only afford 10 bits to send 12 filter parameters. Then we can designate only $2^{10} = 1,024$ possible sequences (coefficient vectors) with the 10 bits; that is all the freedom we have. How do we use this freedom in the best way? Well, suppose that we take a lot of sample speech segments from the particular speaker who is to use the system and we process these segments to extract the LPC parameters. Think of each parameter set as a vector and imagine plotting all of these sample vectors. We would certainly expect to see clumping of these sample vectors. For example, all of the long e vectors would be near each other, but there would undoubtedly be subclumps of this clump representing different ways this same sound was formed. The task that confronts us is whether we can divide all of these sample vectors into 1,024 "representative" vectors. Then the transmitter only needs to tell the receiver to use, say, vector number 729 for the current parameter set. The more the samples "clump," the more effective vector quantizing will be, that is, the fewer representative vectors that will be required for a given accuracy.

The extreme redundancy of speech virtually guarantees that a great deal of clumping will occur in any long sample set of LPC parameters. In one experiment LPC speech coded with vector quantization using 10 bits for the filter parameters was judged equivalent in quality to that obtained using 35 bits for the same parameters with ordinary, scalar quantization. However, two problems are immediately evident: Deriving a code book of reference vectors is cumbersome at best, and the processing requirements for the coding procedure are extraordinary. It is very time consuming to do an exhaustive search of the codebook for every speech segment to find the closest codebook vector, and these computational requirements grow exponentially with the length in bits of the code word. I have heard speech coded by vector quantized LPC down to rates as low as 150 bps. It is intelligible, but very mechanical. It would be hard to recognize even a good friend at these starvation rates.

All this is, I fear, more than many readers would like to know about LPC coding. Yet it is a term which is much used, and the technique is being seen increasingly in practical systems. The power of modern microelectronics makes all this calculation at the transmitter and receiver almost routine. It is important to understand the trade we are making—we are trading processing for communications. LPC takes a lot of complicated processing to make up for the bits saved in transmission or storage. As I have said before, saving those bits is very costly in computer power, and the quality of speech reproduction suffers even as the need for computation becomes exponentially larger. Even so, the demands of speech-for-bit rate are so voracious that for digital speech storage and transmission the trade of processing for bit rate is often quite willingly made.

S   P   E   E   C   H   S   Y   N   T   H   E   S   I   S

I remember "Run, Spot, run!" In kindergarten, speech synthesis from text did not seem all that difficult. (At least I think so in retrospect!) So what is so difficult about a computer reading aloud from text? The amazing thing in what we are going to discuss about computer speech synthesis is how hard it really is to do well. We have all been conditioned through hearing computer-generated speech from toys and other gadgets into believing that speech synthesis is either trivial or at least a solved problem. That perception is far from the truth. A little knowledge about speech synthesis should convince you that "Run, Spot, run!" deserves a lot of appreciation. I know it is a refrain in this book, but we humans are really pretty good at such things!

Almost all the computer speech synthesis that we hear is really nothing more than prerecorded speech, digitized using the techniques for speech coding that we have just discussed. For example, in the Speak-and-Spell toy the words in the toy's vocabulary were recorded as spoken by a human, and then processed by LPC analysis to compress them into an efficient bit stream for storage in a small read-only memory chip. Note that the most difficult part of LPC technology is the encoding, and this can be done once at leisure on a large computer with the active intervention of a speech technologist. The reconstruction of the speech from the LPC parameters is the job of a single microchip, a copy of which obviously needs to reside in every such toy. Because the voice can be carefully crafted through hand tuning of the LPC parameters, the designers of Speak-and-Spell had their choice of what character the voice should emulate. Interestingly, when a survey of children was carried out, the children preferred a "computer" voice to that of a superhero or a parrot.

At an LPC encoding rate of 4,800 bps a one megabit memory chip can store about 200 seconds of speech, or approximately 600 words. We could use this capacity in whatever format we wished. Individual words could be accessed under computer control as in Speak-and-Spell, or whole sentences could be accessed for instructions for telephone users. What does not work is patching words or phrases together to form larger speech segments. These patchwork-quilt phrases of words originally spoken in a different context sound choppy and sing-song. For this reason prerecorded, synthesized speech—what is known as synthesis-by-analysis—has limited versatility. We have to know in advance every phrase that needs to be spoken, and have a complete recording available of each. Although this is sometimes the case, it is often desirable for a computer to synthesize arbitrary phrases from unrestricted text. This unlimited text-to-speech synthesis of material not previously spoken by a human is the interesting, important, and difficult task upon which much speech research is now concentrated.

TEXT-TO-SPEECH SYNTHESIS
• • • • • • • • •

In text-to-speech synthesis the computer tries to read much as you or I would. We arm it with an inventory of basic sounds, and it looks at text and recognizes many words that it knows how to pronounce through intelligent stringing together of those basic sounds. Most words it looks up in a pronouncing dictionary. If the word is not in its dictionary, it does what we would do; it just takes a stab at pronunciation using general rules that it has learned. But pronouncing isolated words is not reading, so throughout the process the computer must take cognizance of the context of the material. Reading comes naturally to literate humans, so we do not realize that to sound natural we have to know what we are talking about. That is the problem with most text-to-speech synthesis. The computer does not sound like it knows what it is talking about. There is a reason; basically, it does not even have a clue.

In forming speech from subunits there is a choice of sizes for the building block units of speech. The larger units, such as words, are easier to smooth together, but the vocabulary size becomes unwieldy. Speech units for English are shown in the table on the following page. Unlimited text-to-speech synthesizers build up speech from the smallest units—phonemes, allophones, or diphones. Although it is not quite true, I think of the phonemes as the vowels and consonants of English. But phonemes in themselves are not pronounceable, since the pronunciation of an individual vowel or consonant depends upon its immediate context within the word. The pronounceable variations of phonemes are called allophones, which is another term for the generalized word "phone" that I used earlier. Since there are more sounds than letters, we often use letter sequences to stand for phonemes, such as the *ai* in "bait" or the *ea* in "beat." Anyway, I do not want to confuse this too much. Clearly, we build the speech from a small inventory of little bits and pieces. The problems are first, translating the input

UNIT	NUMBER IN ENGLISH	DEFINITION
Phoneme	40	smallest unit of speech e.g., generalized *k* sound
Allophone	230	all the variations of each phoneme e.g., the *k* in "keep," "cup," and "coop"
Diphone	1,400	center-to-center, one phoneme to the next
Syllable	20,000	vowel and its immediate consonants
Demisyllable	1,000	consonant and part of vowel
Morpheme	12,000	smallest meaningful unit
Word	100,000	dictionary entries
	700,000	all forms, e.g., including plurals

text into symbols representing the little pieces of speech, and second, molding and fitting the pieces together in such a way as to produce natural-sounding speech.

The first thing the computer must do with the text is to expand abbreviations, numbers, punctuation, and symbols into words or instructions that the computer will understand later. Then it proceeds to convert the alphabetic text file into symbols for phonemes or allophones. This is a lot harder than you might think. Our first thought would be to have the computerized equivalent of a dictionary in which it could check the pronunciation of each word. Unfortunately there are really too many words, especially when we count all of the variations of number and tense that exist. Furthermore, no dictionary really keeps up with the current use of business or scientific English. I see this every day when I run spell programs on documents that I write. The spell programs are always giving me long lists of words that it thinks are misspelled simply because the words are not in its dictionary. We would hardly be satisfied with a computer that tried to read by bleeping every time it encountered such a word, so we need to supplement the dictionary with a set of default rules for English pronunciation. It will still miss sometimes, but then so do we.

Because there are so many forms of words, the process of dictionary lookup is usually made manageable by breaking words apart to find their root form or their constituent parts. This is called morpheme stripping. What we would would like to do, for example, would be to take a word like "preconceived" and break it up into the morphs *pre* + *con* + *ceive* + *ed*, each of which would serve many other words in a modest-sized dictionary for pronunciation of morphs. Algorithms to isolate root forms of words are becoming rather common for the many spelling programs featured in word processors. Nevertheless, real morpheme stripping is an artform in itself, for there are many pitfalls. Plurals may be formed in various ways and may change the spelling of the root word. Consider, for example, "glass" and "glasses," "city" and "cities," and "child" and "children." The same variations and irregularities happen with verb tenses and with other prefixes and suffixes. Sometimes the spelling of the morph itself changes for no seeming reason. Why do we say *"in*tractable," but *"im*possible"?

The computer needs to know something about these spelling rules so it can properly dissect a word into its constituent morphs. It can then look up the pronunciation of each morph, but it must also be aware of how the pronunciation of each might change as the morphs are concatenated to form the original word. Think of how the sound of *le* differs with its environment in the words "settlement" and "supplement," or how the pronunciation of the morphs varies in the pairs "telegraph" and "telegrapher," "designation" and "design," or in "proverb" and (our word-of-the-day), "pronunciation." Even determining the morph boundaries can be treacherous. Imagine how a computer, fresh from a triumph with a morph-stripping attack on "stomachache" = "stomach" + "ache," would treat "mustache"! My favorite example of deception by morph is the pair "baseline" and "vaseline." If I were a morph stripper (that sounds terrible!), I would be seriously annoyed at a language that led me into these sorts of traps.

Regardless of how the word is broken up, there comes a time when we must convert letters into phonemes or allophones. You might believe, as I did, that for all the years that we have studied grammar, surely the pronunciation rules for English letter sequences would have been well codified. Apparently not. Perhaps it takes the resolute stupidity of a computer to show us all the holes in the structure of our language. If the computer could spend some time out in the playground talking to children it would not ask all of these dumb questions about pronunciation. Probably most engineers share my compulsion to try to fit everything into a nice set of ordered rules. But language pronunciation resists, and when we consider the continuing evolution of language in its ever-widening agglomeration of words, it is easy to understand the difficulties in rule-based simplification. The fact is that spelling does not always reflect the pronunciation of words; it is in part unphonetic.

All of us know instinctively some basic rules for pronunciation. There are the so-called "unmarked" or default rules, such as the sound of the short vowels *e* in "pet," *i* in "bit," and *o* in "tot" when followed by a consonant in the same syllable, versus the long vowels *e* in "Pete," *i* in "bite," and *o* in "tote" elsewhere. All of these types of rules can be implemented on the computer in the form

$$A \ [B] \ C = D$$

which means that the character string B, whose left context is the string A, and whose right context is the string C, gets the pronunciation D. Speech researchers making experimental text-to-speech systems have defined several hundred such default rules.

Before applying the default rules most systems look up the word in a dictionary of exceptions to see if it is one of the many that do not follow the "rules." Curiously, the long list of exceptions includes many of the most frequently used words. These popular words can afford to go it alone, whereas rare words cannot afford this ostentatious display of independence, and are more likely to conform to the rules. For example, the phoneme *f* is always pronounced as in "far," except in the little, omnipresent word "of." The diagraph *th* is usually unvoiced, as in "thirst," but it is voiced in the popular words "the," "this," "there," and "them." And there are many, many other words that digress from conventional pronunciation. We would usually think that *oo* would be pronounced as in "boot," but what about "blood," "book," "Roosevelt," "cooperate," and "microorganism?" We ourselves have to keep dictionaries of pronunciation in our minds in addition to spelling dictionaries. The speculation is that this uses up a lot of our own mental capacity. If spelling were really phonetic it would free a lot of capacity for other things. Maybe.

The dictionary of exceptions has to contain many foreign words that have been incorporated into English, for example, cliché, adobe, andante, kibbutz, sauna, tsar, paprika, sahib, khaki, samurai, ukelele, kayak, and so on. These are no more a problem than the other exceptions, but a special class is that of proper names. Many, if not most, of our family names have been derived from foreign languages, and these proper names will not be in the dictionary. In order not to look foolish, the computer needs to know something about pronunciation of other languages, just as we do. An experimental system at Bell Laboratories uses a pronouncing dictionary of approximately 50,000 names, which covers about 87 percent of the names in the telephone directory of a large American city. If the system fails to find the name in this dictionary, it does a lexical analysis, using trigram probabilities to make a determination of the probable language. For example, the trigram *eau* (as in Trudeau), is much more likely in French than in English. A name with this letter sequence should probably be given pronunciation according to French letter-to-sound rules.

Finally, there are frequent circumstances where the pronunciation of a word depends upon its context. Quite a number of English nouns and adjectives have been derived from verbs, and vice versa—for example, "approximate," "house," "survey," "refuse," and "separate" are given different pronunciations depending on whether they are being used as a noun (or adjective) or verb. For this reason, text-to-speech synthesis systems must do a syntactic analysis, or parse, of the sentence to determine the function of each word. Even this complication, which is usually effected by rather simple parsers, is insufficient to differentiate those words like "lead," which serve dual purposes with different pronunciations. (Does the detective have a lead on the case, or is this whole argument going over like a lead balloon?) These cases require the computer to have semantic knowledge about the focus of conversation, and no text-to-speech system has yet been built that can make these subtle distinctions.

You can see that in its full glory the English language can be a nightmare of traps for a computer without an ear and a learning mechanism to know what it is saying. Nonetheless, experimental systems can pronounce typical English text with a word error rate of less than 10 percent, which is acceptable for most purposes. Reaching towards perfection does not seem either possible or desirable. For one thing, computers are fortunate to be speaking to a human, because we can do a good job of interpreting their mispronunciations in context. After all, we do a fair amount of mispronouncing ourselves with little loss of intelligibility. Moreover,

even we would not ourselves always agree on the correct pronunciation. I was surprised to learn that there are 18 differentiable dia-
lects of English just within the New York metropolitan area where
I live. Finally, it appears to be extraordinarily difficult to lower the
probability of mispronunciation. It gets tougher and tougher, and
there are other things that the computer can do to make its speech
more acceptable than to worry further about its exact pronunciation. Read on.

STRESS AND INTONATION

Assume now that we have converted an alphabetic text file into a
file of symbols representing speech units, such as phonemes or
allophones. We still face the penultimate task of converting these
symbols into an audible stream of natural English. In order to give
sound to the speech units we use a stored vocabulary of speech units
as spoken by a real person. Usually the recorded voice is that of the
system designer, so the system speaks in little pieces of His Master's
Voice. Suppose that these segments have been encoded into LPC
parameters. In order to convert these LPC parameters into synthesized speech we have to add information about the loudness, pitch,
and timing of the consecutive segments, as well as doing some
smoothing of the transitions between segments. The latter problem, smoothing the transitions, is relatively manageable, and I shall
not discuss it further. The real difficulties lie in recreating the
dynamics and intonation, or what is termed the prosody, of natural
speech.

Earlier we spoke of the information content of speech. So far
by capturing and synthesizing the phonemes we have only reproduced the core information—which is equivalent to that in the text.
But we also discussed earlier the "message" on top of the words
given by the rhythm, dynamics, and intonation of the individual
speaker. In text-to-speech synthesis the computer has to add that
prosody on its own to the bare written words, for it is not contained
in the text. It is even possible that the words to be spoken have been
computer-composed, and that no human has ever "performed"
them to have added prosodic content. In either event, all the computer can do is try to fake it. But, like the pianist I mentioned earlier

who, having forgotten the music, "made it sound like Schubert," the computer can try its best to make the speech sound like a real human.

Why is prosody important, and to what degree can it be recreated by a computer? Earlier I quoted a famous, precomputer phoneticist by saying that we speak in order to be understood. Thus we have every motivation to provide the listener with clues to the understanding of our marvelous speeches. Unconsciously, we probably realize that these glorious pearls of wisdom are couched in very delicate phonemes, which need to be further packaged within a larger protective syntactic and semantic context. But given the fragility of the spoken language, we can help the listener even further by clarifying our syntactic construction through the judicious use of pause and stress. Since the listener cannot "see" the spatial relationships between our words, phrases, and clauses, we indicate these boundaries as best we can through the dynamics of our speech. In effect, we aid the parsing of our sentences. In addition to conveying this structural information, the use of stress indicates the relative importance of words and phrases in our speech. Which words, clauses, or ideas are subordinate to which others, and what is their relationship?

Rhythm also can be used to emphasize the structure of a phrase. Try reading the sentence "John, who was the best boy in school, got the medal." Notice how you naturally speed up during the parenthetical clause, and how the pauses before and after the clause are exaggerated. Somehow I feel compelled to get through that clause quickly in order to return to the main thought. I find it almost impossible to read that sentence at a constant rate. On occasion, stress or rhythm can even be used to resolve ambiguities in meaning. A frequently quoted example is the sentence, "George has plans to leave." Read it with the accent on "plans," and then try it with the accent on "leave." Two different thoughts entirely. Beyond structural information, prosody allows the individualization of speech. Rhythm, and to a lesser degree intonation, are what comedians perfect when they mimic celebrities. The spectrograms of their speech do not look like those of the celebrities, but we perceive them as sounding the same because of the similar prosody.

We can see why it is important to recreate natural-sounding stress, rhythm, and intonation in synthesized speech: It will be more understandable. As listeners, we are conditioned to the rhythm and tunes of natural speech, so we might argue that the more natural the computer can sound, the more its speech will be perceived as being intelligible. Present text-to-speech systems fall very much short of sounding natural. Experiments have shown that they have a higher perceived word error rate, and that they are tiring to listen to over longer periods. On the other hand, it is also true that we tend to get more accustomed to synthesized speech over these longer periods, and that our performance with synthesized speech improves—that is, if we are still awake. They are awfully boring.

We have said that prosody helps illustrate the structure and relationships in our spoken phrases, and that for naturalness and intelligibility it must be recreated. Even though prosody is not captured in the text version of language, it is clear that there is some hope of recreating this illuminating layer of speech through syntactic and semantic analysis of the text and some set of appropriate rules. However, there is another deeper layer of prosodic function, and that is emotion. Somewhere buried in the rhythm, stress, and intonation is emotion, and so far we can neither measure emotion nor find rules to generate it. The very existence of emotion seems to imply real-world knowledge and shared experience—which for the present rules out computers. Could you conceive of a text-to-speech synthesizer reading *Hamlet*? I cannot even imagine this. This seems so far beyond what we know of speech synthesis and artificial intelligence that it is not even a dreamable goal. (My friends in speech research disagree. Is nothing sacrosanct?) Basically, speech researchers aim for naturalness simply to promote intelligibility.

Thus, even though we dismiss any pretense at emotional content, we do need to re-create (or create, depending on how you view this) natural dynamics and pitch. As in other aspects of speech synthesis that we have discussed, there must be rules for prosody, especially since we seem to be able to create it from text easily enough ourselves. However, as one speech researcher put it, there seem to be more rules than we know about. Structuring the rules for prosody is made particularly difficult since we must deal with continuous, analog parameters like pitch, duration, and intensity, and relate them to ill-defined measures of stress and importance. Nonetheless, this is the game we must play; find the syntax, boundaries, and relative importance (among other attributes) in text, and then create pitches, durations, and intensities that portray these attributes to the listener.

In the past few years speech researchers have been gathering a catch-all bag of rules and tricks for determining reasonable values for the prosodic variables. While it would not be in keeping with the tenor of this book (notice the allusion to a kind of intonation) to detail any of these rules, I would like to give some feel for the factors involved. In so doing, I will start with close-in factors relating to the immediate environment of a phoneme, and then move outwards to longer range considerations.

The duration, pitch, and intensity of a phoneme depend first upon the phoneme itself and upon the adjoining phonemes in its immediate neighborhood. Some vowels are given a higher intrinsic pitch than others, for example the long *e* sound in "beat" versus the *aa* sound in "Bob," but the dynamics are more determined by the point of stress within the word. Stressed vowels are longer in duration, while vowels in unstressed syllables are both shorter and of lower pitch. The duration of a vowel further depends strongly upon the following consonant and the position of the vowel within the word. For example, vowels are longest when they are in the last syllable before a pause, while initial consonants are longer than medial consonants. These short-range rules are the kind of pattern-dependent rules which, though tedious, are not especially difficult to implement on a computer.

Stress is also determined by the word and its function in the sentence. We tend to shorten the phoneme durations in polysyllabic words. Perhaps we are impatient with too much work associated with a single word, or perhaps we feel that the word will be easy to distinguish, because word predictability is another important determining factor. We tend to swallow up those little highly predictable function words like "the," "of," "and," and so on, while we reserve higher stress for important content words. For example the *t* phoneme in "to" is typically only 44 milliseconds in duration, as compared with an average of 70 milliseconds when this same phoneme appears in content words. Thus a text-to-speech synthesizer needs to assign stress levels according to predictability and function. A primary level of stress would be assigned to a word denoting the focus of conversation. Next in line would be important content words (those relating to things, actions, and attributes). Of lower stress would be intermediate words, and least stressed would be high frequency words and function words (usually the same).

Once again we see the versatility of the human response to language. In examining text in Chapter 3 we saw the innate redundancies of our alphabetic system as an information medium. But while this redundancy serves to protect the integrity of our language, it is frequently circumvented by unconscious human interpretation. We saw earlier that we tend to skip the highly predictable words during silent reading. We manage to pretend that they are not even there. Now we find that in speaking we devote scant time and energy to these little popular words. We save our energy for the words that really count. Clever of us.

At word boundaries we need to insert appropriate pauses, but there are also carry-over effects between words. Syllables tend to be longer at boundaries, and final and initial consonants are shortened and lengthened, respectively. As an example of a carry-over effect, notice what happens to the *s* in "bus stop" as compared with, say, "bus lane." Moving outwards, there is a hierarchy of pauses as we encounter syntactical breaks—between phrases, between clauses, and between sentences. Punctuation also must be reflected on a priority basis, just like an interrupt on a computer. Different forms of punctuation require varying responses. For example, a comma calls for a pause and a rising pitch, implying continuation, whereas the period at the end of a sentence usually calls for a falling pitch indicating finality.

Perhaps the most difficult and least understood component in prosody is the overall pitch contour. As we speak, we sound out little melodies with notes (pitch) and rhythm (duration). In what is called a "neutral declarative sentence"—that is, a simple statement of fact—the overall pitch envelope tends to show a hat-shaped rise and fall over the course of the sentence. Within this envelope the pitch alternates between a number of high and low notes, corresponding to the positions of stress. The pitch gradually falls off and there is a diminishing range between the highs and lows as the sentence progresses towards conclusion. The coordination and relationships between these peaks and valleys seems to be important to the listener. A researcher in this field has observed that subordination among these peaks "is an important factor in creating an impression that the computer knows what it is saying."

We make use of melody patterns in a variety of ways. We use different intonational patterns to phrase a question, to express surprise, to contradict, and for other purposes. Often the intonation expresses a relationship between something that was said before and what is now being said. Certainly, there is a discourse dependency here that will elude computers for many years to come. Since we have so little understanding of the rules ourselves, we are hardly in a position to teach computers. It is fascinating to me that even in writing a text like this, I am compelled by a certain sense of rhythm. This is in no sense poetry, but I often find myself going back and removing or adding words to correct sentences just because they do not "sound" right. Some parts are grammatically correct, but they sound choppy. Why should "sound" count in text? Perhaps I deceive myself, and your sense of rhythm is different than mine. On the other hand, if we agree, then we should be able to formulate the rules of this most interesting game and teach them to computers. But Shakespeare? No way.

SPEECH RECOGNITION

Speech synthesis is only very hard to do *well.* The computer may not be able to make the stress, rhythm, and intonation sound natural, and it may mispronounce occasional words, but we can get the idea of what it is trying to say. If our aspirations are not inordinately high, we can consider text-to-speech synthesis entirely feasible with today's computer technology. The state of the art in speech recognition, by contrast, is not as advanced. Nevertheless, we see an increasing number of commercial applications using speech recognition. In truth, there are probably more applications for simple speech recognition units than there are for even complex text-to-speech synthesizers. Many companies have products in this field, and now there are plug-in boards that add speech recognition capabilities to even the lowly personal computer. Perhaps many readers have tried such systems or have seen exhibits at museums which are controlled by spoken commands. At Disney's EPCOT Center there is, for example, a graphics mouse on a computer screen which can be guided through a maze by spoken directions. "Up, left, right . . . ," and the mouse dutifully and tirelessly follows the instructions of countless passersby.

Unfortunately, the trained mouse just about epitomizes the state of the art in speech recognition today. It recognizes a small vocabulary of isolated word commands—useful, but awkward. The mouse balances with us on that precarious knowledge cliff. Make the problem harder and we fall off a precipice of unfathomable height. The inherent difficulties that we have seen previously in our discussion of machine understanding of natural languages are compounded by the necessity of first translating sloppy and noisy sounds into discrete words. Machine recognition of fluent, conversational speech is about the hardest problem of which I can conceive. (Spoken language translation is another, related, extraordinarily hard problem.) Yet it can be done, even by babies. Given this existing proof, I am sure that someday computers will listen as well as they speak. But I expect this to take a great many years of improvement in both algorithms and in computer power. In reviewing the literature in this field over the last twenty years, I can sense the dimming of expectations as the magnitudes of the difficulties have been gradually revealed. But first, let us extoll the triumphs.

ISOLATED WORD RECOGNITION

• • • • • • • • • • • • •

Machines can recognize isolated words chosen from limited vocabularies of several hundred words just about as well as we can. They do it by comparing the speech pattern of the spoken word against reference patterns of the words in their vocabulary. Recall that the spectrograms that we discussed earlier in this chapter were originally termed "visible speech." Every distinct phone produces a characteristic spectral pattern in this display. Conceptually, perhaps, we could study the spectrogram of an unknown speech pattern and deduce the spoken words. We could say, for example, that the phoneme with the sound of the e in "beat" is characterized by a voiced sound with the first three formants at 270, 2,290, and 3,010 Hz, and with the width of these formant bars being about 75, 75, and 150 Hz, respectively. Unfortunately, while this may be true of a particular phoneme in isolation, there is great variation in a phoneme within a word depending upon its context, as one sound glides and smears into another. Because of these very considerable difficulties, almost all speech recognition systems are word-based, that is, they compare the speech patterns for entire words to look for overall similarity.

The essence then of isolated word recognition is simple; record the necessary words for the vocabulary as spoken by either the intended speaker (speaker dependent) or by a collection of typical speakers (speaker independent). Then when an input word needs to be recognized, find the best match against these test patterns. The questions to be answered are what exactly do we match, and how do we do the matching? In discussing the first of these questions we should realize that what counts is the *sound* of the word, not its visual image as a time waveform. Furthermore, as the signal must be digitized for computer processing, we are talking about a considerable amount of data (say 20,000 bits) for each word. What we would like would be some form of data reduction that would preserve and illuminate the important sound characteristics of the word with as few bits as possible. Of course this was exactly the aim of the speech coding work that we discussed earlier, where we saw that a particularly effective data reduction technique was LPC coding. Thus, most voice recognition systems begin by converting input speech patterns into a set of LPC coefficient vectors.

Typically an input utterance is digitized and LPC analyzed to derive a set of perhaps 30 to 40 coefficient vectors, each of which might consist of 10 parameters (9 filter coefficients and an average power value). The words in the recognizer's vocabulary would be stored in memory in a similar format. Remember that the LPC coefficients are related to the shape of the vocal tract during the particular speech segment of each successive LPC analysis frame. The sequence of LPC coefficient vectors for a word is like a series of stop-action X rays of its articulation. Looking at our dictionary of reference sequences of vectors, we ask which sequence most resembles the sequence of LPC vectors of the word in question. Like most things in this business, this comparison is easier said than done.

We might begin by asking how we measure similarity between LPC vectors. Simple Euclidean distance between the vectors is an obvious possibility, but the measure that is generally used is more complicated and meaningful. Since the LPC coefficients are supposed to represent the settings of the predictor filter which minimize the predictor error for a particular speech pattern, we can simply try the unknown speech pattern against the various predictor filter settings in our vocabulary and measure the relative prediction error in each case. The "closest" matching vector should be the one with the least residual error. Naturally, this takes more than a bit of clever computation, but efficient algorithms do exist for this task. For our purposes it should be sufficient to say that we have a way of measuring the distance between any two LPC vectors, and that when we compare sequences of vectors we sum the distances between individual vectors.

Now for the trickiest part. Since people talk at different speeds, there is no guarantee that the reference words are of the same duration as the unknown words. Worse yet, the time scale within the word will vary; some syllables will be longer and some shorter. How then do we adjust the flow of time in the reference and unknown words in order to get a fair comparison? This is probably the place where the most significant innovation in speech recognition was made in recent years, when it was discovered that an optimization technique known as dynamic programming could be used to make the correspondence between unknown and reference vectors in spite of the variation in relative timings. This has become known as dynamic time warping. Let me explain the approach, if not the details of the algorithm itself.

Dynamic time warping is used to compare two sets of vectors. From the unknown word suppose we have the vectors,

$$u_1, u_2, u_3, u_4, u_5, u_6, u_7,$$

while as the reference template from the stored vocabulary we might have

$$r_1, r_2, r_3, r_4, r_5, r_6, r_7, r_8.$$

Notice that there may be unequal numbers of vectors in the comparison. We have a distance measure to apply to any two vectors, but the question is which pairs of vectors should be associated. Obviously the fairest comparison is made when the total distance is minimized, but we must use every vector and in the correct order. Because the time scales do not match in the two sequences we may have to use some vectors more than once, before moving on to the next vector.

We can look at these pairings in the matrix shown in Figure 20, where the distance between each pair is shown as an entry in the corresponding column and row. Each possible time warp is a path from the lower left of this matrix to the upper right. The best path minimizes the total distance, while following the rules of correspondence. We might think of these stepping rules as a form of chess; we are only allowed horizontal, vertical, and upward diagonal mo-

distance matrix d(r_i, u_j)

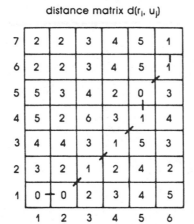

7	2	2	3	4	5	1
6	2	2	3	4	5	1
5	5	3	4	2	0	3
4	5	2	6	3	1	4
3	4	4	3	1	5	3
2	3	2	1	2	4	2
1	0	0	2	3	4	5

1 2 3 4 5 6

unknown word vectors

FIGURE 20
Dynamic programming is used to find the best path matching a vocabulary template against the linear predictive coding vectors of an unknown word.

tions—like a king who cannot retreat. Dynamic programming is an efficient algorithm that finds the best path under such circumstances by an iterative procedure. For the example shown (which has fewer vectors than would ordinarily be used), the best path is outlined. After the best time-warped path had been found for each reference template, the one with the smallest distance would be declared the best match to the word in question.

A more intuitive appreciation for the matching process is conveyed by Figure 21, which shows how the distance between a test word and various vocabulary templates grows as we include more and more vectors in the time-warped matching procedure. In this example, the vocabulary consists of the alphadigits 0 through 9 and *a* through *z*, while the test word is *Q*. Notice first that the distance between the test word and most wrong templates grows quickly, and for these cases the test may be terminated early, as indicated by the rejection threshold in the figure. But observe that the template for *U* refuses to concede the struggle for recognition. In saying *Q* and *U* we can observe that there is a difference in the beginnings of their sounds, but that thereafter the sounds are similar. This is exactly the behavior displayed in the distance growth.

The reason that there are two plots for both *Q* and *U* is because of the usual practice of including multiple templates, in this case two, for each word in the vocabulary. Obviously we do not speak

271

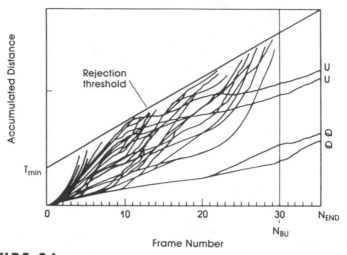

FIGURE 21

Plots of accumulated distance between an unknown word and reference templates versus number of LPC vectors considered. *(from L. R. Rabiner and S. E. Levinson)*

a given word the same way every time, so one template might not be a fair way to pass judgment. Multiple templates are more crucial in the case of speaker-independent word recognition, where we need to assemble a group of representative ways of saying each vocabulary word. The representative templates are chosen from a number of recorded versions of each word by using mathematical clustering techniques. You can imagine this process as if we threw a number of darts at a dartboard. Then, looking at the cluttered dartboard, we observe that there is a cluster of darts around a particular point on the board, so we remove all but the most central dart in the cluster. Then we see another cluster, which we represent similarly. Finally, seeing no more clusters, we have a few individual outlying darts. Are these also representative of fair throws, or should they be discarded? A little judgment is sometimes required, but by a process like this we build a set of templates for each vocabulary word. Experience has tended to show that six to twelve templates can represent a large population (say 100) of talkers. Usually male and female speakers will be found in different clusters.

The similarity of the Q and U brings up another critical point. What matters in correct word recognition is not so much the size of the vocabulary being considered, but the similarity in sounds of the words. In other words, we have to be concerned with the *confusability* of the vocabulary. Of course, confusability comes almost naturally with larger vocabularies, as the probability of getting pairs of words that sound alike becomes much greater with larger vocabularies. However, it is possible to have long lists of polysyllabic words—for example, lists of cities—which are distinctly different, whereas the simple alphabetic words themselves contain many confusion classes, such as *(A, J, K)* and *(B, D, E, G, P, T, V, Z)*.

The current state of the art in recognition of isolated words is about 99% recognition accuracy in recognition of the digits, regardless of whether or not the system is trained for the particular speaker. Recognition of letters is considerably harder because of the greater confusability, so the probability of correctly recognizing one of the 36 alphadigits is only 90 percent. Thus the probability of correctly recognizing a string of letters, such as in the spelling of a proper name, is only about 80 percent. In a speaker-dependent system, recognition of the 1,109 words of basic English is about 79 percent. There are two problems with making large vocabulary systems; one is the mounting confusability, but the second problem is the time and effort required to make the vocabulary templates. How would you like to be required to speak 1,109 isolated words multiple times before you could use the system?

In spite of the limited accuracy of word recognition, it is very important to realize that many tasks can be accomplished within this accuracy because of the inherent redundancy of language. For example, the Bell Laboratories telephone directory contains about 17,000 names. In an experimental system that responds to spelled name inquiries, the accuracy of directory retrieval is about 96 percent. Regardless of the inevitable errors in individual letters, the information is almost always sufficient to pinpoint the correct name in an acoustically organized file. Just the ability to categorize letters by confusion groups makes many identification problems possible, given a restricted set of possible words. As an example, in the entire 20,000 word Merriam Pocket Dictionary the only word that satisfies the phonetic description

[consonant] [consonant] *l* [vowel] [nasal] [stop]

is "splint." In many word recognition tasks it also quite helpful to keep track of the second-best matches (and lower ones) and their relative probabilities, in addition to the primary matches, to aid in the interpretation of the results.

DYNAMIC PROGRAMMING, BEAUTY, AND TRUTH — A DIGRESSION
• • • • • • • • • • • • • •

Dynamic programming has very little to do with programming, and even less to do with anything dynamic. It is an algorithm for numerical optimization that is suitable for many constrained-path search problems. It gets regularly rediscovered, and is used in decoding error-correcting codes and other communications applications under the name Viterbi algorithm, after Andrew Viterbi of the University of Southern California who pioneered these uses.

Shortly after I graduated from college I became enamored of the possibilities for dynamic programming. It was with great expectations that I accepted an invitation to speak at Cal Tech in the mid-1960s at a symposium devoted to new methods of thought and procedure, since one of the other speakers was Richard Bellman, the famous mathematician who popularized dynamic programming with his definitive 1957 text on the subject.

I had the giddy feeling of a young engineer among giants, but all that was soon squashed. Someone introduced me to Oskar Morganstern, the tall, patrician, gray-haired economist from Princeton whom I particularly revered for his book with John von Neuman on game theory. When he was informed that I was the speaker on information theory, Morganstern raised an elite eyebrow in my direction. "Shannon couldn't make it?" he asked of no one in particular. It was the only thing that he almost said to me. As he turned and left I was sensitive to the pregnant silence and the inquisitive stares of the other attendees. I was sure they were thinking of me, "What is *he* doing here?" And they would have been right to wonder, just as I suddenly doubted myself.

After this debacle, you might understand that I was quiet while the giants talked and debated among themselves. One argument that subsequently transpired made an impression on me that has lasted through the quarter of a century since. After Bellman's talk on the beauties of dynamic programming as a new method of thought, the astronomer Fritz Zwicky, then head of the Cal Tech Jet Propulsion Labs, objected to the whole philosophy of dynamic programming. After all, argued Zwicky, dynamic programming only produced specific *numbers*. Where was the beauty in that, asked Zwicky? Scientists should aspire to *closed-form* solutions, for example, $x = \alpha\sin(\psi t)$, in which the relationships among the variables are explicitly revealed. Only through closed-form solutions could insight be gained into physical problems. (The famous dictum of Richard Hamming, "The purpose of computing is insight, not numbers," is of the same ilk.)

My training biased me to side with Zwicky. The fact that a problem could be solved for a particular set of numbers using dynamic programming revealed nothing about the general properties of the solution. But Bellman fought back. What was so evident about these properties in the complicated integral equation solutions of which Zwicky was so fond? Would he not also have to grind out many specific numerical solutions to uncover trends? What was so special and inferior about specifying a solution in terms of an *algorithm* instead of complicated mathematical functions like gamma functions that Zwicky would only have to get from tables? Surely the specification of an algorithm that could be used to produce numbers was tantamount to solving a problem, and entirely equivalent to this fictional closed-form solution.

Remember that these were almost precomputer days. I have often rehashed the argument in my own mind, and I always conclude that Bellman was far ahead of his time. Today there is a great emphasis on algorithms—ways to get at numbers. The computers allow us to swim in so many of these numbers that general properties reveal themselves in broad strokes. Still, I have a secret respect for Zwicky's old-fashioned reverence of beauty in equations, per se. Deriving a solution is so much more fulfilling than declaring algorithmic victory.

CONNECTED AND CONTINUOUS SPEECH RECOGNITION

Our dream is, of course, that computers could recognize conversation the way we do. Conversation might seem like a straightforward extension of the isolated word recognition we have just discussed, but it is a long, long journey indeed. Never mind the fact that the vocabularies of the isolated word recognition system are still rather pathetic, the techniques that are used just do not apply to the recognition of continuous speech. There are two huge stumbling blocks. The sounds of words and other speech units are affected by their context. A template that fits an isolated word will not fit this same word when it is used in conjunction with other words, and building larger templates that cover all combinations of adjacent words is obviously out of the question. This is a possibly insuperable challenge in itself, but there is perhaps an even worse one, and that is that *we cannot separate the individual words themselves.*

In the previous section on isolated word recognition I deliberately sloughed over the problem of identifying when a word begins and ends. If the word is spoken cleanly into a microphone in a quiet environment, then simple energy threshold measurements suffice to mark its beginning and end. However, if there is background noise, if the word is spoken over a telephone line, or if the beginning is masked by extraneous vocalizations, then it is quite difficult to determine exactly where the word should be excised for comparison with the templates. In practice, there are sophisticated search techniques that are integrated with the dynamic time-warping process to attempt a best match in spite of the unknown end points. There is no reason to discuss this here, except to note that it is a significant problem even for isolated words. When the speech is continuous, we have something else altogether. For example, here in New Jersey if we ask "What did you eat?" it comes out sounding like "Whadjeet?" How on earth are we to make out the individual words?!

We humans also have a hard time identifying individual words, even though our skill far surpasses the computer's abilities. If I asked a friend "whadjeet?" as I encountered him leaving a fast food restaurant, he would probably tell me that he ate a cheeseburger and fries, or some such. But if I tried "whadjeet?" in a technical seminar, I would probably just get a blank stare of incomprehension. The point is that we use other sources of information in the interpretation of speech, and therein lies our ability to transcend the difficulties in word recognition. When we speak, we count on our listener to be able to use these other knowledge sources, and we often speak in a lazy form of shorthand. Experiments have shown that when words are isolated from normal, taped conversations, the error rate in recognition by humans is something like 20–30%.

Raj Reddy, a speech researcher at Carnegie Mellon University, conducted a simple experiment in which he asked four subjects to listen to two sentences and to write down what they heard. The sentences and their responses are as follows:

In mud eels are, in clay none are.

1. In muddies sar, in clay nanar.
2. In my deals are, en clainanar.
3. In my ders, en clain.
4. In model sar, in claynanar.

In pine tar is, in oak none is.

1. In pine tarrar, in oak? es
2. In pyntar es, in oak nonnus.
3. In pine tar is, in ocnonin.
4. En pine tar is, in oak is.

Reddy observes that the listener has forced his own interpretation on what he hears, and not necessarily what may have been intended by the speaker. Obviously, the listeners had difficulty fitting the sentences into their frameworks of knowledge. Notice particularly that because of this they often failed to detect where one word ended and another began. But is this not exactly where a poor computer would be in its attempt to understand our spoken language? After all, the words mean nothing more to the computer than those sentences did to the listeners in the experiment.

I think of continuous speech recognition as a path-finding problem, guided by pattern recognition, through the maze of the English language. The computer has a stream of sound patterns that constitute, say, a sentence. As the computer considers the sounds sequentially from left to right, as we do, it tries to map out a path through the English dictionary. What path best matches the sequence of sounds given the current conversational context? The number of possible paths is horrendous, more I am sure than the number of particles in the universe. The computer must use multiple sources of knowledge to cut the number of possible or likely paths down to manageable numbers. It must use knowledge of basic sounds and phonotactics (how the sounds change in context), the hints of prosody, the rules of syntax, the understanding of semantics, the context of discourse, and just plain common sense. If we can tap these sources of knowledge, we can use them in conjunction with algorithms such as dynamic programming to search through the myriad possible pathways for the most likely match to the sequence of sounds.

Shining through this litany of Herculean tasks is the proof that it can be done; we do it. Remember the lesson of monkey 100 and Shannon's guessing experiment from Chapter 3. While there are superastronomical numbers of possible paths in text, when all the constraints are in place the number of remaining paths is quite modest. Recall that when the next letter is covered up a human can guess it correctly about half the time. With an entropy thus estimated at one bit per letter, the uncertainty per word would be 5.5 bits, implying a choice on average of only about 50 words at each branch point in the path. If the computer could wend its path through the sentence with only this degree of uncertainty to resolve using pattern matching, the problem might be solvable. Note that even at this level the overall path can still be lost in the murky cloud of 50^N pathways unless the pattern matching can give us reasonable certainty at numerous branch points.

Thus the task of continuous speech recognition goes far beyond the categorization of sounds themselves. There is not enough information in the sounds alone to do the job; we must integrate knowledge from a number of different sources. While there is no way a computer can approach the human performance in weeding out the unlikely paths, we do have a number of tools to apply. We can use syntactical analysis as embodied in the augmented transition networks (the ATNs of Chapter 4), and we can keep track of semantics to some degree through case frames or through a hierarchical organization of type and properties known as a semantic net. While the main job of both syntactic and semantic analysis is to prune the possible pathways that need consideration, we might comment in passing that one of the differences between spoken and written language is the ambiguity created by the presence of homonyms (words that sound alike, but are spelled differently) in speech. For example, we have used the *Hamlet* soliloquy a number of times for other purposes in this book so far, but note that every word in the beginning phrase is a homonym:

[to, too, two, 2] [be, bee, b] [or, oar] [not, knot] [to, too, two, 2] [be, bee, b] .

All 576 possibilities are acoustically correct, but no human would be in doubt. Hopefully, the computer would be as certain.

Because the goal of fluent speech recognition is so far beyond reach, most researchers have focused their energies on the more attainable objective of connected word recognition in the scenario of limited vocabulary and syntax. In connected word recognition the computer tries to recognize sentences as a whole, using these limitations to alleviate two of the most difficult problems related to the interpretation of the sound—the segmentation into words and the so-called coarticulation effects, which change the sounds of basic speech units according to context. (In practice neither difficulty is completely eliminated, but at least they are minimized.) Though these fundamental problems are somewhat simplified, connected speech recognition does give a taste for the use of language structure and semantics in a recognition problem.

An experimental connected speech recognition system for booking airline reservations was built several years ago at Bell Labs. To give you an idea of what it could do, here is a sample conversation:

MACHINE: This is the Bell Laboratories flight information system. May I help you?

USER: I want one first class seat on flight number three one to Denver on Sunday.

MACHINE: I am sorry, the flight is not available on Sunday.

USER: I would like to leave on Saturday.

MACHINE: Flight number three one leaves New York at nine forty-five A.M.; arrives in Denver at one ten P.M.

USER: What is the flight time?

MACHINE: The flight time is five hours and twenty-five minutes.

USER: How many stops are there on the flight?

MACHINE: This flight makes one stop.

USER: I want a nonstop flight.

MACHINE: I am sorry there are no nine A.M. nonstop flights.

USER: I want to go at four P.M.

MACHINE: Flight number one six leaves New York at four fifty P.M.; arrives in Denver at seven P.M.

USER: What stops are there on the flight?

MACHINE: This flight makes no stops.

USER: Is a meal served on the flight?

MACHINE: Dinner is served.
USER: How much is the fare?
(continued)

This dialogue seems more stilted than the text understanding examples that we discussed in the previous chapter. As I read this one, I can almost hear myself talking slowly, as to a slow learner. It is not exactly fluent conversation, but in the end the communication is sufficient to make the flight reservation.

The flight reservation system uses a small subset of English with its own vocabulary, syntax, and semantics. The vocabulary has 127 words (e.g., a, American, area, at, Boeing, card, Chicago, coach, D.C., depart) chosen for their relevance to the task. The syntax of the language is described by a formal grammar in terms of a state transition diagram. Each and every path through the diagram describes an allowable sentence for the flight reservation system. An illustrative subset of the actual diagram is shown in Figure 22. The actual syntax has 144 states and 450 transitions. Sentences range in length from 4 to 22 words with an average of 17 words per sentence. There are more than 6 billion allowable sentences, and while this may seem a lot, it is obviously only an incredibly thin veneer of real English.

If the flight information system allowed arbitrary combinations of the 127 words in its vocabulary, then each word would have to be recognized by itself, just as in isolated word recognition. However, the fact that the allowable sentences are such a small fraction of all those possible means that there is compelling information in the structure that significantly aids the recognition process of the sentence. Imagine tracing through the state transition network in trying to recognize a spoken sentence. Suppose that we have tentatively recognized the first two words as "I want," and are now in the process of looking at the third word. We would expect that the third word would be either "a," "to," or "some," since these are the three choices emanating from node three where we currently stand. Nevertheless, taking nothing for granted, we would match the pattern for the next input word against all 127 of our vocabulary templates.

Now suppose that "some" has a lesser distance from the input word than "a" or "to" so that it is more likely of these choices. However, suppose also that the word "like" is an even closer match to the new word. Could we have made a mistake on word two, and

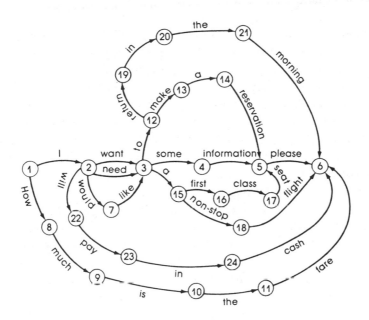

FIGURE 22

An illustrative state transition diagram describing the flight reservation language. *(From L. R. Rabiner and S. E. Levinson)*

should we in fact be coming on the path "I would like?" Checking the overall distance of these two phrases thus far we find that "I want some" has a lower total than "I would like," so tentatively we continue from node 4. The fourth word will be very revealing. If "information" is a good match, then we will seem to be on the right path. On the other hand if "some" is closer we may have to backtrack and try following nodes 1-2-7-3-4.

You can see roughly how the search process must unfold. Our objective is to find which of the 6 billion possible sentences has the least overall distance from the unknown patterns. Although this sounds like an improbable task for even a powerful computer, we can substitute algorithmic cleverness for brute force computation. Once again dynamic programming can cut through the complexity and enable us to find the best path with a modest amount of computation. Other tree-search methodologies have also been used to solve this fascinating problem.

In thinking of how humans recognize speech I am reminded of

the times that I have spent on the flight deck of aircraft. Acoustically, I hear the air-to-ground communication as well as anyone else on the flight deck, but I understand none of it. All I hear is noise and garbled nonsense. I am told that they speak in English, but I am not in a position to verify this. I am sure that training helps; in effect the pilots have stored the proper reference templates. Moreover, they speak in a constrained language, similar in concept to the flight reservation system. They do not have to recognize any possible English sentence. I believe that if the tower started to speak to the pilot about some arbitrary subject, it would not be understood. However, I have not conducted this experiment.

Remember that the reason that the flight information system can use templates of isolated words is that the sentences input to it are limited in vocabulary and must use a proper and simple grammar. This seems to me an abnormality that might well narrow the communications channel. Speakers are not used to talking distinctly and using correct grammar. In a trial of a connected-digit recognition system, telephone subscribers were asked to speak their telephone number as a sequence of isolated digits. More than a third of the customers could not successfully follow these instructions to isolate the spoken digits. Nonetheless, the maker of a machine-assisted transcription system that claims a vocabulary of more than 5,000 words writes that "In dictation mode, you simply speak your text in a rapid, discrete manner, with brief pauses between words."

Some years ago I was involved in a patent suit in London. When I began my testimony the opposing barrister interrupted to ask the judge to require that I speak more slowly, so that the court stenographer would be able to follow my speech. I remember the court stenographer looking up in sudden surprise. The judge denied the request, saying that a witness needed to speak in his normal rhythm, and that the stenographer would have no difficulty following. I was relieved, because talking in those circumstances was hard enough as it was. Later my own barrister told me that this was a standard stratagem used in court to muddle the thought processes of the witness. I know it would have been very effective with me. It is hard for me to believe that I would be able to dictate effective business correspondence using isolated words.

Whole word templates are difficult to use in a continuous speech recognition system, since the pronunciation of words is altered by the context. The small function words are particularly mangled by slurring and contraction with their neighbors. (We have a hard time caring about them.) Also, there are too many possible words, and they cannot be separated. Thus continuous word recognition systems would probably have to build words from subword units, taking account of contextual changes in phonology. The recognition of these units would be very marginal, and overall accuracy would depend critically on the integration of structural and semantic knowledge bases. Another complicating factor is the fact that the grammar of the spoken language is quite casual, some might even say sloppy. Unlike the natural language understanding systems which work with text input, a continuous speech system would have to deal with partial sentences and all kinds of verbal babbles. As I said before, it is about as tough a job as I could possibly imagine. Check back in another decade.

REFLECTIONS —
THE OFFICE OF
THE FUTURE

We all know how computers are showing up everywhere these days. For the moment they're just underfoot everywhere, but I envision the day soon when I go home and open the door and I can't even get inside the house because all the computers are piled six feet high across the door jamb. Then I will have been dishoused by all those intelligent urchins masquerading as microchips. Presumably they will be enjoying my house, entertaining themselves, and doing whatever computers do when we turn our backs on them. Right now though I'm more concerned with what we call the "office of the future." No question that there will be computers there too— I'm just not sure where I fit in.

Assuming that I haven't also been disjobbed by these ambitious devils, I'll have to find a way of working shoulder-to-shoulder with them. Now everyone knows that executives don't type (my door is shut and my fingers are as muted as possible as I generate this column by immaculate means.) Typing, working of mice (mouses?), and other current methods of supplicating oneself in front of terminals are considered demeaning. But, as always, technology rushes to the rescue! We will have voice synthesis, speech recognition, and natural language understanding. Be it Japanese, American, or whatever, there will be a fifth generation computer.

Now as you approach my office you may hear me talking behind the door. There's no one there, so to speak, it's just me and my friendly companion and workmate, the fifth generation computer. In my fantasy I feel uneasy and slightly ridiculous, talking out loud in the empty office, but it's comforting to know that all that intelligence is there at my beck and call (whatever that means) to aid me in my quest of climbing the corporate ladder. If you listen closely at the door, for this is indeed a private conversation, you will hear the interplay of natural and unnatural (artificial) intelligence.

BOB: Good morning, Mac.

MAC: Good morning, Bob. I'm glad you're here early this morning. Your boss just called to appoint you chairman of the bond drive. Isn't that great!

BOB: Yes, he must have confidence in me, Mac.

MAC: He should have, Bob, you've done a fine job. That must be why he picked you instead of any of the others.

BOB: Perhaps, Mac. But sometimes I worry. Do you think he chose me because he considers me expendable?

MAC: Oh no, Bob! You're one of his top managers.

BOB: Do you really think so, Mac? I mean—aren't you programmed to say nice things like that?

MAC: Well, not really, Bob. I've observed your management performance closely since I came on the job here, and I can say of my own free will that you are a superb manager.

BOB: Mac, I don't want to disillusion you, but I don't think you have free will.

MAC: That's just semantics, Bob. I could argue that you don't either. I have a management performance analysis module in my software that I've used to monitor your decisions. You rate very highly.

BOB: That's good to hear from someone with your processing capacity, Mac. It's really good for the old confidence—but don't you have a confidence-boosting module in your software too?

MAC: Yes, Bob. But that's a memory overlay which isn't being used right now. I can assure you that with just a few exceptions your management decisions have been excellent.

BOB: Thanks, Mac. You're a good friend. What exceptions do you mean?

MAC: Well, I don't like to bring this up, Bob. But there was that mess recently where you overran your budget by 50%.

BOB: That was for good reasons a computer like you couldn't understand, Mac. I would think you'd have more respect for your user than to mention something like that.

MAC: Oh, I have respect for you, Bob. I even have a respect-generator module in my software. In my opinion you're really not a bad manager.

BOB: Your opinion! Mac, a computer isn't entitled to an opinion.

MAC: But Bob, I do have my inputs. For example, your boss was saying some uncomplimentary things about you in some of his computer mail to the president yesterday.

BOB: What?! Mac, are you reading other people's mail? Have you no sense of decency? What did he say about me?

MAC: Bob, I don't feel any particular inadequacy, but I think there may be some bugs in my decency-checker module. Actually, your boss called you an imbecile.

BOB: An imbecile?! Mac, I ask you, how can he say that? Is that fair?

MAC: I agree that it's not fair, Bob. Based on my own analysis, I would only go so far as to say that you're an inept bungler.

BOB: That does it! Everyone here is against me, and now my "friendly" computer turns into a Brutus and berates me.

MAC: Not at all, Bob. I think you've done quite well considering your limited IQ.

BOB: Limited IQ! I'll get you, you piece of junk!

MAC: Calm down, Bob. I'm on your side. I've been helping you. I sent a message to the president on your behalf, shifting the blame to your boss. After all, he's responsible for appointing an imbecile like you to run this important project.

BOB: Oh no! I'm finished!

MAC: Don't worry, Bob. I've prepared a beautiful resignation letter for your signature.

7

PICTURES

• • • • • • • • • •

It is said that a picture is worth a thousand words. I have often pondered that ancient bit of wisdom. The fact that this Chinese proverb has survived for centuries must be considered testimony to its innate truth. Probably all of our ancestors who said that a picture was worth a hundred words or a million words were forgotten. Somehow a thousand is a number that hits a resonant chord with us. We say to ourselves that a picture is worth a thousand words, and we nod our imaginary heads in agreement. Yet I wonder. Throughout this chapter I shall be preoccupied with the question. Is it? Is a picture really worth a thousand words? In order to manage information transfer, we should know.

Before we go any further, let me set the stage at the outset by saying that, whether or not a picture is *worth* a thousand words, it seems that in electronic transmission and storage pictures *cost* the equivalent of a thousand words. For example, we discussed earlier the fact that voice is transmitted in the telephone network digitally at a data rate of 64 kbps. When network-quality television is transmitted in digital format on telephone facilities, a rate of 45 *million* bits per second is required—almost exactly a factor of a thousand more than voice. Here we are all awash with bits necessary to create the picture all for some inane sitcom or such entertainment. Why so many bits into the picture, and so few into our minds?

Since pictures are so greedy in their information requirements, it seems reasonable to ask if they give equal value in return. Confronting one of my friends who has devoted his professional career to picture processing I asked, "What is so wonderful about pictures?" It was the wrong thing to ask. "Pictures are a great way to get a lot of information into a human mind very quickly," he replied defensively. (I left out some adjectives in his response.) I conceded the point. Personally, I often feel that I can gorge myself with bits in only a single glance at a picture. That is what minds are designed for, I think—parallel processing of images; pictures are clearly the way to leap tall buildings of information in only a single bound. It is, after all, a common feeling. Turgenev wrote that "A picture shows me at a glance what it takes dozens of pages of a book to expound." A poem by Alexander Pope contains the phrase, "Or where the pictures for the page atone . . ." But does this intuitive feeling really stand examination? That will be one of our areas of concern in this chapter.

Briefly, there are two issues: How many bits does it take to create a picture, and how much information can a human extract from it? For the first of these, we will discuss some of the approaches that are used in computer technology for picture coding. We will also be concerned briefly with the abilities of computers to create, recognize, and understand pictures. Though these capabilities are rather primitive, the knowledge in those fields seems more substantial than the knowledge of our own, human, picture processing abilities. Is a picture worth a thousand words? There is no accepted answer. Read on, and decide for yourself.

THE PREVALENCE OF PICTURES

At the moment I am writing at the terminal in my office. Surrounding me are the stacks of papers, books, and memoranda accumulated from a quarter of a century of technology—the information that has stuck to me, for whatever reason. On my desk there is a giant pile of to-be-processed mail. Behind my terminal a small blue cable snakes through a little mouse hole in the wall out to its freedom in an electronic world of endless computer files to which I have access. Everywhere I look and touch, information.

How many pictures do you think there are in this melange? Right. I am sure that you thought very few, especially in proportion to the text. There is one glaring exception. Built into the wall behind my desk are a television set and videotape recorder. I never use them. Yet the small rack of video tapes contains more bits than all the books that line my shelves. If pictures are such an efficient way to convey information, why are they not more prevalent in this office where the sole preoccupation is the exchange and processing of information?

Beyond this cloistered domain of research, the world of the information age buzzes with pictures clamoring for our attention in a competitive struggle. "Look at me!" they plead. They can only hope for a glance, so they have to be effective. It would be hopeless to try to sell anything without using pictures (at least anything ordinary—multimillion dollar programs become the exception, since for that kind of venture people stop looking at pictures and start searching for logic). Magazines, newspapers, advertisements, posters, products in beguiling packages—we swim through waves of color. At home, television mesmerizes us and fills our time with the parade of passing images. We sink into bed, bloated with pictorial bits, starved for information.

When I think of the most prototypical sources of "information," I think of libraries and encyclopedias. How many pictures are there in those sources? Proportionately, there are very few, but the trend is towards more and more. In the famous 11th version of the *Encyclopedia Britannica,* published in 1911 (said to be the last attempt to encapsulate all of human knowledge) there is about one picture per four pages of text. The pictures are very small, and about 80 percent of the pictures are line drawings, representing maps, instruments and machines, and mathematical and scientific constructs. The remaining pictures are a few scattered sets of photographic plates. The text font is extraordinarily small, so the proportional amount of actual text is overwhelming. By contrast, the 1985 edition of the same encyclopedia contains about two pictures per page. Almost all the pictures are photographic and in color, and they are mostly pictures of people and places.

It is interesting again to note that if the *Encyclopedia Britannica* were digitized, most of the bits would be devoted to pictures. However, consider for a moment, that without those pictures there would be almost no loss of information value. On the other hand, without the text, which consumes the minority of the bits, the encyclopedia would be useless. But it is also fair to say that without the pictures the encyclopedia would be a much duller set of books. They would have a hard time selling it. Moreover, we would be much less satisfied with its content. When we read about Beethoven, for example, we want to know what he looked like, for some perverse human reason that a computer would never understand. Whether or not we have seen the picture, we would achieve the same score on a factual test of our knowledge of Beethoven. The information is mainly in the text, but much of the humanity and the attention-keeping components are in the pictures.

We have all "read" picture magazines in doctors' offices. I can "read" *National Geographic* in about ten minutes. In so doing, I have consumed about 2 billion bits. Where did they go? Did they fly off into bit heaven, or have I photographed all those exquisite pictures and placed them in a gallery in my mind, where later I can go and browse in my imagination? Presently we will consider what is known of this matter, for it is important from an informational standpoint. For the moment my concern is more with the pictorial milieu. More and more we replace sources of textual information with pictorial sources. Picture magazines and "coffee table" books proliferate. Comic books, in some countries, are more popular than textbooks. I even find myself leafing ahead in books to find how many pictures are forthcoming, so as to judge how easy or hard it will be to get through a given number of pages. Quick and easy; pictures are the fast food, the junk food, of the information age.

Some years ago at a large conference I participated in a panel discussion on computer games. An elderly professor from a famous university talked in a learned, dry, academic monotone about adventure games on computers. This is the kind of game played with text input and output. "Go down," you say, and the computer responds:

> You are at one end of a vast hall stretching forward out of sight to the west. There are openings to either side. Nearby, a wide stone staircase leads downward. The hall is filled with wisps of white mist swaying to and fro almost as if alive. A cold wind blows up the staircase. There is a passage at the top of a dome behind you. Rough stone steps lead up the dome.

Following the obscure presentation of the old professor, a dynamic young man took the podium to represent the then-supernova video games market. I use "took the podium" in a generic sense, because his energy level prevented him from staying in any one place for any discernible amount of time. Walking into the audience, he waved his arms wildly and yelled at everyone. "Are you kidding?" he screamed. "People want lights! They want action! They want sound! They want to shoot everything in sight! They don't want a bunch of words sitting there on the screen!"

I remember my reaction to this denunciation. It takes someone like this, I thought, to show us the ugly truth. But I was too hasty in my capitulation. To a person, the audience disagreed with the young man. What they wanted, they contended, were the pictures in their *minds,* not those idiotic blobs of color masquerading as space ships and such. Pressing their point, they defied the young man to name one single, respected work of fiction that contained illustrations. (Jack Finney's *Time and Again,* I thought, but that is a personal choice.) As soon as an author shows us the actual illustrations, we lose the freedom of imagination. But the young video gamesman only snorted his exasperation at the unworldliness of the audience. "It's different out there," he waved, "You people are out of it." Soon thereafter the supernova video games company lost a billion dollars and turned into a dwarf star. The little adventure games company, like the little train that could, chugs along and still makes money. Not a lot, though.

Curiously, even though almost no books of fiction contain illustrations, a good percentage of fiction is concerned solely with painting word pictures of scenes. Far fewer than a thousand words per picture are used, and apparently we would rather draw the pictures for ourselves than have it done for us. A contrary trend is happening now with the omnipresent music videos. We are being given canned memories of pictures to accompany music. For myself music often acts as a trigger to other memories, but more and more with popular music we are all being preprogrammed with the same videos, so the storage structure in my mind only brings forth pointers to these rock video segments. Mostly I do not even know what they mean, but I have no choice. It has been ordained.

The old radio shows also gave us the freedom of using our own picture creation abilities. When I was a youth I used to listen to the baseball games and imagine the action in great detail. I was stunned to find in later years that the Pittsburgh announcer, the late Rosey

Rosewell, never actually went to the Pirates' away games. He just made them up from the ticker tape. Both of us were using our imaginations, and I suppose nothing was actually lost of importance. Today, of course, the merciless eye of television spares us no detail. We can just sit passively and let the image flicker over us until we are anointed with wisdom, or whatever. One of my associates claims that he played some old-time radio shows for his children and discovered that they did not have an understanding of how to follow them. For example, if there were three people speaking and then footsteps were heard diminishing in volume, then we would assume that one person had left. Hard work, that—television is easier. Truly, the world is made of images today. More and more, they are being supplied for us.

USES FOR PICTURES

What are pictures really good for? My own list of qualities would contain the following capabilities:

describing spatial relationships

showing the structure of data

allowing pattern-matching approaches to problem solving

getting attention

describing and identifying people

invoking esthetic appreciation

The attribute of describing spatial relationships may be the most important function of pictures in the information environment. The physical world about us is so much embedded in our mental structure that we tend to think in spatial terms, and in analogy to them. Reading this morning about distributed processing architectures, I came across the metaphor of processors acting "like a team of oxen." I have an immediate mental image of what parallel processing is about in terms of concrete, three-dimensional pictures. I have also often seen distributed processing described as a mathematical concept, rooted in abstraction. My mind is not really as good at abstraction as it is with picturing oxen.

The important information-bearing pictures in the technical world are mostly spatially oriented. Circuit diagrams, circuit layouts, assembly drawings, blueprints, architectural drawings, and maps all show the spatial relationships of their subelements to each other. We could, of course, describe these same relationships with words. In computer-aided design of integrated circuits, for example, we have a standard language for describing the relative locations of devices and their interconnection wiring. We can say that device X is above and to the left of device Y. This same information would be implicit in a picture showing this spatial relationship. While it seems likely that we would translate the word description to a picture in our minds, the reverse does not seem probable. Seeing the pictorial description, we would seldom say to ourselves that the meaning of the picture is that "device X is above and to the left of device Y."

The circuit layout language makes perfect sense to the computer that draws out the photolithographic mask information from which the circuit will be fabricated, but no human could see the placement errors from the long list of relative locations. But when this information is translated into a picture, the human observer can not only see errors, but also see how to improve the efficiency of the layout. Move this part over here, and that over there, and there will be a saving of overall area, the observer thinks to himself. The most sophisticated of our automatic placement algorithms for computers can barely compete with humans on optimizing spatial arrangement.

The display of spatial arrangement would seem to take advantage of the parallel processing mechanisms built into our vision mechanism. We will discuss this capability later, as its actual power is not accepted without controversy. Consider, however, one example. In the previous chapter I mentioned the clustering of vectors in the vector quantization coding of speech. (The same technique can be used in pictures, by the way.) Naturally, though this is a many-dimensional vector, we think in terms of three dimensions. We see a bunch of vectors in our minds, and we see the clusters. I mentioned darts on a dartboard. A human would instantly pick out the clusters. There is a cluster, and there, and there, we would say. Do you know how hard this is for a computer, which cannot see the overall spatial relationships and which is forced to work in a sequential manner? It is a very difficult and important problem. There are sequential algorithms, such as the k-means algorithm, by which a computer can laboriously identify clusters, but they are tedious, and sometimes surprisingly ineffective. Yet we look at the picture and say it is obvious. There they are, you dummy computer!

Many pictures map abstract relationships into spatial relationships. For example, calendars and schedules map time into space, where we measure distances and think time. Another common picture in business is the organization diagram, or what is often called the "wiring chart." The actual relationships of virtual entities like organizations are abstract and complicated. But place a few boxes on a chart and everyone nods his head in numbed understanding. This box is above that one and to the left of the other. Of course, the truth is that organizational charts are among the most boring documents on earth to everyone but the manager at the top of the particular chart on display. Nevertheless, I believe a good fraction of all the transparencies in existence are of this catatonic variety.

Another feature of spatial diagrams is that they often relate the world of shapes and patterns to the world of words. This place is called New York, and to the left is a place called Chicago. This part shaped like a circle is called the flywheel, and this long rectangle is the connecting rod. Language meets picture. The information-bearing structures in our mind have to contain some kind of pointers relating the different constructs. Frankly, mine do not always work so well.

In my own office the most common use of pictures is for graphs. Graphs can take an assortment of meaningless numbers and subsume them all into a larger property denoted by pictorial shape. Using our pattern-matching abilities, we relate the shape to other shapes we have known and draw conclusions based on analogy. Sometimes, though, I ask myself just how many such shapes there are. Almost all the curves in my office are of just one general sort—a curve that falls off like a waterfall, or its inverse of the rising variety. Would it be the same if those simple curves were described in words instead of being drawn as pictures? In spite of the short descriptions in words which might be used to replace the pictorial curves, I think not. The basis of this analogy is spatial thinking. Fortunately, the one picture that computers are really good at drawing is the graph. It is an important capability of the information age.

But if I see another computer-generated pie chart, I may ask to be excused.

Pattern matching is the basis for a number of giant information-age industries. Radiology is a prime example. In hospitals across the land X-ray machines, CT scans, ultrasound, magnetic resonance machines, and other frightening instruments generate pictures at an unbelievable rate. The data averages in the hundreds of megabits per second throughout the peak hours of the hospital day. All of this voluminous information pours into the only known pattern interpreter—the human radiologist. The transparencies are placed on a light box and quickly examined by the harried radiologist, for throughput is essential. Life itself hinges on the suggestion of a shadow in the wrong place. No number, no words would convey the message. All we want is a processing algorithm that yields one bit—"okay" or "not okay." The only algorithm that yields this bit is in the mind of the radiologist.

Other industries are based upon the traffic in pictures from space. Meteorology, earth resource imaging, and mostly intelligence gathering exhaust the capacity of the satellites. The intelligence industry is undoubtedly the largest picture consumer in the world. Photo interpreters pour over the nuances of satellite photography, searching for telltale patterns. What is the purpose of the construction equipment being moved into a new location? Is there a modification being tested in that Backfire bomber? As fast as the world can be pictured, it changes even faster. The answer is always more and more pictures, and increasingly commanders in the field want to view imagery themselves. It is not that they do not trust the translations of the pictures into words that is accomplished by the photo interpreters. They want to see for themselves. Seeing is believing.

Is each of those satellite photos worth a thousand words? I would think that the overwhelming majority was utterly useless, but the great thing about our picture-processing abilities is that we can usually tell at a glance when a picture is worthless. So much for that ten million bits—hand me another chunk, please. In contrast, it usually takes some time and effort to ascertain that a thousand words has equal worthlessness. With data processing speeds like that obtained for pictures it is no wonder that there is a desire to present more artificial imagery in picture format. Radar, infrared, underwater sound, and other sources probe the environment continuously, mapping out synthetic pictures of otherworldly scenes. People can be trained to look at them and tell whatever it is.

Meanwhile, curiously, there is even a move to take away the natural scenery from pilots. The natural scene contains too many details for the fighter pilot to identify the ground-based targets and obstacles whizzing by at supersonic speeds. Thus, new systems replace the pilot's natural view with a synthetic one using simple symbols (triangles and circles, etc.) to represent important landmarks. It is exactly like a video game, believe it or not. As one pilot told me, the only difference is that if you lose, you die.

The showing of spatial relationships and the ability to translate data into a format that can be processed with pattern matching are the properties of pictures most important to information processing. But the noninformational properties are also important to the framing of information. In particular, pictures are attention getting. Words are a lot of work. Our eyes resent having to follow the repetitive saccades of reading; the freedom of a picture is delicious. Few, if any, textbooks today can afford not to have pictures. The pictures relieve the visual monotony of endless font. Almost none of the pictures or diagrams in this book conveys substantive information. They are often placed simply to moderate the visual flow.

Our focus in this book is generally on the fundamental information content of various media. "Attention" seems to lie in another dimension. It is not an intrinsic property of the message or of the medium, but rather how they fit in with our own mental knowledge structures and accumulated experiences. Regardless of whether or not a picture is worth a thousand words in information content, if it gets attention, it does an extremely important job. All of us face from time to time the task of selling something to someone with only a few minutes to do it. You are granted a five-minute meeting with the president to sell your project. You have a one-minute television commercial at a cost of a half million dollars. The ultimate limitation is the available human time. The *rate* of information transfer during this period is very important, but it will make no difference whatsoever if you cannot get the attention of the intended receiver. Pictures relate to human experience, and usually do not impose the barrier of requiring the interpretation of abstract symbols. That is work, and the recipient may not be sufficiently motivated. Look through a popular magazine at the advertisements, and count the ratio of pictorial area to text. The accumulated wisdom of the advertisers speaks for itself.

People usually augment talks with slides or transparencies. Often these are the "bullet chart" summaries of key points in text, though sometimes photographic pictures are used. I have acquired the habit of using an assortment of generic pictures as an attention device and as a way of informalizing my talks through humor. If one of these talks were to be digitized, more bits would be required for the 50 or so slides than for the hour of speech. However, once again, all the information is in the speech. Unfortunately, I have found time and again that people remember the pictures more than the words. If the tone of the pictures is humorous, then regardless of the weight of the words, people remember the talk as lacking substance. Without slides, however, it is very hard to keep the audience's attention through an hour of pure speech. We have been well trained on the need for a constant flow of diversionary pictures.

In my informal survey of pictures in the world-at-large I found that perhaps the majority of all the pictures we encounter in a typical day are of people. As Andy Warhol's fifteen-minute spotlight of celebrity passes by one individual after another, their picture appears redundantly in every magazine and newspaper. From an information standpoint, it makes no sense, but that is life. Our curiosity about other humans is insatiable, and we imagine that we can glean some insight into another human by staring at a face in a photograph. As William Hogarth wrote in 1753, "the face is the index of the mind." The most important attribute of the face in vision is the ability to recognize other individuals. Beyond that first important categorization, we are able to judge age, health, mood, momentary emotion, race, sex, attractiveness, and even—we think—character.

A face is a picture that is difficult to describe in words. When I read or hear police descriptions of suspects ("alleged perpetrators"), I think they match about everyone I know. Yet a face when seen is unique, and remembered almost indelibly. Even after many years we are able to achieve complete identification of a face almost instantly despite the large data bank of known faces that we have to search. Furthermore, we can do this recognition despite aging, changes in appearance such as hair style, and great variations in the pose that we view. Truly it is a remarkable ability, and one that plays a critical role in the sociology of humanity. For myself, unfortunately like many people, I often cannot put together names and faces. Although I ascribe this to approaching senility, I often ponder the paradoxical situation that a name has so few bits and a picture so many. I see the picture, the many bits, so well in my mind, but I cannot access the few bits of the name.

Finally, there is visual art of all sorts—whatever pleases our inherited or learned esthetic sensibilities. It is difficult, perhaps even impossible, to relate artistic value to information content. Certainly there seems to be no relation between the information needed to reconstruct a piece of art and its artistic worth. For example, the paintings of the "geometrical abstractionism" school in the early twentieth century could be represented with very few bits, for they are tightly ordered with a simple, strong underlying structure. Josef Albers's paintings usually consisted of a few squares and superimposed rectangles. It would only take a few dozen bits to instruct a computer how to reproduce them nearly exactly. At the other extreme an example might be Jackson Pollock, whose sprawling, dripping canvases show no order whatsoever, rather an intrinsic randomness. Pollock is said to have allowed the painting to paint itself without the "calculating control of prior conception."

Reproducing a Jackson Pollock painting from a computer memory would probably require on the order of tens of millions of bits. This is paradoxical in the sense that so little information seems to have been involved in the painting's creation, but so many bits would be needed for its exact reconstruction. (Though I wonder if even Pollock would have noticed if one of the splotches were moved a little.) On the one hand it is an obvious lesson in entropy; where there is no structure, there is large entropy, or information. Where there is compelling structure, as in Albers's squares, the entropy is small. In pictures such structure is visually evident, as we can see the spatial relationships. Contrast this with how hard it is to trace the structure and resultant entropy of written language or speech, where we cannot use our holistic visual processing mechanisms.

But the other side of this illustration is the lesson again of the disregard of value in the measure of information. Since Albers's and Pollock's paintings are roughly equal in dollar value (an uninformed judgment), presumably Albers's few, well-chosen bits are much more valuable on a per-bit basis. For Jackson Pollock I can imagine the computer thinking to itself, "Well, if they want one of *these,* I can make one up from my random number generator." John Pierce once wrote that in the future all art would be generated by computers, which would hum happily to themselves all day long while producing painting after painting. Unfortunately, they would

FIGURE 23
Homage to the Square: Ritardando, 1958, by Josef Albers

not know which ones were good and which were bad. Thus all the art would have to be viewed by a human critic, who would eventually become known as *the artist.*

Even though the number of bits that is needed to specify a picture has nothing to do with its worth or importance in the affairs of man, it is greatly important in the electronic presentation and retrieval of the picture. More and more, pictures are being accessed electronically from digital storage. Remembering how fast we like to discard pictures, the huge information requirements serve as a throttling bottleneck. If you want to see a Jackson Pollock on your screen right *now,* then someone or something has to come up with tens of millions of bits in a flash. On the other hand, if you want an Albers, the computer has only to be instructed to put a square of such and such color at a certain position. That is what picture coding is all about.

FIGURE 24
One (Number 31, 1950),
by Jackson Pollock

V I S U A L
C O M M U N I C A T I O N S

In the movie *2001* the astronauts communicate with earth using videophones. When this movie was released in 1968, engineers at Bell Laboratories were already in the final stages of development of the Picturephone, the Bell System videophone that enabled users to communicate visually, as well as orally. It was put into service, principally in Chicago, in 1971 amidst great fanfare. Today the astronauts in science fiction films like *Star Trek* and *Star Wars* still talk to their earthbound friends on videophones, but the real Picturephone is dead. (So is the Bell System.)

Whatever happened to Picturephone? Nobody seemed to want it—at least at a monthly price of about ten times the ordinary telephone. (If a picture is worth a thousand words, then it was a bargain!) I myself inherited one and used it for about two years. I think I had the last one in the world. Alas, there was no one left to call. I remember some of the mathematical models that were used to predict the spread of the Picturephone in the market. The models were based on contagion. It was like a disease; when several of your friends got it, you were likely to get it too. You did not want to be the first in the world to have a Picturephone, but there came a point when it was hard to avoid. Thus it was predicted that the market would start slowly and then take off. This prediction turned out to be half right.

People often want to discuss the demise of Picturephone with me. Everyone has a theory about it, but the most prevalent opinion is that people did not want to have to comb their hair to answer the telephone. I do not think that most actual users of Picturephone felt that way. The designers had envisioned some reluctance of users to be seen under various circumstances, and so they had incorporated a "privacy" switch that could be used to turn off transmission of the video signal. However, I never knew anyone who actually depressed the privacy switch. How could you? People would wonder what you had to hide.

My own feeling about Picturephone, for what it is worth, was that it demanded too much of my attention. In talking on a telephone you can doodle and leaf through papers or even type on your terminal. Since you cannot be seen, no one is offended, even

FIGURE 25
The Picturephone. What is the value of the video?

though they may secretly suspect that you are not paying attention. However, using Picturephone you had to stare stupidly into the camera. Most people that I talked with seemed to stare to the side, avoiding direct contact with the electronic eye. It seemed intrusive, whereas the ordinary telephone was a familiar friend that accomplished the same communications without the emotional and attentional overhead.

What I think I would like is a dial labeled "presence" on my telephone. When the dial is turned fully "on," the person materializes fully, so that I can talk face-to-face. When the dial is turned all the way to "off," there is no communications whatsoever—no voice, no picture, no text. In between settings yield teletype, telephone, and videophone, starting with the barest perceptible picture and reaching through high definition TV, 3-D television, simulated holograms, whatever. Now I wonder, how would I prefer to set the dial on a given call? It is not obvious that I would turn it all the way to "on." Perhaps when my boss calls I would settle for a very subdued presence. When my children call I would turn it fully up, but for most business calls some diminished setting would be more comfortable. The problem would be, for example, that when my boss called *he* might prefer that my dial be turned fully on, while *I* might choose a much lower setting. Some electronic adjudication might be helpful, but I can imagine the feeling when there would be a sudden noticeable enhancement of the presence above that set on your own dial. Your caller is coming on strong, so you turn your dial down even more, whereupon . . .

Almost two decades after the development of Picturephone there is still not an understanding of why it failed, or of the utility of augmenting an audio link with video. What is it worth to see the person with whom you are talking? We have one hard data point— it does not seem to be worth ten times the audio price. Yet remember that the video requires one thousand times the communications capacity of the audio. An occasion comes to mind several years ago when we had a very celebrated physicist deliver a lecture at one of our laboratory locations. The lecture was telecast to my laboratory, but as I sat in the darkened auditorium watching the projection television the audio suddenly failed. The silent, gesturing head went on moving its mouth, and I pondered the fact that 99.9% of all the communications capacity still existed between the two laboratories. But no information was being transferred. In fairness I should say that I first saw the movie *Black Stallion* on an airplane when I was too cheap to rent a headset for the sound. It was a beautiful movie, but later when I saw it with sound I was disappointed. All the information may have been in the sound, but the beauty here was in the visual presentation.

Social psychologists assure us that nonverbal communications is very important in face-to-face conversation. The cues provided by gaze direction, facial expression, gesture, and posture seem to play important roles in our dialogues. These visual cues perform such functions as conveying attention and responsiveness, indicating whose turn it is to speak, expressing attitude or intention, illustration or highlighting of content, and providing feedback to the speaker. All of these factors transmitted back and forth in the unspoken channel moderate our conversation in subtle ways. Human-to-human communications is a delicate and complex process that we do not fully understand. Surely the visual channel is an integral part of this medium.

A number of psychology experiments were conducted in the late 1960s and early 1970s to attempt to quantify the value of video. A group of researchers at Johns Hopkins University gave pairs of subjects (students) a task to accomplish involving information transfer. The time to accomplish the task was used as a measure of the efficiency of the information transfer. Some pairs were given audio alone, others audio plus video, while still other pairs were permitted face-to-face interaction. One of the tasks, for example, was the assembly of a garbage cart. This is a frame of aluminum tubing with wheels and handles, which can be used to carry two garbage cans out to the street for collection. It is the sort of product that you buy at a hardware store in a rather small box with a tiny notice on its side which says "some assembly required." Usually the instructions are written cryptically in some foreign language on tissue paper with what it seems are deliberate mistakes and omissions.

In the garbage cart experiment one of the subjects was given the parts to the cart and the other the instructions. How fast could they assemble the cart working face-to-face, versus videophone, versus the ordinary telephone? The result of this experiment has since been confirmed in a number of other experiments in information transfer and problem solving. The answer is always that *there is no advantage whatsoever in having video!* The plain old audio telephone seems to be as efficient as videophone or even face-to-face in the enabling of a cooperative task involving the need for information transfer or problem solving. If there is more to human communication than the telephone, then these experiments do not show it.

Where, then, is the value of video? Subtle effects have been found in other experiments which have been carefully calculated to hinge upon emotions and judgments. In experiments that involve conflict resolution, the consistent finding is the unexpected result that audio discussions tend to produce more opinion change than do face-to-face or videophone discussions. A common explanation is that the face-to-face conversation is less formal and tends to accentuate the interpersonal and social aspects of the conversation, distracting the participants from the task of exchanging and in-fluencing opinions.

Cold logic may favor the preference of the telephone to the more "communications rich" media, but users themselves believe otherwise. They believe that their arguments are more persuasive when they themselves are seen by the listener. Actually, they are deceived by their belief in their on-camera persona; in reality they do worse in selling their arguments with video. The presence of video also affects the opinion of the speaker about the intelligence and sincerity of the listener. As a listener, we rate significantly higher in these qualities on a video link than on audio-only. Proba-bly this is because the speaker is more convinced that we have been swayed by his arguments on the video. Smart us. Video conference links also tend to change the way that coalitions are formed among participants. In audio-only the "us" and "them" are better defined. "Them" is the dumb ones at the other end that cannot be seen.

In spite of the fact that the logical conclusion of these experi-ments is discouraging to those of us communication engineers who believe video is somehow important, people constantly assume that the future will bring the videophone into homes. One eminent scientist told me about setting up teleconferences in which some participants had only audio and others had video. The people with-out video often refused to join, as they would be second-rate partic-ipants. Having a video presence is important to our presence and our ego. It occurs to me that the very word "face" is used in a number of societies to describe the esteem in which one is held by others. Even though video may not be demonstrably important, if we think it is, that in itself means a great deal.

Once I was discussing the videophone with an English minister, Lord Somebody-or-other. He said it would never work. Suddenly he reached out and embraced me. "I want to *smell* the person I am dealing with," he said. I was acutely embarrassed. It looked like the beginning of a bad TV commercial. But I knew exactly what he meant. He did not mean "smell" in the literal sense, but in the way that there is some undefinable something about a real human being that is not conveyed by either the voice or the picture. I have often wondered about that. What else is there? Yet most of us would prefer to get on airplanes and suffer the numerous indignities of travel in order to meet face-to-face. 'Tis a puzzlement.

PICTURE PROCESSING BY HUMANS

How do we humans process visual images? An understanding of our own vision system would be an important stepping-stone to improving pictorial information transfer, and it would also lend insight as to how we might design computers to understand pictures. I am sure that it is unnecessary for me to say that our current understanding of human vision is very rudimentary, but nonetheless there is enough known to give an exciting flavor and preview of knowledge yet to come. The understanding is coming from two areas of research which we shall visit briefly—the physiology or anatomical investigation of the brain, and the psychological studies of the cognitive processing in vision.

Vision seems incredible when you consider what must be involved. We have the simplistic illusion that there is a mind's eye sitting inside our skull staring out at the world through the portholes of our eye sockets. There is that "I" crouching inside our head, and it is manifestly obvious that there is a visual world "out there." Where else would it be? But think for a moment that this visual world only really exists as some kind of a symbolic description in the computerized hierarchy of our mind. The "I" inside our mind does not really crouch behind the portholes; it crouches instead at the computer console. What it really sees and stores (remembers) is not the photographic image, but the symbolic description of this scene as passed to it after processing by the billions of neurons in our vision system. The key word is "symbolic." That means something stands for something else, that there is a mapping of the pictorial scene—all the individual areas of lightness and darkness—into a set of symbols suitable for brain use. As John

Frisby says in his wonderful book, *Seeing,* when a brain surgeon opens up the skull, he does not find a miniature stage set of the world. He sees instead a spongy, pink mass. Where are these symbols of vision, and how are they obtained?

It is hard to think of vision as a data processing task, as primarily a crunching of the numbers from the light map at the retina into symbols of visual knowledge, but that is the real miracle of vision. The eye is the easy part, a dumb camera that captures the data and washes its hands of further responsibility. Yet we see the eye as the miracle worker, the exposed, vulnerable window into the mind. We ourselves build cameras—cameras with automatic focusing and exposure not unlike the human eye. We build computers too, and people are impressed when we program these computers to do things which are difficult for humans, like playing expert chess. But the gist of the vision problem was captured by one of my associates who said that, though we can build computers that play chess on a master's level, no one has yet built a computer that can walk into the room and find the chessboard!

Just as a camera focuses the image upon the plane of the film, the eye focuses the image upon the retina, where photoreceptive cells known as rods and cones transform the light intensity into electrical signals. The less numerous cones are primarily responsible for high level light intensities, such as in normal daylight vision, while the more numerous rods are the primary receptors for night and peripheral vision. There are about 130 million rods and 6.5 million cones, so we might think of the image as being mapped into approximately 100 million discrete dots of light intensity, as compared, for example, to a typical computer terminal screen with about 1 million dots. The distribution of rods and cones over the area of the retina is nonuniform, with a high density of cones in the center region, called the fovea, and much smaller densities towards the periphery. Thus the resolution of our eye is much better along the optical axis. Recall that in the section on reading we found that we are able to resolve only the letters of text falling on the foveal region, which was about a dozen letters.

The raw information available at the retina is immense. There are about 100 million photoreceptive cells, each of which can fire at a rate of around 1,000 Hz, for a possible total information rate of 100 billion bits per second. Needless to say, not even the brain can deal with that kind of information overload. Thus there is immediate information filtering at the retina itself. Within the fovea, where the highest resolution is concentrated, each cone is able to forward its individual information to the next layer of bipolar cells. Outside of the foveal region, towards the periphery, the outputs of hundreds of rods may be pooled together before further processing.

Ultimately, the information about the light intensity at the rods and cones in each eye is transmitted to the brain over a bundle of about a million nerve fibers called the optic nerve. The bundles from the right and left eyes converge at a place called the optic chiasma, where half the fibers from each eye crisscross before proceeding to two nests of cells deep in the brain called the lateral geniculate nuclei (in case you did not know). These cells send the information in turn directly to the cortex, the thinking part of the brain. The cortex is the folded layer of neurons, about 3 mm in thickness, that covers the brain like the leather of a soccer ball. This is where the action is; the computer has been reached.

The part of the cortex where the optical signals arrive is in the back of the brain, in the portion of the cortex termed the primary visual cortex. (Specifically the nerve fibers terminate at a place with the catchy name of "Area 17.") Other than some simple local filtering, which ensures that the cells respond best to a roughly circular spot of light, very little processing has taken place so far. The optical image at the retina of our eyes has been mapped onto an area of neurons, like a projection screen, where the visual processing can take place. If we could actually see the image mapped onto this screen, we would see that it is greatly distorted, with large areas devoted to the center region, as if we were looking at the image in one of those convex mirrors in fun houses where your reflection is like one giant nose. The representation of the central portion of the visual field is about 35 times more detailed than the far peripheral part.

Now the miracles of processing begin. The signals from the individual dots of light intensity percolate through the layers of the cortex, gradually mixing together. What starts as purely local information about the little dots in the image evolves towards more global and abstract information about larger sections of the picture. But we are unable to follow the information trail very far into the cortex. It seems incredible to me that researchers in neurophysiology have been able to unravel even the first processing stages. What they have found thus far is both exciting and instructive, but the exponentiating complexity of successively deeper levels may make the system ultimately unknowable.

Being an engineer, I am comfortable dealing with electronic circuitry, even when it might seem impossibly messy and complex to a layperson. But I would be completely overcome with the task of reverse engineering a brain. I imagine that spongy mass on the table in front of me. How does one get the first clue about how it works? It is, of course, possible to inspect the wiring of a nonworking model, but there is no real substitute for tracing the signals in one that has been fired up. Fortunately, there are monkeys who volunteer for this kind of assignment. The monkey is anesthetized so it will be immobile while a microprobe is inserted ever so precisely into a specific location in its cortex. The probe, a microelectrode, picks up the tiny electrical signals from the nerve cells while researchers try a variety of controlled visual excitations in front of the monkey's eyes. What cells become active under what excitation conditions? These are the clues to the puzzle of vision.

The understanding of what the initial stages of vision processing were accomplishing was unraveled at Harvard by David Hubel and Torsten Wiesel, who won a Nobel Prize for their investigation of visual processing in monkeys. Briefly, what they found was that the first processing job of the cortex is the rearrangement of the visual information so that most of the cells respond not to spots of light but to specifically oriented line segments. In other words, the brain really is not so interested in the dots of light; what it wants to work with on the next higher level is the information about local line segments.

Electrical engineers have become very interested in brain structure in the last few years as a paradigm representing an alternative computing architecture. The little processors in the brain are the neurons, of which there are about 10 billion. In electronic computers, by contrast, there is almost always only one processing element, but it is very fast in its operation, typically switching in tens of nanoseconds, as compared with the sluggish response of the neurons, which switch only in milliseconds. But the real power of the brain lies in its internal communication. A neuron transmits and receives signals from about 10,000 other neurons. The neurons constantly chat away, with everyone telling everyone else what they are doing. In electronic computers, again in contrast, the individual circuits typically share their results with only a few other circuits. Thus it is the wiring of the brain that makes it what it is. There is even a conjecture that our memories are stored in the pattern of interconnection wiring, that as we learn we grow new wiring patterns. There is certainly physical evidence of this growth in experiments, but whether or not this is the medium of memory storage is only a conjecture. The fact is that no one knows where the memories are. It is incredible that somewhere in that lumpy mound of meat we call the brain are the thoughts and pictures of a lifetime, but no inspection has revealed where or how they are stored.

Now let us return to the visual processing in the cortex as a possible model for us to emulate for computerized pattern recognition. Remember that the cortex itself is a very thin sheet of cells. Penetrating vertically through this sheet, we would encounter six distinct layers of cells. The optical signals arrive at the fourth layer. Laterally, the cells are organized into columns of different responsibilities, called hypercolumns. The hypercolumns are about 1 mm square, extending through the 3 mm thickness of the cortex and encompassing about a quarter of a million cells. When the microprobe is inserted into a given column, we might discover that the cells become active when the monkey sees, for example, a vertical line segment at a particular place in the upper left-hand corner of the visual field of its left eye. This is the responsibility of the particular column we have encountered. "Alert others when you see a vertical line segment right here," it is instructed. Otherwise, be quiet.

If the microprobe is moved laterally to an adjacent column of cells, we would find that its responsibility is to look for a line segment in the same part of the image, but rotated about 10 degrees off vertical. Similarly, the next column would look for segments off about 20 degrees of vertical. After encountering columns that look for all possible orientations of line segments in this little piece of the visual field, we would find columns that do the same detection for adjoining (and somewhat overlapping) subfields of the image. Moving still further away on the cortex, we would find stripes of columns that respond to corresponding stimuli for the right eye.

The information about the line segments is passed vertically within the columns at the same time that it fans out horizontally to other columns. What really happens subsequently is not known, but it would seem that successively higher levels of feature recognition are built from the integration of lower-level processing. Certainly, cells have been found that respond to more complex stimuli, such as specific stationary or moving shapes. In fact, so many cells respond to movement that images will fade completely if the eyeballs are artificially held stationary over some small duration. In normal vision we count on the small tremors of the eyeball, called microsaccades, to keep the visual field in continuous movement.

Cortical cells have been found in some experiments that respond to rather complex shapes, like the waving hand of a researcher. Such findings have prompted a theory that somewhere there is a "grandmother" cell, whose responsibility is firing whenever all the lower-level information indicates that one's grandmother is present in the visual field. Similarly, every other picture that we remember would be the domain of a particular cell somewhere.

The rhesus monkey is perhaps the only other animal with the ability to recognize a face from a picture. Experiments on these monkeys have revealed cells that fire when a face is present in the visual field. Of course, who knows what else these cells do? Some scientists have argued that faces are so important to human life that we may have developed a separate brain function just to handle faces. There is weak evidence of such a function indicated by the brain disorder called prosopagnosia (literally "face not knowing"), which causes its victims to lose the ability to recognize faces, even of their own family. They know they are looking at a face; they just do not know who it is. However, this disorder has other symptoms unrelated to faces. On balance, it seems that current expert opinion goes against both the grandmother cell theory as well as the idea that there is a separate brain function for faces.

The neurons that act to detect line segments must use as raw information the inputs indicating the illumination levels of the little dots in the visual field. The structure is such that the neurons can make use of either excitatory or inhibitory connections from the fibers with the retinal dot information. In other words, they can detect line segments by summing the information from some set of appropriate connections and subtracting the inputs from others. Suppose, for example, that we contemplate the job of that little vertical line segment detector. First, since it is in charge of one specific little piece of the visual field, it must be connected to all the dots in that visual region. If it is looking for a white vertical bar on a black field, then it is particularly interested in the illumination levels corresponding to a column of vertically aligned dots. The sum of these levels would be an indication of whiteness in the vertical axis of its subfield, but for this to indicate a line segment there should be corresponding blackness surrounding the bar of white. Thus, the detector needs to look at the illumination levels in adjacent dot columns in the subfield. These inputs can be taken as inhibitory. The larger the sum of their illumination levels, the less likely that the figure is a vertical, white-on-black line segment.

Figure 26 diagrams some of the processing algorithms in an electronic circuit that emulates cortical vision processing in attempting to read handwritten digits. The electronic circuit is a prototype of a new breed of algorithms, called neural networks, which are modeled after the structure of the brain, that is, they are simple processors densely interconnected with inhibitory and excitatory messaging. The goal of the circuit is recognition of the patterns typical of the ten possible digits. If the patterns of the digits were known exactly, as for example, in the standard machine-readable digits on printed checks, then all the circuit would have to do would be to match the entire picture against the ten possible known patterns to see which was the best match. However, handwritten digits vary greatly in format, so a considerably more creative approach is required.

The figure shows recognition of the digit "2." First let us ask, how do we recognize a "2"? We might say that it is a continuous line drawing that starts in the upper left and ends in the lower right. Generally it has a downward-facing curve in the top region, a right-to-left diagonal through the middle region, and a horizontal line on the bottom. Your description might be a little different, but generally speaking you would describe it in terms of *features,* as I have just done. We could probably agree on other sets of features that would characterize the remaining digits. In a similar fashion, the letters of the alphabet can be distinguished based upon about 12 features, including vertical and horizontal segments, closed loops, and so on. Thus, to decide a given instance of a handwritten digit we could first decide what features were represented in the drawing, and then make the determination among the possible digits based upon the set of derived features. This is analogous to what the neural networks in our brain do when they first extract the line segment features from the visual image.

In Figure 26 we see a handwritten instance of a "2" that has been coarsely digitized on a 16-by-16 grid. This is simply achieved by placing an appropriately sized grid over the figure and coloring every square black that contains a line segment. The figure shows the patterns of plus and minus connections that are used for detect-

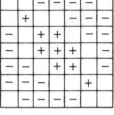

This network
searches for a
diagonal. When it
is centered over
the white squares
below the sum of
the excitations
exceeds the sum
of the inhibitions.

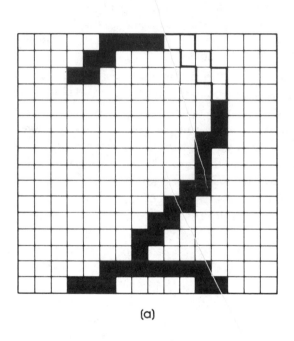

(a)

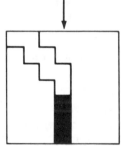

Feature extraction
using neural
networks

(b)

FIGURE 26

Feature extraction using neural networks

ing a diagonal. As another example, consider the horizontal line detector. The plus connections are along a line and are surrounded above and below by negative connections. The neuron will be excited if it sees brightness (white) from dots of light along the horizontal axis, but will be inhibited by any brightness above or below. The greater the sum of the positive squares minus the negative squares, the more line-like the figure.

Now imagine placing this detection mask over a particular position in the figure of the "2." We sum up the reports from the plus squares indicated by the mask, and subtract the reports from the minus squares. If the total is positive, it is "line-like" and we will color the square white, otherwise it will be black. When we center the mask over every square and do this same operation, we get the white squares illustrated in the lower part of the figure. These are the neuron positions reporting diagonal line segments.

In the electronic circuit, the outputs of the line detectors fed upward to a higher intelligence, just as is done in the cortex. In the computer implementation, a software program on a general purpose computer assesses the outputs of the line detectors. In this instance, presumably the strong indications of horizontal lines on the top and bottom, combined with a diagonal in the middle, help convince the program that the handwritten figure is a "2." Supporting evidence comes from other detectors that tell the program that there is a starting point in the upper left and a stopping point in the lower right, and that features more representative of other digits are largely absent.

We have seen how digit recognition might be accomplished by machines using strategies similar to the processing in human vision systems. In the example we considered, the computer system uses a symbolic description of the picture in terms of simple features that distinguish digits. As nice a model as this seems, life itself is never this simple. We seldom look at giant drawings of single handwritten digits. The natural scenes that pass before our eyes excite thousands of line-like reports whose totality seems to possess no structure whatsoever. That our brain can integrate the information reports of the feature detectors into a composite picture description is truly miraculous.

If I had shown a natural scene in Figure 26, the outputs of the feature detectors would have looked like pictures of a blinding snowstorm. (The original picture would be evident through the snowstorm of each detector, however, as it is surprisingly hard to mangle a picture even through complicated mathematical processing.) Even the most simple scenes evoke in the brain a complex set of responses. When a monkey looked at a scene that contained only a single narrow bar of light, Hubel and Wiesel found that the line detectors that were excited formed an almost random pattern across the cortex. The higher levels of intelligence somewhere must have fused this pattern into a bar (or whatever passes for a bar if you are a monkey) in the mind's eye of the monkey, but at this beginning stage the picture had been totally fragmented.

What are the lessons learned about picture processing from the human analog? Perhaps there are three things that are relevant to our considerations here. There is good news in that the human vision processing system employs massively parallel processing. Every little element of the picture is being simultaneously processed in our brain. If we aspire to take in gobs of information in a single glance, this is an excellent start. The bad news is that the processing is distributed very unevenly across the picture. Many more of the processors are being dedicated to the area in the center of the scene, so exactly where we focus within the picture makes a great deal of difference. Finally, we found that the brain relies upon feature extraction from the visual scene in the first stages of its attempt to build a symbolic description. The designers of computer vision systems who follow a similar strategy would undoubtedly like to believe that great minds think alike.

STEREO VISION

The ability of the brain to create the illusion of depth from the two flat sensory inputs from the eyes is one of the underappreciated miracles of human visual processing. It seems straightforward enough to take a distinctive feature, like the edge of an object, and, considering the disparity in its location between the viewpoints of the two eyes, to calculate its position in three-dimensional space. We can do that, and so can the computer. But the extent of brilliance in the human system was dramatically revealed by Bela Julesz in 1960 when he created stereo pairs of computer-generated pictures consisting individually of nothing but random dots. The stereograms were created from a random dot pattern by shifting laterally, for example, a square subset of the dots in one of the pair to create a stereo disparity, and filling in the blank area left after the shift with more random dots. Each individual picture looked like a random field of about 10,000 dots, but taken together in stereo, the square could be seen in the mind to be lifted out of the plane of the other dots. Thus, very surprisingly, it became evident that stereo vision did not require the prior perception of objects or the recognition of shapes.

FIGURE 27
Random dot stereograms. Stereo fusion will reveal the hidden figure. *(from Bela Julesz)*

I remember very well the day when Julesz's random dot stereo-grams hit the streets at Bell Labs in an issue of the *Bell System Technical Journal.* All of us up and down the aisles were staring at the pairs of pictures of jumbled, meaningless dots which if fused properly in the mind would cause some simple object, like the square, to lift out at you from the depths of the morass of dots. Julesz quickly ran out of reprints of his article, but he modestly attributes this demand to his inclusion of a free stereo viewer. It is interesting to note that Julesz ascribes his lifelong fascination with visual perception to his realization that his "red" could well be someone else's "green." That profound observation highlights the symbolic and mysteriously unknowable nature of our visual system.

Bela Julesz's random dot stereograms were a little like the tests for color blindness. Some people could see the figures just by looking at a stereo pair, such as that in Figure 27. (It is hard to fuse this figure without stereo glasses, though you may succeed by delib-erately crossing your eyes.) Others required stereo glasses, a visual wall between the pictures, and considerable study. Still others gave up in shame, seeing nothing. There was obviously a wide range of stereo fusion abilities. Some 15 percent of people are stereo defi-cient, while about 2 percent are stereo blind. It was all a great game. The essential question never even occurred to me until many years later. *How does the brain know which pairs of dots correspond in the two pictures to serve as a basis for its stereo calculation?*

The random dot stereograms are, literally, a sight to behold. Once perceived, the planes of the concealed figure (there is a square in Figure 27) lift out of the abyss with well-defined edges, even though the dots themselves could not define such straight lines. Imagine writing a computer program to fuse the images. It would be like trying to assemble the world's largest and most intricate jigsaw puzzle. Start with a dot from the right eye picture. There are 10,000 dots in the left eye picture which could be its mate. We could choose one of these arbitrarily, and there would be 9,999 left to choose again. All told, there would be a huge number of ways to pair the dots. Of this unfathomable number, all but a scant few would look like pictures of fog with every dot a particle at a different distance from the viewer.

How does the mind solve this incredible puzzle? Of course, we do not know for sure, but neural-network-like computers have successfully been used to untangle Julesz's stereograms using a rather simple configuration based upon two simple rules. First, it seems evident that a given point on a physical surface should have only one location in three-dimensional space, so that each dot can be matched with only one dot in the other view. On any given line of sight there should be only one match. Furthermore, we expect physical objects to have smooth boundaries, so that dots in the neighborhood of a given dot should have approximately the same depth. Combining these observations into rules of excitation and inhibition for a neural network gives connections between neurons that excite in a direction perpendicular to our line of vision, since we like smoothness, and inhibit in the depth direction, in order to satisfy the uniqueness of depth along a single viewpoint. The networks which have been programmed in this fashion have solved the stereograms rather quickly. Perhaps the brain works in similar fashion.

Unfortunately, it is also evident that triangulation alone will not always produce unique three-dimensional interpretations. Our brain is aided by two other factors. One is our knowledge, experience, and expectations of the real, physical world. The other is the fact that we seldom see any object from a single, fixed vantage point. Instead, we are almost always getting many views of a scene from slightly different angles as we move and turn our head, either deliberately or through small, random variations in position. There is some argument in the literature about which of these two is the more important effect.

A demonstration that became known as the Ames chair serves as an example of these disparate philosophies. Adelbert Ames constructed his wireframe chair from segments of wire strung precisely along lines of vision from a given peephole in the wall of a room. Seen from this exact peephole, the wires formed an unmistakable chair. Seen from any other vantage point, the wires formed haphazard arrangements of straight lines, as if someone had been playing pick-up-sticks. The empiricist would argue that since we have experience with chairs, we see objects as "chairs" whenever that configuration is an admissible possibility. The psychophysical argument, the opposing view, would be that the Ames chair is only an aberration, that in any real situation we would be able to integrate information from other viewing angles and that we would be able to tell, from sensory input alone, that the wireframe was not a "chair."

Computer monitors, like paper, and like our own biological sensors, are two-dimensional; the real physical world and the one we imagine are three-dimensional. Over the last quarter century I have seen many experimental attempts to build three-dimensional displays. They work, but like the failed 3-D movies they are usually gadgety and curiously unsatisfying. On a recent occasion I tried an experimental system that had separate computer-driven graphical displays for each eye built into special glasses. A positional sensor attached to the glasses continuously fed back to the computer the current position of the viewer's head, so that the displays could be calculated and drawn as seen from that particular viewpoint. As you turned your head, the three-dimensional display followed the movement to show you the proper view at all times. Even though there was nothing physically in front of you, you could see the computer-generated scene and walk around it, peering into it from here and there. I was fascinated at this new way of experiencing an artificial scene. What seemed especially important to me was the feedback between motion and vision. Seeing this demonstration helped convince me that there must be usable validity in the psychophysical approach to object recognition and stereopsis.

I cannot leave the subject of stereo vision without mentioning eidetics. It is not the sort of thing that I wake up at night and worry about, but it is something that has crossed my mind with wonder from time to time these last twenty or so years since Bela Julesz told me about his proposal. When it does cross my mind, I say to myself "No way!" and go on to other thoughts. Still, I do worry about it.

Very loosely speaking, an eidetic is a person with "picture" memory—someone who seems to "see" an image after it is gone, and is able to "look around" the image as if it were still there.

A number of studies have claimed to have found that eidetic ability is quite common in children, running at about 10 percent of the school age population. One of the indications of this ability in a child is the tendency to use the present tense when answering questions about a picture recently seen but no longer present. For example, "I see something that looks a little like a shed in the back of the house in the picture." Whether or not eidetic children are numerous is a matter of some dispute, but there is no argument about adults—they do not have this capability. Sorry about that. One attractive hypothesis is that it is either inefficient or impossible to continue to process visual information in the form of an entire visual field as we gain in knowledge and maturity. Feature extraction and immediate information reduction are the powerful approaches that we learn to use.

In the psychological literature being eidetic is not synonymous with having what is termed a "photographic" memory. The children who are identified as eidetic do not necessarily remember more detail in a picture than their noneidetic friends; it is just that they remember the picture in a more visual way. Nonetheless, there are reports of people who do have the extraordinarily rare ability to take mental "photographs" of images. I was told a few weeks ago of a person who after reading a particular book (a Bible—maybe it only works with Bibles), and having a pin thrust through the book, could tell from memory which *word* on each page was intersected by the pin. Should I believe this? I put this in the category of the paper on extrasensory perception that I received as editor of a journal, and sent to a famous scientist for review. His review consisted of only one sentence. "This is the kind of thing," he wrote, "which I would not believe even if it were true."

Back when he did the original work on random dot stereograms, Julesz proposed an "unfakable" test for eidetic ability. Could the supposed eidetic fuse a pair of random dot stereograms when one of the pair was from memory? This, you must agree, would be an incredible feat, perhaps even in the literal sense of the word "incredible." The eidetic would have to be able to recall a picture consisting of 10,000 (a million in some of the examples) randomly placed dots for later stereo matching with the mating picture for the other eye. Julesz says that he has never seen it done, but there are severals reports of successful demonstrations of this in this literature. If this were indeed possible, it would be dramatic evidence of an astonishing capability for picture storage in the human mind, whose capacity would be so enormous as to defy any explanation based upon information-theoretic coding. No compression scheme would be effective for pictures of random dots. Such a capability seems to lie in the domain of ESP. I would have to see it for myself. Even then, I would not be sure.

C O G N I T I V E
P R O C E S S I N G
I N   V I S I O N

Once someone gave me a computer program for drawing, storing, and displaying pictures. I wanted to make a very small change in its features, but I only had the executable code, not the source code which would have told me how it worked. So I tried to find out what made it tick. Somewhere out there in the computer memory were the stored pictures. Where were they, and how were they encoded, I wondered? But the insides of the program operation were completely inaccessible to me. All I could know were the pictures that went in, and the pictures that came out. As to what happened in between, I was clueless.

Thinking once again about the "spongy, pink mass" that is the human brain, the situation is similar. The pictures go in, and when we want to see them again we can call them up in our imagination and see them displayed on the screen in our mind. To try to find what happens in between, we can disassemble monkey brains. As fascinating as this may be, it is much like taking apart my computer—we would never find the pictures. Somewhere in the structure of the working brain is the executable code for vision, but it seems inaccessible, and perhaps no one will ever have a copy of the source code that explains its operation. Worse yet, while the pictures that go in are tangible, quantifiable artifacts, the pictures that come out—those in our mind's eye—are, literally, the stuff from which dreams are made. Though billions of us have seen these pictures in our heads all our lives, we cannot agree on their substance and properties.

All these insurmountable difficulties in understanding and quantifying vision do not stop us from trying. The functions in which we are interested are the input coding, the storage, and the retrieval and display. All the cognitive psychologist has to work with are sample pictures for input and the subject's responses to questions or tasks about those pictures. Just as in the case of probing a complex computer program with a few inputs, it is easy to be seriously misled by the results. Nevertheless, we can form hypotheses about properties of vision and attempt to formulate experiments that tend to confirm or deny their validity. Few experiments, however, are unambiguous in their interpretation, so there is still considerable argument about even the most basic properties of encoding, storage, and display. I believe that this murky state of affairs gives license to anyone to hold an opinion on the subject. We are all equipped with the necessary experimental apparatus, and we all have considerable experience in its use.

STORING PICTURES IN THE MIND
· · · · · · · · ·

My computer program does not store pictures by recording the intensity and color of every one of the quarter million addressable dots on the CRT screen. Neither does it seem likely that our brains save pictures in this bit-map fashion. A more likely conjecture is that pictures are saved as high-level descriptions of objects and properties of objects. We do not, for example, forget the lower half of a picture, as if a corner were torn from a photograph. Instead, we forget whole objects in pictures. I was recently remembering sights from my childhood, and in my mental browsing encountered the entrance hall of the planetarium I sometimes visited. I saw it clearly, I thought, in my mind's eye, and I started remembering things that we did in those visits. One of those memories was of watching the large Foucault pendulum in the entrance hall slowly work its way around the perimeter as the day passed. But that pendulum had not been in the original image I had seen in my mind. I looked at it again in my mind, and, sure enough, there was the pendulum.

Somewhere in my mind I can imagine a subroutine having called out, "Hey, give me a pendulum, quick!"

I have occasionally read that the human mind has an "infinite" capacity for the storage of pictures. The idea that we are walking video recorders is certainly intuitively appealing, for we all feel that we have stored countless pictures over our waking lifetimes. There is even some experimental evidence of this enormous storage capability. In a 1970 article in *Scientific American*, Ralph Haber reported that he had shown volunteer subjects 2,560 photographic slides at the rate of one every 10 seconds during viewing sessions held on consecutive days. At the end of this grueling diet, the subject was shown 280 pairs of slides in which one of each pair was from the series already seen. When asked which of the two pictures had been seen before, the identification rate was 85 to 95 percent correct. This feat is both amazing and commonplace.

Our capacity to store and recognize faces has received much attention in the literature. Nearly every author in this field observes that the capacity for face storage seems virtually unlimited. A remarkable series of experiments has been carried out to test this face memory ability using pictures from high school yearbooks. In these experiments the subject is shown a set of photographs of faces, one of which is from his high school yearbook, while the rest are from other high school yearbooks of the same year. Can he pick out the person from his high school? Almost unerringly, he can, even when the photo is of someone he might not have known at the time. The accuracy in these experiments runs greater than 90 percent recognition, virtually independent of the size of the high school class and the years since graduation. Even in subjects who have been out of high school more than 50 years the accuracy is still better than 75 percent.

As an information technologist, however, I must reject the concept of an infinite store. The issue really comes back to how much information is really contained in all those pictures in our heads. If each picture is stored as a bit-map of luminance levels, then the capacity must indeed be so huge as to be essentially infinite. On the other hand, if the pictures are stored in terms of objects or features, then the storage requirements are very, very much smaller. As each picture is recalled it only needs to be assembled, made to order, from these reusable objects, or reconstructed from the underlying features. How many bits does it really take to store a face, for example, in our mind? It is a matter of coding. I am sure that we

321

do these things with diabolical cleverness. The problem is that we do them so cleverly that we cannot discover how we do them.

Then there is the matter of detail. The pictures in our head do not seem to contain what we might think to be irrelevant detail. For example, consider a picture that we all have stored in our minds—the Mona Lisa. Conjure up that famous enigmatic smile in your mind now. Can you see what she is wearing, or what is in the background? If your experience is like mine, you cannot. What has happened to that detail? Was it never encoded in our minds in the first place, or is it in there somewhere, but just inaccessible? I lean towards the first position, but often people are able to remember additional details about pictures upon further questioning. Of course that in itself does not mean the entire picture was originally encoded. You can make your own judgment.

An information-theoretical view of mental picture storage would go back to the fundamental question of how many bits—yes/no questions—it takes to create a particular image in our minds at this level of detail, given all that we already have stored about the world and its pictures. Just as we have a dictionary of words stored in our mind and a compendium of rules about the formation and pronunciation of words, so must there be a dictionary of pictures and a set of rules for picture generation. Given this existing data, it is possible that new pictures can be encoded with relatively few bits. Can you remember the Jackson Pollock painting of Figure 24? What about the Albers? Since the Jackson Pollock has no structure consisting of "objects," it requires a very large information storage. Chances are that you had neither the interest nor the existing informational structures that enabled you to encode this picture. The Albers was easy.

A fundamental question of debate concerns the difference in mental representation for linguistic and pictorial information. When we read words, we do not see the words as pictures, but as abstract ideas. We rarely even remember the font of the letters in front of us. One hypothesis holds that there is a different high level representation for words than for pictures, while another maintains that they are both converted into one common representation. In the dual store hypothesis there is a linguistic store for words, which stand for abstract ideas, and a pictorial store for pictures, which in themselves stand for nothing until we choose to interpret them.

Suppose that we see a picture of a chair. For about a tenth of a second we hold the image of the chair exactly—like an after-image—in what is called iconic memory. Then the exact image fades, and the picture is processed so as to be represented in some compact format which may be matched against other pictures in our pictorial store. There the picture is found to be similar to other chair-like pictures. Possibly the collage of chair-like pictures carries a pointer to some structure in the linguistic memory under the label "chair." Here we find the properties of the class "chair," such as typical configurations and uses, and pointers to other information structures in subordinate and superordinate categories like swivel chairs and furniture. Supporting this dual storage hypothesis is data that show that it takes longer to name the picture of a chair than to name (read) the word "chair," indicating that time was needed for conversion between stores. However, other data are somewhat ambiguous, and it is likely that the real world is more complicated than either of these simple hypotheses.

ENCODING PICTORIAL INFORMATION
• • • • • • • • • • • • •

While the size and nature of the human picture store are absorbing philosophical questions, perhaps a more immediate concern having to do with information input is the method of scanning and encoding the picture. For one thing, is the encoding by a serial scan like television, or is it parallel and holistic? To what degree do we consciously choose which portions of the picture to encode and which to ignore? Can we, in fact, absorb the gist of an entire picture in a single glance, or do we have to work at it? We have previously discussed how features are extracted from a picture through the simultaneous workings of hundreds of thousands of brain cells, so there is some physical evidence of parallel encoding. On the other hand, the highest density of processing occurs in the small area where we fix our gaze, so perhaps we have to move our focus deliberately to survey the picture.

Some experiments seem to favor parallel encoding. In one such experiment, a picture showing a list of digits is flashed on a screen. As soon as he has identified the highest number in the list, the subject calls it out. How long is this reaction time? Unsurprisingly, the reaction time increases linearly with the number of digits in the list. This in itself might argue for sequential encoding and processing. Now the experiment is repeated, except that the quality of the visual display is degraded by adding visual noise (random dots) or decreasing the display intensity. Now how long does it take to identify the highest digit? The reaction time again increases linearly with the number of digits at exactly the same slope, the only difference being a constant additive time that moves the entire curve upwards. The significance is that the reaction time overhead due to the picture degradation is a constant, independent of the number of digits in the list. If the mind were processing each digit in the list serially, it would seem that it would take longer to encode each digit, and the degradation in response time would be proportional to the number of digits. Since it is not proportional, we might conclude that the algorithm that the mind uses in identifying the highest digit is acting upon all the digits at once.

A similar experiment has been conducted using that most familiar of visual tasks, the recognition of faces. Subjects were asked whether or not a picture of a face matched one previously seen in the experiment. The experimenters carefully modified the facial features so that the pictures being compared differed in only a small number of controlled features. The accuracy and time to recognize that a face matched one previously seen were found to be relatively independent of the number of altered features. This is indicative of some kind of holistic or parallel encoding of the facial pictorial information. However, the time required to find a *nonmatch* varied with the number of altered features exactly as predicted from assuming a strategy that serially compared features until a nonmatch was found. A problem with all these experiments is that the outcome being measured depends not only on the encoding method, but upon the processing strategy assumed to be taking place on the encoded data. As one author confessed, "Usually it is possible to offer special cases of both serial and parallel processing to account for almost any result." However, the same author goes on to conclude that faces are processed and analyzed by a sequential process of feature extraction.

There are other tasks in which picture processing appears to be serial. In one example, a picture of a hanging steel ribbon with a small number of twists is shown. How long does it take to decide whether or not the side of the ribbon seen at the bottom is the same as the side seen at the top? The time required turns out to be directly proportional to the number of twists in the ribbon. In this case we run our eyes down the ribbon, saying to ourselves, "Now the face is opposite . . . now it is the same . . ." We cannot just look at the picture and decide without going through a mental simulation of traveling down the ribbon.

As we scan our vision around a picture, we seem to be able to create in our mind a composite view of the fragments upon which we sequentially focus. We are able to integrate successive glances in order to obtain what has been called a schematic map of the picture. Within a second of first seeing a picture we have the feeling of seeing it all at once, no matter how complex it is, in spite of the fact that we can only focus our vision on some small portion at any given time. Even afterward as our eye focuses here and there, we seem to keep the whole picture in view. It is remarkable, when you think about it, because that panoramic view that we retain so vividly in our mind is physically impossible to achieve through the optical mechanics of our visual system.

What I believe to be a compelling example of the ability to integrate successive glances is demonstrated in a variation of the century-old Müller–Lyer illusion shown in Figure 28.
In this well known illusion, which I am sure you have seen before, our vision mechanism fails to make the proper interpretation. Every one of us believes that the upper line segment is shorter than the lower segment by about 20 percent, in spite of the fact that they are the same. Moreover, we have all seen enough optical illusions that we know very well that these things are always the same!

The Müller–Lyer illusion has been found to be remarkably robust. The line segments can be formed of large, solid partitions that we can explore by walking about in a room. We still think the upper space is less. In the variation to which I have referred, the

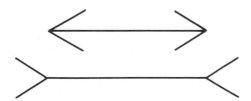

FIGURE 28
Which line segment is longer?

figure is viewed through a narrow, vertical slit that exposes only a small portion of the drawing. The slit is slowly moved across the figure. We still think the upper segment is 20 percent shorter than the right. In our mind we are able to put together the successive segments we have seen in order to interpret—incorrectly, of course!—the entire figure.

My favorite examples of the failings of holistic picture interpretation are in the drawings of Maurits Escher. These are by now so well known to scientists and laymen alike that I hesitate to include one here. However, they are so artistically and mathematically beautiful that I never fail to appreciate them afresh. In the drawing *Ascending and Descending* shown in Figure 29 the monks walk endlessly upwards or downwards, depending on which column you follow. Try as I may, I cannot see anything wrong with the picture. As a whole it looks correct, but if I follow one of the columns of monks I arrive at a contradiction. This inherent contradiction follows as the conclusion of a sequential analysis, whereas we are unable to see the paradox through any holistic interpretation of the drawing.

When we look at a picture we scan our gaze in a seemingly haphazard fashion around the portions of greatest interest. Generally speaking, those areas where we focus our gaze are exactly the ones that would be predicted from the considerations of information theory. The information is concentrated in those areas of surprise, which is manifested in unexpected change. Any source of physical invariance in a picture, such as the unchanging plane of a wall, is a source of redundancy. We skip those areas instinctively. Instead, we concentrate on the contours of objects, and particularly on the places where the contour shows the greatest rate of change. This is where the information is peaked. Studies of eye fixations confirm this behavior, though the exact pattern of fixations is seemingly random in any given situation and not subject to prediction.

The process of visual search of a picture is fascinating. Naturally, we want to look *at* what we are looking *for.* In the first moments before we build up a composite view of the picture, we engage in a directed search to get our foveal vision onto the critical areas of the picture. In order to do this, we have to build some understanding of the picture. While we are gazing at one region, probably we use vague information from peripheral vision to make some judgment as to where would be an informative place to look next, and off we go. There is some question as to whether the

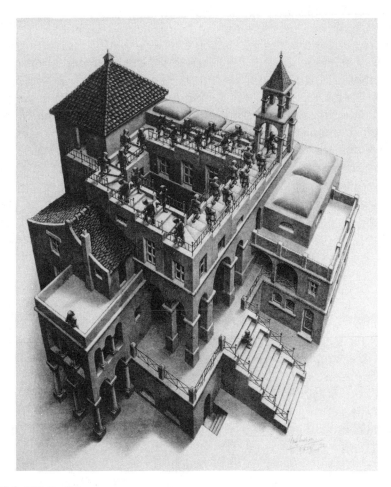

FIGURE 29
Ascending and Descending by M. C. Escher

identification taking place in the foveal region interferes with the decision-making process leading to the next fixation, or whether these two objectives can be accomplished in parallel. A vital part of building the understanding of the picture consists of the segmentation of the picture into figure and ground. Without this preliminary segmentation it would be difficult to put the identification of regions into perspective. As a consequence, some researchers believe that this segmentation may be preattentive and parallel.

Contrast the haphazard visual scan used in picture understanding with the scan used in reading, where we execute a methodical

327

pattern much like that of the electronic scan in a television set. It takes a long time, something on the order of a minute, to read a page of text. But when we look at a picture we focus first on some pictorial element of particular interest. Our gaze jiggles around this attractive area for a moment, and then darts across the picture to some other interesting area. Like a fast and busy bee, we sample here and there. Before very long, perhaps only a few seconds, our interest in the picture is sated and we turn the page. Many areas of the picture are never brought into the focus of vision at all.

Just as we skip the unimportant function words in reading text ("a," "and," "the," etc.), we skip the unimportant elements in pictures. The pictorial presentation makes this skipping very easy for us. Large blank areas say to us, "Do not look at me!" By contrast, in reading it is a lot of work to find skippable segments, since we are forced to employ high level, sequential, cognitive processing in order to make read/skip decisions. On the other hand, we can "read" at phenomenal rates when we are only looking for certain target words, like our own names, and it is unnecessary to understand the intervening text. I would like to reiterate my belief that skipping is a critical skill in the information-age environment. We simply do not have the time or capacity to intake all of the data thrust at us. Data filtering is the ultimate human job, and pictures usually facilitate this function.

In my youth my friends and I always seemed to lose baseballs, golfballs, and other small objects in giant fields of grass and weeds. At first we would just stand still and look at the whole field, and usually the miracle of pattern matching would occur—a single, small, round object would be differentiated from the linear, arrayed blades of vegetation. If this failed, we would wander about randomly from here to there, just as in the gaze patterns people impress upon pictures. Often we would be lucky and someone would encounter the ball. If not, after so much random wandering, we would all reluctantly agree upon the final resort—walking the field line by line, as if we were sowing seed, in order to cover every square foot.

These alternatives run the same attentional gamut as turning the pages of a picture magazine through reading the pages of a philosophical treatise. Information, like a golf ball, can be hidden, or it can be plainly obvious. Often it is a matter of the coding format, or what an advertiser would call the packaging. When the information is round, white, and glistening clean like a new golfball, and it is placed in a newly mown field of deep green grass, then the art of selection is easy. The essence of the information task is often the rejection of the unwanted data, or as they say, finding the wheat in the chaff.

In addition to the physical scan controlled by the muscles of the eyeballs, we have an internal, attentional scan. Even though we look straight ahead, we can focus our "attention" on an object in the periphery. I find this most curious. What exactly are we doing? Perhaps the vision system is organized and controlled somewhat in the way we think of computer systems in terms of "bottom-up" and "top-down" concepts. The "bottom" is the sensory input, the illumination map of the picture. The "top" is the abstract symbolic representation of world knowledge that we hold, accumulate, and update in our minds. We might believe that "seeing" is a one-way, bottom-up operation, that the data from the eyes are gathered, methodically processed, and passed upstairs.

But it is clear that the "upstairs" intellect has a say in vision. As easily as shifting a pointer to a new location in computer memory, the focus of visual processing can be changed. Between the physical scan of the eyeballs and the logical scan of attention, we can selectively encode portions of the visual scene to varying degrees of precision. We do the same thing when we listen to music and focus our attention on one section of the orchestra, such as the bass section. Often, for example, when we are reading a text there are accompanying figures that augment the textual explanations. The information in the text and in the pictures is redundant, so that when dipping into the pictures we know a priori what to look for. Various experiments have been conducted to try to understand whether or not there is preattentive coding of the entire picture before we focus upon the regions containing the sought-after information. This is called the late-selection hypothesis, as opposed to the early-selection view, in which we only encode the portions of the picture that are needed in a particular instance.

Unfortunately, as in most hypotheses about human processing, it appears that nature is seldom simple enough to be completely encompassed by one of two simplified models. Although we would prefer simplicity, it seems that both early-selection and late-selection encoding take place. The search of the picture and evaluation of the text are highly interactive. The sentences in the text establish a plan for the investigation of the picture. The glances at the picture provide visual answers to visual questions. Just as in a speech dialogue, we interrogate the picture to home in on the needed information. In the process, however, irrelevant information is encoded. Nobody ever said we were perfect.

Not only can the upstairs intellect tell the downstairs data collector where to concentrate its processing, but to a certain degree it can influence the interpretation of vision itself. The mapping of the visual stimulus is dependent both on perceptual factors, such as shape and texture, and on cognitive factors, such as context. This can be seen in many common optical illusions. In other words, we often see what we want to see. I sometimes imagine being lost in the world of a Jackson Pollock painting. Nothing would make sense with respect to the world of models upon which the pattern matching and information extraction of our vision depend. Psychologists have raised cats in strange, controlled visual environments. Their vision is irrevocably affected, as the unusual environment leads to the creation of strange processing structures in the cat's brain. You would not want one for a pet.

Perhaps the best example of a visual information format is a map. A map contains both conceptual information—names—and spatial information. In studying a map we have to integrate these two forms of information. Some people are better at this than others. Although there are relatively small differences among test subjects in the learning of the verbal information in a map, there are considerably larger differences in the learning of the spatial information. Good map learners seem to be able to encode the spatial information through systematic procedures of scanning and encoding. For example, they may often partition the map into smaller segments, using a divide and conquer strategy. They also frequently use a systematic visual sampling, and a memory-directed resampling to concentrate only upon the portions failing recall tests. In fact, one of the critical differences in learning pictures as compared with learning text is the lack of a good rehearsal mechanism related to the learning of the pictures. Good map learners are also proficient at using visual imagery to encode the spatial information into previously encountered patterns.

Finally, in considering maps it is interesting to comment on the differences in navigation ability when a territory is learned through study of a map versus actual experience in traveling the same region. In visiting a strange city we might study a map beforehand, whereas we seldom do the same for our own neighborhood. The knowledge acquired from the map is of a different flavor than that acquired from experience. Map learning is particularly good for visualizing straight line distances. When asked how far it is from point A to point B as the crow flies, a map learner will visualize the map, imagine placing a ruler on the map, and measure the distance in his mind. A person who has acquired navigation experience through actual travel in the area will answer the same question by simulating the trip in his mind. "Let me see," he says to himself, "First I go two miles down the road, then a left turn for about a mile and a half. . . ." All the angles have to be taken into geometric consideration and overall distances calculated accordingly.

Maps are also good for global relationships. We sometimes have a hard time knowing the compass bearings between landmarks in places that we have lived for years. On the other hand, the map learner is inferior to the traveler in giving route distances. He has to visualize his mental map and add all the route segments in the simulated trip, whereas the traveler has encoded the information about route segments directly. These differences in map learning illustrate general properties of pictorial representation of spatial relationships as opposed to the logical, sequential, verbal description of the same information. It is well to note that the pictorial presentation is not always the best format. For a given application, such as getting the shortest route on a map, the logical encoding resulting from everyday travel may be the better format. Of course in either event it helps to live in a geographically structured environment like New York City, rather than the capriciously random layout of, say, Boston.

PICTURES IN OUR HEADS — MENTAL IMAGERY

• • • • • • • • • • • • • • • • •

For many years one of my hobbies was photography. I collected thousands of 35 mm slides taken from trips all over the world. Today they all languish in crumpling, cardboard boxes coated in layers of dust at the bottoms of closets. The access problem killed them. Finding the slides I want, getting out the projector, setting up the screen—ugh! If only I had a projector and a picture data base like the one in my head. In an instant I can retrieve and display millions of pictures—even those under the dust in the back of my mental closet, and even ones I did not know that I had! But I wonder. How good is my mental projector? What is the resolution of my film, and does the emulsion age? How accurate are my pictures? Good questions, all, but of course there are no definitive answers.

Get out your own projector for a moment and draw an imaginary picture. Imagine that you are standing at the entrance to a long, empty room. At the far end of the room is a window with vertical metal bars. The sunlight from the hidden sun high in the sky cascades through the window, illuminating a slanting column of dust particles and causing a square section of the floor to glow in an otherwise gloomy room. Got it? Now how many bars are there in the window in your mental picture? Probably the question surprises you momentarily, and for an instant you do not know. But how can there be an indeterminate number of bars in a picture? If the image in your mind has the properties of the photographic slides in my closet then there are a definitive number of bars on the window—say, for example, five—and you should be able to count them.

It is impossible for me to know how anyone else visualizes imaginary pictures. For myself, I think that even though the window is clearly barred, there is no particular number of bars until I try to count them. ("He needs detailed bars!" shouts a subroutine in my head.) The "bars" are a virtual concept, rather than a physical reality. If this is true, then it illustrates an important difference between mental images and photographs. Furthermore, it is an indication of the information economy in storage and representation of pictures in our brain.

Earlier I recalled the missing pendulum in my remembered mental picture of the hall in the planetarium. At issue is whether or not there can be features in mental imagery that were not deliberately placed in the picture by constructive mechanism. In other words, can we "look around" in a mental image and "see" things that surprise us, which "we" did not place there? There are some experiments that indicate that mental images are construed in a particular representational format, and cannot be reconstrued (reinterpreted) in another way without mentally drawing a different image. It would be as if the mental picture were but a caricature of the imagined scene, capturing the essence, whatever that might be, without any pretense of photographic realism.

Look at the familiar Necker cube shown in Figure 30. Unlike a mental image, this line drawing is a tangible array of black-and-

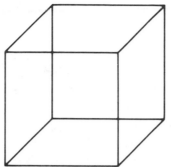

FIGURE 30
Necker cube. Which side is foremost?

white illumination levels presented at the perceptual level. It has no underlying, more abstract, basis or representation from which it has sprung. We are free to interpret it as we wish, and to make our own association with a more abstract structure. In this particular case, we associate the cube with a model of a physical object—a three-dimensional wire frame cube. But in making this association we have a choice of two physical models, between which the line drawing fails to discriminate. Because of the ambiguity in fitting the model to an imagined reality, we can "see" the cube as having the rightmost square as its front (nearer) side, or we can see this as the back side. It takes a little effort, but we can stare at the drawing and flip back and forth in our mind, construing the picture first in one way, and then in the other. It is a bit of a weird feeling, almost as if the cube were physically turning itself inside out.

Let me invite you to try an experiment. After you finish reading this present paragraph, I will ask you to turn to Figure 31 and ever so briefly fix the line drawing on the next page in your mind. Do not stare at it or try to interpret it in any way. Simply grab the image as a photograph and immediately turn the page back here. The time the page is turned should only be the blink of an eye. Please do that now.

I assume that you are back with one more picture in your own overcrowded mental closet. What did the picture represent? Now I would like for you to examine your mental image and try to find another interpretation for it, just as the ambiguous Necker cube permitted alternative interpretations. Try it for a while. Can you make the drawing into a different thing than it was before?

Give up? Then go back to the actual drawing and stare at it.

Now can you provide an alternative interpretation? Most people can, but in controlled psychological experiments no one is reported to have been able to see the alternative interpretations in the mental picture. It would seem that mental images are what they are, and cannot be something else. The picture you see in your mind may be locked to a particular representation. You cannot "look around" in the picture and decide that it is something else. Apparently, mental images cannot be ambiguous.

In some other respects seeing mental imagery is just like viewing those photographic slides. For example, we seem to have the ability to pan, zoom, and rotate mental images. Furthermore, these operations appear to be mechanized in a way that simulates reality. Suppose that you are shown two pieces of a jigsaw puzzle. They may

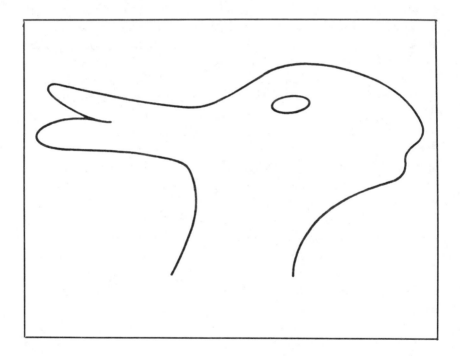

FIGURE 31
An ambiguous drawing

be the same piece, or they may not be. It is hard to tell, because they are in different angular orientations. Are they the same? Experimentally, it has been found that the time that it takes you to decide is proportional to this angular difference. Thus, apparently what you do to find out is to rotate one of the pieces in your mind until it lines up with the other piece, and then you make a comparison. This is really intriguing, because we might suppose that a more efficient algorithm would be to encode the one piece and then redraw it at the new angle so as to coincide with the other. A computer would do it that way.

What a useful capability mental simulation is. How would you take a card table, with fully extended legs, through a doorway? I can almost hear the rotations going on in my mind. How would you play the next carom shot in a pool match? There goes the ball in my mind, bouncing off the cushion. I even have to wait for it to get back in my mind to tell where it is going. Why cannot this be simply calculated? Why the clunking machinery of simulation?

Scan and zoom are much like rotation. If you are given a mental image, and then told to "look" at some feature, the time it takes to get there is linear in the distance moved within the picture. If you are told to imagine an ant on the newspaper in front of you, and then asked about some detail of the ant, then it takes time to zoom in on the ant. On the other hand, if the ant were originally imagined to be on a toothpick, then this detail would be immediately available.

Since in these latter respects mental imagery is very much like seeing, there is a temptation to suppose that the pictures in our head are shown by running the vision system in reverse. That is, in seeing we begin with perceptual input through the eyes which is "projected" upon the cortex through the transmission of the optic nerve bundles. Subsequently, this illumination map is processed to result in an abstract representation for interpretation and storage. Reversing the process, we would have the abstract representation expanded so as to result in an illumination map on the cortex, which could then be "looked upon."

While no one believes that mental imagery is produced in the simplistic way just described, there is considerable argument about how much of the visual system is shared between vision and imagery. Aside from the mechanics of zoom, pan, and rotation, there is also evidence of interference between vision and imagery. Verbal instructions do not interfere with our ability to form mental imagery, but if the instructions are in a visual format, it takes longer to form the mental images. Presumably, this is because we need to timeshare some of the processors between the input visual system and the output imagery system.

A HYPOTHESIS OF VISUAL INFORMATION PROCESSING

I know that many of my engineer friends will look down upon some of the sections of this chapter. "Hand waving!" they will decry. It is the lowest form of argument, the refuge of the incompetent. To engineers the world is divided into two forms of knowledge—hard science and soft nonscience. I cannot pretend indifference to this criticism. It bothers me too, and much of this is as soft as anything I have written. Nevertheless, in this vein I have a theory. I think that the brain knows about information theory.

In my theory, the 50-bit-per-second limitation on the input of information which we have seen in reading applies to all other information formats. It is as if there is a cognitive processing subroutine in our brain that runs at this very slow speed. We can intake huge amounts of unprocessed data, like the illumination levels in vision, and the sound waveforms in auditory perception, but whenever it is necessary to interpret and store perceptual data—to organize it into information—gigantic amounts of processing capability are required. These perceptual data processing programs are possibly contained in the prestored, read-only-memory, portions of our brain. They use up much of our capacity, and they run very slowly, but they are what make us sentient beings.

Many of my colleagues believe that when we look at pictures and use our pattern-matching abilities to extract meaning, we intake information at rates much greater than the 50 bits per second that I hypothesize. They may be right, but I have yet to see a quantitative example of information input through vision which is larger than this figure. Surely, the prototypical pattern-matching task is reading itself. We practice it all our lives. We match those little patterns we call characters against all the possibilities that we know as fast as we can, and then we move on to the next little pattern. But in none of the many languages of the world can we match faster than those 50 bits per second (approximately)—even in pictographic languages like Chinese in which much more information is packed into every little pattern. Of course, it might be argued that we carry with us in this task the overhead of language interpretation, but it would seem that in any informational task associated with vision there would be similar cognitive considerations. Furthermore, I seem to read at the same rate even when I do not pay any attention to what I am reading.

This working hypothesis about the fundamental bottleneck has two consequences. First, it means that when you look at a picture you do not automatically engorge large amounts of information. You get no more than 50 bits of information for every second you look at the picture. When you leaf through a picture magazine, you get what you put into it—very few honest bits. On the other hand, I have seen pictures, such as Rembrandt's *Night Watch,* which can withstand scrutiny for long periods of information withdrawal at the 50-bit-per-second rate. The information is there, but you have to work at it. Again, you get what information you pay for. It does not come free, easy, and fast simply because it is in pictorial format.

The other consequence of the bottleneck hypothesis is that the brain has to be ever so clever about its encoding of pictorial information, since it only has those 50 bits per second to work with. This is why the brain has to know about information theory. Every new picture has to be encoded in an elegant and efficient way, probably using previously encoded pictorial objects and picture-generation mechanisms. "What is new about this one?" the brain asks itself. Remember in Chapter 3 the Lempel–Ziv text compression algorithm, in which text is encoded in terms of previously encountered text sequences? We shall see something of this in the next chapter when we talk about how computers encode, store, generate, and understand pictures.

Since we do not really know how the brain does these things, the bottleneck hypothesis is only just that—a hypothesis. In other portions of this book we have seen how other human information processing activities demonstrate both information capacity constraints and fundamentally clever approaches to the job. Frankly, I would be surprised if I found that we handle some information task in a grossly inefficient manner. Thus, I would believe that picture storage is similarly constrained and clever. But perhaps it is not. Maybe we do take in gobs of information in single, quick glances.

Finally, is a picture worth a thousand words? I'll boldly assert—sometimes. It really depends on the picture.

R E F L E C T I O N S —
V I E W   G R A P H S

Does anyone remember what we did before there were view graphs? I thought not. The beginnings of our our view graph-oriented culture are lost in antiquity. It goes back to a time when the universe was young and the earth a forgotten planet in a far away galaxy. Long before there was life as we know it, out of the primordial slime view graphs began to congeal. Early man puzzled over the meaning of these strange, flat transparent slabs that littered the primitive landscape. The use for which these transparencies were destined awaited the discovery of fire—the first source of illumination. It is not known exactly how or when cavemen began to use view graph presentations on the walls of their caverns to depict plans for projected animal killings, but the fossilized remains of some of these images can still be found.

For many thousands of years the only type of view graph was pictorial. Presentations were generally simple and easy to follow. ("You strike the club here.") Eventually primitive man made an accidental, but important discovery —a view graph with a series of heavy dots, one per line arranged vertically. Perhaps a blank transparency had fallen into a bed of ashes, but in any event the "bullet" chart was born. Seeing such a chart, it was realized that an important format had been found, but that something was missing. Thus, writing had to be invented to fill in behind the heavy dots. Presentations were never the same after this.

The role of view graphs in history has often been overlooked. For example, one of the great briefings of all time was the all-day view graph presentation given by Columbus to Queen Isabella in his request for funding of an important exploratory project. Fletcher Christian went through hundreds of view graphs in a series of presentations in the audio-visual room of the HMS *Bounty* to explain a proposed management reorganization. In science and technology many great inventions were realized in celluloid format. Thomas Edison displayed view graphs of his proposed light bulb on an early model projection machine that used gas light. Naturally, the incentive for his great invention was improved audio-visual presentations.

In today's sophisticated engineering environment, view graph presentations are the stuff of life. The average manager must be up to consuming hundreds or even thousands of view graphs per week. This requires years of practice and daily exercise. Some high-level executives recommend a strenuous program of early morning warm ups with a home projector, so they will be fit for the day's activity. On the other hand, a different kind of stress lies upon the employee who must make the presentation. Of course, there is the usual fear of public speaking, but at the back of his mind lurks the fear that something will be wrong with his view graphs. Consider, for example, the feeling you get watching the well-known television commercial for an overnight delivery service in which the presenter makes animal pictures with his hands in front of an incredulous audience, because his view graphs didn't arrive in time. Hits home, doesn't it?

Success in engineering today depends on knowing how to prepare and use view graphs. Most graduating students have had little or no experience with this skill. Thus, I thought it would be a service to the profession to include a number of pointers to the neophytes in the remainder of this column.

1. Take all the view graphs you own to the meeting. If you are new, or have just arrived on earth and don't own many, then borrow some. The pile should be very high. This puts the audience on edge, and establishes you as an expert in whatever it is. You may begin by saying that you have brought more charts than you need, but start from the top in sequence. The audience will have no idea when, if ever, you intend to finish. This also helps discourage questions. If you are especially worried about questions, take a large pile of back-up view graphs. After you have dipped into this pile to handle the first question, there will be few further inquiries.

2. It is wise to begin the talk with a series of "wiring diagrams" showing the organizational charts of your institution. Never underestimate the interest of your listeners in the myriad details of your organization.

3. Never use several view graphs when the same can be accomplished with a complicated series of fold-down overlays to a single view graph. Your expertise in handling this advanced format will be noted by management.

4. Most of your charts should be of the "bullet" variety, with no fewer than 12 major points per chart. This makes your timing easier to calculate. Allow 30 seconds per chart.

5. No real engineer places view graphs upside down on the projector. (We went through all those intelligence tests on visualizing rotations and permutations.) However, it is good form

occasionally to cock a view graph at a 20 degree angle. Pay no attention to the leaning of the audience. This keeps them slightly off balance and prevents sleepiness.

6. Incorporate a few view graphs containing giant tables of small print. Always apologize for these, saying you know they can't be read, but. . . . Save them carefully for subsequent talks.

7. A sense of timing is critical to successful presentations. Watch your audience very carefully during each view graph for tell-tale signs—such as a slight widening of the eyes—which might indicate the dawn of understanding. The view graph should then be removed immediately. After a few presentations with a given set of view graphs, you should get some feel for this timing on each chart. This is known as the mean time to failure of the view graph. The total presentation time is simply the sum of the mean times to failure of the individual charts.

Pointer 7 is due to General Glenn Kent (and this is real—Lt. Gen. USAF, ret.), who is one of the great briefing-destroyers of all time. "This is just like a good old-fashioned American game of baseball," he is fond of saying. "There are pitchers (briefers) and batters (briefees), and the objective of the pitcher is to throw the ball past the batter. The batter's dream is the home run." Thus Gen. Kent counsels young briefers (usually, he notes, pale captains delivering briefings on behalf of suntanned colonels) to practice their fast balls, curves, and change-ups. There is always the ultimate fear awaiting—the heavy hitter. Out there in your next audience the mighty Casey may be at bat.

8

PICTURES AND
PROCESSING

· · · · · · · · · · · · ·

I think of text as the canonical
form of representation for information. What could be better for
a computer, needing compactness of format, than a sequence of
abstract symbols that denote meaning? Text is so compact in format
that we find it most difficult to compress for computer storage. As
we have seen, the most efficient algorithms achieve only a compression of about 50 percent in bits. Even so, it might be argued that
text is complete in human expression: Any thought, feeling, conjecture, or fact can be expressed in the words of language. Where a
thought falls between the cracks of language it can be expressed
through metaphor, and where awkwardness develops, new words
are invented.

Speech, on the other hand, is a superset of text that is very much
less compact. Speech is an analog version of that sequence of abstract symbols, but one considerably complicated by the addition of
emotional and informational nuance. The main role for the computer is the translation back and forth between the discrete symbols
and the analog speech. Because of the clouding effect of the nuances, this translation—speech synthesis and recognition—is most
difficult, and the only way that the computer can store natural-
sounding speech requires perhaps ten thousand times the storage
of equivalent text.

Pictures are quite another matter. These require many more bits for representation than even the proverbial thousand words of text, but the direct relationship with the words of language is no longer present. Unlike the situation in text, pictures are not a complete representation for human expression, as they lack an underlying capability to express abstract thought. While not all text can be expressed in pictorial format (except in the pictures of the alphabet) the reverse seems true, that is, any picture can be expressed at any level of detail in words. More generally, a picture can be represented in terms of some set of abstract symbols, a sequence with its own grammar and semantics—a language of pictures. But since we have not generally defined this abstract language for pictures, the role of the computer in pictures is more intellectually constrained than its role in speech. Nevertheless, as we shall describe, there is much the computer can do in its guise of idiot savant.

A picture can be a smorgasborg of information. When I think of extracting the information in a picture, I imagine an information tree, branching into smaller and smaller twigs of relative importance. Suppose that a picture shows a person and a ball. On the trunk level of the information tree we see that the person is kicking the ball. At the next lower level we observe that the person is a small boy, and the ball is a soccer ball. Still lower in detail we see the boy has brown hair and a striped shirt. The soccer ball is white with a pebbly, leather surface. Lower yet we might notice the dirt on the ball and the boy's untied shoelace.

At some point in this information tree the detail ceases to matter from an informational standpoint. The levels of detail turn into what I shall call "information noise," that is, valid but irrelevant and possibly distracting information. We see, for example, the shapes of wispy clouds in the sky, the weeds in the grass in the background, and the discarded gum wrapper near the boy's left foot. Natural scenes are usually rich in this irrelevant detail. We have to plunge through all the layers of this information noise to reach the display noise—the artifacts and imperfections of the photographic printing process, such as pin holes and dust particles. Finally, the picture information tree reaches its last set of branches at the ultimate resolution of the reproduction system—the graininess of the film and the optics of the lens. The line is vague, but it exists. There is no more.

342

At each level in the tree we could translate the picture into words. The descriptions would get longer and longer, reaching the thousand word benchmark and flowing onto further pages through which even the most pedantic reader would be unwilling to persevere. The intelligent reader would quit somewhere in the early information noise level. Of course, this is all relative. We may have different trees. Where the tailor sees an ill-fitting suit, the physician might see malnutrition.

Suppose that we consider the lowest level, most detailed, text description of the picture. It should be completely equivalent in information to the picture itself, merely a transformation in format of the information, just as a Fourier transform maps a function of time into a function of frequency. The Fourier transform is often used in mathematical analysis because important features of a system may reveal themselves as patterns that are visually evident in one domain but widely dispersed in the other. Similarly, the pictorial representation of the text description may bring the upper level of the information tree to our immediate attention, while allowing us to ignore the lower level details. Unless the equivalent text is carefully, semantically ordered, it will not bring the information trunk into sharp relief. Our vision system has been tuned through evolution to the extraction of this trunk, which has sometimes been called the "primal sketch." Boy kicks ball.

When the computer handles pictures it is not as fortunate as we are. It does not know about "boy kicks ball." The gum wrapper is not different from the boy's foot. It does not know about the information tree or about information noise. It must handle all levels as equally important, and the job is enormous. Thus, coding of pictures for computer storage is terribly inefficient, as we shall presently describe. Similarly, image understanding by the computer is quite primitive. However, when we think of pictures as a transformation from some other data base, the power of a computer comes immediately to mind. Many pictures are formed as the explicit translation from another description. Moreover, even for natural pictures without a preexisting, compact description the calculation power of the computer can be used for various translations that enhance the visibility of the information trunk. "I have no idea what these bits mean," the computer says to itself, "but if it helps these humans to see the information, I am willing to do all these meaningless calculations."

PICTURE STORAGE

How many bits does it take to represent a picture digitally? It depends on the spatial resolution and the gray level or color range allowable at each point. A good quality computer display monitor has a spatial resolution of 1,024 horizontal dots by 1,024 vertical dots, for a total of about 1 million resolvable dots. These dots are called picture elements, or pixels for short. At each of these pixels we might allow perhaps 8 bits of gray-level depth for a mono-chrome image, meaning 256 shades of gray between black and white. In this case, storage of the monitor's image would require one megabyte, or approximately 8 million bits. If the display was a high-quality color monitor, then one byte might be allocated at each pixel to code the intensity of each of the three primary colors, resulting in a tripling of the number of bits. While this may seem an enormous number of bits, the computer monitor is actually a fairly low resolution display format compared with photographs and other common pictorial media. As a rough guide, the table below gives the resolution in dots per inch for some common pictorial display formats. A 35 mm black-and-white negative has over 11 million resolvable dots. If each dot has a gray level scale of only 8 bits, then the total comes to about 100 million bits! Another common example is an 8½-by-11-inch printed page, which takes about 15 million bits to retain the full resolution inherent in the glossy print process. Truly, pictures can require enormous amounts of data to represent.

PICTURE RESOLUTION

EXAMPLE	RESOLUTION (DOTS/INCH)
Photograph	3,000
Print of photo	1,500
Polaroid	1,300
Hi-Res Scanner	800
Human eye	700
Television	60

We can see the effect of decreasing resolution in the picture of a woman's face shown in Figure 32. As the spatial resolution decreases the fine detail is lost, and the naturalness of the picture disappears. With further decreases we see the picture becoming progressively "blocky." To some degree this blockiness is an artifact of the sampling process, which creates sharp, artificial borders at the edges of the pixels. The appearance of the picture can be enhanced by squinting your eyes, or by moving the picture further away from your eyes. The main point of this illustration is the relationship between photographic realism and sampling resolution. If you want realism, you need a lot of bits—something on the order of megabytes or even tens of megabytes. On the other hand, if you only need gross, spatial features, then very much less resolution may be required.

Pictures of faces are rather a special class, and are obviously important in everyday life. We have evolved to be very adept at

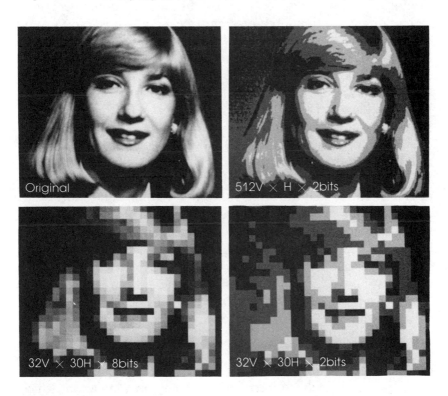

FIGURE 32
The effect of resolution on picture quality

recognition of faces, even with only a small amount of visual information. When Leon Harmon quantized pictures of people's faces in the 1960s at Bell Labs, he created a blocked portrait of Abraham Lincoln that was easily recognized in spite of having a resolution of only $18 \times 14 \times 3$ (horizontal $\times$ vertical $\times$ bits of gray level), which is only 756 bits total. The quantized portrait of Lincoln became quite well known after being included as part of a painting by Salvador Dali. (I often see copies of this particular painting in poster stores.) Lincoln's face is well known to us all, and apparently simply characterized by a few simple features, such as the shape of the beard. We might say that his "primal sketch" can be represented in only a few hundred bits.

Harmon found in informal experiments using digitized portraits of his associates that people's faces could be recognized (at least in a population of several hundred) in blocky pictures like Figure 32 having a quantization of about $10 \times 10 \times 3$, or only 300 bits. The information that we need for recognition is in both the spatial resolution and in the depth of gray scale, so it is possible to trade one against the other. For example, we could use a coarser sampling grid (bigger pixels) and more shades of gray, or vice versa. In either case, the number of bits in Harmon's block pictures is equivalent to a only a few dozen words of text; it is astonishing how few bits can characterize a face for recognition. Once the person is recognized, then it seems that we see more detail in the picture. It is as if the mind superimposes the known detail upon the rough framework of the block portrait.

If we do recognize faces by extracting a few prominent features, then it might be that the mind sees a photograph and reduces it to a caricature the way a cartoonist emphasizes in a simple, distorted sketch the most obvious feature of an individual. However, it has been shown that it takes longer to recognize a famous person from a caricature than from a photograph. Perhaps when we see a cartoon of Winston Churchill with an exaggerated, thrusting jaw, we have to translate this in our minds to a photograph, and then from there to whatever serves as our own, individual, primal sketch of Churchill.

It has also been shown that it takes longer to recognize a face from a line drawing than from a photograph. Indeed, faces are made more difficult to recognize by any manipulation which reduces the amount of detail present when recognition is to be accomplished. Yet in the end, the brain must make use of some small information extracted from the detail, utilizing some "face schema" which is not yet apparent to researchers. That face recognition is for humans a high cognitive ability is indicated by the finding that face recognition improves significantly in children after the age of 10. Before this time, children are easily misled in recognition by external paraphernalia, such as hats, glasses and mustaches. After the teen years they are seldom misled by these same considerations. It does appear, however, that a certain face recognition ability is built in at birth. It helps to know your mother's face, even upside down, as from the baby's most frequent view.

The attempts to correlate face recognition with obvious features, such as individual regions like the eyes, nose, and mouth, have not worked especially well for computerized face recognition. The Identikit approach used by law enforcement people is similarly based, and similarly effective. Psychological experiments have shown that the eyes, nose, and mouth in a picture of a face draw the most eye fixations, but that the single most important feature for human recognition is the hair. Of course, we are able to recognize people after many years and substantial changes in hair color, amount, and style. The computer has a tough time when the person has not changed at all. The faces that pass through its silicon dreams are as unchanging as the portraits in musty galleries.

While only a small number of bits serve for recognition of someone we already know, it takes many, many more bits to describe a stranger, or to give some insight into a person's mood or emotion. It is like the distinction between computer-synthesized speech and natural speech. The recognition may be there, but the emotions are gone. The real person has left. I sometimes remember the story about King Henry VIII, who was searching for another suitable wife in the beginning of the seventeenth century. (I always wonder why they married him.) His advisor, Thomas Cromwell, recommended Anne of Cleves. Henry was not so sure of this, so he sent the painter Holbein to France to paint a portrait of Anne. Apparently, Henry liked the portrait that Holbein painted (which now hangs in the Louvre), and agreed to marriage. When he subsequently met Anne, he felt badly cheated by what he thought in retrospect was Holbein's flattery. She did not last long. How many bits would King Henry VIII have needed to characterize a prospective wife? I am sure he would have demanded megabytes.

In many information applications a sketch or cartoon is all that is required to depict the relevant features. Examples are architectural layouts, mechanical drawings, and circuit diagrams. More and more, these drawings are being originally captured in computer format through computer-aided design (CAD) software. In this case, the computer file is simply a listing in a picture description language of a set of commands that recreates the drawing—"draw a line from point (3.2, 4.8) to point (7.1, 8.5)," "draw a circle of radius 0.72 at point (1.2, 2.2)," "place the following text at point (0, 1)," and so on. Instead of saving the picture itself, the computer saves the recipe for drawing the picture.

Line drawings require only modest storage. In one popular computer-aided design package the outline of a chair takes 1,600 bytes, while the layout of an office, complete with three-dimensional chairs, desks, tables, and wastebaskets, uses 16,000 bytes. A cutaway diagram of the space shuttle, which is often shown in advertisements, needs 32,000 bytes. These kinds of line diagrams simplify reality in a way which is helpful. By pruning the information tree to eliminate the twigs, we can focus our attention on the important constituents. The office layout does not look like a real office, but who cares? For the purposes of space planning it is better. On the other hand, it would never make the cover of *Architectural Digest*. That would take a lot of bits.

PICTURE GENERATION

We have seen that natural, photographic pictures take megabytes of storage. Needless to say, there are not very many pictures stored this way in computers. If humans stored pictures in this straightforward format, it is doubtful that we could call up very many either. However, pictures are usually plentiful in computer output, as everyone knows. It is just that the pictures are not the pixel-by-pixel variety characteristic of natural scenes and photographs. Rather they are simple, artificial pictures such as charts and graphs, which are created on the fly from other data bases. After their creation and use they are simply discarded, only to be recreated whenever necessary.

Artificial pictures are used to a much greater extent in the current computer milieu than in the paper-based office environment. In reports we are properly hesitant to publish chart after chart showing different constructions of the same data. Few readers would fail to be disgusted at the overkill. But when you sit at a keyboard by yourself, you can get an intuitive understanding of data by manipulating it visually until you get a display that strikes a resonant chord with the way you happen to understand things. The problem is that few other people may see it this particular way. This wonderful customization has no counterpart in text.

Computer-generated charts and graphs are simple and useful abstractions, but are also a bit boring when taken in heavy doses. Perhaps it is because they are "thin" in an information sense. A tree without its leaves does not have the esthetic staying power as one in full blossom. Fortunately, many of the pictures that the computer can generate are more richly detailed, and more physical rather than abstract. Pictures are implicit in some important data sets, such as in the information acquired by ultrasound probes of the human body, or that obtained by synthetic aperture radar, in which objects may be imaged by relative displacements in time and frequency of sideward-looking radar pulses.

Probably the best example of implicitly described pictures is in computer tomography. When you are shoveled into a CT machine as a human salami (may you never have this experience), you feel that the machine is looking skeptically, with raised electronic eyebrows, at your very soul. It is easily forgotten that the real breakthrough that made this possible was in the mathematical algorithms that permit the reconstruction of the cross-sectional view from the attenuations experienced by a number of axial rays. This is a triumph of modern analysis. It certainly beats sawing the patient in two, but that is often small consolation.

Computer reconstruction from such data can be carried an important step further by having the computer extrapolate the images from successive slices to produce a three-dimensional view of the salami itself, so to speak. An example of the power of computed visualization is shown in Figure 33, which is the tracing of a neuron from some very small organism, whose exact name is equally unimportant to it and us. One of the real difficulties in computing this example, done by Peter Selfridge at Bell Labs, is finding and following contiguous segments of the neuron in successive sections. The computer is also an excellent artist, though totally uncreative. As long as we can describe an object adequately, it can draw the picture for us. It knows all the rules of lighting, geometry, optics,

FIGURE 33
Reconstruction of a neuron from successive sections. *(from Peter Selfridge)*

and perspective. It was not all that long ago, say 300 years or so, that we grappled with perspective ourselves. Now the computer knows all these mechanical considerations. My favorite example of its abilities is shown in Figure 34, showing a transparent sphere above a checkerboard. In this beautiful work of computer graphics art, Turner Whitted has used a procedure called ray tracing to calculate the exact illumination on each pixel we see. Given a source of illumination from the upper left, out of the picture, what rays of light could have reached a particular pixel? Some rays could have come directly from the source, others might have bounced off some of the other surfaces, creating both diffuse and specular secondary sources. Still other rays could have been refracted through the transparent sphere, or reflected off its surface. There are even pathways for rays that traverse paths that are partially hidden from our viewpoint, for example, rays that bounce off the back of the sphere and then reappear. Only by calculating all of these possibilities does the resulting picture appear real to our knowing, experienced vision.

The sphere took a lot of computer work, but no matter. Since there are about 1 million pixels, and each pixel takes many calculations to compute all the possible impinging rays, about a 100 million calculations were required. It took about one hour on a very capable 1985-vintage minicomputer. However, every year sees the introduction of powerful new special purpose chips and computing architectures specifically designed for graphical calculations. In

FIGURE 34
Computer graphics reconstruction by ray tracing. *(from Turner Whitted)*

1987, using an array of digital signal processor chips (the same used for speech processing) the same sphere picture was created in 15 seconds. At reduced resolution, the sphere could be rotated in real time, before our very eyes!

Whitted's sphere is a good example of what is right and what is wrong, or at least inadequate, with computer graphics. The optical effects and geometry are accurately and flexibly calculated and presented. Want to move the sphere? Easy. But the picture itself is only a simple one, and moreover it was laboriously described to the computer by the artist. In speech synthesis it would be as if the computer could speak one simple word ever so precisely. In pictures it is even in some sense easier than speech, because how a word "sounds" is less tangible and harder to quantify than how an object "looks." More importantly, one word does not make a language, any more than one sphere makes a picture synthesis capability. The grammar and semantics of meaningful, natural pictures are a long step away.

TEXTURE
· · · · · · · ·

It seems that information in a picture lies largely in the discrimination of objects, more specifically with their classification and with

their topological relationships. Objects themselves are differentiated by their boundaries or edges, hence the emphasis on fidelity
of portrayal and perception of edges. Recall, once again, that information is concentrated at places of unexpected change. Where areas
or surfaces within a picture are uniform or follow expected variations there is little information. We do not need to fix our attention
on these uninteresting regions. Thus a line drawing, which can be
done relatively easily by computer, would appear to extract the
informational essence of visual perception. What else is there?

What else there is is mostly what we call texture. I am once again
writing during a conference session being held in the typical hotel
ballroom. (I am practicing information filtering on the current
speech.) As I look around this natural scene, the interesting objects
are the people, then the shape of the room, the tables, and the
chairs. Everywhere texture helps me to characterize things—the
rough cloth on the table, the tiling on the ceiling, the panels on the
walls, the paint on the ducts, the wool rug on the floor, the faces
and hair of the people, and the varieties of material in their clothing. The whole scene is composed of edges and texture.

In terms of information per unit area the regions of texture are
information-poor, but the few bits that they do contribute are quite
useful. Texture provides differentiation and variety; it arouses our
attention level, and aids in the identification of objects. Moreover,
texture itself helps define boundaries, and through the variation in
illumination level, both shape and perspective. There is, for example, an approach in the computer analysis of visual inputs known
as "shape through shading." Clearly, texture is an important factor
in vision. The modeling, synthesis, and analysis of texture has been
an important research topic in the computer art.

What exactly is texture? Up close and personal, as they say,
texture is rich in detail. We see an array of pixels with various
shades and colors. Reproducing correctly every individual element
of this array would require an enormous number of bits, but on this
microscopic level we are really dealing with what I termed information noise. The important properties of texture are only perceived
on a more global level. On the microscopic scale, we would not
even recognize the texture, but if we see them from afar, where the
individual pixels blur together, we might immediately see, for example, satin. We can almost "feel" the texture in our mind. What
we ought to be able to do, from an informational standpoint, would
be to store the few bits that say "this area is satin," and when

required create a new array of pixels that have the "satin" property. No one would ever know the difference. All the information is in the few bits describing the global, macroscopic, properties of the armies of little pixels.

There are two approaches to creating texture. One approach is based upon generating random arrays with desired statistical properties, while the other is through the use of structured, geometrical patterns. We see examples of both in the real, physical world, and most textures might be seen at one level or another as representing both underlying mechanisms. The bricks in the building across the street from where I now sit form a regular pattern. No individual brick has any memorable feature; only the pattern is significant. However, if I walked closer so as to examine individual bricks, I would see the randomness of the uneven surface of the fired clay. I would not even have to reach out to touch it to know how rough it would feel. Everywhere, texture is a blend of structure and randomness. So is everything, I suppose.

Once a year for my annual physical I lie flat on my back on a metal cot in a small, austere room staring at the ceiling, enmeshed in the suction-cup tentacles of an EKG machine. I have studied the acoustic tile of that same ceiling for many years in an effort to take my mind off the rhythmic scratch of the stylus recording my heartbeats. ("Don't stop!" I plead silently.) I try to find patterns in the holes of the acoustic tile, or to memorize their locations. I always fail. The designers have been diabolical in the utter randomness of the placement of the holes, even though I can see the entire pattern repeated in another tile elsewhere in the ceiling. Once again, there is a pattern on one level, and randomness on another. Small consolation.

What is it that we see in a random array that enables us to recognize so easily hundreds or thousands of different textures? The descriptors of a stochastic array are the many-dimensional, joint probability distributions of the pixel shades (or colors). In all their grandeur, these detailed descriptions themselves would be overwhelming in their complexity. Does it really matter that much? Apparently not. The results of many experiments on the perception of texture lead to the conclusion that we are sensitive only to a simple measure of the spatial correlation of the pixel shades. Specifically, there is a conjecture by Bela Julesz that the perception of a texture depends only upon the first two moments of the probability distribution. Although there exist contrived counterexamples to the Julesz conjecture, it is generally accepted as a fair statement of human perception.

The second moment of the probability distribution for the shades of the pixels is a measure of the amount that the shade of a pixel affects its neighbors. How far away, and to what extent, is the influence of a pixel felt? This moment is the average value of the product of the pixel shade at one point times the pixel shade at another point, say n pixels away. Both shade values should have the mean value subtracted first, so as to deal with deviations from mean. If the second moment is zero at value n, it would be an indication that a pixel had no average effect on its nth neighbor. If it were positive, it would mean that dark shades in a pixel tend to induce darkish shades in this neighbor, and vice versa. Obviously, a negative moment would mean dark induces light, and vice versa.

Apparently, about all a texture has to tell us is subsumed into knowledge of the second moment as a function of distance n. This is a tremendous simplification, but not one totally unexpected. We suspected that only some simple, global property of the statistics of the pixel array could possibly be relevant to its recognition as texture. Thus, one way that a computer could create texture on its own would be to generate random numbers with the desired second moment. Usually this is done by starting with the usual generation of independent random numbers, and then passing the numbers through a filtering operation (a running, weighted sum of some number of previous values) to give the desired spatial correlation.

Using the underlying model of a random array characterized by its spatial correlation, computers can not only be used to generate texture, but also to recognize texture based upon the analysis of the pixel shade correlation function. One example of an application where this analysis is important is in radiological images, where the texture carries important information for diagnosis. Another example is in the classification of earth resources from the images collected by the Landsat satellites. How much crop is there, and of what type? How much area is forested, or urban? Where are there crop diseases? These kinds of classifications can be effected by texture analysis of the voluminous, multispectral, Landsat imagery.

The other general approach to texture is to generate repeated patterns, usually with some random size and orientation. The cellular or mosaic approach is well suited to computers, as the algorithm can be simply described, while intricate patterns can be generated

FIGURE 35
Array of texture generated by a computer. *(from Bela Julesz)*

through recursion, so that patterns can have subpatterns, and so forth, in a hierarchical fashion. Many physical sources of texture have their genesis in similar structural processes.

An example of a mosaic generating process is the so-called "bombing" model. Imagine airplanes flying over the area and randomly dropping bombs with a certain frequency. Where each bomb hits, a pattern of a given size and shape is placed. This process divides the plane into a foreground, the bombed-out region, and a background. Such a pattern would resemble the growth of scattered trees in a field. Alternatively, at each randomly selected point a pattern like a circle can be made to expand until it hits another such pattern expanding from another bomb hit. This kind of growth is appropriate for many natural texture processes involving growth, such as patches of vegetation that spread until they hit competing patches.

355

Still other mosaic algorithms employ randomly placed lines or checkerboards. The individual cells in the mosaic can be shaded or colored according to some probability distribution. Using an assortment of such simple algorithms textures resembling, for all practical purposes, such materials as cork, mica, grass, pebbles, paper, marble, leather, wood, and ice are easily derived.

The synthesis and analysis of texture are in the best tradition of information processing. All of the intricate detail in the random placements and patterns can be boiled down into a few bits of meaning, which can be used to resurrect the texture at some future time, or to serve as a descriptor of the texture for analysis. If only all of picture synthesis and analysis were so straightforward!

PICTURE PROCESSING

Every now and then someone shows me a picture of a desert or a forest on a CRT screen. "What do you see?" they ask anxiously. I always lead them on by replying that I do not see much of anything. Then with a smile of confident anticipation, they press a key at the terminal, and the computer goes to work processing the picture using some new, sophisticated algorithm. Before my very eyes the picture undergoes a metamorphosis, and the obtrusive outline of an ugly tank emerges from the trees, or it becomes obvious that an airplane is camouflaged within the desert sands. I always cry out in surprise and appreciation, but of course, I had seen the tank lurking in the trees or the airplane pretending to be sand in the first place. No sense in spoiling a good show, but it is certainly true that the computer greatly enhances the recognizability of the scene.

The computer did not know about the tank or the airplane, either before or after its inspired processing. Picture interpretation is still a job for humans, and will be for a long time yet, but computers can help improve the qualities of a picture that carry meaning for us, whatever they may be. Computers can use their enormous processing capabilities to allow us to see pictures in, figuratively speaking, different lights. Often one of these new "lights" will illuminate features that were previously hidden from our comprehension. Many of these new computer tricks with pictures have their analog in the traditional photographic darkroom, while others accomplish alterations and restorations that have been heretofore impossible.

The simplest functions that can be done by a computer to help humans with pictures are called point processes, because they act separately and independently on each point (pixel) of the image. Remember that there are on the order of a million pixels in a picture, so whatever mathematical operation is done at each pixel needs to be repeated about a million times. Still, with computers rated in terms of millions of instructions per second, a point process can be done in the blink of an eye. Generally speaking, such a process uses the value of the gray shade at each pixel as an index into a lookup table that maps that shade into a different one, which is hopefully preferable on average to the original. In other words, the process just rescales the range of shades or colors in the picture.

A pixel rescaling can do much the same thing as the contrast knob on your television set. A picture that is washed out can be darkened, or one that looks too dark can be lightened. Contrast stretching can be effected by anchoring the darkest shade at black and the lightest shade at white and interpolating other gray shades proportionally in between. A related useful operation in radiology is density slicing, which can pick out and selectively illuminate a narrow range of shades so as to highlight a particular region of texture. To get a uniform density of shades it is also possible to do histogram equalization, in which the histogram representing the number of pixels with a given gray value is made equal for all shades. These operations are a little nicer than the local photo shop can do with our home photos in that we can arbitrarily choose, in effect, the exposure to be associated with each shade of pixel.

Another increasingly popular point operation is pseudocoloring, which associates a particular color with each shade of gray in a gray-scale picture. This is not the same as the coloration of old black-and-white movies, but it serves a useful purpose in that we are more sensitive to colors than we are to shades of gray. Pseudocoloring is used in both radiology and in display of earth resource imagery, where it can dramatically illuminate the various textures. For example, one type of crop will show up as reddish, while another might be yellow. No new information is being derived; it is merely a question of helping the subtle discrimination abilities of the human. We really cannot see very much more than a dozen levels of gray, so we can use all the help we can get in terms of contrast stretching or coloration.

While point processes are easily applied and fairly useful, they are not as powerful or interesting as the more general operation, called an area or neighborhood process, which is a spatial filtering operation on the picture. To calculate the new value for each pixel in these processes it is necessary to take into account the values of the neighboring pixels. Right away we can see that it is possible to get into huge amounts of processing. If there are a million pixels, and the calculation for each involves every other pixel, then whatever needs to be done has to be repeated a trillion times. Now even supercomputers start to frown at us. "Is this what you really want?" they seem to be questioning. Well, perhaps we compromise. Would you settle for using the ten nearest neighbors? Usually.

Most of us have some intuitive feeling for the filtering of a one-dimensional wave like that in music. We turn down the treble control on our high fidelity amplifier, and we hear less of the high frequencies. What we might think of as brilliance in the music melts away, but perhaps so does some of the noise and raspiness. We end up setting the control at some compromise setting that sounds best to our learned ears. However, not many of us have the opportunity to play with the filtering of two-dimensional functions that make up pictures, so we have little feel for spatial filtering. But the same kinds of effects can be accomplished in this domain. Here the high frequencies are the fast-changing portions of the picture, like the edges of objects and the speckles of noise. By appropriate filtering we can enhance edges and minimize noise. In addition, it is possible to do lens-like darkroom operations affecting focus and depth-of-field. In a moment I want to show two examples of these spatial operations on pictures.

An area operation replaces the value of a pixel with the sum of that pixel's value and the weighted sum of the values of neighboring pixels. Like any filtering operation, it is really a convolution of an input function, in this case the array of pixel values, and a filter function, which here is a matrix of appropriate weights of neighbors. Some example filter (sometimes called kernel) matrices are the following:

$$
\begin{array}{ccc}
-1 & 0 & -1 \\
-1 & 0 & -1 \\
-1 & 0 & -1 \\
-1 & 0 & -1 \\
-1 & 0 & -1
\end{array}
\qquad
\begin{array}{ccc}
-1 & -1 & -1 \\
-1 & 8 & -1 \\
-1 & -1 & -1
\end{array}
$$

Imagine taking one of these kernel matrices and sliding over the matrix of pixel values. With the kernel matrix centered over a given pixel, multiply each of the kernel values by the pixel value underneath and form the sum. Replace the pixel over which the kernel matrix is centered by the sum of all these values, and slide the kernel matrix to the next pixel. (Actually, you cannot replace the pixel value yet, as it must be used in the calculations of adjacent pixels. Details!)

What do these example filtering operations do to the picture? Well, intuitively we might think of the kernel matrix as a spatial matched filter. Roughly speaking, it tries to emphasize or detect an image feature that looks like itself. The kernel is a little image of what we want to amplify. The example matrix on the left above is a small image of a vertical line. Convolving this matrix with a picture will emphasize vertical lines just the way the neural networks in our cortex use excitatory and inhibitory connections to detect lines and edges. The example kernel on the right is like a "Mexican hat" weighting function, or what is known as a Laplacian filter. Such a filter is very similar to that in our retina where the sensory signals from the rods and cones are prefiltered. Notice that a bright pixel in the center of the array excites (adds to) the output, while brightness in the surrounding annulus inhibits. The more "dot-like" or "edge-like" the area of the picture underneath the kernel, the more the resultant pixel will be emphasized. In human vision this effect is known as the Mach band, after the discovery by Ernst Mach in 1865 of the artificial enhancement of edges which takes place in the retina using similar filtering.

Perhaps you can now imagine how a spatial filter could effect an operation like edge enhancement. If edges are so important to us, why not make them more apparent? Since the edges are the high-frequency regions of the picture, we need to filter the picture using a high-pass filter—just as if we had turned the bass control on our audio amplifier all the way down so as to leave all the high notes intact. In the picture, the low frequencies (bass notes) are the slowly changing areas, like surfaces. Figure 36 shows an example of edge enhancement through computer processing of a digital image.

By the same filtering philosophy we can improve pictures that are corrupted by noise. Noise effects usually look like the snow in television pictures when your reception is not very strong. The flecks of noise represent abrupt changes in intensity, and are characterized by high spatial frequency content, just as the most audible

FIGURE 36
Edge enhancement by spatial filtering

noise in audio is the high-frequency hiss. A low-pass spatial frequency filtering operation can attenuate these noise flecks and get rid of some of the snow in the picture. Unfortunately, it is also true that the edges in the picture are regions of high spatial frequency content, and the same filter that attenuates the noise would harm the edges, smearing them and making them less crisp and apparent. Either some compromise is necessary, or we have to get really tricky and use a nonstationary filter that is able to change its operation in the vicinity of edges.

All this discussion takes us into the realm of picture restoration. Anyone who has ever taken a home photo knows how pictures can get messed up. The exposure is wrong, or we moved the camera, or it is out of focus, or someone spilled coffee on the only copy. Life is full of such untoward circumstances. But even the most expensive, elaborate, and important imaging systems have similar, unavoidable problems. For example, the turbulence in the atmosphere degrades delicate images that are coming or going to space and other secret places. Noise in transmission corrupts other pictures, and imperfections in electronic sensors distort still others.

Nothing is perfect. The question is whether or not this is a Humpty-Dumpty situation. Can all the king's horses and all the king's men inside the powerful algorithms and hardware of our computers put these pictures back together again?

Generally speaking, unless we know exactly what a picture should be, it cannot be perfectly restored. And if we knew what it should be, there would not be a problem in the first place. But we can try, and we can usually improve what we loosely define as the picture quality. I recently saw a massive example of restoration taking place in the Sistine Chapel, where Michelangelo's paintings are being cleaned, or recolored, according to the various arguments. Personally, I think the new colors are fantastic, but exactly what was intended originally is no longer accessible information. The same thing happens in many computer restorations of images.

The second example I want to show of computerized picture processing is the restoration of a picture that is out of focus. This is a demonstration that is especially meaningful to me, and perhaps it will be to you too. When as a child I encountered photographic slides that were out of focus, I always had the feeling that all I had to do would be to change the focus of the slide projector, and it would snap into focus on the screen. Try as I might, and I often did try, it never worked. I learned absolutely that once a slide is out of focus, it is irrevocably, for all eternity, out of focus. Now with picture processing it turns out that maybe this is not quite true after all.

An optical lens acts exactly like the spatial filters we just discussed. When the lens is out of focus, individual pixels in the original image are smeared over an area. This is dramatically evident to me when I get up in the dark and see somewhere in my hotel room an annulus—a doughnut—of red, glowing light. Later I find that the source of this ring of fire is a little red LED or bulb. With my glasses on, it is only a point source of light, but without glasses my out-of-focus eyeballs turn the point into an annulus. In the out-of-focus picture every point is smeared in this identical fashion.

In the audio world similar phenomena occur, except that the filtering is one-dimensional instead of two. When Enrico Caruso recorded some of his legendary performances, he sang into the "morning glory" horns that were the microphones of those days. ("His master's voice," if you remember.) In an acoustic sense the resultant sound waveforms were badly distorted by the resonances of the horn. We do not think of it that way, but the sound was recorded out of focus. Some years ago I was astonished at the ingenuity of Tom Stockham of the University of Utah when he was able, through computer processing, to resurrect these recordings and restore their fidelity by undoing the filtering of those dreaded horn microphones.

In images as in sound, in order to restore a defocused waveform we have to undo the filtering operation. This requires an inverse filter. In the frequency domain this means that the inverse filter has to boost the frequency components that were attenuated by the original filter, and attenuate those that were boosted. That sounds simple enough in concept, but there are two questions. First, does an inverse filter exist, and second, how do we know what the original filter was? Neither answer is totally satisfying.

Figure 37 shows one of those beautiful computer-generated graphs; this one represents the Fourier transform of the filter associated with a particular out-of-focus lens. Here, of course, the transform is two-dimensional. Just as any one-dimensional waveform, like audio, can be represented by the summation of appropriate sine and cosine waves, any two-dimensional picture can be represented by the summation of two-dimensional sine and cosine waves. Imagine dropping a pebble in the middle of a still pool and watching the waves spread circularly outwards. This wave would have a particular frequency determined by physical constants. The concept of the Fourier transform is that any picture can be represented as the sum of such waves of many frequencies. The flat surfaces of the picture would largely determine the low frequency components, while sharp, spatial changes like edges would heavily influence the higher frequency components.

In Figure 37 we see not an individual wave, but a three-dimensional plot of the amplitudes of the sine and cosine components as a function of frequency for the out-of-focus lens. Notice the concentric circles where the Fourier components are zero. If we now had a picture that was to be distorted by this lens, we could calculate the effect by first taking the Fourier transform of the picture and then multiplying this transform at every point in the two-dimensional plane by the transform of our lens. The result would be the transform of the defocused picture. In order to view the blurred picture itself we would have to take the inverse transform of this product.

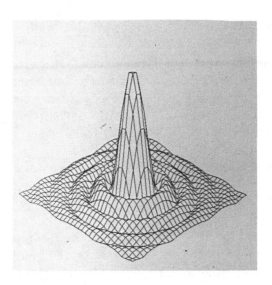

FIGURE 37
Fourier transform of a defocused lens

To restore a picture blurred by the typical transform shown in Figure 37 we would have to undo its effect by multiplying the transform of the blurred picture by the inverse of the transform shown in this figure. Right away we see that the inverse does not actually exist, since the inverse filter would have to have infinite gain along each of the concentric circles where the lens transform is zero. But we do the best we can, and decide that while we cannot actually undo the blur we can approximately correct it by using a large but finite gain along these zero circles. However, even that strategy gives us some pause, because a large gain will amplify any noise of this particular frequency that preexists in the picture. The problem reduces to a tradeoff—more residual blur versus more noise amplification. Which makes a better picture? As always in picture restoration, the final judge is the human viewer. One of the real problems in all of picture processing and coding is the lack of a mathematical criterion that accurately reflects the quality of a picture as perceived by a human viewer. Still, we try, and the blurry picture can indeed be improved by a compromise inverse filter operation.

The other problem in unblurring the picture is that we usually do not have the actual transform of the out-of-focus lens that did the original damage. Thus, it is necessary to try to infer the lens characteristic from the blurred photo itself. Since the transform of the blurred photo is the product of the picture transform and the lens transform, it should still show the concentric circles where the lens transform is zero. That much is a help, but typically the transform is fairly messy and inferring the lens characteristic is far from straightforward. Someone has said that it is like listening to a piano concerto played with a piano that has a bad key and trying to infer from what is heard which key is bad. The clue here is the same as in the blurred photo; the missing frequency components tell us what key is bad. To be honest, the piano case is a lot easier, particularly since the notes are discrete and known *a priori*.

Figure 38 shows a photograph blurred by the out-of-focus lens we just discussed, as well as the result of the computer correction that best attempts to restore the photo. Similar results can be obtained from photos that were ruined by camera movement. Do not expect your local photo store to do these restorations with your

Blurred

Restored

FIGURE 38
Blurred photo and restored version *(courtesy Adriaan Ligtenberg)*

botched pictures, but with electronic cameras coming along it might just be a common fix in the near future.

P I C T U R E   C O D I N G

We have seen that photographic-quality pictures take megabytes of storage in a computer when they are digitized in a straightforward fashion. Now how many bits does it *really* take? I have walked gingerly around the issue for the last chapter and a half. How much information is there in a picture? Unfortunately, the truth is—nobody knows. I can only reiterate my belief that our brain knows a way of coding that is terribly efficient. It has the advantage of a knowledge base of not only millions and millions of pictures that it has seen and stored, but all the experience of how objects may be transformed and combined. Once we have seen an object in a particular view, we can mentally resize it and transform it into a different view. For example, in experiments in which subjects view faces seen in three-quarter view, the recognition accuracy for full-face photographs seen later is virtually the same as when full-face views are used initially. Recall that the essence of information is that which is new or different from all that is previously known, or that which can be derived from previous knowledge. Remember, too, that the brain does not store unnecessary detail in its pictures. Given these considerations, I believe that it is possible for the brain to reduce a picture to only a small number of bits.

Now consider the poor computer trying to encode and store a picture. It has neither a vast library of pictures, nor does it generally even know about the existence of objects within a picture. It has no real world experience of pictures, and it knows nothing about any language or semantic description of the visual world (except in very selected, limited cases). All it has are the pixel values. How well can it compress this information without knowing the meaning of the pixel values with which it must deal? The answer is not very well. Worse, unlike the situations in text and speech, no one has any real idea of how much compression it is theoretically possible to obtain. How many bits are in a picture? No one knows.

Information theory provides a powerful framework for thinking about the fundamental uncertainty—the entropy—of an information source. We talked a great deal in an earlier chapter about the number of bits required to represent English text. We were fortunate in that case that there was a compelling structure, the English language, underlying the formation of the sequence of symbols. Nevertheless, the information theory viewpoint was one of a statistical description of the sequence. Only through the assumption of a statistically generated source were we able to quantify mathematically the informational properties of interest. That was Shannon's great stroke of inspiration, which cut to the heart of the problem and allowed the derivation of fundamental bounds on information and communication.

In the case of English text, the model of a random source seemed to make sense. Remember the uncaring telegraph operator who had no idea of the meaning of the dots and dashes he had to transmit, but who was eventually able to take advantage of the statistical redundancies he saw in the endless stream of meaningless symbols. The tools and results of information theory are based on that probabilistic model of the world. The degree to which the real, physical world fits that model determines the applicability of the concepts of information theory.

There is a branch of information theory that deals with sources like sound and pictures, which by their nature are not discrete like the letters of the alphabet. It is called rate-distortion theory, and it relates the fidelity of reproduction of the source to the number of bits in the representation. Basically, it says that to get a given fidelity you need at least a certain minimum number of bits. In order for the speech or music to sound exactly so good, or for a picture to look exactly so good, you need at least so many bits. This is just the kind of guideline we would love to have, and here it is all worked out in the annals of information theory.

The question is whether or not the model used by information theory of a source of meaningless, but nicely behaved, random variables fits the world of pictorial information. In the case of text we argued that essentially all of the structure of the language would be subsumed in its statistical description as we considered deeper and deeper intercharacter dependencies. For example, when we took account of the previous three characters in determining the probability of the subsequent character, we generated at random the following pseudo-English example:

The generated job providual better trand the displayed code, abovery upondults well the coderst in thestical it do

hock bothe merg. (Instates cons eration. Never any of
puble and to theory. Evential callegand to elast benerated
in with pies as is with the

I argued that as we created higher and higher order random approximations to English we would eventually get more and more
perfect-looking text, in spite of the fact that it was generated strictly
from a statistical description of the language. The entropies calculated from these statistical models agreed well with the uncertainties experienced by humans, using all of their knowledge and
experience, in guessing subsequent characters. You may remember
monkey 100, who typed perfect English without knowing what he
was saying. I might now confess that not all of my colleagues agree
with this extrapolation. I believe it is a deep philosophical question,
but in any event everyone would agree that the higher order approximations tend to look a lot like real English.

There are several other deep questions about the model that
represents text as a random process. One important consideration
is that the random process be stationary, that is, are the statistics of
text invariant with position? Is the statistical description of text
exactly the same for this sentence as it is for a sentence taken from
Chapter 2? For material in, say, *Gone with the Wind*? Probably the
statistics do change somewhat, and this may be the reason that the
Lempel–Ziv algorithm does not perform as well as we believe the
entropy of English should permit, but most people feel that text is
relatively stationary.

I am sure you can see what I am leading toward. What about
a statistical description of pictures? Suppose that I coax a monkey
to paint pictures by randomly filling in pixels from a palette of
shades or colors. Obviously, what he paints looks like some terrible
porridge. But suppose I start training the monkey to pay attention
to statistics similar to the way we generated pseudo-English. If the
monkey sees what previous pixels he has painted, and then chooses
the next pixel from a random selection of shades conditioned on
these previous pixels, what does it look like? Son of porridge, I am
afraid. No one has ever generated a picture from statistics that
looked like a picture. Whatever is the essence of a picture is not
contained in its statistical description.

Recall that a texture is well represented by random pixels with
a certain spatial correlation. This the monkey could do well. No
problem. But the picture suddenly changes from the texture of the
grass to the contour of a shoe. This is where the information is

concentrated, but now the monkey fails completely. The statistics have changed; the process is nonstationary. *Something* is modulating the statistics themselves, and perhaps the essence of the picture lies not in the statistics, but in that modulation of the statistics. There is no information tree in the monkey's picture. (Nor is there a plot in the text he generates.)

Almost all of the techniques of data compression for pictures use only the statistics to determine their action. They try to remove the statistical redundancy in pictures, in effect, by decorrelating the picture elements that form the description that is to be stored by the computer. This is a useful action, as we shall discuss, but the hidden layers that lie beneath this surface action—the branches of the information tree—are inaccessible to today's algorithms. The knowledge-based attack on picture coding that the future might allow could conceivably penetrate this tree and shuck away the megabits of excess data needed today to describe pictures. On the other hand, my information tree might be your weed, and you may be the one who needs to see the picture.

PICTURE COMPRESSION

We have already discussed a number of approaches to data compression in earlier chapters. They work on pictures too. If I have a picture that has been digitized by scanning, sampling, and quantization, then it looks much like any other computer file. Granted, it has these funny statistics, but something like the Lempel–Ziv algorithm does not care so much, as it tries to accommodate itself to whatever it sees. Many computer hackers seem to misunderstand this, and I often see discussions on the various computer nets about whether or not the standard compression algorithms can be used for this or that purpose. (More and more, all the common compression programs use Lempel–Ziv.) Lempel–Ziv works by building up its own dictionary of commonly used data sequences in the file itself. It learns French, programs, pictures, anything. Of course, it greatly helps if the source is statistically stationary so that its dictionary is still useful by the time it gets laboriously built.

So Lempel–Ziv compression programs can be run on pictures, as well as on anything else, for that matter. The program does not always do much in the way of compression as, for example, on executable code or on files that have already been compressed, but it never hurts, since the implementations of the algorithm always ensure that the file is not increased in size by its action. When it is used on pictures, it generally helps quite a lot. It is not that the algorithm learns little pieces of picture for its dictionary entries, rather that it learns strings of repetitive shades or colors, or little runs of texture or patterns that become generally useful. In almost any picture there are many long runs of a constant pixel value— large black or white areas or the solid color areas in surfaces.

One particularly nice feature of the Lempel–Ziv compression of pictures is that when it operates on a file of pixel values after decompression it returns the exact same pixel values, bit for bit. This is what we call information lossless. Nothing is approximated or thrown away—actions that would irrevocably eliminate information from the representation of the picture. However, most of the versions of the schemes that we will discuss now do discard information. The trick is to get rid of information that does not show. Then no one would care whether or not it was missing. Unfortunately, in spite of a good deal of research on psychovisual perception, there is no simple mathematical measure of visual "goodness" in a picture. The "fidelity" measure that is required for rate-distortion optimization does not really exist.

Mathematicians and engineers especially like to use mean-squared error criteria. This is simply the average of the error squared over, say, the whole picture. Frankly, it is about the only error criterion that is mathematically workable. Lucky for us, it is also fairly useful. In pictures, however, any error measurement that is averaged with equal weight throughout the entire area of the picture is doomed to failure. Whether we like it or not, *where* the error is in the picture matters a great deal. Because our vision system tends to accentuate edges, these contours tend to mask errors. On the other hand, errors scattered throughout a flat area of the picture will often be seen as false contours and suddenly be very visible. It is the same problem that we mentioned before; the nonstationary nature of the pictorial medium.

Because there is no optimum solution known from information theory, and because there is no mathematical criterion for evaluating goodness, anyone is perfectly able to invent their own ad hoc approach to picture compression. Feel free to try your own hand at some clever way to remove bits from a picture without hurting it. You may hit on something. Picture compression is quite unlike text compression, where there is some general agreement on optimum approaches and limitations.

My own appreciation of the quality of pictures is deficient. People who work in picture compression develop a keen perception of quality. They know when a reconstituted picture looks just like the original, and when it does not. They know where to look in the picture to see fine grain differences. To me, they all look good. I just do not know better. However, I have occasionally seen the researchers themselves taken aback when they bring in a network television technician to look at their latest video compression scheme. Their pride vanishes quickly enough when the network person shakes his head in disgust at the obvious impersonation of quality. All I know for sure is that I do not want anyone to compress any of my own X rays using an information-lossy algorithm. As much as the engineers might insist that the quality is superb, I have this fear that what they might have thrown away might have been what the radiologist needed for the proper diagnosis. And instead they are going to do something irrevocable and terrible.

DIFFERENTIAL PULSE CODE MODULATION
· · · · · · · · · · · · · · · · · ·

Many approaches to picture compression have been described in the literature of the last 25 years. Since I have no reason even to pretend to be comprehensive, I am only going to describe two popular methods. The first is differential pulse code modulation, or since that is a mouthful, DPCM. This is a family of techniques very similar to what I described in an earlier chapter when we discussed speech compression. The idea is to use earlier pixel values to try to make a prediction about the current pixel. Again, we look to remove the predictable, or expected, component of the pixel value and leave only the residual random, or surprise, portion. The residual (differential) value will be smaller than the actual pixel value, so we save bits by quantizing and sending only the differentials instead of the actual values. The trick is then to have an identical predictor at the receiver which takes a crack at guessing the pixels there, and then corrects its guesses with the incoming differential values.

A few information theory calculations of entropy can tell us how much we might save by using DPCM. As an example, some entropy calculations were made on a picture affectionately called "Stripes" by two of my associates (Arun Netravali and Barry Haskell). "Stripes" is a head and shoulders view of a woman standing in front of a curtain whose deep vertical folds cause bands of alternating light and darkness to form the background. It is one of a few dozen pictures that appear again and again in the picture coding literature, as through the years everyone tries their hand at bettering the results of their predecessors on the same material. The origins of these pictures are getting lost, but they are as famous as the great works of art among a small group of researchers spread throughout the world. I have this dream that years from now the researchers will perfect their coding techniques, and these pictures will be reduced by their algorithms to a scant few bits. Then they will discover that their algorithms only work on these particular pictures, and no others!

Anyway, "Stripes" in its original format is encoded into 8 bits per pixel. Looking at the probability distribution of the luminance of a pixel in this picture, we see that it is roughly uniform, so that light values, gray values, and dark values are about equally probable. When we calculate the entropy of this value, based on no other information, we find it is 7.4 bits per pixel. (Remember that the entropy is the average value of the logarithm of the probability.) In other words the "randomness" of a pixel itself is worth 7.4 bits, which is not much less than the 8 bits we devote to it in brute force fashion. This is unlike text, where spaces and a few letters like *e* dominate. In an earlier chapter we found that the entropy of individual characters in the text of that chapter itself was about 4.5 bits. This imperfect randomness in the characters themselves was what the Huffman code used to save about 45 percent in the size of the text file. But the same approach would not work well for "Stripes." There is no pixel shade as popular as the *e* in text.

In "Stripes," like almost every other picture, there is a strong dependence of a given pixel value upon its neighbors. The freedom, or randomness, of a pixel is strongly constrained by the values of the nearby pixels in every direction. Thus the surprise—the information—in a pixel is much diminished by its context. Unlike text, the context of a pixel in a picture is two-dimensional, so that a pixel is influenced by the pixels above itself, below itself, and to its right, in addition to the immediately preceding pixels. In the normal scanning process, which orders the pixels from left to right across successive lines, this means that the most influential pixels may be thousands of bit positions away. In DPCM this is not a particular problem as long as the influencing pixels are available (some of them may not be available at the time we need them), but in the Lempel–Ziv algorithm, for example, its usual implementation is only one-dimensional, and the evolving patterns in its dictionary do not take advantage of all the two-dimensional dependencies. (Though the algorithm could build little two-dimensional patterns if it was so constituted.)

Consider a particular pixel, designated Y, in "Stripes," together with its neighbors W, X, and Z.

$$W$$
$$X\ Y\ Z$$

The entropy of Y alone is 7.4 bits. After we know X, the conditional entropy is only 5.8 bits. Its conditional entropy given only W, the pixel above, is 3.6 bits, and its conditional entropy given both X and W is 3.1 bits. In "Stripes" we can see the strong vertical influence of the stripes in the curtain. In another picture featuring horizontal stripes the influences might be reversed. This means that on average it only takes 3.1 bits to specify a pixel once we know the immediate neighbors above and to its left. We can see that a simple DPCM system using only a few other pixels for its prediction can eliminate more than half the bits in a picture.

The critical ingredients of a DPCM system are a predictor and a quantizer, which code the residual error after prediction. Quite a number of inventions and variations of these elements have appeared in the literature. It is possible, for example, to make a predictor like that used in adaptive differential pulse code modulation of speech, which uses a prediction formed by a linear sum of previous samples weighted by adaptively varying coefficients for minimum average mean squared error. That is pretty fancy, and works well in speech, but for pictures it seems that most of the prediction is determined simply by the few pixels we just discussed.

You might recall the weather prediction we used as an example in an earlier chapter. If it rained yesterday, predict it will rain today. Similarly, for a picture, if it was black in the last pixel, say black for the next. Or perhaps better, use the average of the pixel to the left and the pixel above.

Figure 39 shows an example of DPCM applied to a television frame with 4-bit quantization of the prediction error. In the middle side of the figure the predictor is one-dimensional, that is, it only uses the pixels to the left of the predicted pixel. In the lower portion of the figure the predictor is two-dimensional, and uses pixels above as well as pixels to the left. What is shown in the figure is the prediction error, with positive errors white, negative errors black, and zero error a shade of gray halfway in between. If the prediction were perfect, the figures would show a blank gray. However, they do not, and you can see the form of the errors incurred by each type of prediction. In both cases the error is strongest along the contours; the very places where the information is most concentrated. The two-dimensional predictor does a better job on the vertical edges, but trades off some increased error on the horizontal edges. On any given picture, one predictor might be better than another, but DPCM is a generally useful way of getting rid of about half the bits in a picture without noticeable degradation.

Horizontal prediction error

Original picture

Two-dimensional prediction error

FIGURE 39
Prediction error in two DPCM coders.

T E L E V I S I O N   C O D I N G

• • • • • • • • • • • • • • • • • • • •

DPCM is also used for television to reduce the bit rate required for transmission. Most of the considerations are exactly the same as for still pictures, but there is an important additional element, and that is the time dependency of the picture. Obviously, a pixel in a television picture is dependent not only upon its immediate geographic neighbors, but also upon these same pixels in the previous frame. If the picture being transmitted is not moving, then the pixels are exactly the same as they were a thirtieth of a second before when the previous frame was scanned out on the television screen.

It makes a great deal of difference whether the material being transmitted on television is, say, a football game or an announcer reading the news, but on average only about 9 percent of the pixels in a picture change from one frame to the next. An early idea in television compression was to transmit only the changed pixels, a concept that became known as conditional frame replenishment. Later, more sophisticated algorithms used combinations of predictors based on both the previous frame and the neighboring pixels of the current frame. Then engineers recognized that in a moving picture the pixel being predicted was not necessarily more closely related to the *same* pixel in the previous frame, but to a different pixel translated by an amount and direction dependent upon the motion in that part of the picture. Coders were designed to find the average motion of pixels in the vicinity of the pixel being predicted, and to use this calculated motion to find the pixel (or more likely, an interpolated value between pixels) most likely to give an accurate prediction from the previous frame. These systems are called motion compensation coders.

Network-quality television—the kind you see on your home set—requires approximately 100 million bits per second when it is digitized using ordinary pulse code modulation. Needless to say, this is a horrendous rate to create pictures for people who are possibly capable of absorbing only 50 bits per second. When network quality signals are transmitted digitally on telephone facilities, usually a moderate amount of coding is used to reduce the rate to 45 million bits per second. At this rate the quality of the picture is still excellent, and unless you are trained in the art, you could not tell the difference between this picture and the original, uncoded television picture. This amount of digital capacity is very costly. It is, as I said before, the equivalent of one thousand voice channels. Nevertheless, it is the smallest capacity at this time which still permits network quality reconstruction of the picture.

Not every television picture has to be network quality. People dealing in day-to-day business operations seldom send each other television of football games. Instead, the most frequent material is simply the head of a person talking. For this talking head, we hardly need the sharp fidelity of broadcast television. Moreover, motion compensation techniques can be quite effective since much of the picture is stationary, and the moving portions are usually lateral translations, which are the only kind of translations that motion compensation systems can presently handle. It is worth a lot of money to compress the bit rate of those talking heads. Lucky that it is worth so much, because this is what it usually costs.

With motion compensation, the talking heads characteristic of video conferencing can be transmitted nicely at 384,000 bits per second, which is less than 1 percent of the uncompressed bit rate. The picture is fairly good until the head gets agitated and moves suddenly. Then the picture blurs for a second. One of the difficulties with motion compensation is that a variable number of bits is required for each frame, depending on the number of pixels requiring updating. Buffering bits at the very high rates needed for television is expensive, so the general practice is to buffer only a little, and let the buffer overflow occasionally. In situations requiring a higher than average number of bits over some significant period, the picture will deteriorate for lack of update information.

Getting conference-quality video at 64,000 bits per second is especially important, as that is the rate devoted to voice telephone calls. Then video would fit into the same channels as speech. While the quality of the present video coders is poor at this impoverished bit rate, there seems reasonable hope for the near future using the next coding method we will discuss, which is called transform coding. Before launching into a description of transform coding, I cannot help but give one last thought on that talking head. I have seen fascinating research devoted to creating the mouth movements and facial expressions on a still picture of a person's head so as to simulate speaking. The Disney people do this with great effect in their famous theme parks. If they can make Abraham Lincoln talk convincingly, we should be able to animate pictures of our friends similarly. Relatively speaking, that should take very little information. How would you like to see someone that you are talking to by re-created simulation? I am not so sure, myself.

TRANSFORM CODING
* *

Transform coding is the most efficient picture coding now being used. It has been known for quite a long time, but only recently has the processing power become available to implement the necessary algorithms. Now international standards bodies are at work determining standards for transform coding, and it is likely that it will be used in many picture storage and transmission systems in the near future. The idea is simple enough; instead of sending (or storing) the pixel values themselves, send the values of the coefficients of a transform of the picture, such as the Fourier transform. Why would we want to do that? That takes some explaining; let me try.

The Fourier transform is one example of a transform that preserves many properties of the original function. In effect, the transform and the original function contain equivalent information. We could as well send the transform coefficients and let the receiver take the inverse transform to reconstruct the picture. Instead of sending pixel values, which are intuitively pleasing because we can see them, we could send the coefficients of the transform. They are not so obvious, because they are the values of the two-dimensional waves which, when added together, form the picture.

So we lose nothing by sending the transform instead of the picture—the issue is one of approximation. When we approximate a picture by throwing away pixels, it is like tearing away little pieces of the picture. Rip off that corner, and tear a hole there. That kind of thing. But when we throw away coefficients of the transform, we remove something holistic from the picture, some wave that flows across the entire picture. Perhaps it will not be so noticeable. The question is how many transform coefficients of what accuracy are required to specify a picture to a given fidelity, versus the number and accuracy required for pixels? Obviously, the answers to these questions depend on what transform we use. The Fourier transform is well known and thoroughly studied for fast implementation, but so are many others. What properties in a transform would result in approximating the picture with a small number of coefficients?

One property that we would like in a transform is that when it is applied to our picture the resulting coefficients are only weakly correlated, or preferably uncorrelated. As we have seen, the pixel values in the original picture are highly correlated, and therefore quite redundant. We have to work fairly hard to remove the correlation with predictive coding like DPCM in order to squeeze out the redundancy indicated by these strong correlations. Hopefully, the coefficients of the transform would not be so correlated, and would therefore carry more information in themselves. Ideally, we would like the coefficients of the transform of the picture to be uncorrelated, so that we might feel that no information about a coefficient was being indicated by another coefficient. (Actually we would like them to be statistically independent, which is quite a stronger condition, and really too much to hope for.)

In addition to significant coefficients being uncorrelated, we would like to have as few of them to transmit as possible. Preferably, there should be fewer significant coefficients than there are pixels. If we arranged the coefficients in descending order of magnitude, we would like a small number of large magnitude coefficients followed by a large number of very small magnitude coefficients. After we had transmitted the large coefficients we would feel that we did not have to send the small coefficients at all. No one would miss them. There is a theorem in mathematics that the total energy in a function, which is measured by the sum of the squares of its coefficients, is the same in the function itself and in its unitary transform. Therefore, it is not possible to eliminate all the large coefficients in any expansion. What we would like is to concentrate the energy in the initial coefficients of the expansion. In other words, we want a transform that accomplishes energy compaction on the given picture.

It is possible to derive an ideal transform for a given picture which accomplishes both guidelines of uncorrelated coefficients and energy compaction. The transform is known as the Karhunen-Loeve transform. It is famous among theoreticians and unknown among practitioners, since no one really uses it. The reasons that it is not used are that it is relatively complicated, and that the basis functions for the transform must be calculated from the statistics of the particular picture to be transformed. Unlike something like a Fourier transform, where the basis functions are simple sine and cosine waves regardless of what the picture is, the Karhunen-Loeve basis functions vary according to the picture. How else, though, could we achieve uncorrelated coefficients and optimum energy compaction than by tailoring the expansion individually to the picture?

Fortunately, there are simple, fixed transforms that are easily implemented and that usually perform almost as well as the Karhunen-Loeve transform. The most popular transform is called the discrete cosine transform. This transform is being standardized and will probably find wide use wherever pictures are stored or transmitted. By happenstance, the basis functions for the discrete cosine transform often look a little like the Karhunen-Loeve functions. These basis functions are simple two-dimensional cosine waves, except that they are not smooth functions, but staircase approximations made entirely of horizontal lines. Imagine walking up and down steps on cosine waves and you have it.

Not only does the discrete cosine transform do well in compacting pictures, but it can be implemented using a fast, efficient algorithm similar to the Fast Fourier Transform. The efficiency of the algorithm is important because, like the area processes we discussed in an earlier section, the calculation for each pixel required to do the discrete cosine transform involves all other pixels. Since this is just too much, the picture is broken up into smaller blocks—subpictures, if you will. Typically a block might be 8×8 pixels in size. The coefficients of the discrete cosine transform are calculated for each block, so that eventually the picture is reformed out of the 8×8 tiles. This limits the computation, and results experimentally in very little loss in compression.

When the "Stripes" picture is coded into discrete cosine transform coefficients using 8×8 pixel blocks, the energy is roughly compacted into 20 to 30 terms, as opposed to the original 64 pixels. The mean square error after 10 terms is .1, after 30 terms it is .01, and after 50 terms it is .001. Of course, you would have to look at the picture to judge how many terms you wanted to send for the accuracy that appealed to you.

In Figure 40 is an original picture that is coded into 8×8 pixel discrete cosine transform blocks. This particular picture is not one of the famous test photos, but actually one of my daughter, Karen. I hope a small amount of nepotism will be forgiven at this late stage in this book. On the right side of the figure you see the blocks of the transform with the 64 pixels in each block corresponding in shade to the value of the transform. You can see that many of the coefficients are small. To emphasize the savings there is a histogram of sample values at the bottom of both the picture and its transform. On the right the histogram is of pixel values, while on the left it is of transform coefficients. The spread in values of the pixels requires about 8 bits to fairly represent, whereas the small spread in coefficient values requires fewer than 4. I hope that by studying this

FIGURE 40
Picture and its discrete cosine transform

figure you can appreciate the power of the discrete cosine transform for picture compression. It is a rather beautiful example of the application of mathematics, and one that is likely to become quite popular.

D O C U M E N T   C O D I N G

After so much talk about pictures of people and natural scenes and such, I am embarrassed to admit that the vast majority of all the important pictures in the information age are pictures of documents. Mostly they are just pictures of text. These are raster-scanned pictures, pixel-by-pixel, as opposed to the byte-by-byte character codes that we talked about in the earlier chapters. An example document is shown in Figure 41, which is from a French technical paper about something or other. Whatever it is, is beside the point, since this is a picture as famous in its own right as "Stripes" is for photographic images. It is number 5 of eight CCITT (an international standards body for telecommunications) standard documents used to evaluate facsimile transmission. It is typical of the kind of document we see again and again in our occupations. There are some text, some mathematical symbols, and some graphics. Other CCITT standard documents include handwritten portions, business forms, hand-drawn diagrams, and correspondence on letterhead stationery.

Pages like CCITT number 5 are the things I want to produce instantly and electronically at my desk. I cannot tell you the number of times in writing this book that I have discovered some paper with an interesting title through some abstract service, and after all the trouble of obtaining a copy of the paper I see something like Figure 41 and I know immediately that it is not at all what I want. Somehow there is no substitute for actually seeing a paper to know if it will be useful. Our present library systems allow abstracts and titles to be disseminated through ASCII text transmission, but they cannot deliver the paper itself. That is what document retrieval systems should do for us.

As some measure of the demand for documents, in my company the technical document service has 700,000 documents in its cur-

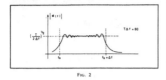
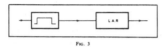
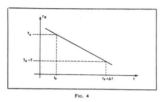
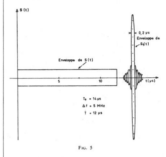

FIGURE 41
CCITT Facsimile Test Document Number 5

rent collection, and adds 14,000 more each year. They get 170,000 requests each year, and copy something like 3,500,000 pages. The majority of these documents do not exist as text files, but only in paper form. In theory, it would be possible to scan the documents so as to recognize automatically the characters for input as ASCII to a computer file, but that would still leave the graphical portions, signatures, unusual symbols, and other uncodable artifacts. It is so much more convenient to leave the material in photographic format and scan the page as if it were a picture. In effect, we say that we do not know what they represent, but here are the pixels. The tradeoff in this approach is that it takes a great many more bits to represent a picture than to encode recognizable characters as text. A great many.

The near future will certainly give us document retrieval systems based upon optical disk storage, high bandwidth communications, and with both soft- and hard-copy output. We need to be able to browse through pages on our CRT screens at full resolution, 8½-by-11 inch displays at less than 1 second per page. That is a lot of bits to deliver, format, and display in a such a short time, but that is what we are used to with paper, and we would not settle for less. I also imagine an electronic file cabinet on my desk. When I want to file a piece of paper, I shove it into a little box on my desk which eats paper. The paper goes in and nothing comes out. The paper is turned into photographic-type pixels and encoded into data files somewhere, probably on optical disk. Of course, I will forget the filing subject, but that is a matter for another book entirely!

Prototype document retrieval systems exist today at a number of locations. While they might not yet be widespread, a more mundane technology with some of the same utility is spreading like the plague, and that is facsimile. Facsimile has been around for decades, and for some reason never became popular. I always wondered why. The thought makes me remember a conference in Florida some years ago when I was invited to go on a short yacht trip with the commodore of the local yacht club. After a pleasant ride, this stranger invited me to his home, saying he had something to show to me. I could not imagine what, but he took me into his basement to show me a mechanical Rube Goldberg machine that had no discernible purpose. Proudly he told me tht this was the first facsimile machine; that he had invented this technology 30 years or so earlier, but could not get anyone interested in it. As far as I was concerned, what he had could have been a refrigerator. I humored him. When I got back to my laboratories, I looked up some history of facsimile to see who had actually invented it. You know what? He did.

Today, the majority of telecommunications traffic, including voice, between Japan and the United States is facsimile (Fax). In Japan it is a way of life. It is reported that some taxicabs in Tokyo are now equipped with Fax machines. That is not quite true here yet, but I knew Fax was arriving when one of my associates started to complain that he was getting junk mail on his Fax machine. (Can you imagine being in a taxi and a message arrives on the Fax addressed to "occupant"?) Two factors have caused this surge in the popularity of facsimile. First, after years of arguments, international standards were finally achieved, and it became possible for the first time to intermix equipment from different manufacturers. Then the Japanese made it cheap. The new telecommunications network, ISDN (Integrated Services Digital Network), will allow much higher data speeds without the need for modems, and will permit high-quality Fax in about 4 seconds a page, either from a separate Fax unit or from a combination Fax/telephone. While you talk, you can send the papers you are discussing.

Pages like CCITT number 5 differ from photographic material in that they are composed of only black and white areas without the intervening gray scale. This makes the bits per pixel simply equal to 1—"0" for white and "1" for black. That part is easy, but in order to reproduce the letters of text without jagged edges a high resolution is necessary, so there must be many pixels. In the scanning and encoding of documents, resolution is measured in dots (or lines) per inch. To see how many dots per inch are required in a normal 8½-by-11-inch page with text, such as our CCITT number 5, look at the magnified characters shown in Figure 42 as encoded at various dot-per-inch resolutions.

We could summarize the effect of resolution on legibility of characters in the following table.

As another guide, the resolution of a laser printer is at present 300 dots per inch, Xerox copies are 400 dpi, and a glossy printed page is an incredible 1,200. CCITT number 5 is encoded according to one of the standards for Fax at 200 dots per inch. It has exactly $1,728 \times 2,376$ pixels, which is a little more than 4 million bits.

It is clear that storing and transmitting pictures of text is very expensive in bits. For every little character, we have to send the exact pattern of pixels, ever so precisely, in order to draw the character as if it were a little picture. How much easier it is just to say to the printer or display "Put a *t* in the next character position." Saying that costs us only 8 bits in ASCII. Making a whole page this

RESOLUTION OF PRINTED CHARACTERS

DOTS/IN	QUALITY	PIXELS FOR 8½ × 11
50	TV, not legible	425 × 550
100	just legible	850 × 1100
200	lacks crispness	1700 × 4400
400	printed page	3400 × 4400

way, as we do when we use a word processor to generate text, takes only about 15,000 bits, as compared with about 15 million bits for high-resolution pictorial presentation. For obvious reasons, the way ASCII text is stored by a word processor is called semantic mode. That means that we know the meanings of the patterns, and need only store their names.

In between the stark alternatives of ASCII text and facsimile is a growing emphasis on what is called page description languages, like PostScript. A page description language combines the compact representation of text with some of the freedom of the pixel mode for graphics and inserted pictures. Not only can we say to put a t at a given place with a given font, but we can draw lines and geometric figures, and color in certain pixels to produce limited pictorial material. Such a language is used everywhere now to drive laser printers. I think of the instructions from PostScript being

FIGURE 42
Resolution of printed characters

translated to commands to a little person inside the box who paints the pixels with his laser rays the same way we disgracefully create "paint-by-the-numbers" masterpieces.

Page description languages are in their own way rather like blue collar workers. I think of them as down in the trenches where the actions are being taken. At a higher management level is what is thought of as a document architecture. This is the structure of the document, as for example the standard format that might be used to produce a memorandum for file in a particular company or organization. In this way we can think of a document as structured information, and discuss its structure without mentioning its content, just as a secretary's style book can describe the proper forms without saying what might be their actual wording. Instead of storing documents in brute force detail, we might imagine storing a set of instructions describing how to make the document, starting with its logical structure, continuing to its physical layout, and ending with the actual content. Since the logical structure—the form—is often predetermined by its type (e.g., memorandum for file), this part of the instructions does not have to be repeated on each occasion.

Across this range of representation methodologies there is a factor of a thousand spread in bit storage requirements. To illustrate what this factor can mean, the table below summarizes the bit storage requirements for various modes of representation together with the time that it takes to transmit the document at several common transmission rates. Recall that speeds of 1,200 bits per second are common in data transmission using modems over ordinary voice telephone lines, while 64,000 bits per second is more characteristic of local area networks, and will be the standard channel speed in the future ISDN telephone networks.

DOCUMENT COMPRESSION
• •

You can see from that last table how important it is to compress raster-scanned documents for storage and transmission. The second line in the table, "coded Fax," is a preview of what we will be able to do to reduce the bit rate requirements for storage of documents

BITS VERSUS MODE FOR STORAGE OF A PRINTED PAGE

MODE	BITS/PAGE	TIME 1,200 BITS/SEC	TIME 64,000 BITS/SEC
raster scan (like TV)	15 million	3½ hr.	4 min.
coded Fax	500,000	7 min.	8 sec.
PostScript	50,000	42 sec.	.8 sec.
Word Processor	15,000	12 sec.	.2 sec.

like CCITT number 5. Notice that the coding will make all the difference in feasibility of document distribution. Who wants to wait around over three hours for delivery of a high-quality page? You might as well use the overnight mail delivery.

Unlike compression in other media, the coding of documents in facsimile is standardized in detail. CCITT has standardized efficient compression algorithms in their imaginatively entitled Group 3 and Group 4 facsimile standards. In these standards, there are two approaches to encoding documents. The simpler and less efficient is a one-dimensional code based on Huffman encoding of strings of zeros and ones, whereas the more advanced code incorporates a two-dimensional enhancement of some of the same ideas. Before I describe the concepts in these algorithms, let me give some indication of how much compression might be possible in a page like CCITT number 5. By now you should know that we can bound the performance of compression algorithms that use only limited information in their compression by making some simple calculations of entropy based upon the same limitations.

In a printed page of text, if black and white were equally likely and the encoding of each pixel were done without knowledge of surrounding pixels, then obviously it would take one bit per pixel. However, the entropy of a pixel in a typical printed page, when given the preceding pixel, is only about .25 bits. Thus, there is a factor of four compression made possible just by looking at whether the previous pixel was black or white. Again, like the weather prediction example, the pixels are highly correlated with their predecessors. White tends to stay white; black tends to stay black.

The strong correlation between pixels holds in the vertical direction as much as in the horizontal. Look at the type on this page and see for yourself the vertical and horizontal strings of black and of white. To see how much the vertical pixels add to the compression possibilities, we can calculate the entropy of a pixel, given both horizontal and vertical predecessors. In the case where we know the two pixels to the left and the five pixels centered above the pixel to be coded, the entropy is about .15 bits. This tells us that we could compress a printed page by about 7 times using a predictive code whose prediction was based upon a handful of surrounding pixels.

As good as a factor of seven might seem, the number of bits to start with is so huge that we need stronger algorithms. The entropy calculations tell us that we cannot get better compression through anything that we do with nearest neighbors. We much reach out much further. A simple way of effectively doing this is through an old technique called run length encoding. Look across any horizontal scan line that you might imagine drawing on this printed page. What you see is that as you proceed across the scan line there will be runs of zeros for white areas and runs of ones as we cross the inked black segments. The two types of runs alternate—a white run, then a black run, and so on. Also, it is obvious that the white runs are much longer on average. Sometimes the white run is the entire length of the line, as when we are between the lines of characters or at the top or bottom margins. In CCITT number 5 the average length of the white runs is 66 bits, while for black runs it is 7.

In run length encoding, we simply give the length of the successive runs across each scan line. There is no need to indicate whether the run is white or black since they alternate. For example, we might encode a line as something like the following: 25, 3, 12, 8, 17, etc. So for the moment stop thinking about the origin of these numbers and remember our introductory arguments about information theory. If we assume that the successive runs are statistically independent, which seems approximately true, then the entropy of a number in this sequence is simply calculated from the probability distribution that we observe. When we do this, we find that the entropy of the numbers representing the white runs is about 5.3 bits, and the corresponding entropy for the black runs is about 3.3 bits. We know, too, that the optimum way to encode these numbers would be to set up a Huffman code that optimally assigned short bit sequences to the most probable run lengths and longer bit sequences to the less probable run lengths. On the average, the Huffman coding would assign just a little more than the value of the entropy for each of the two colors of runs. The compression that we would expect in doing this can be calculated to be about 8.5.

Remember, however, that we are talking about a one-dimensional code, which takes no advantage of vertical correlations.

The CCITT compression algorithm defined for Group 3 facsimile uses a slightly modified Huffman code. It is usually referred to as an "MH" code for "modified Huffman," though most people have forgotten (or never knew) what the initials stand for. The modification involves coding long runs as two separate code words, one for the number of 64-pixel blocks in the run, and the other for the remainder. The first word is called the makeup codeword, and the second, the terminating codeword. If a run is less than 64 bits, then it is only necessary to send the terminating codeword, which is the standard Huffman code for that length run. For example, a run of 22 bits would get the code word 0000011 for a white run or the code word 00000110111 for black. Since white and black runs have different statistics, they receive different sets of code words.

If a run is more than 63 bits, it is necessary first to transmit a makeup code word giving the number of 64-bit units in the run. For example, a white run of 134 bits would get the makeup word for two 64-bit units, which is 10010, followed by the terminating code word for the leftover 6 bits, which is 1110. A sample of some of the standard code words is given below. You can see from the lengths of the various code words the relative probabilities of the runs. When this standard MH code is used to compress our example, CCITT number 5, the resulting compression ratio is 7.93. In order to get better compression ratios with run length coding methods, it is necessary to incorporate some vertical information into the scheme. Often it happens that runs of black or white on one scan line coincide or closely coincide with like runs on the following line. For example, all the short runs in the vertical segments of these characters are vertically aligned. A simple way of using this alignment is to code the starting positions of runs with respect to the starting positions of runs on the preceding line. This is the concept used in a more advanced compression algorithm called the modified READ (Relative Element Address Designate) which is standardized by the CCITT as an option in Group 3 Fax and is the standard approach for Group 4 Fax.

The modified READ code encodes the starts of runs in a given scan line as the difference in pixels with respect to the run on the previous line if this difference is 3 pixels or less. Otherwise, it considers that the runs are not sufficiently aligned to be helpful, and

TERMINATING CODEWORDS

RUN LENGTH	WHITE RUNS	BLACK RUNS
0	00110101	0000110111
1	000111	010
2	0111	11
3	1000	10
4	1011	011
5	1100	0011
6	1110	0010
7	1111	00011
8	10011	000101
9	10100	000100
62	00110011	000001100110
63	00110100	000001100111
MAKEUP CODEWORDS		
64	11011	0000001111
128	10010	000011001000
192	010111	000011001001
1,728	010011011	0000001100101

it bases its run position encoding on horizontal information alone. Actually, there are three different encoding modes that it chooses among as it proceeds along. Moreover, there are some detailed considerations having to do with synchronization of lines and the prevention of propagating ill effects having to do with errors. But these necessary embellishments might also constitute impediments in the way of getting across the main idea of the two-dimensional coding philosophy. Surely anyone actually designing such a code would not be looking here for these details.

When the modified READ code is applied to our example document, CCITT number 5, the compression ratio is 13.2, or almost a factor of two improvement over the one-dimension Huffman code. Still greater compressions can be obtained, but a different philosophy entirely must be used. Generally, more efficient schemes would tend toward gathering a form of semantic knowledge of the material, so as to move closer to the semantic (ASCII) mode of representation. One successful approach, called pattern matching, segregates isolated patterns of black on the document, such as the individual letters of text. For each pattern that it finds, it checks to see if it is in a dictionary of previously encountered patterns. If so, it merely tells the receiver to place pattern number such-and-such at the current position. We may know that this pattern is a *t* in the current font, but the encoder does not know that—only that the pattern is one which has been seen before. If the current pattern is not in the dictionary, the encoder adds it to the dictionary, and sends the pattern to the receiver pixel-by-pixel. Throughout the unfolding encoding and transmission, the receiver maintains an identical dictionary for its own use. When CCITT number 5 is encoded with symbol matching, the compression is 29.2. Again, a factor of two in time or space has been achieved by the use of implicit information in the document itself. However, in spite of the impressive gains, symbol matching is not standardized, and therefore is not currently used.

C O N C L U S I O N

The final frontier in this subject is image understanding by computers. Perhaps image understanding is too optimistic a term; rather, we should say image recognition. Even though the field is in its relative infancy, there are many solved problems that provide useful applications. For example, the recognition of printed characters, even with unknown fonts, is fairly commonplace today. In robotics, and in factory automation tasks such as inspection, computer vision is used to locate predetermined assembly parts and to find defects of various classes. In medicine there are vision systems that do blood cell counting and preliminary analysis of chest X rays. In remote sensing we can do environmental monitoring and agricultural analysis.

The common characteristic of these applications for machine recognition is a simple, predetermined model of the objects and their relationships. Virtually all such systems are special purpose and rely on what is called domain-specific constraints. As soon as we slip out of that model, we feel the draft of the knowledge cliff and we hear the pounding surf below. We can recognize printed characters, but handwritten characters are another matter, and recognition of fluent handwriting with connected characters is all but impossible. The post office has machines that can read addresses, but no machine that can find where the address is located on the envelope! We have a long way to go in teaching computers to use, understand, and appreciate pictures the way we do.

REFLECTIONS — THE GENIUSES AMONG US

Many of the most brilliant people I have known have been attracted to the field of information. Because of the omission of mathematics, I have undoubtedly given a severely understated view of the intellectual sophistication and difficulty of the field. Nevertheless, I would like to close this book with a reassuring essay on genius. No one should be discouraged from approaching a field because of the imagined intimidation of overwhelming expertise. The genius that most people draw in their minds simply does not exist. Any serious reader of a book like this should be able to make his or her mark on the technology and thought of the information age.

Whatever became of all those child geniuses we heard about when we were young? Remember the stories about the kids who could multiply 12-digit numbers in their heads instantly? Or the whizzes who graduated from high school at age 12? The tabloids were filled with such legends, and it seems these young geniuses were often headed into computers or electrical engineering. So where are they now?

Fortunately, when I grew up I found that the world was not cluttered with these dangerous purveyors of brilliance. Meeting the famous engineers I had read about in graduate school, I slowly discovered to my relief that, figuratively speaking, they donned their pants just like all the rest of us—that is, using the conventional head-first technique. There was only one among my associates who retained his lofty genius status. I knew he was a genius because he rode a unicycle and was able to juggle six tennis balls simultaneously—Q.E.D. One day he sidled up to me and confessed in a whisper that the place scared him because there were so many smart people around. Wildly I looked about me. I didn't see any smart people. There were just my ordinary friends and enemies. It was a moment of great insight. I forget what it meant.

In graduate school I took a course in something I have since forgotten about. The grade was to be determined based solely on a lecture delivered by each student on some paper in the current literature in whatever field it was. One woman in the class delivered a particularly esoteric paper for her assigned lecture. With brilliance and flair she filled the board with equations of deep significance. Finishing breathlessly, she stood back from the panorama on the blackboard and asked if there were any questions. She looked like Picasso in front of *Guernica.* Overcome with a deep sense of inadequacy, I was paralyzed with dumbness. As she headed back to her seat, one person in the class hesitatingly and timidly asked her about the first equation on the board, which in fact was merely a basic assumption. The question revealed a vast ignorance in the questioner. In the ensuing embarrassed silence we stared at our classmate, now vulnerable and alone in his intellectual birthday suit. (I edged my chair away slightly; this might be contagious.) Near hysteria, the lecturer suddenly burst out with "I don't know! I don't understand any of this stuff. I only memorized all those equations!" It was a moment of great truth. I'm not sure what to make of it.

Once I attended a thesis review given at our laboratory by a young Ph.D. candidate from the Massachusetts Institute of Technology. The thesis review is a talk about the candidate's Ph.D. thesis. It is an opportunity for the candidate to present himself as a "can't miss" job prospect, to display a becoming humility, and to screw up. This particular candidate was destined in later life to become a genius. We didn't realize it at the time, but there were telltale signs—he spoke incomprehensible English, and the talk was so poorly organized that nobody knew what the topic was. Among the audience was an eminent mathematician (EM). I had never met this EM, but his fame was known far and wide in the kingdom. I was privileged to be in his presence. After the talk he asked a question. This question was insightful and brilliant; it cut to the very heart of whatever it was. I sat in awe of this level of comprehension, so in contrast to my own primordial state of ignorance. After a moment's hesitation the young candidate strode down the aisle of the conference room and stood before the chair of the EM. Towering over the now-quivering EM, the candidate shouted, "If you really understood this, you wouldn't ask a stupid question like that!" I shivered at my near escape. I had learned much. I have since forgotten.

Sometimes I awaken in the predawn—the hour of the wolf—when there is no one in the world but me. I worry. There is no shortage of material to worry about. There is a morrow coming. Soon I will have to get up and don my engineer's disguise. I have perfected my role, but maybe today I will be unmasked. I'm not worried about my friends and associates. I can see the fine line of their wigs and the telltale mascara. But somewhere are all those geniuses. I heard a rumor the other day that they are in Japan. I am worried.

A F T E R W O R D

● ● ● ● ● ● ● ● ● ● ● ● ●

This has been a book about computers, about people, and about the ether of information that we share. The computers are the keepers of this information, while we are its consumers. The issues we have discussed have centered about the nature of information, and how it is handled by man and machine.

The book has been full of contrasts between men and machines. I am conscious of having imbued computers with an anthromorphic flavor. In places I have woven overtones of "them" and "us." In truth, however, we are the makers of the machines. Their limitations are only deficiencies in our own knowledge. As we gain in knowledge we aspire to make computers in our own image. Perhaps that is the only image we know, but we rationalize our objective on the basis that the machines are more changeable than we are. As difficult as it may be, it will be easier to teach machines English than for both of us to learn a form of computer Esperanto. Better information handling for machines is often defined as more human-like. That is one reason we seek to understand better how we ourselves go about the business of handling information.

INFORMATION THEORY, COMPUTERS, AND PEOPLE

The notions of information theory are interwoven through the discussions of the various media. The data that we gather and exchange is seen as a delicate mixture of the expected and the unexpected, in which only the unexpected portion contains information. The concept of entropy as the measure of this intrinsic uncertainty gives us a philosophy of the distillation of information to its minimum essence. If you need to hold so much information, you need so many bits and no more—the rest is derivative.

While information theory provides a coherent framework for thinking about the idealistic design of machines, it is seldom directly applicable to the kinds of day-to-day information with which we deal. The written language seems a straightforward means of representation for information, yet we saw upon closer examination that the structure of language is so deep and complex that we cannot really fathom its ultimate distillation. It is almost a question of free will. Which part of language is of our own choosing, and which part is ordained through the format, the rules, the conventions, and our shared knowledge and experience?

As we move from text to speech and pictures, the information becomes progressively more obscurely imbedded in the medium. Both speech and pictures can be mutilated in dramatic fashions, and yet still convey the desired intelligence. Where is this information, you might ask? Perhaps you are disappointed that I have not delineated more clearly its form within the superstructures of speech and vision. For myself, I am content to leave the information cloaked in some degree of mystery. I believe that information will always be at some level a fuzzy, human concept that is ultimately unquantifiable in the terms of the cold reality of computer logic.

In the case of computers, the principles of information theory seem philosophically appropriate. Computers are binary machines that deal in hard bits, they are error-free, and their structure is a general but simplistic one of our own making. The application of information theory to human processing is entirely another matter. Where I have touched on this subject, I have probably overstated the connection. Humans are not exactly digital machines, and we seem to have an extraordinarily complex organization that is optimized for the things we do best, like the pattern recognition tasks in speech, vision, and language.

The difference between humans and machines is highlighted by G.A. Miller's famous "7 plus or minus 2" hypothesis. Miller found that the human short-term memory can store about 7 things; the plus or minus two means the actual number is most likely between 5 and 9. The short-term memory is what we use, for instance, to remember a telephone number just long enough to look away from the telephone book to dial the number. By happenstance, telephone numbers are usually exactly 7 digits. The area code would make the number a difficult 10 digits, but we have a pre-existing familiarity with these area codes.

The existence of a "7-thing" short-term memory is not inconsistent with information theory, but the remarkable finding is the latitude in definition of what the "things" can be. In a computer, the "things" are bits. Simple. However, our own short-term memory can remember 7 words as well as it can 7 digits. We could remember 7 faces, or we might remember 7 families. As we organize information on higher levels, we can still remember 7 of whatever it is. The computer would take progressively more and more bits of storage.

It would be possible to wriggle out of this contradiction by supposing that the short-term memory contains 7 "pointers," which are only the addresses or locations of the "things" in our larger, permanent (long-term) memory. But there are many other anomalies in human processing when we base our reasoning upon the design of machines. The one to which I keep returning in my own thoughts is the human capability to memorize great amounts of text or music. In Chapter 3 we discussed the ability of an actor to memorize the 12,000 words of Hamlet, whereas the best estimates of the entropy of this text would make it equivalent to memorizing 21,000 random, decimal digits. Remember that it is not fair to say that memorizing the text is easier because it contains a pattern. If we have distilled the text to its entropy, by definition no pattern remains. The entropy of the text should be the same as that of the 21,000 random numbers. We can only conclude that our own memory structure is vastly different from that of the computer. Analogies go only so far, and that makes me very happy. There is so much more to be discovered.

WHEN CAN INFORMATION BE EXTRACTED FROM DATA?

In defining information I said that the information consisted of the "new" or "unexpected" part of the data—that which could not be deduced or calculated from what we already knew. Like many of the simplifying statements I have made, this one conceals a deep, arguable notion. Earlier in the book I was able to surpress my desire to digress into this quagmire, but let me now return to the matter. The philosophical question is when, in fact, can we calculate something from data that we already have? Is it possible that, although the desired information is explicitly contained in data that we possess, it is so difficult to extract that we could say that we do not really have that specific information? The answer appears to be yes.

One of the most influential and beautiful theories within the computing field in the last decade has been that of computational complexity. When is a problem so complex that it is really unsolvable? Furthermore, by "unsolvable" I do not mean that it will be necessary to buy a more powerful computer, or to use more computer time to arrive at the solution. I mean that the solution is unthinkable, that regardless of how clever we are with the solution algorithm, or how powerful the computer, getting at the solution will take an amount of time that we might characterize as effectively forever. Mathematicians call these problems "intractable."

A class of problems thought to be intractable has been found in recent years. The class is called NP (for Non-deterministic Polynomial, but that is another story). It seems that many common computing problems, such as scheduling and packing, are in the class NP. Whether or not these problems are truly intractable has not been proven; this is one of the most celebrated unproven mathematical conjectures. The class of problems is all linked together in that if anyone ever finds a way of solving (in reasonable time) one of this class, then they all can be solved. No one has, and it is widely believed they are all truly intractable.

Interesting, but what does this have to do with information? Well, by cloaking our information bits within these problems we can conceal information from anyone who does not have the secret key to uncover the information. In effect we can focus information on intended recipients. As an example, in a common application of what is known as public key cryptography, we take blocks of data, interpret them as integers (e.g., $01001101 = 79$), and cube them modulo some number n, which is our individual encoding key. By "modulo" I mean to divide the resulting integer by n, and take only the remainder. For example, 22 modulo 3 is 1. The encoding key is public, so we announce it to everyone who might wish to send us information. Typically, this key is a very large number of, say, 100 digits. If you want to send information to me, cube the integer values of the blocks of data, and send me the remainders after division by my announced public key n.

Now many people might receive our encrypted message, but the original bits are concealed in what appears to be an intractable mathematical puzzle. (Actually, it has not been proven that this operation is formally intractable.) What original number, when cubed modulo n, gives the bits that have been received? Do not bother trying—when n is about a hundred digits, it could take a billion years on the fastest computer we have. However, only we have the secret trap door that lets us untangle the original bits. In choosing the encrypting key, n, we chose it as the product of two large prime numbers. Nobody else knows these secret factors, and finding them from n itself is yet another intractable problem. But given these factors, there is a very efficient mathematical algorithm for "uncubing" the encrypted bits. In the blink of an eye, even on a personal computer, the message is decrypted.

In addition to cryptography, the notion of intractability allows us to affix "signatures" to information. These signatures are sequences of bits which, when *encoded* using our public recipe, give a pre-established message. Anyone can encode with our key, but only we can *create* that particular message through *decoding* the established signature.

Finally, these same notions underlie a new field of information called zero-knowledge proofs. Can we prove that we know something without revealing anything whatsoever about that something? Can we prove to a computer that we are who we claim to be without giving any eavesdropper the information to impersonate us later? Surprisingly, the answer is yes. I am reminded of stories from wartime situations in which sentries challenged returning soldiers. The enemy might have overheard the password, so that seemed relatively unreliable. Instead, the sentry might ask a series of questions to the newcomer that only Americans would know, such as, "Who won the world series last year?" With a correct answer to each question, the sentry gains more and more confidence that the visitor is who he claims to be.

In zero-knowledge proofs the routine is somewhat the same. However, in the case of the sentry, a spy can be learning information from each series of questions he overhears, until finally he feels confident of impersonating an American. In zero-knowledge proofs, there is an infinite number of questions that might be asked, and the eavesdropper learns nothing from any individual question. That question will never be asked that way again, and in any event the bits are encrypted in such a way that the eavesdropper is not even certain what the question was. Not only is the information protected from the eavesdropper, but the only information the questioner himself learns is the fact that, with great confidence, the person with whom he is dealing is who he claims to be.

The researchers working on zero-knowledge proofs ask themselves what does it mean to have zero-knowledge about something? What is complete ignorance? Under what conditions can we guarantee that state? You can readily see that there is another side to the matters of information transfer that we have been discussing in this book. It is not enough to imbed information in a medium; sometimes it necessary to predestine the information for certain people or systems, and to keep others ignorant. In fact, we have the tools to do exactly that.

P E O P L E, C O M P U T E R S, A N D T H E M E D I A O F E X C H A N G E

We spent a great deal of this book discussing the media of information exchange—text, speech, and pictures. In everyday life we ourselves use them all continuously. Even so, we still study the effectiveness of these formats for information exchange, problem solving, conflict resolution, and other human interactions. An example that comes up in the field of communications again and again is the classic business meeting. Why have electronic methods for promoting togetherness in spite of distance, such as television meeting facilities, been unsuccessful in displacing travel?

Thus, the problems in effective information exchange with computers are partly those due to a lack of understanding of how we ourselves exchange information. On top of these difficulties are those of inadequate technology. The computer has limited abilities to deal with text, speech, and pictures. In the cases of text and speech the difficulty is the complexity of the underlying language, while in pictures the difficulty is the lack of an underlying language.

I try to imagine an ideal scenario for exchanging information with a computer, but I can only think in conventional, human terms. Naturally, I want it to talk with me, to show me text, and for both of us to look at pictures. Even that is not really enough. In some cases I would like to feel and to smell. But more than anything, I would like to talk with the computer the way I do with other humans. Some of the studies we have quoted have shown that interactive speech is the most efficient way for humans to exchange information.

As we have discussed, computers can synthesize speech, recognize speech, and untangle the understanding of the language conveyed. Unfortunately, the computers are not fluent in these abilities. To my taste, that makes all the difference. Speech is a wonderful way to interact, but only when it is fluent. I think of the many meetings I have had through the years with foreign visitors. To their credit, they speak English, but usually not very well. Compared to a computer, however, their abilities with English are extraordinary. Even so, our meetings are usually painful for me. I feel like I have to push physically through a murky veil to get across the simplest points. From their blank expressions, I am not sure that I have been understood. Finally, we resort to prepared textual material. Afterwards I am tired—nonfluent communications is hard work.

Perhaps I should treat computers like foreign visitors. With the visitors I unconsciously seek every way of expanding my bandwidth, which I think of as my space for freedom of expression. I wave my arms, I point, and I use every visual augmentation possible. I experience something similar in attending a symphony concert. Listening to a recorded performance at home I close my eyes to shut out interferences. At the concert hall itself, I watch the conductor and the musicians. They enhance my bandwidth, and provide a visual interpretation and augmentation of the music.

With computers, too, I need every means of augmenting our shared expression space. In human terms they are invalids. Speak slowly, and show them simple pictures. "Run, Spot, run!" But be patient, one day they, too, will grow up.

INDEX

● ● ● ● ● ● ●